THE THANKS
OF THE
FATHERLAND

THE THANKS

OF THE FATHERLAND

German Veterans after the Second World War

JAMES M. DIEHL

The University of

North Carolina Press

Chapel Hill & London

The paper in this book meets the guidelines for
permanence and durability of the Committee on
Production Guidelines for Book Longevity of the
Council on Library Resources.

Portions of this book appeared earlier, in different form,
in "Victors or Victims?: Disabled Veterans in the Third
Reich," *Journal of Modern History* (December 1987),
© 1987 by The University of Chicago, all rights
reserved, and "Germany in Defeat, 1918 and 1945: Some
Comparisons and Contrasts," *The History Teacher*
(August 1989), and are used here with the permission of,
respectively, the University of Chicago Press and the
Society for History Education.

Library of Congress Cataloging-in-Publication Data
Diehl, James M.
The thanks of the fatherland : German veterans after
the Second World War / by James M. Diehl.
  p.   cm.
Includes bibliographical references and index.
ISBN 0-8078-2077-6 (alk. paper)
  1. Veterans—Germany.   I. Title.
UB359.G3D5   1993
362.86'0943—dc20   92-50811
                                              CIP

97   96   95   94   93   5   4   3   2   1

For my mother,

who first taught me

the virtue of trying to

understand the points

of view of those with

whom you disagree

CONTENTS

Contents

PREFACE

Like most books, this one took much longer to complete than its author expected; also, as is often the case, it is a compromise. Both were caused in part by deliberation and vacillation over what the scope and structure of the book should be. Originally, it was conceived of as an extended essay dealing with the fate of German veterans after the Second World War. As research proceeded, however, the siren call of writing a comprehensive history of German veterans in the twentieth century began to beckon. This authorial version of the "totalitarian temptation" was alternately encouraged and checked by archival finds that, on the one hand, revealed the richness of the topic and, on the other, made manifest its immensity. Eventually I concluded that I had neither the time nor the desire to become involved in what could easily become a lifetime project. The idea of a comprehensive history was abandoned and a compromise was made. This book is the result. It makes no attempt to recapture the experience of *all* veterans during and after the two world wars. Instead it focuses on the activities of organized veterans, always a small proportion of the entire veteran population. The book's main emphasis is on the problems facing German veterans after the Second World War and the ways in which they were addressed in the decade following Germany's defeat. The primary focus is on the major pieces of veterans' legislation passed in the early years of the German Federal Republic. Historical context is provided by the first two chapters and the conclusion, which attempts to compare and contrast the fate of veterans and their sociopolitical impact on German society following the two world wars. A full account of the experience of German veterans and their impact on German society in the twentieth century remains to be written. I hope that this book will provide a useful contribution to that story.

In the end, the writing of a book is a solitary enterprise, yet it is rarely possible without financial and personal support, both of which I have received and take pleasure in acknowledging. The main financial support came from a National Endowment for the Humanities Fellowship for Independent Study and Research, which permitted an uninterrupted year of archival research. Summer research trips were assisted by two DAAD Fellowships, an Indiana University Summer Faculty Fellowship, and grants from the West European Studies program. As any author knows, time is as valuable as money, and I am especially grateful to my departmental chairperson, M. Jeanne Peterson, for arranging a semester's time-release from teaching responsibilities at a crucial stage in the writing of the book.

I also want to express my appreciation to the staffs at the Bundesarchiv in Koblenz, the Bundesarchiv-Militärarchiv in Freiburg im Breisgau, and the Parlamentsarchiv in Bonn for their helpful assistance. I owe special thanks to Dr. Hans-Dieter Kreikamp of the Bundesarchiv, who provided invaluable assistance in gaining access to needed material in the Zwischenarchiv and in the process destroyed the negative stereotype of German *Beamtentum* that American scholars alternately curse and cherish. My work in Germany was also greatly aided by the Institut für europäische Geschichte, Mainz, which graciously provided space to work and the use of its library facilities.

Finally, as always, my greatest debt is to my wife, Bobbi, who remained a constant source of understanding and encouragement throughout the many years consumed by this project.

ABBREVIATIONS

The following abbreviations are used in the text. For abbreviations used only in the notes, see page 243.

BdK	Bund der Kriegs- und Zivilbeschädigten, Sozialrentner und Hinterbliebenenverbände Deutschlands
BDKK	Bund Deutscher Kriegsbeschädigter und Kriegerhinterbliebener
BDS	Schutzbund ehemaliger Deutscher Soldaten
BhK	Bund hirnverletzter Kriegs- und Arbeitsopfer
BP	Bayernpartei
BVG	Bundesversorgungsgesetz
BvW	Bund versorgungsberechtigter ehemaliger Wehrmachtsangehöriger und deren Hinterbliebenen
CDU	Christlich-Demokratische Union
CSU	Christlich-Soziale Union
DDSB	Der Deutsche Soldatenbund
DGB	Deutscher Gewerkschaftsbund
DKOV	*Deutsche Kriegsopferversorgung*
DNVP	Deutschnationale Volkspartei
DOB	Deutscher Offiziersbund
DP	Deutsche Partei
DSZ	*Deutsche Soldaten Zeitung*
FDP	Freie Demokratische Partei
HKG	Heimkehrergesetz
HIAG	Hilfsgemeinschaften auf Gegenseitigkeit der ehemaligen Angehörigen der Waffen-SS
KgfEG	Kriegsgefangenenentschädigungsgesetz
KPD	Kommunistische Partei Deutschlands
LAG	Lastenausgleichsgesetz
NDO	Nationalverband Deutscher Offiziere
NDS	Nationalverband Deutscher Soldaten

NSDAP	Nationalsozialistische Deutsche Arbeiterpartei
NSKOV	National-Sozialistische Kriegsopferversorgung
NSV	Nationalsozialistische Volkswohlfahrt
RDO	Reichsverband Deutscher Offiziere
ROB	Reichsoffiziersbund
RVG	Reichsversorgungsgesetz
RVO	Reichsversicherungsordnung
SA	Sturmabteilung
SPD	Sozialdemokratische Partei Deutschlands
SS	Schutzstaffeln
ÜBG	Gesetz zur Verbesserung von Leistungen an Kriegsopfer (Überbrückungsgesetz)
VdH	Verband der Heimkehrer
VdK	Verband der Kriegsbeschädigten, Kriegshinterbliebenen und Sozialrentner Deutschlands
VdS	Verband deutscher Soldaten
VfA	Verwaltung für Arbeit
VNS	Verband nationalgesinnter Soldaten
WAV	Wirtschaftliche Aufbau-Vereinigung
WEFVG	Wehrmachtseinsatzfürsorge- und Versorgungsgesetz
WFVG	Wehrmachtsfürsorge- und Versorgungsgesetz

THE THANKS
OF THE
FATHERLAND

INTRODUCTION

The development of mass armies in the late nineteenth and early twentieth centuries produced a new social group—veterans—that quickly became an active force in the rapidly emerging arena of mass politics. In Germany, a nation with a strong military (indeed, militaristic) tradition, veterans played an important part in domestic politics. Before the First World War, organized veterans were a major pillar of support for the authoritarian sociopolitical order of the German Empire. After World War I German veterans continued to play an influential role in domestic politics. Through their propagation of authoritarian, militaristic values and mobilization of antidemocratic sentiment, they did much to undermine the Weimar Republic and, as I have previously argued, the violent paramilitary subculture that emerged in Germany in the 1920s helped greatly to pave the way for Hitler's Third Reich.

In the Third Reich the paramilitary subculture of Weimar became the dominant culture. Military virtues were equated with the highest ethical principles, and society was militarized. The armed forces were enlarged, and opportunities for military careers burgeoned. At the same time, pension benefits for career soldiers, especially noncommissioned officers, were expanded during the 1930s in order to enhance the attractiveness of a military career. With the collapse of the Third Reich and Germany's subsequent territorial (and administrative) reduction, large numbers of former career soldiers saw their hopes for pensions and secure civil service jobs destroyed. Thus, after the Second World War, veterans again formed a large and potentially disruptive segment of the population. Yet this time the story was dramatically different: although the German people were responsive to the veterans' socioeconomic needs, former soldiers never exercised a decisive political influence.

Most of the literature on German World War II veterans has treated them as part of the larger problem of the revival of right-wing radicalism in postwar Germany. The authors of these works, primarily political scientists and journalists, have been mainly interested in the political aspects of veterans' activities, particularly their involvement in neo-Nazi movements. My approach is more comprehensive; it treats veterans, including disabled veterans and their families, as a historical and social phenomenon as well as a political one. The changing political fortunes of veterans are used to measure other important changes in the socioeconomic and political fabric of Germany.

The problems confronting veterans in postwar societies are universal and of universal significance. They include compensation for war-related disabilities, reentry into the labor market, pensions for professional soldiers, and the reintegration into society of late-returning prisoners of war. In post–World War II Germany, these problems were compounded by defeat, occupation, division, and the extensive damage that the country had suffered as a result of fighting and aerial bombardment. The nation was destitute, and many segments of the civilian population (for example, air raid victims, refugees, and expellees from former German territories in the East) had equally compelling grounds for compensation. The manner in which these competing claims for state assistance were presented, defended, perceived by society as a whole, and, ultimately, resolved provides illuminating insights into the sociopolitical milieu of postwar Germany. The main focus of this book is an examination of the place of veterans within this larger context during the decade following the war. In addition, by comparing their activities and treatment after the two world wars, it is possible to identify significant continuities and discontinuities in German history and to illustrate some of the important social and political changes that have contributed to the success of the Federal Republic.

The first two chapters are introductory and cover the years 1914 to 1945. Chapter 1 traces the emergence of veterans as a social and political force after World War I, analyzes the veterans' legislation of the Weimar Republic, and briefly explores the ways in which the activities of veterans' organizations helped to undermine Germany's first experiment in democracy. The second chapter deals with the treatment of veterans in the Third Reich, a classic example of National Socialist control and manipulation of social groups. Although there was much rhetoric celebrating the glory and honor of veterans after 1933, the material benefits provided to the war-disabled under the Third Reich were less generous than those provided by the much-maligned Weimar Republic; only during the war were they expanded, piecemeal, in an effort to sustain support of the war by servicemen and their families. Since benefits were predicated on victory and conquest, the collapse of the Third Reich left veterans with nothing. The "thanks of the Fatherland" bequeathed to veterans by the National Socialist regime consisted of material impoverishment and international disgrace.

The remaining chapters of the book deal with the period 1945–55. Chapter 3 covers the occupation period, 1945–49. Allied policy toward German veterans, especially disabled veterans and survivors, was a casebook study of misapplied lessons drawn from the past. Determined to root out German militarism, Allied policymakers not only abolished the pensions of career soldiers but also dismantled the existing system of war-disability benefits, incorporating it into social security or industrial accident disability programs. This produced great hardships for the war-disabled and the families of servicemen killed in the war. German officials charged with the administration of the new systems fought to change them, and the ensuing struggle with representatives of the military governments offers an interesting example of the dialogue between victors and vanquished in postwar Germany, a dialogue that was less one-sided than is usually assumed. In the end, the misguided and unnecessarily harsh policy of the occupying powers did have a significantly positive effect: the immediate postwar discontent of the war-disabled and former career officers was focused on the occupying powers instead of on German officials, who, as advocates of the interests of former soldiers, gained political capital that would later prove to be of considerable value in the difficult early years of the Federal Republic.

Chapters 4 through 6 deal with the emergence of veterans' organizations after the formation of the Federal Republic and the passage of the formative pieces of postwar veterans' legislation. The major German veterans' organizations after World War II can be grouped into three categories, representing, respectively, the interests of the war-disabled, former prisoners of war, and former professional soldiers. Three corresponding types of veterans' legislation were enacted during the years 1950–54: legislation providing benefits for the war-disabled and survivors, compensation for former prisoners of war, and pensions for former career officers. Functional counterparts of the post-1945 veterans' organizations existed after the First World War, but there were significant differences in the nature of those that emerged after World War II.

The public debate that accompanied the passage of veterans' legislation reveals important areas of consensus and conflict in postwar German society. Since virtually every family had been adversely affected by the war, there was general agreement that the victims of the war should be compensated for their losses; at the same time, in view of the limited resources available for social programs in devastated postwar Germany, there was considerable disagreement over how benefits were to be distributed and costs apportioned. The government, anxious to establish its legitimacy and to demonstrate its ability to provide social services, responded favorably to the competing demands of veterans but was constrained, at least initially, by limits on its fiscal capacity and its political freedom of movement. The resulting legislation was consequently based on a number of hard compromises. Though none of the groups of veterans affected by postwar veterans' legislation felt their needs had been fully met, they were satisfied enough to continue to work within the system. The veterans' and war victims' legislation of the early 1950s thus succeeded in defusing social and political unrest and facilitating reintegration, processes that were aided by the subsequent "economic miracle," which permitted the steady expansion of benefits.

Chapters 7 and 8 discuss the ideological and organizational evolution of veterans' organizations after the passage of the major pieces of veterans' legislation. Once the specific needs of the various organizations' memberships had been met through legislation, they began to face a crisis of legitimacy. Although they could—and did—justify their existence on the basis of the need to fight for improvements, their future was threatened by the fact that their constituencies were discrete, increasingly inactive, and, for demographic and other reasons, declining in numbers. New missions had to be defined to ensure organizational survival, and, with the exception of the organizations of the war-disabled, this took the form of attempting to expand membership beyond the ranks of the original interest-specific group to encompass all veterans. These efforts naturally led to competition; the organizations not only vied with one another to attract previously unorganized veterans but necessarily became involved in raiding each other's ranks. This interorganizational strife was further compounded when it became clear that the government, seeking support for its policy of rearmament, was interested in the creation of a single veterans' organization. Thus the stakes were high and competition was bitter; the results, however, were disappointingly meager. New members did not flock to the veterans' organizations, and the attempts to increase political influence through unification failed. Moreover, unlike the Weimar era, the larger programs and political appeals of the veterans' organizations found no resonance among the population at large. While willing to accept veterans' organizations as legitimate representatives promoting specific material interests, most Germans firmly rejected their attempts to assume the role of political savants.

A powerful veterans' mystique did not develop after 1945. In 1918 veterans returned to a relatively intact society as alienated outsiders. They joined together immediately after the war when the collective veteran consciousness was high, and in later years veterans' organizations helped to sustain a separate veteran identity that became highly politicized. After 1945 veterans' organizations were banned during the occupation, and in the years of hard economic struggle that followed the war, veterans were forced to form new economic and social ties—ties that worked to reintegrate them into society as individuals. Social reintegration therefore preceded activity in veterans' organizations, and this helped to foster pragmatic policies by the latter when they were again permitted. The desire to avoid the mistakes of Weimar also played an important role in determining the different outcome of veterans' politics after World War II. Government policy was consciously designed to appease the legitimate demands of veterans while weaning them from extremist positions, a goal that was achieved through an astute combination of threats and concessions. The parties acted similarly. Finally, veterans and their leaders had also learned lessons. Leaders who attempted to pursue ideological and political goals at the expense of bread-and-butter issues were repeatedly reined in by the rank and file. While in some cases the process was slow, veterans' organizations generally came to accept the fact that more could be gained through cooperation than through confrontation. In the area of veterans' politics, therefore, Bonn is definitely not Weimar. Perhaps lessons *can* be learned from history.

ONE

WORLD WAR I, VETERANS,
AND THE WEIMAR REPUBLIC

Even before the First World War's voracious demands on manpower irrevocably transformed the nature of veterans' politics, veterans in Germany had played an important role. At the outbreak of the war the veterans' associations, with nearly 3 million members, represented by far the largest of the many nationalist organizations that dotted the political landscape in Wilhelmine Germany. Although veterans' groups had existed in Germany since the eighteenth century, they did not become mass organizations until after the Franco-Prussian War of 1870–71. Whereas the earlier associations had limited their memberships to front-line soldiers and therefore had declined by the middle of the nineteenth century into little more than burial societies for former comrades in arms, the new veterans' organizations founded after the wars of unification opened their ranks to all men who had completed their military training, thereby creating a mass, self-perpetuating base. In spite of the fact that they owed their origins to the wars that had united Germany, the new veterans' organizations themselves remained divided. Efforts to incorporate them into statewide organizations during the 1870s and 1880s were generally successful, but no single nationwide organization existed until 1900 when, after much effort, the Kyffhäuser League of German State Veterans' Organizations (Kyffhäuserbund der Deutschen Landes-Kriegerverbände) was founded.[1]

German veterans' organizations were originally unpolitical and accepted veterans from all walks of life. During the Wilhelmine era, however, they were increasingly politicized and became active agents for the mobilization of support for the existing social and political order. Under the leadership of Alfred Westphal, a classic example of Eckart Kehr's "feudalized" reserve officer, the Kyffhäuserbund, and with it the entire prewar veterans' movement, was converted into a tool for the "class struggle from above."[2] According to

Westphal, the primary tasks of the veterans' organizations were to cultivate "monarchistic and patriotic feelings" and to counter "the revolutionary and traitorous Social Democratic movement with a monarchistic and nationalistic mass movement of former soldiers."[3] These goals were actively supported and encouraged by government officials and military authorities, who considered the veterans' organizations a useful means of continuing the fight against social democracy following the lapse of Bismarck's antisocialist legislation and a way of propagating the "spirit of the army" in the ranks of civilian society.

During the final decades of the empire, socialists were systematically purged from the ranks of German veterans' organizations. Not only those who belonged to the Social Democratic Party (Sozialdemokratische Partei Deutschlands [SPD]) were excluded, but also those who dared to vote for Social Democratic candidates. Similarly, socialist unions were attacked. In 1909 members of veterans' organizations were prohibited from belonging to the socialist Free Unions. During elections the veterans' organizations, ostensibly nonpartisan, campaigned vigorously against the SPD and actively supported the nonsocialist parties. In the view of the Kyffhäuserbund, being "nonpartisan" simply meant that political issues dividing the middle-class parties were to be avoided in the interest of building a firm front against the Social Democrats.

Not surprisingly, the bitter hatred of the Kyffhäuserbund was returned in kind. Social Democratic publications decried the "terrorism of the veterans' organizations," and the tactics of the enemy were frequently adopted by denying members of the veterans' organizations membership in Social Democratic organizations. By the outbreak of the war in 1914, the Kyffhäuserbund and the Social Democrats faced each other like two hostile armies: on the one side, a leading exemplar of the dominant militarized culture of Wilhelmine Germany; on the other, the main exponent of the antimilitarist, pacifistic subculture.[4]

The chasm between the two sides, like other divisions in German society, was temporarily covered over by the *Burgfrieden*, or social truce, that was concluded among the contending social and political forces at the outbreak of the war. As a result of the *Burgfrieden*, as well as the fact that its ranks had been thrown into disarray by the calling up of over one-half of its members, the Kyffhäuserbund largely discontinued its antisocialist activity during the early years of the war and instead limited itself to general patriotic support of the war effort. Never suffering from modesty when it came to evaluating the importance and efficacy of their organization, Westphal and his colleagues concluded that the unity of the German people and the positive response of the Social Democrats to the war were in large part the result of the Kyffhäuser-

bund's activity. Impressed by the patriotism of the working class, they decided
to open the Bund's ranks to Social Democrats. This, it was hoped, would
strengthen the latter's commitment to the monarchy and win them away from
the pernicious influence of Social Democratic organizations.

Directives urging a reconsideration of the exclusionary policy were sent out
in May 1915, and in October the new policy was tentatively adopted by the
executive council.[5] Although there was some opposition to the new course, it
was ineffectual. In September 1916 the Kyffhäuserbund held its first annual
meeting since the outbreak of the war and voted to accept the executive
council's decision. Social Democrats who were "patriotic" and "loyal to the
monarchy" were now eligible for membership, and an extensive recruitment
campaign was launched.

The reversal of the Kyffhäuserbund's policy came as a shock to many of its
members, as well as to outside observers. Yet its about-face was not as surprising as it seemed. When it occurred, in late 1916, the German people's war
weariness was becoming increasingly visible. The *Burgfrieden* was breaking
down. The liberal forces of movement were beginning to reemerge after their
temporary eclipse, and increasing pressure was being put on the government
to define its war aims and to fulfill its vague promises of a "New Orientation,"
that is, domestic reforms. The conservative forces of order responded by
seeking to mobilize support for their own policies of annexationist war aims,
which were designed to preempt demands for postwar reform. The main
vehicle for this was the Fatherland Party (Vaterlandspartei), founded in September 1916, but others were also enlisted.[6] The "new orientation" of the
Kyffhäuserbund was, in short, an attempt to mobilize veterans against the
government's putative "New Orientation" and to prevent it from becoming
reality.

The Social Democrats were well aware of the implications of the renewed
activity of the veterans' associations. Soon after the Kyffhäuserbund's official
endorsement of its new policy, the question of whether Social Democrats
should respond by founding veterans' organizations of their own became a
widespread topic of debate in the party's publications. An article of 9 November 1916 entitled "The Organization of the Veterans" in *Vorwärts*, the leading
Social Democratic newspaper, stated that "veterans will consider the common
representation of their interests after their return home. They will, especially
if . . . disabled by the war, justly claim for themselves far-reaching welfare
measures, and they will decisively oppose any attempt to reduce their political
rights with respect to other segments of the population." Since "in their
present form the veterans' organizations are hardly organizations for the
representation of social and political interests," it was concluded, it would be

necessary to create a new organization "from scratch." The reference to the need for "far-reaching welfare measures" for the war-disabled and the necessity for veterans to "oppose any attempt to reduce their political rights" pointed to the two issues that were to provide the basis for Social Democratic involvement in veterans' politics.

Two years of war fought with mass armies and modern weapons had produced an unprecedented number of casualties. This in turn had placed an unbearable strain on nineteenth-century institutions for the collection and distribution of funds for the war-disabled and next of kin of those killed. Although new measures were introduced during the war to provide medical care, pensions, and vocational rehabilitation, a comprehensive system of welfare for the war-disabled and their families was never developed. Instead, responsibility remained divided among a number of semiofficial and voluntary organizations. Many gaps existed, and more importantly, disabled veterans and their families had no legal claim on many of the services that did exist.[7] In 1917, as war-weariness mounted and civilian morale was declining, the inadequacies of Germany's programs for aiding the victims of the war became increasingly obvious. The raising of mass citizen armies sounded the death knell of voluntarism. More and more, disabled veterans and their families began to demand recompense from the state, to insist that the ubiquitous official promises that they could be sure of the "thanks of the Fatherland" be given concrete form. The cry for "justice, not charity" prompted the formation of new types of veterans' organizations, not only in Germany but in all of the belligerent nations. If either side in the domestic political and social struggles that began to reemerge in the warring nations of Europe during the winter of 1916–17 had previously been unaware of the importance of winning the allegiance of soldiers and veterans, such ignorance was impossible after March 1917; the events in Russia dramatically demonstrated the political power of soldiers as well as the advantage—indeed, the necessity—of winning the support of veterans.[8]

In Germany, the breakdown of the *Burgfrieden* was accompanied by renewed pressure for reform of the unjust suffrage system that existed in Prussia.[9] An important weapon in the arsenal of those advocating reform was the argument that one could not deny an equal vote to soldiers who had fought and bled to defend the state. The moral weight of such reasoning, combined with the vast numbers of veterans and war-disabled, represented a political force of potentially enormous power, a fact realized by those who were urging the Social Democrats to form veterans' organizations.

The driving force behind these efforts was Erich Kuttner. Kuttner had served at the front, been wounded, and then returned to Berlin in 1916 where he joined the staff of *Vorwärts*.[10] His interest in veterans' affairs was a result of both humanitarian and political considerations. In an article entitled "The Return Home," for example, Kuttner discussed the difficulties that would face returning soldiers, especially the disabled. The problem of providing aid to the disabled, he argued, would be an enormous one that could only be dealt with through the active intervention of the state. It was the state's duty to ensure that provisions be made for employing the disabled, that they be given fair wages, and that they receive adequate pensions. Kuttner then turned to the broader question of their political needs, stating that "the war-disabled will not only make economic demands, but also political demands on the state. Whoever has sacrificed an arm or a leg, been seriously inconvenienced or afflicted with sickness for the rest of his life as a result of defending the whole of the population will not have the slightest understanding for a situation in which another person has more rights in the state because he pays a somewhat higher tax." Kuttner rejected the arguments of those who contended that existing organizations could handle the problems of the war-disabled—that their economic demands could be looked after by the unions and their political demands could be met by the party. In Kuttner's view this was unsatisfactory, since it meant that the war-disabled were simply to stand by while others acted on their behalf. The disabled veteran, he concluded, wanted not only to be an "object but also a participant. . . . The fundamental fact that the disabled themselves must represent their cause . . . should be clear to everyone in the party."[11]

Initially unheeded, Kuttner's arguments began to gain ground in the spring of 1917. By then the implications of the stepped-up activity of the Kyffhäuserbund were becoming more apparent, and, in addition, there were indications that the forces of order were preparing to make a direct appeal to the war-disabled in the form of organizations modeled after the yellow unions.[12] Fearing that unless they acted soon their own members as well as potential new recruits might be lured into the ranks of their political opponents, Kuttner and his colleagues were given the go-ahead. On 23 May 1917 the League of War-Disabled and War Veterans (Bund der Kriegsbeschädigten und ehemaligen Kriegsteilnehmer) was founded. The Bund claimed to be nonpartisan and disavowed any connection with the Social Democratic Party or its unions. Nonetheless, its program, which combined specific economic and social interests with general political demands, clearly reflected its origins. For the war-disabled, the Bund demanded a fundamental reorganization of the military disability system, a voice in the determination of public welfare benefits for the disabled, laws compelling employers to hire a certain percentage of war-disabled workers, and the prohibition of the practice of basing wages on pensions. In addition, it demanded in the "name and interest of all veterans" the removal of discriminatory political practices "which put the veteran in an unfair position with regard to other segments of the population," the transformation of the army into "a true peoples' army" (an old Social Democratic demand), and a foreign policy "which would prevent the outbreak of future wars."[13]

During the final eighteen months of the war, the struggle for the allegiance of German veterans intensified as political differences in Germany sharpened and both the Bund—after Easter 1918, the Reichsbund (National League)—and the Kyffhäuserbund sought to mobilize veterans in support of their respective political programs.[14] While the Social Democratic organization demanded social and political reform and urged a negotiated peace, the Kyffhäuserbund argued that domestic reforms had to wait until after the war and demanded a decisive victory. The Kyffhäuserbund was an active supporter of the annexationist war-aims policy of the Pan-Germans, the Fatherland Party, and other diehard conservatives. A permanent feature of the propaganda of these elements was the promise that once German victory had been achieved veterans would be given land for settlement. The land in question was to be provided by Germany's conquests in the East, a policy that was to be revived during the Second World War by the National Socialists.[15]

GERMANY'S DEFEAT and the subsequent November Revolution completely changed the framework and nature of veterans' politics. The Social Democratic Reichsbund continued to exist after the war, but as a result of the changes introduced by the revolution, its major political demands were fulfilled and the need to mobilize veterans on political issues declined. Thus, while the Reichsbund still continued to accept nondisabled veterans—in order to keep them out of the grasp of the Kyffhäuserbund—the percentage of nondisabled veterans among its members remained low; after the war it devoted its attention almost exclusively to representing the interests of the war-disabled and survivors of those killed during the war.[16]

In addition to fulfilling the political demands of the Reichsbund, the revolution also helped it to achieve the social reforms it desired. In December 1918 the Reichsbund organized a demonstration in Berlin that led to a raise in disability pensions. In the following month the elections to the National Assembly produced a democratic majority dominated by Social Democrats, which assured the Reichsbund of a sympathetic hearing for its demands on behalf of the victims of war. During the next two years Germany's outdated system of aid for the war-disabled and their families was thoroughly over-hauled and expanded.[17]

Although drafted hurriedly and in many regards imperfect, the National War Victims' Benefits Law (Reichsversorgungsgesetz [RVG]) of May 1920 incorporated many of the demands made by the war victims' organizations during the war and represented a significant improvement over the previous war-disability system in Germany. Animated by social welfare rather than military principles, the RVG abolished earlier distinctions between profes-sional and nonprofessional soldiers as well as pension differentials based on military rank. To further underline its civilian character, the new system was placed under the jurisdiction of the Labor Ministry, which also was responsi-ble for the administration of old-age and industrial accident disability pro-grams.

The main thrust of the RVG was not simple monetary compensation for injury but physical rehabilitation and the reintegration of disabled veterans into society and the economy as productive citizens. The first component of the law was therefore the guarantee and provision of free medical care to cure or alleviate the suffering associated with war-related injuries. Provisions were also made for vocational rehabilitation.

For veterans who were permanently disabled and for the survivors of those killed in the war, an elaborate system of pensions was established. As the most tangible and costly component of the RVG, these pensions were the most controversial aspect of the new law. The pensions were calculated in a complex and multilevel manner. The base allowance of the pension was established on the basis of the disabled person's decrease in earning capacity as determined by a doctor, who, among other things, took into account the victim's education, prewar occupation, and social standing. Pensions began with a disability of 20 percent. Men with a disability of 50 percent or more received a severe disability allowance in addition to the base allowance. A further supplement, the equal-ization allowance, compensated those who had had—or, barring their war-time injuries, could reasonably have been expected to attain—positions of particular responsibility. The base allowance plus the severe disability and equalization allowances comprised the full pension or *Vollrente*. The *Vollrente* could be increased further through additional allowances that were geared to family status, place of residence, and the need for in-home medical care. Widows' pensions were calculated at 30 percent of the husband's *Vollrente* or at 50 percent if the widow was over fifty years of age, herself disabled, or had children to support.[18]

For all its virtues, the RVG contained flaws that—especially under the precarious economic conditions of the Republic—generated considerable discontent among its beneficiaries. During the war the issue of war victims' benefits had been strongly politicized, as the treatment of war victims became intertwined with the larger question of postwar political reform. Yet, in contrast to other countries where postwar legislation for war victims was accompanied by extensive political debate, the drafting of the RVG was curiously unpolitical, more the product of bureaucratic intervention than a political act.[19] The law was drawn up by civil servants and was accepted virtually without debate by the Reichstag, partly out of humanitarian concern and partly to preempt a source of social discontent in a period of revolutionary unrest.[20]

As a result of its bureaucratic origins, many aspects of the RVG were shaped more by administrative concerns than by attention to the sensibilities of the war victims, which in Germany were sharpened by the psychological burden of defeat. Whereas in the victorious countries the self-esteem of the war-disabled (as well as their sociopolitical bargaining power) was strengthened by their "success," that is, victory, German war victims were haunted by the fact that their sacrifice had been in vain and that many of their countrymen saw them not as heroes but as highly visible and painful reminders of the nation's defeat. Thus, even though the material benefits of the RVG were in many aspects superior to those provided by the French or English systems, the RVG failed to meet the psychological needs of German war victims. It promised vocational rehabilitation, but it did not confer the legally sanctioned special status that, for example, war victims in France enjoyed.[21] The special place in society that German war victims felt was their due as a result of their sacrifice seemed unrecognized, a fact that was further underlined by the Republic's refusal to award a commemorative medal to veterans and the failure to create a national monument honoring the nation's war dead.[22]

The main source of discontent with the RVG was its bureaucratic imper-sonality and complexity, which constantly put the war victim in the position of an anxious supplicant.[23] The process of establishing eligibility was often arduous and humiliating, and the frequently mandated reexaminations—designed to eliminate fraud and cut expenses—were a constant irritation. The war victims' lack of a positive sense of identity was compounded by the fact that the Labor Ministry also administered other, more mundane welfare programs. Although the change of administration of war victims' benefits from the War Ministry to the Labor Ministry had been a key demand of the war victims (at least of those affiliated with the Social Democratic Reichs-bund) and the RVG was administered through a separate section within the Labor Ministry, many war victims resented the association with industrial accident victims and welfare recipients. This resentment was exacerbated by the universal character of laws regulating the employment of severely disabled workers, which equated the war-disabled with accident victims, and the war victims' sense of separateness was further diminished by the administrative cutbacks and merging of social services that followed the governmental cuts in expenditure connected with the revaluation of 1924.[24]

Like most large welfare programs, the program connected with the RVG was an object of suspicion among those who did not benefit from it, and the prejudices of Germans outside the system were often exploited by Reich officials to keep expenses down and to justify cuts. Charges of fraud by "welfare cheaters" and accusations that the RVG promoted a "pension psychosis" constantly harried the war victims, and these allegations proliferated with the onset of the Great Depression and the accompanying intensified struggle for a share of the state's steadily diminishing resources.[25]

WHILE THE REICHSBUND, with over half a million members by 1920,[26] was by far the largest organization representing the interests of the war-disabled, it was not the only one. Like virtually every sphere of activity during the Weimar Republic, that of social welfare for war victims was divided along political and other lines. In addition to the Reichsbund, there were three other major organizations of war victims: the United Association of German War Disabled and Next of Kin (Einheitsverband der Kriegsbeschädigten und Kriegshinterbliebenen Deutschlands), the International League of Victims of War and Work (Internationaler Bund der Opfer des Krieges und der Arbeit), and the Central Association of German War-Disabled and Survivors (Zentralverband Deutscher Kriegsbeschädigter und Kriegshinterbliebener). Although the Reichsbund's relations with the first were comparatively cordial, the only basic difference being over the question of accepting nondisabled veterans, its relations with the other two were far from harmonious.[27]

The Internationaler Bund was a Communist organization that had broken off from the Reichsbund in early 1919. At the time of the revolution, the Reichsbund's leaders had quickly rallied to support the new government and made it clear that they opposed any radicalization. A number of its members, especially in Berlin, were more radically inclined, however. In early 1919 these elements tried unsuccessfully to gain control of the Reichsbund and put it on a more radical course. The dissidents subsequently left the Reichsbund and in February founded their own group, the Internationaler Bund. The group followed the Communist line, arguing that the problems of disabled veterans could only be settled in the context of the general class war. In the following years relations between the Internationaler Bund and the Reichsbund were marked by the peculiar animosity and suspicion endemic between competing Communist and Social Democratic organizations.

The Reichsbund's relations with the Zentralverband were, if anything, worse than those with the Internationaler Bund. The Zentralverband had been founded in late June 1918 and in organization and purpose seemed to be little different from the Reichsbund. The reason for this similarity was simple: it had been created specifically for the purpose of competing with the Reichsbund. The Zentralverband had been formed under the auspices of the Christian and Hirsch-Duncker unions and was backed by prominent figures in the middle-class parties. Just as the founding of the Internationaler Bund introduced the Communist–Social Democratic split into the ranks of the war-disabled, the founding of the Zentralverband introduced the divisions that existed in the German labor movement. Thus, in spite of their functional similarities and common goals, the war victims' organizations (*Kriegsopferverbände*) remained divided.[28]

IN ADDITION TO new organizations devoted to the needs of the disabled, the First World War also produced another type of special interest veterans' organization in Germany—the officers' associations. Whereas the former dealt with the casualties of the war, the latter represented the casualties of the Revolution of 1918. In the empire there had been no officers' organizations because there was no need for them.[29] The officer corps was recruited almost exclusively from the nobility and the upper levels of society. Professional officers enjoyed enormous prestige in prewar German society and, upon retirement, officers were provided with pensions. In addition, since many were already independently wealthy or were at least guaranteed remunerative positions after their retirement because of their social connections, most former officers enjoyed secure and comfortable lives after their days of service were over. Assured of economic security and social prestige, they felt no need to unite organizationally to defend their interests during the empire. Not only was such activity unnecessary, it would have been considered demeaning in the view of the aristocratic ex-officers.[30]

Germany's defeat and subsequent revolution transformed the position of officers in German society and with it their reluctance to band together in defense of their common interests. The revolution was accompanied by a widespread wave of anger and revulsion against the old system, and as the most visible representatives of the old society and as symbols of both prewar oppression and wartime hardship and suffering, the officers were frequently subjected to harassment and abuse. Furthermore, the Treaty of Versailles limited Germany's postwar army, the Reichswehr, to 100,000 men, of which only 4,000 were to be officers. As a consequence a number of older officers were retired, and scores of younger ones were dismissed so that more experienced officers could be retained. Faced with unemployment and a Republic dominated by Social Democrats—their bitterest enemies before the war— former officers considered their futures to be precarious indeed. In response, they founded organizations to defend their interests. Although united in their suspicion, resentment, and hatred of the Republic, as well as in their desire to secure their financial and social needs, the ex-officers were unable to unite in a single organization. Like those for disabled veterans, postwar associations of officers were divided along social, political, and professional lines.

The largest of the officers' associations was the German Officers' League (Deutscher Offiziersbund [DOB]). The DOB was formed in November 1919 on the heels of the revolution.[31] By 1922 its members numbered about 100,000, and membership remained near this figure throughout the Republic. The DOB concentrated primarily on securing economic and social benefits for its members, which included retired as well as active officers. Although strongly conservative, nationalistic, and hostile to the Republic, the DOB tried to avoid becoming openly involved in politics so as not to endanger its effectiveness as an economic interest group or to violate military regulations that prohibited active members of the military from belonging to political associations. As a result of its prudence, it became the foremost representative of the economic interests of the officer class, both past and present, and played an influential role in drafting legislation relating to pensions and benefits for retired as well as war-disabled officers and their families. Officially nonpartisan, the DOB, once it had become established and the immediate threat of revolution had passed, became less reserved in political matters. During the middle and later years of the Republic, it began to cooperate more openly with radical organizations and purged what few Republicans there were in its ranks.

Similar to the DOB, but more limited in scope, was the Naval Officers' Association (Marine-Offiziersverband), which had about 5,000 members. Like the DOB, the Naval Officers' Association, although hostile to the Republic, maintained a nonpolitical stance, included active as well as former officers, and concentrated primarily on obtaining economic and social benefits for its members.

To the right of these two organizations was the National Association of German Officers (Nationalverband Deutscher Offiziere [NDO]). The NDO, which had about 10,000 members, was formed in December 1918 by a group of diehard officers who rejected what they felt to be the opportunistic attitude of the DOB, that is, its acceptance of the new conditions in Germany and its emphasis on economic matters. Less interested in economic and social questions than the others, it openly devoted itself to anti-Republican political activity. According to the NDO, the main task was not to secure economic advantages but to carry out "the political fight against the conditions created by the Revolution." After that, it was argued, "the problem of the individual's [material] existence would take care of itself."[32] The NDO was thus a rightist counterpart to the Internationaler Bund, subordinating economic matters to counterrevolution rather than to revolution. True to its word, the NDO waged an active and open fight against the Republic, rejecting any compromise with the new state and demanding the restoration of the Hohenzollern monarchy, as well as a return—with certain radical-conservative modifications—to the constitutional framework of the Bismarckian empire.

Another important officers' association was the National Officers' League (Reichsoffiziersbund [ROB]), which numbered about 10,000. The ROB was originally founded in October 1919 as the League of Sergeant Major Lieutenants (Bund der Feldwebelleutnants) but changed its name at its first convention in October 1920. While ungainly, the original name reflected the particular character of the ROB more clearly than the later one. The ROB's members were not former professional officers but officers who had risen through the ranks or had otherwise been commissioned during the war. In order to maintain the elite social character of the officer corps, these men were rarely given the status of regular officers. Instead they were appointed to the temporary rank of sergeant major lieutenant (Feldwebel-Leutnant). While they served as officers during the war, it was always made clear that they were neither militarily nor socially the equals of the regular officers, and that once the emergency was over they were likely to be demoted.[33]

Discrimination against these officers continued after the war. The DOB's membership, for example, was limited to professional career officers and, as a consequence, the ROB was founded. In addition to pressing for equality of treatment in officers' economic benefits, the ROB also demanded that former sergeant major lieutenants be recognized as lieutenants of the Reserve (Leutnant der Landwehr a.D.). Once this demand was fulfilled, the social resentment of its members seems to have cooled somewhat. The Republic's generosity in this matter, however, did not earn the ROB's support. Officially, the ROB was politically neutral, since a large number of its members were state officials, who, like active military personnel, were prohibited from belonging to political organizations. In practice, however, it was far from neutral. Although it tried to avoid becoming openly involved in political questions, the ROB was heavily influenced by the NDO, to which a number of its members also belonged.

BY THE STANDARDS of the times and in view of the difficult circumstances under which it labored, the Weimar Republic's treatment of veterans, including former officers, was not ungenerous.[34] That this was generally unappreciated, however, was shown by the emergence in the 1920s of the pervasive political myth that Germany's returning veterans had been scorned by an ungrateful Republic.[35] Fashioned and adroitly manipulated by the right, the myth found wide currency. It was given at least superficial credibility by the Republic's failure to offer the usual public symbols of respect and gratitude to veterans of the Great War. In reaction against the militaristic excesses of the empire, the drafters of the Weimar constitution prohibited the award of military medals and decorations. The absence of an official state medal honoring their wartime service offended many veterans who were not in principle hostile to the Republic and opened the way for attacks by veterans' organizations who claimed that the Republic's failure to issue a commemorative medal proved its lack of respect for veterans. Several associations, in what was interpreted as an act of anti-Republican defiance, struck their own commemorative medals.[36]

Political divisions and regional rivalries also blocked efforts to create a national monument to honor the nation's war dead. The lack of consensus over the meaning of the war and the politicization of the war experience was also revealed in squabbles over the nature and symbolic content of local war memorials.[37] These debates reflected the war's divisive impact at yet another level: Was the war to be memorialized as a glorious chapter in the nation's history or as a disaster? Were the soldiers who had fought in the war to be considered heroes or victims? Veterans on both sides of the issue felt they had been betrayed and swindled. Those on the left felt they had been victimized by the prewar authoritarian, militaristic elite, who now, unrepentant, continued to play a large and negative a role in the Republic; those on the right were convinced that they had been betrayed by the prewar pacifistic subculture, which had subverted the war effort, plotted the revolution, and now, undeservedly, controlled the state.[38]

Dissatisfaction with the postwar world was also fueled by the feeling of many veterans, from all walks of life, that their idealism and sacrifice had been exploited by the nation's leaders and the civilian home front and that their contribution to the wartime "economy of sacrifice" had been vastly disproportionate and unappreciated.[39] Such resentments against superiors and civilians—often tinged with misogynist feelings—were not unique to German veterans.[40] Yet in Germany they were sharpened by defeat and politicized by the subsequent traumas of revolution and civil war.

Bewildered by defeat and faced with an uncertain civilian existence, many veterans blamed the Republic for Germany's and their own misfortunes. As a result of the stringent military provisions of the peace treaty, the Republic was forced to demobilize many soldiers, especially young officers, who wanted nothing more than to continue their military careers.[41] Defeat and revolution, with their attendant economic dislocation, meant limited opportunities for employment. This was especially true for young middle-class veterans who had no skills and who could not rely on the help of trade unions after the war as could their working-class counterparts.[42] Social resentment and patriotic outrage combined to turn many middle-class veterans against the Republic and its new leaders. Humiliated by the Treaty of Versailles, and unwilling or unable to acknowledge that Germany had lost the war or that their sacrifice had been in vain, many veterans—as well as many civilians—became prey to the infamous "stab in the back" (*Dolchstoss*) legend, which attributed Germany's defeat to the betrayal of an undefeated army by a cowardly home front led by traitorous leftists.[43]

It is difficult to say with certainty whether German veterans as a whole supported or opposed the Republic. The overwhelming majority of *organized* veterans, however, unquestionably opposed it and were among the most vociferous of the Republic's many right-wing detractors. With the exception of the organizations for the war-disabled (and even here political factors played a role), the mass-based postwar veterans' organizations in Weimar Germany were animated more by political than by economic concerns. Although united in their opposition to the new democratic order, the rightist veterans' organizations, like the political right in general, were divided along generational and ideological lines.

The Kyffhäuserbund continued to be the largest single veterans' organization throughout the Weimar Republic. Although it survived the tumultuous events of 1918–19, the Bund was shaken and its recovery was slow. Its previous obsession with promoting the monarchy and combating social democracy had given most people, including its own members, the feeling that this was the Bund's only purpose, and its belated entry into the field of social welfare during the war had done little to dispel this impression. Faced with the prospect of an organizational collapse and dwindling membership, the Bund's leaders launched a widespread recruitment program in order to win over new members from among the returning veterans. Above all, efforts were made to promote the Bund's "new spirit" by emphasizing its newly found role as an organization devoted to serving the social and economic interests of veterans. In addition, local groups were urged to get rid of old, out-of-date leaders and replace them with younger, more dynamic men who would have a greater appeal to young veterans. As a final means of gaining new members, the Kyffhäuserbund opened its ranks to civilians who had served under military supervision during the war. Once consolidated, the Kyffhäuserbund returned to its prewar practice of excluding Social Democrats.[44]

Although the Kyffhäuserbund survived and eventually returned to its prewar strength of between 2.5 and 3 million members,[45] it never regained the prestige and influence it had enjoyed in the empire. The loss of state support and of its former monopolistic position were without doubt important factors in its relative decline, but an even more crucial cause was the failure to appeal to the new generation of veterans. In general, the activities of the Kyffhäuserbund consisted of building monuments and celebrating the anniversaries of great events in Germany's past. Wrapping itself in dreams of the golden days of the empire, the Kyffhäuserbund was unable to adapt to the present. Like the other prewar nationalist organizations, it was considered too old-fashioned, too "bourgeois," and too tame by the younger, more activist veterans. Instead, they were attracted to the new, modern, and more radical organizations that emerged after the war.

The history of one of these, the Association of Nationalist Soldiers (Verband Nationalgesinnter Soldaten [VNS]), was short and stormy.[46] Originally founded as a veterans' organization in September 1919, the VNS soon became a radical political organization more dedicated to the overthrow of the Republic than to the representation of veterans' interests. While its membership consisted primarily of ex-soldiers, the VNS also accepted as associate members "nationalistic Germans" who had not served in the war. The VNS was closely linked to the ultraradical *völkisch* wing of the German National People's Party (Deutschnationale Volkspartei [DNVP]), and its heavy involvement in politics eventually proved fatal. When in 1922 the *völkisch* wing of the DNVP, which included a number of the VNS's leaders, broke away to form its own party, the German Völkisch Freedom Party, the ranks of the VNS were split. The ultraradical *völkisch* faction retained control of the organization and began to steer it on an activist, putschist course. This alarmed the more moderate members, and in June 1922 they seceded and formed a new organization, the National Association of German Soldiers (Nationalverband Deutscher Soldaten [NDS]). As a result of its continued and virulent anti-Republican activity, the VNS was banned in late June 1922, following the assassination of Walther Rathenau, the Republican foreign minister. Shortly thereafter the

NDS was also banned because of its anti-Republican activity and the suspicion that it was merely a cover for the VNS. Although both organizations continued to exist in some states and were later revived in others, neither played a significant role in veterans' politics after 1922.

The most dynamic, well known, and successful of Germany's postwar veterans' organizations was by far the Steel Helmet, League of Front Soldiers (Der Stahlhelm, Bund der Frontsoldaten), founded in December 1918 by Franz Seldte, a former captain who had fought on the western front and had lost his left arm in the battle of the Somme.[47] As indicated by its subtitle, membership in the Stahlhelm was limited to soldiers who had fought at the front. According to the minutes of its founding meeting, the new organization had three major goals: to promote comradeship among former front soldiers, to support the mutual interests of its members, and to work for the maintenance of law and order or, as Seldte bluntly put it, to stop "this *Schweinerei* of revolution" from going any further. Thus from the beginning the Stahlhelm had political objectives as well as the more common goals of promoting comradeship and representing material interests.

Although opposed to the revolution, the Stahlhelm was by no means a reactionary organization. During the course of 1919, its role as a defender of law and order increasingly gained the upper hand, however; this, combined with general political developments, such as the signing of the Treaty of Versailles, drove the Stahlhelm further and further to the right. The shift in emphasis from the representation of veterans' interests to general right-wing political activity was reflected in a letter written by Seldte in 1920, in which he characterized the three main goals of the Stahlhelm as now being the "encouragement of the old comradeship, support of law and order, and reconstruction [Aufbau]."[48] By 1920 "reconstruction" had become a general code word on the right for opposition to the Republic. Like many other rightist organizations in the Weimar Republic, the political profile of the Stahlhelm was in large part formed by its activity as a paramilitary "self-defense" organization, and by the mid-1920s it had become the leading element of a virulent paramilitary subculture that plagued the Republic from its inception.[49]

The seeds for this subculture were inadvertently provided by the Ebert government in the form of the volunteer units, the so-called Free Corps (Freikorps), which it authorized the General Staff to raise to suppress leftist uprisings in late 1918 and early 1919.[50] The Free Corps had provided a temporary shelter for many veterans while at the same time giving numerous young Germans who had not served in the war a taste of military life and a "front experience" of their own. Following the dissolution of the volunteer forces because of Allied pressure, their members—many of whom were unable, as

Robert Waite has put it, to "psychologically demobilize"—were forced to return to a civilian society that was alien, disliked, and distrusted.[51] Militarily disenfranchised, these "military desperados" found new homes in a profusion of so-called military associations (*Wehrverbände*) that flourished in the early years of the Republic: Bund Oberland, Wiking Bund, Young German Order, Wehrwolf, and increasingly, the Stahlhelm.[52] With the exception of the Stahlhelm, these were, strictly speaking, not veterans' organizations since they also included nonveterans. Nonetheless, they were recruited primarily from veterans, and their leaders were almost exclusively former officers.

In 1920 a young Free Corps officer about to leave service wrote a letter to his commander outlining what he felt had to be done by the war generation: "We must enter politics and try to create a generation of leaders which unites the courage to act, the character, the firmness, the energy and the composure of the soldier with the spirit, flair, cleverness, and snake-like cunning of the politician. This is the task of the generation of the trenches."[53] This desire to combine military virtues with political activity was embodied in the *Wehrverbände*.

The military associations combined open propagandistic activity with programs of clandestine military training. The former was carried out under the guise of patriotic organizations dedicated to the national cause in general and, in particular, to the preservation and propagation of German military traditions; the latter was supported by the Reichswehr, which felt the *Wehrverbände* were necessary to supplement Germany's reduced armed forces, and by large segments of the middle class who saw the paramilitary formations as counterweights to working-class organizations. Eschewing traditional political activity, the military associations sought to achieve their political aims through military action. The ultimate goal was a war of liberation against France à la the 1813 revival against Napoleon. Such a war against Germany's "external" enemies, however, was considered blocked by the "internal" enemy, a term initially used to describe the Communists but that soon came to mean virtually all those who supported the Republic.

The hopes of the military associations to transform their military potential into an effective political force during the tumultuous early years of the Republic were never realized. The shots at the Munich Feldherrnhalle on the morning of 9 November 1923 marked more than an end to Hitler's abortive Beer Hall Putsch. They also signaled the end of an era in paramilitary politics. Realizing that a direct seizure of power was impossible, the leaders of the military associations began to reverse their priorities. Whereas previously they had put military activity first and perceived political problems in a subsidiary and derivative manner, they now reasoned that the existing "system" had to be changed before military action could again become meaningful. Putschism, in short, had to be replaced by politics. During the middle years of the Republic, the military associations transformed themselves into self-styled political combat leagues (*politische Kampfbünde*), which consciously developed political programs and sought to gain political influence. At the same time, however, they retained their military forms of organization, dress, and action.

The changeover to political activity was accompanied by other changes. Once the hope for an immediate overthrow of the Republic was abandoned in favor of long-term political activity, providing reserves for the thinning ranks of war veterans became critical. In 1924 the Stahlhelm, which previously had limited its membership to veterans who had served six months at the front, created a special section (Landsturm des Stahlhelms) that accepted men who supported the Stahlhelm's goals but because of "age or other honorable reasons" had not served six months at the front.[54] At the same time, the Stahlhelm, like the other combat leagues, formed a youth organization. Such measures not only reflected the Stahlhelm's transformation into a political combat league but also point to a basic difference between it and veterans' organizations in other countries. While veterans in England, for example, quickly abandoned what has been called "external aims" in favor of bread-and-butter issues such as pensions, the Stahlhelm virtually neglected such activity and ultimately even sacrificed its character as a veterans' organization in order to achieve its "external aims," that is, the overthrow of the Republic.[55]

By 1926 most of the former military associations had completed their transformation.[56] Once force had been renounced, however, the combat leagues were faced with the thorny problem of how they, as extraparliamentary organizations, were to influence political developments in a parliamentary democracy. Attempts to pressure the rightist parties into adopting more intransigent positions proved to be frustrating and ineffective. Although the parties welcomed the support of the combat leagues in the fight against their competitors on the left, they soon became annoyed with the efforts of the "nonpolitical" politicians to meddle in their affairs. Moreover, the ill-disguised contempt of the combat leagues for the parties and their patent desire for the latter's eventual liquidation made harmonious cooperation problematical at best.[57]

To the dismay of the combat leagues, politicization was not a guarantee of political success. In their efforts to bring the parties into line, the combat leagues frequently resorted to the threat of electoral blackmail, but the fear of leftist gains usually caused them to back down. There also was periodic discussion among the combat leagues over the possibility of forming their own parties, but, given their antipathy to parliamentary government as well as the hardheaded realization that they could hardly beat the parties at their own game, such talk remained for the most part conjectural and was intended more as a threat to the parties than as a serious alternative. Ultimately, the effort to develop political programs and tactics produced tensions among the combat leagues that made unified action—the fundamental prerequisite for success—impossible.[58]

If political activity divided the combat leagues, they were united in their basic ideological premises that the war had been a decisive watershed in history and that veterans were called upon to be the heralds of a new political age. These views were expressed in the so-called Front Ideology, which had an extremely pervasive effect in postwar Germany, not only among veterans but on the political right as a whole.[59] For many Germans, plagued by a history of disunity, the war—at least initially—had seemed to offer a unifying ideal.[60] This feeling of unity and common purpose was continued and deepened in the trenches, where, in the face of the common danger, differences in civilian profession and position in society were forgotten and men were judged on their skill as soldiers. During the mid-1920s this experience was politicized and made the basis for a powerful anti-Republican ideology.[61] The experience of the trenches was seen in retrospect as embodying all the virtues that were lacking in the present state and that were to be possessed by the ideal future state, which—unlike the Republic—would be capable of reversing and avenging the loss of the war. The politicization of the Front Experience (*Fronterlebnis*), with its stylized and distorted rendition of a heroic past and vague, idealistic pictures of a better future, provided the basis for unrelenting attacks on the political and social realities of the present. Claiming to be the sole guardians of the nationalist grail and the "true" state, the combat leagues and their ideological fellow travelers rejected the existing one. The Weimar Republic, they demanded, must be replaced by a state that was "national, social, military, and authoritarian."[62]

Because they had risked their lives for the nation and proved themselves in the trenches, former soldiers felt themselves uniquely qualified to lead the nation, which by chance and subterfuge had fallen into the hands of civilians whose weakness, lack of commitment, or outright treason had been responsible for Germany's defeat and its current problems. The experience and achievements of the front soldier, it was argued, had created a new type of person who alone possessed the insight, strength, and resolution to save Germany from its present state of weakness and chaos.[63] One expression of this theme of the special role and rights of the former soldier was the contention that the Republic's system of universal and equal suffrage was a mistake, since only those who had performed a service for the state, above all the front soldiers, were entitled to full political rights.[64]

The experience of the front, in the words of the Stahlhelm's leader, Seldte, was to be "the starting point for the transformation of the German state."[65] The combat leagues were in effect an attempt to transfer directly into civilian life the discipline and comradeship of the front. The militaristic, hierarchical, and *bündisch* organizational form of the combat leagues was to serve simultaneously as a model and as a means of overcoming the pluralistic and divided society of the Weimar Republic. The combat leagues felt they were the political vanguard of the new state, not only because they strove for it but because they incorporated the desired new political order in their very being.

Although the virtues of the future state envisioned by the combat leagues were widely advertised, its particulars for the most part remained vague. One thing, however, was clear—it was not to be a return to the empire. The young veterans and other members of the combat leagues who had reached maturity during or after the war had little reason to mourn the passing of the empire. Many, in fact, had already expressed their aversion to Wilhelmine society before the war as members of the German youth movement, and the empire's collapse had only further confirmed their conviction that it and those who ruled it had been corrupt and outdated.[66] Indeed, the young activists often attacked the new Republic not because it had destroyed the old order but because it had *not*. The Republic, they charged, was nothing more than a continuation of Wilhelmine society with all its faults. Foremost among these was the failure to win over the working class to the national cause.[67]

During the empire, it was claimed, the ruling and propertied classes had failed to see this shortcoming and it had cost Germany the war. The bitter class antagonism that still divided Germany, argued the combat leagues, had to be removed before Germany could ever successfully wage the hoped-for war of liberation. To the proponents of the Front Ideology, the war had been a watershed. The front generation, forged in the crucible of the trenches, had overcome the divisions that had separated Germans in the past. The "storm of steel" had obliterated traditional social distinctions. All that mattered now was devotion to the national cause. In order to induce the working class to forsake its previous alignment with the international cause and to join the nationalist ranks, argued the young nationalists, real social reform, even social revolution, was not only permissible but necessary. The national revolution, however, always had precedence. Socialism was not an end in itself but a means to an end; it was to be "the savior of nationalism."[68]

The naive political conceptions that were associated with the Front Ideology had an enormous appeal. For many young veterans the war had been, and would remain, the decisive experience in their lives. That the war experience was the decisive event in the lives of a large cohort was unquestionably true.

The expectation that the interpretation of it would be uniform was not. No matter how unique, how bonding, the war experience had been, it was unavoidably perceived through the lens of prewar political conviction and refracted by postwar political experience. For those, largely middle-class, veterans who stemmed from a prewar "social-political milieu" that was purportedly "unpolitical," "above party," or, simply, "national," this politicization was not always recognized. Thus, wittingly or unwittingly, the invidious— because largely unacknowledged—politicization of German veterans that had begun in the empire was continued in the Weimar Republic under the rubric of the Front Ideology.[69]

Politically unschooled before the war and faced upon their return with a situation that offered them little in the way of political or social security, many young middle-class veterans saw in military forms and virtues the solution to the Republic's problems. The attempt to use the Front Experience as a basis for concrete political activity was, of course, unrealistic. It betrayed a woeful lack of understanding of political and social reality.[70] In the trenches, where all men were united in the struggle for survival, all else was secondary; the normal divisions and differences between men were either suspended or suppressed. In a peacetime society, it was inevitable that differences would again arise.[71] The refusal to acknowledge this and to try to return to the simpler circumstances that prevailed during the abnormal conditions of the war ultimately led to dictatorial and totalitarian solutions, since all interests that seemed to conflict with what was defined as the national good either had to be forced into line or eliminated.

In fact, it soon became clear that the Front Ideology was highly selective and instead of promoting consensus only helped to justify further division. Not only were the "cowardly" and pacifistic civilians of the home front excluded from the new elite, but so were those front soldiers who had failed to draw the proper conclusions from the war experience itself. Ultimately, the claim to the "true" war experience became limited to those on the right who opposed the Republic. The "new nationalism" that the combat leagues so proudly espoused was, as a contemporary observer remarked, "less an intellectual construct than an inner attitude."[72] The division of German society into "nationalists" and "internationalists," instead of bourgeoisie and workers, did little to change existing class divisions but only perpetuated the Bismarckian practice of dividing the nation into "state-supporting" elements and "enemies of the Reich." In practice, the class antagonisms that had ostensibly been obliterated by the war experience and the "storm of steel" remained. Simultaneously national warriors and social pacifists, the combat leagues called for a socialism, be it "national" socialism or "front" socialism, that was in fact little more than an appeal for the total mobilization of German society for the war of revenge that they someday hoped to lead.[73]

The combat leagues and the other rightist veterans' organizations in Weimar Germany were never able on their own to achieve their hoped-for militant, authoritarian state or to realize their dream of a nation totally mobilized for a war of revenge. For this they had to wait for Adolf Hitler and the Third Reich. Not all veterans supported Hitler. Certainly those in the Reichsbund or the Reichsbanner, the Republican combat league formed in 1924 to counter those on the right, did not.[74] Nonetheless, the overwhelming majority of organized veterans either went over openly to Hitler and the Nazis or at least enthusiastically applauded their success. During the final years of the Republic, the rightist combat leagues, with the exception of the Stahlhelm, declined and were essentially subsumed into the Nazi movement. Even though the Stahlhelm was able to hold its own in terms of members, it too came increasingly under the dominance of the National Socialists, as its leaders, mesmerized by the rising political power of the Nazis, sought to manipulate Hitler for their own ends.[75]

WHILE THE National Socialist German Workers' Party (Nationalsozialistische Deutsche Arbeiterpartei [NSDAP]) consistently portrayed itself as a movement that incorporated the "spirit of the front," its avowedly political stance kept it relatively aloof from veterans' politics per se for most of the years of the Republic. Despite the outward similarities of the NSDAP's Sturmabteilungen (SA) to the rightist combat leagues, there was a qualitative difference that was realized by both sides.[76] Veterans' politics remained dominated by the purportedly "unpolitical" veterans' organizations. Although sporadic appeals to war victims were made by the NSDAP during elections in the 1920s, there were no sustained efforts to capture them as a significant interest group.[77] This changed with the onset of the Great Depression. In 1930 the party launched a campaign to organize disabled veterans and the survivors of soldiers killed in the Great War. The impetus was provided by the Emergency Economic Decrees of the Brüning government, the first of which was issued on 26 July 1930. In an attempt to balance the budget in a period of declining revenues caused by the depression, Brüning introduced measures designed to cut government expenditures sharply. Among those affected by the cutbacks were the *Kriegsopfer*: disabled veterans, their dependents, and the survivors of soldiers killed in the war. In addition to outright reductions in pension rates, eligibility requirements for certain benefits were raised and administrative procedures were tightened, all of which produced substantial reductions in the

benefits provided by the Reichsversorgungsgesetz of 1920. The cuts predictably unleashed a storm of protest from the ranks of the war-disabled and their
families, whose outrage was fueled by growing desperation as the depression
worsened and the initial cuts were followed by further reductions in benefits.[78]
The Nazis were quick to seize onto the anger of disabled veterans and to
exploit the discomfiture of the existing war victims' organizations, which
seemed powerless to check the government's dismantling of the pension
program. In September 1930 a special section for war victims (Referat Kriegsopferversorgung) was set up in the party's directorate, headed by a longtime
crony of Hitler, Hanns Oberlindober.[79]

The purpose of the new Referat, which later became the National Socialist
War Victims' Association (National-Sozialistische Kriegsopferversorgung
[NSKOV]), was to exploit the discontent of war victims and, without creating
an actual competing organization, to infiltrate and/or undermine the existing
Kriegsopferverbände. The tactics employed by the NSDAP toward disabled
veterans thus paralleled those employed vis-à-vis other special interest groups
during the final crisis years of the Republic.[80] A directive to the Gau leadership
of 18 November 1930 noted that the recent increase in the party's Reichstag
representation offered the possibility of influencing special interest legislation,
including war victims' legislation, "which the governing parties have up to
now only dealt with as a secondary matter." Gau leaders were informed that
the Referat would be forming branches at the Gau, Bezirk, and local levels.
The new agencies, which were to be set up in cooperation with—and financed
by—local Gau officials, were to be staffed by persons familiar with the legal
intricacies of the Reichsversorgungsgesetz. The agencies were to advise pensioners and to represent them in legal proceedings dealing with veterans'
benefits, proceedings which were proliferating as a result of the government's
efforts to cut expenses associated with the war pension system.[81] The underly-
ing purpose of the new service, of course, was to attract previously unorganized pensioners to the Nazi movement and, if possible, to win over dis-
gruntled members of the existing war victims' organizations. At the same time
the Referat began to publish a series of pamphlets dealing with veterans'
benefits. These were supplemented by a monthly publication, Der Dank des
Vaterlandes (The Thanks of the Fatherland), which in the fall of 1932 was
supplanted by a new periodical, Deutsche Kriegsopferversorgung, eventually the
official publication of the NSKOV.

Although those in charge of organizing the war victims complained in early
1932 that local organizations had not done enough to exploit the "incompara-
bly fruitful field of agitation offered by the embittered victims of the war,"[82]

the party was effectively using the issue to attack the Republic and its supporters. During the final years of the Republic, the National Socialists pursued a
two-track strategy with regard to war victims: on the one hand, they ruthlessly
attacked the Republican government and the existing war victims' organizations, claiming that the cuts in pensions demonstrated the former's lack of
concern for veterans and the latter's inability (or worse, unwillingness) to
represent effectively the interests of their members; on the other hand, they
criticized the "Marxist" RVG for having created a "pension psychosis" that
made disabled veterans think of themselves as welfare recipients rather than as
the military heroes they were. In the final analysis, it was asserted, the plight of
the war victims was the logical consequence of living under a pacifistic regime
born out of the treason of the "November Criminals," who had stabbed the
victorious German army in the back in 1918. Denigration of the accomplishments of Germany's soldiers and ingratitude for their sacrifices, it was argued,
were an integral part of such a "system."[83]

The war victims' dissatisfaction with the existing interest groups was also
skillfully exploited by the NSDAP. The fragmentation of the war victims'
movement, which paralleled that of society and reflected in part the inability to
achieve a consensus on the meaning of the war, served to underline the war
victims' organizations' function as narrow interest groups, weakened their
public image, and lessened their effectiveness. Capitalizing on its position as
the largest non-Marxist party in the Reichstag after September 1930, which
made its legislative support indispensable, and brandishing the threat to form
its own war victims' organization, the NSDAP effectively brought the Zentralverband and the National Association of War-Disabled and Survivors
(Reichsverband deutscher Kriegsbeschädigter und Kriegshinterbliebener),
which had succeeded the Einheitsverband, under its control.[84] The Nazis'
relationship with the leftist war victims' organizations was predictably hostile
and scornful. Those who believed that the Internationaler Bund could help
German disabled veterans were warned that they would experience the same
disillusionment as those who in 1918 had "waited for red flags in the French
trenches and on British warships." The only purpose of the Reichsbund, it was
claimed, was to win votes for the party of "treason and draft dodgers."[85] While
largely immune to such ridicule, the Reichsbund was vulnerable to the charges
of ineffectiveness, since the party with which it was affiliated was, albeit
unwillingly, a key supporter of the benefit-cutting Emergency Economic
Decrees.[86] Founded to exploit the immediate economic fears unleashed by
Brüning's austerity measures, the NSKOV's angry attacks successfully tapped
deep reservoirs of anger and resentment among the war victims and brought

many of them into the Nazi-led coalition of discontent that eventually toppled the Republic and boosted Hitler into power.

THE WEIMAR REPUBLIC'S experience with veterans was a negative one. Organized veterans contributed significantly to the failure of Germany's first experiment in democracy. Veterans' organizations and the combat leagues, whose core membership was composed of veterans, institutionalized instability: they functioned as negative schools of politics, helping to hold the anti-Republican forces of the right in a state of semimobilization during the years of relative prosperity and stability in the late 1920s, which facilitated Hitler's mobilization of them in full after the onset of the depression. The military subculture of the combat leagues militarized politics, undermined the authority of the Republic, and prepared the way—ideologically and psychologically—for the establishment of the violent, militarized society of the Third Reich.

TWO

VETERANS IN
THE THIRD REICH

National Socialist propaganda often proclaimed the movement's affinity with the First World War. The "brown" armies of the NSDAP and SA were portrayed as the heirs of the "field gray" army of the First World War, and the Third Reich was represented as the fulfillment of the legacy of the front soldiers. The fact that Hitler himself had served at the front was repeatedly stressed by party propaganda, as well as by Hitler himself, and one of the most popular roles played by Der Führer was that of the humble, anonymous front soldier who would lead Germany to the realization of the goals for which its soldiers had fought and died before being betrayed by the "November Criminals."[1]

In the Third Reich the front soldier myth functioned as a German version of the American log cabin myth. Just as the latter, by conferring "man of the people" status, enhanced a politician's claim to democratic political leadership, so service in the trenches legitimized Hitler's claim to leadership in a war-traumatized country in which the traditional elites had been discredited and displaced. Hitler in fact owed his political career to the November Revolution, which swept away the class- and caste-bound political system of the empire in which he normally would never have found a place;[2] but since the revolution was condemned by the National Socialists as an unmitigated evil, this could not be acknowledged. Instead, another, more noble progenitor of a new political elite had to be found. This became the war and the Front Experience (*Fronterlebnis*).[3] The positive, emotion-laden image of the front soldier was invoked not only to legitimize Hitler's claim to leadership but to justify the Nazis' unprincipled attack on the "November system" that had presumably betrayed German soldiers in 1918. In the Nazi worldview, the Weimar Republic was accordingly depicted as the negation of all that the front soldiers had stood for, while the Third Reich was portrayed as the embodiment of their virtues and the vehicle for the realization of their—and the nation's—mission.

Invocation of the Front Experience and Prussian military virtues provided the ideological and psychological foundations for the militarization of German society under the Third Reich.[4] Their external manifestations were ubiquitous: in the regimentation and uniforming of virtually every segment of society; in the constant rallies and parades; in the profligate distribution of medals and awards, including those given to mothers for their contribution to the "Battle of Births" being waged in the maternity wards of the Third Reich. Through such measures, the regime hoped to resuscitate and institutionalize the "Spirit of 1914" and the *Burgfrieden* of the First World War in a purer, more effective—and, most importantly, more durable—form, a *Volksgemeinschaft cum Wehrgemeinschaft* that would enable Germany to reverse the defeat of the First World War.[5]

In the militarized society of the Third Reich, the figure of the front soldier assumed a heroic stature. He was ceaselessly presented as a role model for civilians. Military service was transformed into a sacred right and the prerequisite to full citizenship. Disabled veterans were to be honored as the "first citizens of the Reich." In presenting the Third Reich as the antithesis of the reviled Weimar Republic, Nazi propaganda denigrated the Republic's treatment of veterans, claiming that it had victimized the heroes of the war, first by robbing them of victory through the *Dolchstoss*, and then by treating them as second-class citizens. Under the Republic, the Nazis claimed, the victors of the war had become antiheroes—a process they promised to reverse when they came to power. Like most promises of the National Socialists, those made to veterans were specious. Showered with rhetoric, veterans were psychologically manipulated and organized to support the regime's militaristic policies—policies that created millions of new veterans, who were then left to face the ruins of a second lost war.

THE NON-NAZI *Kriegsopferverbände* did not survive long into the Third Reich. Their *Gleichschaltung* had in fact already begun before Hitler became chancellor. By mid-1931 the NSKOV had established a solid framework of counseling centers, and the main office, directed by Hanns Oberlindober and his deputy, Peter Martin, had begun to negotiate with the non-Marxist war victims' organizations.[6] In July 1932 Oberlindober forced the Reichsverband and Zentralverband to merge into a single organization called the Reichsverband deutscher Kriegsopfer. Following the Nazi takeover, the Reichsverband was forced to join a new organization, the National-Sozialistischer Reichsverband deutscher Kriegsopfer, whose formation was announced during a memorial service for the war dead that was broadcast over national radio on 14 April 1933, Good Friday. This was followed by another reorganization, producing the Nationale Kampfgemeinschaft deutscher Kriegsopferverbände, which, in addition to the National-Sozialistischer Reichsverband, included the welfare sections of the Kyffhäuserbund and the DOB. At the same time the Communist-led Internationaler Bund was dissolved. When the hapless leaders of the Social Democratic Reichsbund, seeing the handwriting on the wall, tried to initiate negotiations with Oberlindober, they were brusquely ordered to dissolve their organization and to transfer its membership and financial resources to the Kampfgemeinschaft by 31 May. Following this, the Kampfgemeinschaft was dissolved, and in July the National-Sozialistische Kriegsopferversorgung was declared to be the official "unified" organization of German war victims, which, Oberlindober proclaimed, stood with "its ranks closed, behind the unknown soldier of the World War, Adolf Hitler."[7]

Having gained control of the war victims, Oberlindober raised his sights to his next objective, which was to combine all veterans into a single organization under his control. In part this was simply an expression of the rampant empire building that was encouraged by the bureaucratic Social Darwinism of the Third Reich. At the same time, however, it reflected Oberlindober's conviction that the Front Experience had been the decisive experience of his generation, that it had transcended prewar social reality, and that it had created a unified veterans' community that must be recognized, cultivated, and preserved. As was the case with many of his generation, Oberlindober's vision of the "Community of the Front" was accompanied by a deep and abiding resentment of the traditional aristocratic officer corps of the Kaiserreich, a resentment that was both reflected and fed by his active participation in the SA, of which he remained a member until the end of his career. Like the leader of the SA, Ernst Röhm, Oberlindober had been an officer in the First World War and had emerged from the "storm of steel" with an intense sense of populist equality—at least with regard to the military. If the idealistic views of the Community of the Front formed the positive side of his program to unite all veterans under his leadership, these efforts were given a hard, negative edge by his desire to destroy the influence of the conservative monarchist officers who dominated the leadership of the traditional veterans' organizations, such as the Kyffhäuserbund and the DOB.

Following the Nazi takeover, the conservative veterans' organizations had quickly moved to secure a place for themselves in the new state through acts of accommodation that bordered on "self-coordination." In May 1933 General Rudolf von Horn, the head of the Kyffhäuserbund, placed the Bund under

Hitler's leadership and reorganized it according to the *Führerprinzip*, with half of the positions on the board of directors permanently reserved for members of the NSDAP.[8] With equal alacrity, the Reichsbund der Zivildienstberechtigten, an organization representing former professional soldiers, primarily noncommissioned officers, who were eligible for civil service jobs, reorganized itself, changed its name to the National Association of Former Professional Soldiers (Reichstreubund ehemaliger Berufssoldaten), and placed itself under a new Nazi Bundesführer, Franz Schwede-Coburg.[9] The reaction of the officers' associations was more restrained, though they also pledged their support to the new regime. A willing agent to assist in bringing the officers' associations into line was soon found in the person of Graf Rüdiger von der Goltz, head of the Nationalverband Deutscher Offiziere and the Vereinigte Vaterländische Verbände Deutschlands. If Oberlindober represented the quintessential *alter Kämpfer*, von der Goltz was the quintessential Germannational, *völkisch* fellow traveler. By the fall of 1933 he had succeeded in bringing all but the DOB into a cartel.[10]

The desperate scrambling of the conservative, traditional veterans' organizations only aroused the contempt of Oberlindober. Like other Nazi military populists, he considered the monarchist organizations to be caste-bound and reactionary, perverters of the true lessons of the war, and a threat to the *völkisch* Third Reich of Adolf Hitler. Soon after his takeover of the war victims' organizations, the Reichskriegsopferführer began to infiltrate the Kyffhäuserbund and the DOB with the intent of bringing them under his control. In a May 1933 report detailing the *Gleichschaltung* of the war victims' organizations, Oberlindober noted that he had assumed positions of leadership in the Kyffhäuserbund and the DOB, and that while both groups would continue to remain "temporarily as individual groups" within the newly formed NSKOV, "the transfer of all members into the new unified organization of war victims would follow as soon as possible."[11] Oberlindober's announcement proved to be premature. Whereas his takeover of the *Kriegsopferverbände* had been facilitated by their vulnerability and the fact that his efforts in this area had not attracted any competitors within the Nazi movement, the new targets were stronger and had drawn the attention of Oberlindober's ideological compatriot and SA superior, Ernst Röhm.

In his quest to create a mass-based *Volksarmee*, Röhm was determined to exploit every source of potential military strength, including that embodied in the veterans' organizations. On 6 November 1933 he issued an order that simultaneously broke the back of the SA's main paramilitary rival, the Stahlhelm, and created the organizational framework for the *Gleichschaltung* of the remaining veterans' organizations through the establishment of a two-tier SA reserve system that encompassed all organized veterans. The first level consisted of Stahlhelm members who had not already been taken over into the SA; the second level was composed of the members of the remaining veterans' organizations, including the Kyffhäuserbund, officers' groups, and regimental associations. During the winter other changes were made that further reduced the independence of the veterans' organizations and subordinated them more firmly to Röhm's control: in January 1934 General von Horn resigned as head of the Kyffhäuserbund and was replaced by Colonel Wilhelm Reinhard, the head of the second level of the SA reserve system, and in February the officers' associations were amalgamated into a new organization, the Reich Association of German Officers (Reichsverband Deutscher Offiziere [RDO]), headed by von der Goltz with Reinhard as his deputy.[12] Yet, just as his goal seemed to be in reach, the SA leader's bid to gain monopolistic control of veterans in the Third Reich was brought to a bloody conclusion with his murder and the purge of the SA in the summer of 1934. Thereafter, Röhm's empire disintegrated. The SA was reduced, and, among other things, the second level of the SA reserve system was severed from SA control, which restored the sovereignty—or semisovereignty—of the Kyffhäuserbund and the RDO.

As a high-ranking member of the SA leadership who shared Röhm's desire for a "Second Revolution," Oberlindober was undoubtedly discomfited by the Blood Purge.[13] At the same time, he quickly realized that the collapse of Röhm's empire provided an opportunity to expand his own and to achieve his objective of creating a single veterans' organization under his control. In late 1934 he sent Hitler a twelve-page memorandum on the subject.[14] He began by criticizing the way in which the Kyffhäuserbund and the DOB had managed to avoid being coordinated. As a result of dissimulation, cosmetic changes, and the intervention of well-placed friends both inside and outside the movement, the two organizations had retained considerable independence and—worse—continued to be run by reactionaries. Although the rank and file, in Oberlindober's view, were ready to "acknowledge without reservation the Führer and the new Germany," their leaders were not genuine National Socialists and wanted "to pursue the same reactionary policies they had pursued in the years before Adolf Hitler took the leadership of the nation into his hands." This clearly was dangerous, and the remedy, according to Oberlindober, was the formation of a single veterans' organization "under the leadership of true National Socialists." Such an organization would benefit the state in a number of ways. Militarily, even if the veterans might be too old for active service, they could help to train young draftees and could also be organized into home guard units (Landwehr- und Landsturmformationen) capable of guarding railway stations and providing air raid protection. Moreover, Oberlindober argued, these units would "be the moral backbone for the fighting front at home" and thereby a means of "neutralizing those dangerous forces [Gefahrenmomente] which during the last war led to the collapse of 1918."[15] A second benefit rendered by a united veterans' organization was that it would reunite soldiers into the same sort of *Gemeinschaft* that had existed during the war by once again bringing together enlisted men and officers.

From this "soldierly viewpoint," Oberlindober continued, one came directly to the "political viewpoint," which ultimately was "the most important one for the unification of the German veterans' organizations." A united veterans' movement, Oberlindober contended, would re-create the unity of the war years and demonstrate the solidarity of the Third Reich both at home and abroad. Class and regional differences would be obliterated. Thus, at home, the reconstituted *Frontgemeinschaft* would be a model for the larger *Volksgemeinschaft*. Abroad, Germany's enemies would be made aware that they were no longer dealing with a country divided by partisan politicians and profiteers but with the united Germany that had aroused their fear and respect in the trenches and battlefields of the First World War. Such an organization, in short, would be a useful means of impressing, perhaps intimidating, Germany's foreign enemies. Oberlindober concluded by describing the sort of person who should lead the new organization: he must pursue neither personal, dynastic, or social goals; he must be free from all state and economic ties, including dependence on the Wehrmacht; he must above all be a committed National Socialist and unconditionally loyal to Adolf Hitler. It is not difficult to imagine who Oberlindober had in mind.[16]

Oberlindober's plans apparently did not find favor with Hitler or the Nazi hierarchy, and the Reichskriegsopferführer's wider ambitions remained unfulfilled, if not stilled. While the NSKOV leader continued to inveigh against the reactionary leaders of the traditional veterans' and officers' organizations,[17] Colonel Reinhard, the head of the Kyffhäuserbund, found a protector in the person of the SS-Reichsführer, Heinrich Himmler.[18] Thus fortified, Reinhard resisted Oberlindober's continued attempts to convert the NSKOV into an organization for all front soldiers, not just those who had been disabled, while at the same time working to expand the Kyffhäuserbund's field of activity.[19] The rivalry of the NSKOV and the Kyffhäuserbund provides yet another example of the bureaucratic Social Darwinism of the Third Reich. A pathetic but characteristic expression of this was the fight for control of the organization representing former prisoners of war, a struggle that ended in victory for Oberlindober with the absorption of the National Association of

Former Prisoners of War (Reichsvereinigung ehemaliger Kriegsgefangener) into the NSKOV in late 1936.[20]

ALTHOUGH OBERLINDOBER'S efforts to expand his fiefdom failed, the NSKOV itself flourished, fed by the confiscated funds of the Reichsbund and secured by its monopolistic position.[21] Already battered by the cuts connected with Brüning's Emergency Economic Decrees and faced with the prospect of further restrictions in disability areas deemed "undeserving" by the new regime, disabled veterans were dependent on the NSKOV to represent their interests. These considerations undoubtedly served to attract new members and to keep members of the coordinated *Kriegsopferverbände* in the ranks of the NSKOV, whose membership at the end of 1933 was over a million.[22]

One of the main themes of the NSKOV's early propaganda was the need for a new, reformed RVG. At the 1933 Nuremberg party rally Oberlindober summarized the goals of his organization and sketched the outlines of a new law for war victims.[23] The signers of the Versailles *Diktat*, he claimed, had "preferred to condemn the front soldiers rather than grant them the respect and honor they deserved." Disabled veterans, declared Oberlindober, were not to be considered simply as pensioners, as had been the case under the Republic. With its "fundamental hatred of everything that was soldierly," the Republic had placed the defenders of the nation on the same level as the "unemployed, invalids, and other welfare recipients." In the petty, politically motivated competition of the postwar *Kriegsopferverbände*, "the starting point for the pension system, the sacrifices of the front, had receded more and more into the background and material welfare, rather shamefacedly [verschämt] called social policy, had been thrust more and more into the foreground." The result of all this was that "the honorable and honor-deserving soldiers became unwelcome welfare recipients [unangenehme Rentenempfänger] in the eyes of the tax-paying public." Veterans wanted honor, not just pensions, declared Oberlindober, and to mark these "first citizens of the nation" off from those who "had sacrificed less," he suggested a twelve-point program that included granting front soldiers a special insignia or medal, reserved seats at all public functions, preferential treatment in governmental offices, reduced rates for transportation and cultural events, and preferential hiring (with quotas) in public service jobs. Finally, in a typical Nazi maneuver to appropriate the glory of the war experience for the movement (and to secure undeserved spoils for its members), members of NSDAP paramilitary formations who had been injured during the *Kampfzeit* (as well as the survivors of those killed) were to be accorded identical rights and privileges.[24] Oberlindober's proposals obviously reflected his own resentments, but (with the exception of the last, obviously partisan, one) they also meshed with the frustrations and desires of large numbers of ordinary, non-Nazi war victims, who resented the way they had been treated under the Republic.

On taking power, the National Socialist government immediately sought to demonstrate its goodwill toward veterans.[25] At the official founding of the NSKOV Oberlindober had been solemnly charged by the newly named labor minister, Franz Seldte, the Stahlhelm leader, with the drafting of new legislation for the war victims, and the Reichskriegsopferführer ended his 1933 Nuremberg party rally address with a call for the "immediate implementation of a new law for war victims drafted by the front soldiers themselves." In the following months the press of the NSKOV reiterated Oberlindober's demands, and the upcoming passage of a new law was ballyhooed. Meanwhile, behind the scenes, a battle was taking place between the Labor Ministry and the NSKOV over the administration of the war victims' welfare program. The struggle, which reflected the more general debate about the need for a "Second Revolution," ended in the defeat of the NSKOV.[26] The new law incorporated some of the NSKOV's demands, but the basic structure and content of the RVG remained intact and it continued to be administered by the Labor Ministry.

While Seldte was able to successfully fend off Oberlindober's efforts, he still found himself caught in a crossfire between Nazi zealots in the Reich bureaucracy, on the one hand, and the Reich minister of finance, on the other. The labor minister's first draft for a new law was rejected by Wilhelm Frick, the minister of interior, since it corresponded "so little to National Socialist demands regarding war victims' legislation that it raised severe political reservations," a view that was shared by State Secretary Hans-Heinrich Lammers, the head of the Reich Chancellory.[27] At the same time Seldte's plans to expand benefits were blocked by the finance minister, Lutz Graf Schwerin von Krosigk, who argued that the country's precarious fiscal situation precluded any substantive expansion of benefits. The labor minister called upon Hitler to arbitrate the issue, only to have the Reichskanzler side with the finance minister. According to Hitler, efforts to stimulate the economy (*Arbeitsbeschaffung*) must be given priority.[28] Like Oberlindober before him, Seldte now had to give way, and the law, which was promulgated on 3 July 1934, fell short of the expectations of all who were involved.

The most dramatic feature of the new law was the introduction of the *Frontzulage*, a supplementary pension payment of 60 Reichsmark per year for disabled veterans who had been wounded at the front.[29] In addition, the July law rescinded some of the cuts made under the Emergency Economic Decrees and modified some of the more aggravating administrative practices of the RVG. Those who actually qualified for the *Frontzulage* were few in number,[30] and in view of the immense propaganda buildup that had preceded its issuance, the law's limited scope was bound to be a source of disappointment for many. This was recognized in its preface, which stated that while the government remained committed to a thorough revision of the system of welfare for victims of the war, the need to give priority to a general economic recovery meant that the immediate expansion of benefits had to remain limited.

Oberlindober, who had obviously hoped for more, reluctantly fell into line. Commenting on the new law, he argued that anyone with insight had to realize that the necessary precondition for expanded veterans' benefits was an expanded tax base, which justified giving priority to measures designed to promote a general economic recovery. Taking solace in the government's promise for future changes, he characterized the new law as "the first step on the path that I have outlined." In one area, however, the Reichskriegsopferführer claimed that the law was a "complete success," namely, in the crucial "fight for the honor of the German soldier," which was "as necessary a precondition for a reform of the welfare system as an expanded tax base."[31]

The *Frontzulage* provided for in the July law was complemented ten days later by the issuance of a campaign medal for those who had fought in the First World War. The issuance of such an award conformed to Oberlindober's earlier proposals. In addition to successfully exploiting the longing of many veterans for a tangible symbol of their service, one that had been shortsightedly denied them by the Republic, the "Cross of Honor" distinguished between front- and rear-line service and conferred certain privileges upon its recipients.[32] Yet, while some veterans benefited from the new legislation, others lost out: some 16,000 veterans, the bulk of whom received pensions for nonorganic mental illnesses, were dropped from the RVG's rolls.[33]

In the following years, additional changes were made in the RVG, but they consisted primarily of minor extensions and further reductions in the cuts introduced between 1930 and 1933, measures that were aided by favorable changes in the Reich's economic and demographic circumstances.[34] The gap between the regime's promises and performance did not go unnoticed. In the summer of 1935 Seldte received a letter from a disabled veteran in Berlin reminding the labor minister of the promises made by the NSDAP and the new government at the time of the Nazi *Machtergreifung*. Since then, the writer complained, changes in disability benefits had been so few as to suggest that the authorities believed that "the need of the war disabled no longer—or never had—existed," whereas in fact they "were still in the desperate situation in which they had been placed seventeen years ago." Meanwhile, new positions and promotions at the factories with which the writer was familiar were going not to war-disabled veterans but to SA men, most of whom were undeserving and unqualified. In earlier years, he claimed, Social Democratic politicians had made many promises to the war-disabled and not kept them, thus demeaning and mocking them. This must not be allowed to happen again; such a development, he was sure, most certainly was opposed by the Führer. The war-disabled, he concluded, therefore demanded a "*Gleichschaltung* in the sense of the Führer*," that is, substantive changes in the RVG.[35] Seldte was not immune to such complaints. In October he again tried to push through a series of improvements, including the extension of the *Frontzulage* to veterans who were 40 percent disabled, which he considered to be "unavoidable." His proposals were again rejected by the finance minister, who argued that it was necessary to see what form the benefit system for the new Wehrmacht would take before reforms could be introduced into the existing system.[36]

At this time the labor minister began to receive help from important places. In a November 1935 letter to Hitler, Field Marshal von Mackensen commended the Führer for having introduced the *Frontzulage* but complained that, owing to the many strictures involved, only about half of those entitled to the award were actually receiving it.[37] The elderly field marshal's letter received far more attention than that of the Berlin veteran, and Seldte's plans to extend the numbers of disabled veterans eligible for the *Frontzulage* received additional support from the war minister. According to the latter, suitable benefits for war victims were necessary in order to increase morale in the new Wehrmacht and to "strengthen the *Wehrwillen* of the nation."[38] In December 1935 Seldte launched an all-out offensive in support of granting the *Frontzulage* to all veterans who were 50 percent disabled or more. In its present form, it was claimed, the *Frontzulage* was more of an old-age pension than a front fighter's reward. As the result of the labor minister's having to defer to the finance minister's vetoes, the "moral credit of the Labor Ministry with the war victims had been exhausted" and the failure to fulfill "the great hopes of the 'Oberlindober Program'" had produced a growing radicalism in the ranks of the war-disabled. The finance minister's refusal to make any changes was "politically intolerable," "socially contradictory," and "*wehrpolitisch* irresponsible." Mackensen's request for a removal of restrictions was cited, as was the war minister's support.[39] With this barrage of arguments, Seldte finally prevailed. On 13 December the finance minister gave way, and beginning in 1936 the eligibility requirements for the *Frontzulage* were progressively loosened.[40]

Meanwhile, the NSKOV continued to thunder against the "demilitarization" of benefits under the Republic and to boast of its role in restoring the honor of the front soldier.[41] Although it was admitted that the first two components of the RVG, medical treatment (*Heilbehandlung*) and social welfare (*soziale Fürsorge*), which included vocational rehabilitation, represented an advance over the prewar disability system, the third component, the pension system, continued to be castigated. Under the emotional but misleading slogan "we did not go to war in order to become pensioners [Wir sind nicht in den Krieg gezogen, um Rentenempfänger zu werden]," the NSKOV blamed the RVG's pension system for creating a "pension psychosis," placing material concerns before honor, and having demeaned veterans, both in their own and the public's eye. The importance of pensions during the period of high unemployment, when the disabled veteran had been especially vulnerable, was acknowledged, but with nearly full employment, it was argued, pensions should only play a subordinate role.[42] Yet, while attacking pensions in principle, the NSKOV at the same time publicized and took credit for the piecemeal restoration of earlier pension cuts and other extensions of the pension system, which were often presented as gifts of the Führer in a manner that harkened back to the monarchical era.[43] In some cases a double harvest was reaped: the elimination or raising of thresholds of permissible levels of outside income (*Ruhenvorschriften*), limitations which had always been unpopular with pensioners, had considerable propaganda value among the war victims and at the same time worked to further the regime's objective of mobilizing all available sources of labor for the expanding war economy.

Through the NSKOV the war victims' movement was politicized and psychologically militarized. However, the efforts of the NSKOV's leadership to alter substantially and, in effect, to remilitarize the basic structure of the pension system by replacing its social welfare focus with one that was more militarily oriented were largely unsuccessful. Although the "reforms" of July 1934 placed more emphasis on military criteria, the basic structure of the system remained the same. In concrete terms, the new regime gave little to war veterans that they had not already received under the "pacifistic" Republic. Limited material improvements were, however, accompanied by effective psychological "perks" and highly visible cosmetic measures designed to give the appearance of change. The treatment of disabled veterans thus closely paralleled the manipulative "psychological revolution" employed by the Nazi leadership toward other ideologically favored but expendable groups in the Third Reich, such as farmers and small businessmen.[44]

MEANWHILE, the contest to gain control of veterans continued. After the reintroduction of universal conscription in 1935, the struggle between Oberlindober and Reinhard for the hearts and minds of veterans became more complicated by the Wehrmacht's entry into the contest. Initially this appeared to give Reinhard the edge because of the shared conservative-monarchist political views and the long history of personal and organizational ties between the traditional veterans' organizations and the military. Yet if the Wehrmacht was sympathetic to the more traditional veterans' organizations, it also saw their role as being a limited one, restricted to the organization of veterans of the imperial army. The Wehrmacht had its own plans for the newly created veterans who would comprise its first reserve; as a still-powerful partner in the system of "partial fascism" that prevailed before 1938, it was able to enforce its will.[45] Neither Oberlindober's NSKOV nor Reinhard's Kyffhäuserbund benefited—at least initially—from the bonanza created by the reintroduction of universal conscription. Instead, a new reservist organization was created specifically for younger veterans. In January 1936 the Soldiers' League (Soldatenbund), headed by General Freiherr Seuter von Lötzen, was founded for veterans of the Reichswehr and Wehrmacht, that is, men who had served after 1921.[46] Similar organizations were established for veterans of the navy and air force. With the formation of these groups, the German veteran population was organized as follows: veterans of the imperial army were organized in the Kyffhäuserbund; veterans of the Reichswehr and the new Wehrmacht were joined together in the Soldatenbund; disabled veterans belonged to the NSKOV; and former officers made up the RDO.

Following Hitler's takeover of the armed forces in February 1938, the picture changed again. The final *Gleichschaltung* of the Wehrmacht was followed closely by that of the veterans' movement. On 4 March 1938 Hitler ordered all veterans' organizations with the exception of the NSKOV to be amalgamated into an expanded Kyffhäuserbund, renamed the National Socialist German National Veterans' Association, "Kyffhäuser" (National-Sozialistischer Deutscher Reichskriegerbund, "Kyffhäuser"). The party's control of veterans was further strengthened in January 1939 with the creation of the SA Military Reserve (SA-Wehrmannschaften), which was given responsibility for the post–military service training of veterans. These changes broke the Wehrmacht's control of veterans and completed their *Gleichschaltung*.[47] For the Kyffhäuserbund, the decree of 1938 signified a return to the quasi-monopolistic position it had enjoyed in the Kaiserreich, though its triumph was diminished by the degree of dependence and control imposed by a totalitarian state and made problematical by the creation of the SA-Wehrmannschaften. Theoretically the work of the two organizations was to be divided, with the Wehrmannschaften emphasizing physical training and the Kyffhäuserbund, ideological indoctrination. Yet in view of the Darwinistic bureaucratic practices of the Third Reich, the revitalization of the SA as an active element in veterans' affairs did not bode well for the Kyffhäuserbund. More likely, it presaged a new round in the struggle for control of veterans, which, given the radicalizing impact of the war, might well have ended in favor of the SA.[48]

IF THE SUBJECT of substantive structural reform of the benefit program covering veterans of the First World War was essentially closed by the end of 1934, that of benefits for future generations of veterans was still open. With the reintroduction of universal conscription in 1935, the issue became pressing. Whereas efforts to restructure the RVG along National Socialist precepts had been stymied, the Military Benefits and Pensions Law (Wehrmachtsfürsorge- und Versorgungsgesetz [WFVG]), introduced in 1938 to cover veterans of the new Wehrmacht, incorporated many of the principles advocated by Nazi critics of the "Marxist" RVG.

The WFVG restored a number of the principles associated with the imperial war-disability system and in general reflected the Nazi desire to emphasize military service while deemphasizing the costly welfare aspects of the RVG.[49] The WFVG provided pensions for service-related disabilities calculated on the following basis: whereas the guiding principle of the RVG was the degree of the victim's loss of civilian earning power, the new system was based on the severity of the injury, of which there were four categories. The payment of a flat sum based on the type of disability was a reversion to the type of pension scale employed in the Kaiserreich. The next step in the calculation of a disabled soldier's pension hinged on his employability. Only those deemed incapable of working received the so-called unemployable (*Arbeitsverwendungsunfähig-keit*) pension, which in turn was geared to the recipient's family status, place of residence, and military rank. The introduction of the latter factor in the calculation of pensions represented another reversion to the imperial system, one that had long been advocated by Oberlindober.

The WFVG was designed for a peacetime army. It was supplemented in 1939, on the eve of the Second World War, by the Military Combat Benefits and Pensions Law (Wehrmachtseinsatzfürsorge- und Versorgungsgesetz [WEFVG]), which retained the basic structure of the 1938 law but increased and expanded the benefits accorded to soldiers injured in active combat as opposed to peacetime or rear-echelon duty, a cardinal distinction in the National Socialist view of military disability compensation.[50]

A comparison of the war-disability systems introduced by the Weimar Republic and the Third Reich reveals a definite militarization under the latter. Civilian points of reference in determining pensions were downgraded in favor of military ones. The type of wound and the circumstances from which it resulted, rather than the decline in the victim's civilian earning power, became the primary points of reference. In addition, rank and length of military service became determining factors. In short, the system of 1938–39 emphasized the individual's role in society as a soldier rather than as a civilian. This militarization was reflected institutionally by the creation of a new, separate administrative structure that was subordinated to the War Ministry instead of the Ministry of Labor.[51]

A close look at the WFVG/WEFVG legislation reveals more than just a militarization of the war-disability system. In addition to disability benefits, the new laws also regulated military retirement programs. The new system increased retirement and vocational opportunities for professional soldiers, especially noncommissioned officers.[52] As the war progressed, plans were made to expand these even further. Among the postwar benefits envisioned for noncommissioned officers were positions as teachers in primary schools and as proprietors of state-run tobacco shops and service stations. Hitler repeatedly stressed the importance of noncommissioned officers in the new Wehrmacht and the need to make every effort to attract capable candidates. His sympathy for the noncommissioned officers was coupled with disdain for the traditional elites. This was clear in his plans to open up the bureaucracy to former noncommissioned officers in general and, in particular, in his pet project of reviving the old Hohenzollern practice of using former noncommissioned officers as teachers in grade schools, policies that simultaneously reduced pension costs and worked to permeate the civil service—and thereby society at large—with military values. According to Hitler, after a short training period, former noncommissioned officers, "free from unnecessary academic baggage [Wissensballast]," would be sufficiently prepared to teach young grade school pupils. To enable the state to provide attractive postservice careers, Hitler also considered the creation of a state tobacco monopoly, whose shops would be run by former noncommissioned officers. In addition, there were plans to nationalize the gasoline industry after the war and to establish a network of state-run service stations that would be run by former noncommissioned officers with mechanical backgrounds.[53] Also, during the Second World War the settlement plans of the First World War were revived and, to a certain degree, implemented.[54] While military retirement benefits under the Nazis were expanded, the legislation of 1938–39 effectively reduced benefits for disabled conscript soldiers. The structure of the 1938–39 laws thus provides an indirect but convincing confirmation of Hitler's Blitzkrieg strategy, which envisioned short wars, limited casualties, and territorial gains that would open up new civilian administrative positions for former soldiers.[55]

The front soldier had always been a central figure in the ideology and mythology of national socialism. In the Third Reich soldiers were idealized: their exploits in the Great War were endlessly celebrated in popular literature and film, soldiers were presented as role models for civilian society, and military virtues—duty, obedience, sacrifice—were elevated to the status of primary, rather than secondary, values.[56] During the Third Reich a series of national holidays honored veterans and members of the armed forces. The annual ceremony honoring those killed in the First World War—the Helden-gedenktag—although initiated in the Weimar Republic, became an elaborate set piece of Nazi pageantry. Following the reintroduction of universal con-scription, an annual rally—the Reichskriegertag—was held in Kassel to honor the armed forces and commemorate the outbreak of the First World War.[57]

In the militarized society of the Third Reich, military service was trans-formed from an obligation into a sacred right, the prerequisite to full citizen-ship. The reintroduction of universal conscription was accompanied by tre-mendous fanfare; at the same time, the regime, realizing that not all Germans were enthusiastic about the return of conscription, lightened the burden of military service with a generous system of benefits for military dependents.[58] Yet those who had the misfortune to be injured while fulfilling their military obligations found that when the rhetorical facade was stripped away, the self-proclaimed regime of the front soldier showed itself to be less benevolent—indeed, even less generous—than its much-reviled predecessor. Although disabled veterans were celebrated as the first citizens of the Third Reich, when it came to their treatment and care the regime's performance lagged consider-ably behind its promises. The source of this discrepancy, aside from cynical hypocrisy, was that the Third Reich's treatment of veterans, like most of its social policies, involved contradictory goals and incompatible ideological premises: on the one hand, there was the glorification of war and the promise to reward military sacrifice; on the other hand, there was the regime's preoc-cupation with efficient production (*Leistung*), which favored the strong over the weak and rejected state support of nonproductive elements.[59] Both the RVG and the WFVG/WEFVG sought to reintegrate disabled veterans into the economic marketplace, but whereas the former assisted the process through extensive welfare measures and pensions, the latter relied to a much greater degree on the harsh lash of financial exigency. The work ethic, which provided the philosophical foundation of the RVG, came even more to the fore in the WFVG/WEFVG, and this, combined with the negative features of the Nazi *Leistungsprinzip*, created financial hardships for disabled veterans.[60] Ultimately, continued utility, not past sacrifice, was paramount for the Nazi state. During the Second World War the deficiencies of the Nazi system became abundantly clear, and while war victims were denied the opportunity to openly protest or change National Socialist policies, postwar developments provide an ex post facto referendum on the relative merits of the treatment of war victims under the Weimar Republic and the Third Reich: the 1950 Bundes-versorgungsgesetz decisively rejected National Socialist practices and was openly modeled on the RVG of 1920. The National Socialist treatment of war victims provides yet another example of the immense gap between psychologically manipulated illusion and reality in the Third Reich.

As IN THE CASE OF most NSDAP affiliates, the main purpose of the NSKOV was social control and propaganda. The former was achieved through its monopolistic position; the main vehicles for the latter were its monthly magazine, *Deutsche Kriegsopferversorgung* (*DKOV*), and NSKOV-sponsored rallies and demonstrations. Whereas the publications of the pre-1933 war victims' organizations were rather utilitarian in format and devoted primarily to social policy and related legislation, the *DKOV* was lavishly illustrated and treated social policy in a secondary manner.[61] The main thrust of the *DKOV* was propagandistic—to extol the virtues of the new regime and to glorify Germany's military past, particularly the role of those who had fought at the front in the war of 1914–18. Speeches and statements by Hitler and other leading Nazis were featured, and the Führer's background as a front soldier was repeatedly highlighted, at times in an almost religious manner.[62] Support for various National Socialist ideological positions and programs also appeared in the pages of the *DKOV*, but the main emphasis was on the nobility of the war effort and the heroism of the military. The bravery, sacrifice, and accomplishments of German soldiers, sailors, and flyers were chronicled in numerous lengthy articles.

The *DKOV*, both in format and content, more closely resembled the publication of a nationalist veterans' organization than one devoted to the interests of victims of the war. This, of course, was deliberate. By stressing the heroic military accomplishments of Germany's armed forces and repeatedly invoking the comradeship of the front, while at the same time downplaying social policy and the real problems of disabled veterans, the leaders of the NSKOV sought to obliterate the painful and destructive consequences of the war that had originally united the members of their organization and had frequently contributed to a strongly pacifist strain in the pre-1933 *Kriegsopfer-verbände*. The covers of the *DKOV* featured tanks, airplanes, and scenes of heroic (but remarkably unbloody) combat, not the wounded, mutilated, and dead victims of the war or their grieving families. The pain and suffering of the war were celebrated in a ritualized manner, their reality abstracted and de-natured, while the excitement, glory, and comradeship of the war years were vividly presented. The reasons for membership in the NSKOV were thus manipulated, obscured, and transformed. The basic identity of its members became that of the front soldier—a hero, not a mutilated victim of the war. In this way, war was sanitized and glorified, while the war victims' movement was militarized and, perversely, converted into a vehicle for prowar propaganda.

Although the regime sought to blunt the war victims' memories of their pain and loss, it was also aware of the propaganda value of their broken bodies. In the Third Reich's early years, the NSKOV's membership was regularly mobilized in support of the regime's policies, especially those that were portrayed as righting the wrongs of the Treaty of Versailles. The first major mobilization took place in connection with the Reichstag elections of 12 November 1933 and the simultaneous referendum in support of Germany's withdrawal from the League of Nations. In the weeks preceding the vote, NSKOV rallies were held throughout the country. Germany's action was depicted as restoring the nation's honor and equality, and support for the withdrawal, as well as the regime that had effected it, was demanded. On election day disabled veterans were assembled in their precincts, bedecked with flowers by members of the Bund Deutscher Mädel, and paraded to the polls bearing placards with the inscription: "Germans, have you voted yet? If not, then my sacrifice was in vain." The impact of these long columns of uniformed disabled veterans, many of them in wheelchairs, was powerful, and if the following report of one NSKOV *Landesverband* is accurate, the extent of the mobilization was impressive: "In the mobilization for honor and peace," it claimed, "94,340 flower-bedecked war victims of the Landesverband Mit-teldeutschland, accompanied by 98,643 family members, demonstrated in closed ranks at the polls their loyalty to Der Führer and Volkskanzler Adolf Hitler. Thousands of war victims not yet affiliated with the NSKOV enthusi-astically [einmütig] joined the column."[63]

In his report on the campaign, Oberlindober noted that the election had represented the war victims' "first significant political assignment." It was only natural, he claimed, that veterans should lead the fight for the nation's restora-tion of honor and equality. In the process, the NSKOV had helped to restore the honor of the German soldier that had been lost in November 1918, since "this could only be accomplished through a united demonstration of national loyalty and the mobilization of the nation in support of the political goals of our leader and front comrade Adolf Hitler."[64] The restoration of honor, it turned out, was to be purchased with political conformity and unquestioning support of the regime. Similar NSKOV mobilizations accompanied the referenda of the following years. In addition, the NSKOV staged a number of rallies in border areas, where the unrequited sacrifice of Germany's disabled veterans was used to justify demands for territorial restoration.[65]

By its fifth anniversary, the NSKOV's position on veterans' legislation had become stale and redundant.[66] Its originally avowed purpose as an interest group for disabled veterans clearly had become secondary to its role as an agent for the reinforcement of the general propaganda lines of the regime. The pages of the *DKOV* celebrated Germany's revival, which was attributed to the National Socialist movement and, above all, the genius of its leader, Adolf Hitler. The links between the National Socialist movement and the heroic spirit of the world war were repeatedly invoked. The NSKOV was presented as the first National Socialist *Soldatenbund*, as an organization that had recreated the unity of the front and that, as such, was to serve as a model for the rest of the nation.[67] The war victims' organization also provided a perfect vehicle for Hitler's tactic of coupling bellicose demands for foreign political concessions with professions of peace. Thus, the NSKOV played an integral role in the peace campaigns that followed the reintroduction of universal conscription in 1935. Delegations of NSKOV officials exchanged visits with delegations of veterans' organizations from former enemy states, and the meetings were heralded as demonstrations of the desire of Germany's veterans to improve international relations. In numerous speeches and articles Oberlindober echoed Hitler's line that veterans, because they knew the horrors of war, wanted nothing more than peace—but that it must be a peace based on honor and equality.[68] Germany's withdrawal from the League of Nations, the reintroduction of conscription, and Hitler's later diplomatic demands were all portrayed as necessary and welcome steps on the path to this goal. At the same time Germany's newly found unity, strength, and growing military prowess were trumpeted with the clear implication that, if denied its rightful claims, it would use force to achieve them. The message, in short, was that Germany was strong and the German people stood united behind their leader in his quest to right the wrongs inflicted upon the nation at Versailles, a theme that appeared with increasing stridency as war began to loom on the horizon.[69]

THE OUTBREAK of the Second World War brought increased social welfare work for the NSKOV, coupled with continued and intensified duties as a propaganda auxiliary of the regime. Under the banner of social service (*Betreuung*), the offices and personnel of the NSKOV were enlisted to ease the difficulties of the new generation of war victims and to bolster morale on the home front. In a radio interview with Major General Hermann Reinecke, Oberlindober described how war-disabled veterans and widows of the First World War were working to aid their counterparts in the new war. Although designed to demonstrate the "unity of party and Wehrmacht," the interview also revealed latent tensions between the two erstwhile rivals for control of veterans' affairs.[70] On the whole, however, the NSKOV appeared willing to accept a subordinate role, deferring to the Wehrmacht's control of benefits under the WFVG/WEFVG and limiting its work to filling in the "gaps" that existed between war victims and authorities responsible for their welfare. Since the new war's victims were potential members, the NSKOV had a vested interest in proving its ability to help them obtain pension rights. In addition, much energy was concentrated on activities designed to demonstrate the party's solicitude for the victims of the new war. Thus disabled members of the NSKOV visited wounded soldiers in hospitals, widowed members were urged to visit and comfort the wives and families of soldiers who had been killed, and USO-type functions were staged to entertain wounded soldiers.[71] In these ways the National Socialist war victims' organization worked to defuse discontent and rally support for the war.

National Socialist propagandists began the war with hysterical celebrations of Germany's victories and the regime that had made them possible and ended it with equally hysterical appeals to hold out until the end (*Durchhalten*).[72] The NSKOV was no exception. Yet, as a self-proclaimed front soldiers' organization, it pursued its own distinct line of propaganda, focusing on the role of the soldier and the relationship between the fighting and home fronts. A commonly employed theme was to compare the conditions faced by the men at the front in both wars and to show how much better things were now, thanks to policies of the Third Reich and the understanding of its leader, former front soldier Adolf Hitler. Thus, whereas the soldier of the First World War had gone to war unprotected by any sort of "social safety net," the soldier of the new Wehrmacht, it was claimed, was backed by a comprehensive benefit system that would compensate him fairly in case of injury and provide adequate care for his family should he fall on the field of honor. This knowledge, combined with the thorough inculcation of German society in the ideals of the National Socialist *Weltanschauung*—duty, obedience, patriotism, and unselfish sacrifice—had, it was argued, united the home and fighting fronts in a way that was unknown during the First World War and guaranteed victory in the second.[73] Behind such brave and confident words there lurked the persistent fear that continued sacrifice might lead to a breakdown of morale on the home front and that the Third Reich could suffer the same sort of "stab in the back" that had presumably doomed the Kaiserreich. While repeatedly assured that they had no grounds for discontent, readers of the *DKOV* were simultaneously warned against actions that might express discontent, lower morale, and lead to a repeat of 1918.[74]

As we have seen, two separate systems existed for the care of the war-disabled at the outbreak of the Second World War: that of the RVG, under the direction of the Labor Ministry, which cared for the victims of the First World War, and that of the WFVG/WEFVG, administered by the War Ministry, which covered the newly disabled veterans of the Second World War. Immediately after the outbreak of war, on 8 September 1939, the overall direction of the two systems was transferred to the Supreme Command. Once German casualties began to mount, the inadequacies of the National Socialist legislation became apparent. Men who suffered the same wounds that their fathers had received in the First World War found that their benefits were less; widows of soldiers killed in the Second World War received less than their counterparts in the First World War.[75] In January 1941, Hitler's deputy, Martin Bormann, noted that the reports of the Gauleiters were repeatedly referring to the deficiencies of the WFVG and that the different (that is, poorer) treatment of the disabled of the present war vis-à-vis those of the First World War had become a source of special complaint among the populace. In a memo to party officials, Bormann described the different structure of the two laws, concluding:

> The main thrust of the WFVG is to provide vocational opportunities [Arbeitsfürsorge]. Insofar as he is no longer able to practice his previous profession, every effort should be made to retrain the wounded soldier for a new profession, so that he again becomes fully employable. The law thus proceeds from the sound principle that it is essentially more National Socialist [wesentlich nationalsozialistischer] to make a disabled soldier fully employable than simply to fob him off [abzuspeisen] with pensions and to leave it to chance whether or not he finds work again.
>
> As a result of the different principles of the two laws it is unavoidable that in cases of the same injury lower benefits will be paid under the new law than under the RVG.
>
> It is therefore the task of party officials to point out to those citizens [Volksgenossen] who feel disadvantaged vis-à-vis those disabled in the last war the reasons for their different treatment and to make clear to them the superiority of the new system, which provides vocational retraining and opportunities instead of pensions.[76]

Such efforts apparently remained without effect. Typical Nazi measures such as providing jobs for disabled "front students" in "racially threatened areas [volkstumsgefährdeten Gebieten]," awarding farms to war-wounded soldiers in Gau Wartheland, which was slated to become the "Gau of the Front Soldiers," and training disabled soldiers for future leadership roles in the NSDAP at party academies also failed to dampen the demand for better benefits.[77] As discontent mounted, the leaders of the Third Reich, concerned about morale on both the fighting and the home fronts, responded with an avalanche of ad hoc measures expanding the benefits of the 1938–39 laws as well as those of the RVG.[78] Measures were taken to ensure that disabled soldiers and survivors of soldiers who had had high levels of income before the war did not suffer a social decline ("ihrerer sozialen Schicht erhalten bleiben"), and the distinction between combat and other military disabilities was softened, since "total war" had created conditions in which "virtually all military casualties are now combat related."[79] War widow benefits were extended to the fiancées of soldiers who had met a *Heldentod* in order to maintain the morale of German women, "whose marriage prospects [have been] strongly reduced by the war's steady depletion of men."[80] Benefits for the parents of drafted and fallen soldiers were also extended until by the end of the war they were considered a scandal by many, including officials of the pension system.[81]

The result of these changes was administrative and fiscal chaos. In October 1943 the overall administration of both disability programs was transferred from the Supreme Command to the Labor Ministry, and efforts were begun to unify the two systems. In June 1944 Seldte and Oberlindober convened a meeting of officials to celebrate and discuss the transfer and the imminent completion of the merger. According to Seldte, at the beginning of the war it had seemed logical to place the care of war victims under the supervision of the Wehrmacht; after five years of war, however, the community of war victims, to which the victims of "terrorist attacks," that is, bombing raids, also belonged, had assumed such "a socio-political significance" that it now appeared advisable to organize it under civilian leadership. The war victims had become a united "community of fate [Schicksalsgemeinschaft]," and this had given rise to the view that the sacrifice of the victims of the two world wars should no longer be measured by different standards. With regard to the survivors, Seldte maintained, benefits had to a large extent been made uniform; in the case of the war-disabled, however, the differences in the two laws were so great that their merger could only proceed slowly. Both the labor minister and the Reichs-kriegsopferführer made it clear that they had no intention of returning to the "formalistic," or "schematic," pension-oriented system of old. Work, not pensions, was to remain the principal objective in the care of the war-disabled.[82] By the war's end the merger of the two disability systems had still not been accomplished, and for all practical purposes the system was bankrupt.[83]

The fate of the NSKOV and its leader paralleled that of the regime they so faithfully served. As the casualties of the Second World War increased, exploitation of the mutilated victims of the two world wars became increasingly difficult. Party members shied away from their responsibility of conveying the notice of yet another "hero's death" to bereaved families; even Hitler sought to blot out the sight of wounded soldiers.[84] The immediate exigencies of the Second World War erased the two-decade obsession of the German people with the First World War. The carnage of the First World War became irrelevant; calling too great attention to the carnage being produced by a second, longer, and even more total war became politically inexpedient, if not dangerous. As a consequence, the NSKOV soon felt the pinch of wartime economies: in the fall of 1941 the *DKOV* began to appear every other month instead of monthly, and in early 1943, following Hitler's decree of 13 January ordering total mobilization, the NSKOV was ordered to cease its recruitment activities and to transfer the freed personnel to jobs more vital to the war effort.[85]

An audit of the national headquarters (*Reichsdienststelle*) of the NSKOV undertaken at the same time revealed that Oberlindober had been misusing funds in order to curry favor with leading members of the Nazi hierarchy.[86] Characteristically, such corruption on the part of an *alter Kämpfer* went unpunished. Oberlindober remained Reichskriegsopferführer, and the NSKOV, despite personnel reductions, continued its work. Indeed, the deteriorating military situation allowed Oberlindober to realize one of the goals outlined in his memorandum of 1934. In July 1943 the NSKOV began to form *Marschabteilungen*, paramilitary formations composed of disabled and discharged soldiers still capable of limited military activity.[87] Although he weathered the crisis of 1943, Oberlindober was less fortunate after the Third Reich collapsed. He was interned, then apparently extradited to Poland, where he died under mysterious circumstances.[88]

IN THE END, the National Socialist militarization of the war victims' movement and war-disability system proved to be a double disservice to German war victims: in addition to bringing reduced benefits, it also helped prompt the Allies to dismantle the system as part of their overall demilitarization program. Horrified by the crimes of the Nazi regime and the active participation or acquiescence of the German military in their commission, the victors were determined to root out militarism in Germany. In a series of decrees, military pensions were abolished, veterans' organizations, including those concerned exclusively with the rights of disabled veterans, were prohibited, and the German war disability system was systematically dismantled. Pension payments were stopped, and pension offices were closed. Disabled veterans were forced to rely on benefits accrued in other pension plans or, lacking these, to turn to public welfare.[89] When the National Socialists came to power, they had accused the Weimar Republic of ingratitude to veterans and promised to honor veterans as the first citizens of the state. Twelve years later, German veterans received the true "Dank des Vaterlandes" of the National Socialist state: universal dishonor, obloquy, and a material privation that would have been unimaginable under the Republic.

THREE

THE AFTERMATH OF WAR:
THE OCCUPATION YEARS

Historians of Germany during the occupation face several problems. The first is that there is not one story but four. The division of the country into zones of occupation and the divergent policies of the occupying powers force the historian to describe events in each zone separately. A second problem is the wide differential in the quantity and quality of source material for the different zones. Materials for the Soviet and French zones are scarce, often secondhand, and, especially with regard to the former, politically charged. As a result it is difficult to piece together comprehensive and accurate accounts of what took place.[1] For the Anglo-American zones, the problem is the opposite, though the result is often the same—the sources are abundant but so massive that it is difficult to absorb and synthesize them. The postwar division of Germany meant that the lives of Germans after 1945 were determined to a large extent by geography. This was doubly true for veterans, whose postwar experience was shaped not only by the location of their wartime service but by the zone of occupation to which they returned.

The occupation policy of the victorious Allies was guided by a variety of D's: denazification, demilitarization, decartelization, and democratization.[2] Of these, demilitarization was the most obviously pressing and found the most consistent support of the Allies—and of the Germans.[3] Because of this, demilitarization was achieved more unequivocally than any of the other D's, a fact that was to cause some embarrassment and difficulty when the Allies later changed their minds and began to press for German rearmament.

Demilitarization as an Allied goal was first stated in the Atlantic Charter, then reiterated in numerous wartime statements, including those following the Yalta and Potsdam conferences, and embodied in Joint Chiefs of Staff (JCS) Document 1067, which laid down U.S. and Allied occupation guidelines.[4] According to the latter: "The principal Allied objective is to prevent

Germany from ever again becoming a threat to the peace of the world. Essential steps in the accomplishment of this objective are the elimination of Nazism and militarism in all their forms, . . . the industrial disarmament and demilitarization of Germany, with continuing control over Germany's capacity to make war, and the preparation for an eventual reconstruction of German political life on a democratic basis."[5] Demilitarization consisted of two components, one physical, the other psychological. In the wake of the total defeat and unconditional surrender of Germany, physical demilitarization, comprising the demobilization of German armed forces, confiscation of arms, and destruction of war industries, was carried out relatively quickly and thoroughly. Psychological demilitarization, which entailed the rooting out of militaristic traditions and attitudes, was a more complicated and long-term process.

In the minds of the Allies, nazism and militarism were inextricably linked.[6] Germany's enemies willingly accepted the contention of Nazi propaganda that the Third Reich was the logical culmination of the Prussian military tradition, albeit with differing conclusions.[7] If the immediate cause of the Second World War was Hitler and the Nazis, the long-term cause was German militarism. The failure to stamp out German militarism after the First World War had led to the second. German militarism was a major factor in bringing the Nazis to power and in turn had been fed by nazism. Each had drawn strength from the other, becoming ever more virulent. Of the two, militarism had struck deeper roots and was ultimately the most dangerous. Regimes had come and gone, but militarists had remained and had repeatedly plunged the world into war.

To eradicate German militarism, the Allies set out to destroy everything that helped to preserve or promote military values and traditions. Monuments were torn down; libraries were ransacked for materials that celebrated the nation's military past; veterans' organizations were prohibited; former soldiers returning from POW camps found that the wearing of military insignia was forbidden and that persons wearing the field-gray uniforms of the Wehrmacht could be shot. Since for most veterans the only clothes they owned were their uniforms, this meant a booming business for dye shops and prompted the witticism of a British journalist that it had become a question of "dye or die."[8]

The prime carrier of the virus of militarism was considered to be the German General Staff. This belief was reflected in its collective criminal indictment and the immediate arrest of its members. If the General Staff represented the brain and soul of German militarism, the officer corps as a whole represented its body. The manner in which the victorious Allies grappled with the problem of militarism and the treatment of German officers, who were felt to be its main bearers, provides an interesting example of the way in which the victors of the Second World War sought to learn the lessons of the past and to avoid a repetition of the mistakes that had been made following the First World War.

As the leaders of the Big Three were preparing to meet in Potsdam, where they would reiterate their intention of freeing Germany once and for all from the grip of militarism, military government specialists were wrestling with the concrete measures needed to achieve the goal. The long shadow of the past was clearly visible in their deliberations. In late June 1945 American intelligence experts drew up a report "to analyze the potentialities of the German Officer Corps as a whole in relationship to the demilitarization of Germany and to present appropriate recommendations."[9] The purpose of the report, it was stressed, "was *not* to minimize the importance of the General Staff . . . but rather to emphasize that the General Staff is only part of the problem." A seven-page enclosure traced the history of the German officer corps since the defeat of 1918. In the empire, it was noted, officers had enjoyed high prestige and social status and "were accorded privileges ordinarily denied to civilians." After the war this ended. Not only were officers deprived of their privileges, but

> defeat had hurt their military pride. They were humiliated and embittered. All around them they saw rising elements dangerous to their considered interests. A large number of them were dispersed and were forced to find their way in pursuits that did not carry with them the dignity to which these men, as officers, were accustomed. The members of the old Officer's Corps under the guidance of the General Staff quickly concentrated all their efforts on one aim: the re-establishment of the Army in a State that would bring back to them their position of power and respect. Their motives were rooted more in their own interests than in the interests of the nation as a whole.

Many former officers, "unable or unwilling to adjust themselves to civilian pursuits," joined the Free Corps. The illegal, aggressive, and antidemocratic activities of the Free Corps were then traced, with the conclusion that "it must be re-emphasized here that the activities of the Free Corps would hardly have been possible had they not been organized by trained and experienced officers of the German Officer's Corps."

After 1923, the report continued, former officers had gravitated toward government positions, where they had worked secretly for the overthrow of the Republic, and "their activities in helping to bring the Nazis to power were later openly admitted and applauded by the Nazis themselves." The Free

Corps had "provided a large reservoir of recruits for the Nazi party," and the army's officer corps had been nazified in the Third Reich. Noble officers were displaced, and young officers were recruited from pro-Nazi youth organizations. The nazification of the officer corps of the air force and navy was even more thorough. Reserve officers, "drawn from middle class society to fight the war as temporary soldiers," were less of a threat, since they would be better able to adapt themselves to peacetime conditions, but, the report continued, "it must be realized that many Reserve Officers were strong in their Nazi sympathies and that a considerable number of reserve commissions were given to young men who had not had time to learn any civilian pursuits."

The significance of all this for the present was clear in the light of the aftermath of the First World War. "These officers [that is, nonreserve officers] know only the art of war. Their prestige will be broken and they can only become a dissatisfied and potentially dangerous element in German society." The humiliation of defeat and occupation coupled with harsh living conditions and the fact that the German people were "still sufficiently immature in their political thought to follow any demagogue or movement that promises to better their lot" offered "a most fertile field for a Free Corps, indeed for subversive activity of any kind. . . . Great repentance for their deeds has not been made manifest, and the alternative to repentance is bitterness. Bitterness breeds resistance." Officers, a large number of whom would be "unable to fit themselves into civilian society . . . would be not only willing but quite capable of leading resistance groups."[10]

The recommendation of the report was that all officers were a potential threat and their indiscriminate demobilization was to be avoided at all costs. U.S. military government officials quickly set to work to find ways to implement the report's suggestions. By August two aspects of the problem had been determined: the need to identify those individuals among the approximately 350,000 officers scheduled for release from detention who might be dangerous and the manner of their future disposition. Once the potentially dangerous officers had been identified, three possible solutions were suggested and debated. The first was "banishment or exile of the 'St. Helena' nature." The second was "dispersal, individually or in small groups, throughout the world to places under control of the Allied governments, who would assume responsibility for their domicile and maintenance and for enforcing restrictive measures and exercising surveillance." The third was "retention in Germany under severe restrictive measures prescribed by the Control Council and closely supervised by the appropriate Zone Commander."[11] In subsequent discussions it was determined that of the 345,000 officers to be demobilized, some 58,000 would be "potentially dangerous."[12] An analysis of the advantages and disadvantages of the three modes of disposition of these officers concluded that exile, while advantageous in some regards, was on balance impracticable for a number of reasons.[13] For one thing, "the removal of the outstanding figures of German militarism from Germany might be urged by isolationists as an argument for the too-rapid reduction, or untimely withdrawal of the Allied armies of occupation, since it could be claimed that we had thus rendered Germany militarily innocuous." Moreover, the effect on the German population would also be counterproductive: "Just as Napoleon at St. Helena came to be, for France, a symbol of her vanished glory and the focal point of hopes for future greatness, so might the hope of all Germany be turned to these men 'suffering martyrdom for their loyal service to the Reich.' On the whole, it is considered that the effect on the German population would eventually be other than that desired."

The dispersal of dangerous officers to remote areas under the control of the Allies only differed in degree from the "St. Helena" solution and was rejected for the same reasons. This left the third alternative, retention in Germany under close surveillance. It had several advantages: first of all, while quadripartite unity on the issue was desirable, it would not be necessary—one could act unilaterally; second, public opinion (that is, non-German public opinion) would favor "the idea of solving German problems in Germany rather than . . . distributing them all over the world"; third, the effect of this solution on the German population would be beneficial, "since it integrates the other purposes of the occupation with this purpose, and provides a fitting disposition of these persons before the eyes of other Germans"; finally, it stood the best chance of weathering possible future changes of government in the Allied countries and also "of withstanding assault by proponents of a softer policy, both because it will not be as much before the public eye, and also because it does not lend itself to attack on moral and social grounds." Officers considered to be potentially dangerous, it was agreed, were to be kept in confinement as POWs until conditions had materially improved and then, after their release, closely controlled and watched.[14]

Officers fortunate enough to be released quickly soon found that freedom was a mixed blessing. The material conditions of captivity were generally far better than those experienced outside. Jobs were hard to find, and former officers often encountered discrimination, not only as a result of Allied strictures but on the part of Germans. Those who had counted on pensions to ease their plight were bitterly disappointed. Allied efforts to economize and to demilitarize German society neatly intersected on the matter of military pensions. Convinced that military pensions in the past had glorified and helped to maintain militarism in Germany, the Allied powers abolished them.

The attitude of the Anglo-American forces was clearly reflected in the deliberations of the British Military Government Working Party, which was established at the end of the war to study military pension policy. Starting with the premise that the goal of its policy was to lower the prestige of the Wehrmacht in the eyes of the German people and that the present method of payment was dangerous because pension offices were a potential tool for clandestine mobilization, the committee quickly agreed that military pensions as such should be ended.[15] The cavalier cutoff of German military pensions was not approved by all elements of the British military, however. Responding to the proposals of the Working Party, the Service Chiefs of Staff, representing the view of professional officers, recommended that pensions be continued, since the nonpayment of pensions was unlikely to discredit the Wehrmacht "as there is nothing discreditable in being denied an earned emolument" and there was "no likelihood of the Germans being able to use their pensions machinery as a camouflaged mobilisation office owing to the entirely different conditions today obtaining in Germany and, it is hoped, the effectiveness of our control."[16] Finally, it was argued that considerable harm might be done by discriminating against the Wehrmacht in favor of civilians: "There is little to choose, ethically, between Civil Servants who worked against us and Wehrmacht who fought against us and the pensionable element of the latter is at least as reliable and influential a section of the community as the former. It behooves us, therefore, to avoid victimising and antagonising an element which on the one hand may produce reasonable citizens and on the other, the core of resistance and agitation against us."[17]

The Working Party decisively rejected these arguments. While the first was admitted to be debatable, it was concluded that the withholding of pensions to the Wehrmacht would "undoubtedly show the German people that the Allies were determined to carry out the terms of the Potsdam Declarations that the German armed forces are to be utterly destroyed." While there might be a case in equity for granting pensions, "the political aspect of the matter far outweighed the legal." With regard to the second argument, the Working Party called upon the lessons of history, citing a passage from General J. H. Morgan's book, *Assize of Arms*, which showed how the Germans had used pension machinery for mobilization purposes after the First World War. With regard to the third argument, the Working Party agreed that while there might be little distinction *ethically* between civil servants and the Wehrmacht, the Potsdam Declaration made it clear that the German armed forces were to be destroyed root and branch, whereas the civil service, once purged, was to remain. For this reason, "there is everything to be said for discriminating between Civilians and the Wehrmacht to the advantage of the former." The

Service Chiefs of Staff contention that the Wehrmacht contained elements at least as reliable as among the civil service was categorically rejected with the argument that "it is quite clear that we cannot afford to trust the pensionable element of the Wehrmacht. It has always been the evil influence which has incited the German people to aggression."[18]

The military regulars did not give up, however. In a letter of 27 September 1945 the departmental head of the Naval Division claimed that the distinction being made between military and civil service personnel with regard to pensions was false, since " 'militarism' is a trait which may be found in soldiers and civilians alike and is in no way dependent on the wearing of a uniform. In fact in certain cases the worst militarists are those who do not stand to loose life or limb."[19] Such arguments were to no avail. In its final report the Working Party again refuted the arguments of the Service Chiefs of Staff report and stuck by its original recommendations.[20] Long-service pensions were abolished, and the responsibility for disability payments was to be transferred to the appropriate civilian disability program. Although it was recognized that the Wehrmacht pension was an earned emolument, "the political aspect of paying a pension to an ex-member of the Wehrmacht far outweighs his claim to a legal entitlement." That there could be elements of the Wehrmacht that could be reliable and useful was again rejected on the grounds that "historically their influence had always been an evil one and to pay them pensions did not seem to the Working Party to be consistent with the spirit of the Potsdam declaration nor to accord with the deserts of the individuals concerned." Finally, the committee noted that the Americans had received a directive from Washington that pensions were not to be paid to ex-members of the Wehrmacht and that financial considerations rendered such payments an impossibility in any case.[21]

These ideas were implemented in a series of laws that culminated in Control Council Law 34, issued on 20 August 1946, which officially dissolved the Wehrmacht. In addition, pension offices were closed, pensions for the disabled were transferred to other programs, and long-service pensions were abolished. Veterans' organizations of all types were also prohibited, so that those affected by the legislation were unable to form interest groups to press for rectification of the laws.[22]

Even before the issuance of Control Council Law 34, the situation of former officers was often difficult. In the summer of 1946 British survey teams completed a study in their zone on the adaptation of former officers to their "now demilitarized status." According to American officials, the British report reflected the situation in the U.S. zone as well.[23] "Germans," the survey reported, "have from time to time hinted that former Wehrmacht officers as a class were having considerable difficulty in settling down to civilian life," and there was no question that "the lot of ex-regular officers at present is obviously not a happy one." Lack of experience barred their entry into most public and industrial jobs, and while "the field of commerce is open to them . . . the present economic situation renders it almost redundant." Many former officers and their families were accustomed to a social standard that was far higher than that which they were likely to attain for some time through employment in the civil sector. Older officers were especially hard hit. Younger ones who possessed a little capital were taking courses at the universities, though it was admitted that the limited capacities of the training institutions created difficulties for them, just as those who wished to attend trade schools were confronted by the fact that demand exceeded supply. Many officers were facing the prospect of "unemployment or unskilled work of a type which to them is menial or degrading." One form of unskilled work to which they were being directed—work in the mines—was "a solution which is unanimously unpopular." Nonetheless, the report concluded, "ex-officers do not so far present a separate and specific problem as a class apart from other Germans; ex-officers are having difficulty in finding satisfactory civil employment, but so are many Germans today, and there is little evidence of undue discrimination against ex-officers as such."

Not surprisingly, former officers saw things differently. From their ranks there came countless complaints of discrimination on the part of occupation and German officials and endless tales of woe. According to one source, it was the former soldiers and their families that suffered the most, since "they felt the full brunt of the political and military defeat as well as the economic catastrophe of the time." In abolishing pensions, the Western powers had given in to "bolshevistic pressures that were to prepare the ground in all of Germany for a cold proletarian revolution." As a result of Control Council Law 34, it was argued, those "who had borne the main burden of the war on the front and made a high sacrifice in blood" were forced "to bear the entire burden of the defeat" even though they had done the most to avoid it.[24]

Allied and German officials were flooded with memoranda from former officers complaining of the unjustness of the cutoff of their pensions and chronicling the human misery that followed in its wake. General Wilhelm von Leeb, interned in Allendorf, wrote to General McNary laying out the reasons why he and his colleagues felt the cutting off of pensions was "legally as well as morally and humanely" impossible. Leeb's letter was clearly designed to appeal to a fellow military professional. Pensions, he argued, were a historical and legal right. They had been deducted from pay. With their removal "men were placed helplessly before the void, whose only sin was to have, true to their oath, served their country in the way in which all soldiers of the world do and who possessed neither the political circumstances nor the practical possibilities to prevent the war or influence the conduct of the war in any way." Another general wrote on behalf of men like himself who had retired before the National Socialists came to power, describing their difficulties and arguing that members of the General Staff were not militarists or warmongers.[25]

The most energetic and persistent campaign for the restoration of military pensions was conducted by Gottfried Hansen, a retired admiral who lived in Kiel. The catalog of arguments with which the indefatigable admiral bombarded officials—British, American (both in Germany and abroad), and German—was seemingly endless. Just as the governments of Weimar Germany sought to undermine the "War Guilt Lie" in order to force an end to reparations by destroying the moral claim upon which they were based, so Hansen worked to bring to an end the "defamation [Diffamierung]" of the Wehrmacht that was embodied in the charges brought against the military at Nuremberg and that provided the moral basis for Control Council Law 34. The arguments employed by the defense counsel of the General Staff and Supreme Command at Nuremberg were repeated and expanded by the admiral. According to Hansen, the fact that the two organizations had been acquitted provided grounds for the revocation of the Control Council's measures.[26] The charges brought by the Allies against the General Staff and the Supreme Command, as well as the measures directed against the former members of the military, slandered the German army in general and the officer corps in particular. The officers, Hansen argued, had not been political and had had no decision-making powers. They had simply done their patriotic duty like soldiers the world over. Far from being a hotbed of nazism, the officer corps had provided a refuge from the National Socialist party. Indeed, there had been more resistance to the regime within the Wehrmacht than within any other group in society. The events of 20 July 1944 were invoked to confirm this, an association that was much less acknowledged once pensions were restored.[27] A point of special outrage to Hansen was the fact that civil servants, many of whom had been active Nazis, were receiving pensions, whereas military officers whose records were unblemished and who had been truer and infinitely more selfless state servants were denied pensions. Similarly, while even Communists were allowed to organize, this fundamental right was denied to former officers. Enemies of the state and Western values were thus permitted privileges that were denied those who supported such values. In addition to ceaselessly reiterating the illegality and unjustness of the Control Council's prohibition of pensions, Hansen provided numerous examples of former officers and their families being forced to endure discrimination, degradation, poverty, and even death—often by suicide—as a result of the harsh measures of the occupying forces. Presumably representatives of democratic values, the Allies, the admiral charged, were employing the same sort of unjust, collective punitive measures (*Sippenhaft*) that the National Socialists had used against their opponents. Such actions could hardly be expected to convince former officers of the virtues of democracy. The unwarranted discrimination against this group, whose skills and energies could be used to rebuild the country, would, if continued, only harden their bitterness and turn them against the new state. It could even force them to turn to the East.[28]

Hansen's arguments were echoed in countless letters sent by former officers to officials of the Bizone.[29] They described their difficulties in detail and universally condemned the unjustness of their treatment. If nothing else, the Allied measures appeared to have convinced this group of Germans of the desirability of equality before the law and legal, democratic process, for the offended officers self-righteously stressed that their rights had been violated and that their treatment contradicted the legal and democratic principles espoused—hypocritically, they claimed—by the conquerors. They lamented that they had done less to bring the Nazis to power than civilians and then had been made the scapegoat for Germany's problems. In their attempts to distance themselves from the National Socialist regime, many older officers implicitly (and, at times, explicitly) lent support to the Allies' charges of the military's collusion with the Nazis, a circumstance that contributed to a postwar generational gap within the officer corps that was slow to close.[30] In many cases pathos became bathos. Instances of suicide and joint suicide pacts of retired officers and their wives were frequently cited.[31] According to one correspondent, it seemed that the intent of the measures taken against former officers must be "to starve them or drive them to suicide." If this was the case, then "on the grounds of Christian compassion [christlicher Menschen-, Nächsten- und Feindesliebe] . . . at least give us the necessary cyanide capsules or revolver."[32] Others complained that they were being treated at least as badly (or even worse) than the Nazis had treated their victims. One former officer compared the sufferings caused him and his peers to that of the Jews in the Third Reich and concluded that the plight of the officers was even worse, since "the Jews had been able to count on the support of world-wide Jewry," whereas no one was now willing to help former officers.[33]

Such hyperbole left military government officials unmoved. Although in their zone the French restored pensions to officers who had retired before 1933, the British and Americans continued to enforce Control Council Law 34 strictly.[34] German officials were generally sympathetic, but because of economic and political restraints, they neither could nor would support the full restoration of officers' pensions. Representatives of the bourgeois parties were predictably most outspoken in their support of the officers' claims, but the Social Democrats also agreed that the Allied measures were unjust. Yet while the Social Democrats opposed Allied actions and the violation of innocent officers' rights, they at the same time shared the conquerors' aversion to privileged treatment of the military and opposed military pensions that exceeded those given to civilians. Such reservations were also shared by some members of the Christian Democratic Party (Christlich-Demokratische Union [CDU]). The distinction between acceptance of the demands of former officers in principle and the unwillingness to support full restoration of their pensions was often lost on the officers, who frequently complained that German officials were as vindictive as the Allies.[35]

German officials nonetheless continued to press for some form of relief and by early 1948 were able to achieve a small success when military government officials gave permission for the issuance of Maintenance Grants (*Unterhaltsbeträge*). These payments were to be extremely modest and limited to former officers who had joined the Wehrmacht before January 1933, who were over sixty-five years of age, and who were in need.[36] The drafting of the legislation providing for Maintenance Grants proved to be more difficult than expected. Many German legislators and officials, especially those on the left, believed that for political and moral reasons those who had suffered physical and material damage as a result of the war (for example, the war-disabled, those who had been bombed out, and the expellees) and those who had been persecuted on political or racial grounds during the Third Reich had to be compensated before the claims of the soldiers could be considered.[37] Another obstacle was the fear that the restoration of military service pensions would trigger new demands by the war victims.[38] The legislative process was also interrupted and complicated by the currency reform of June 1948. The majority of members of the U.S. zone's Parliamentary Council in Stuttgart, for example, felt that it was impossible "to single out one group for improved benefits at a time when countless others were similarly facing the abyss as a result of the currency reform—that would 'not be understood by the public.'"[39] Efforts to create a uniform system of grants on either the bizonal or zonal levels failed. Individual state governments began to introduce Maintenance Grants in the summer of 1948, but the process was slow and uneven. A year later, on the eve of the founding of the Federal Republic, the payment of Maintenance Grants was neither uniform nor universal.[40]

Meanwhile, efforts by former officers to improve their situation by forming interest groups continued to be blocked by occupation officials. In late 1948 self-help groups were dissolved by American authorities in Hesse and Bavaria, and the leaders of informal efforts to help former officers continued to be closely scrutinized.[41] British authorities were more lenient. Admiral Hansen was allowed to establish an organization in Schleswig-Holstein, and his colleague, Admiral Raul Mewis, founded a similar one in Hamburg. Eventually, a network of representatives in other states, the so-called "Hansen-Kreis," was formed, and in April 1949 a newspaper, *Der Notweg*, appeared.[42] Hansen's efforts to create a zonewide organization were rejected by British authorities, however.[43]

Allied control measures were eased following the creation of the Federal Republic. In December 1949 Control Council Law 34 was lifted and replaced by a milder decree, Allied High Commission Law 16.[44] Spearheaded by members of the "Hansen-Kreis," *Notgemeinschaften* were formed in the states (*Länder*), and in April 1950 they joined together at a meeting in Bonn to form the League of Pension-Entitled Wehrmacht Personnel and Their Survivors (Bund versorgungsberechtigter ehemaliger Wehrmachtsangehöriger und deren Hinterbliebenen [BvW]), with Hansen as president.[45] Even before the Federal Republic was formed, an office had been established in Bonn and representatives of the former officers had begun actively to lobby the new government for a restoration of their benefits.[46]

THE COMBINED DICTATES of total war and unconditional surrender assured that virtually every member of the German fighting forces became at least nominally a prisoner of war. As the flood tide of Nazi expansion receded, growing numbers of German POWs, like flotsam washed up after a high tide, were caught up and interned in camps located in areas earlier conquered by the Wehrmacht: Eastern Europe, the Balkans, Egypt, and Western Europe. Hundreds of thousands more were transported to Great Britain and the United States. As Germany was systematically conquered, the remaining forces of the Third Reich were brought under Allied control, disarmed, and interned. At the time of Germany's capitulation, over 11 million German troops were in the custody of the victors. Of these, some 8 million were held by the Western powers, the vast majority by the United States.[47] This presented a logistical nightmare for the occupying powers, who, in addition to setting up military governments to rule the war-ravaged country, had to feed, house, and clothe the vast army of prisoners under their control.[48]

Technically, the newly captured German military personnel were designated as Disarmed Enemy Forces or Surrendered Enemy Personnel, a maneuver that permitted their captors to circumvent the formalized rules of treatment for POWs laid down in the Geneva Convention of 1929.[49] For U.S. authorities, the main advantage of the new designation was that it enabled a quick recycling of captured German forces back into civilian life and the removal of a massive economic and administrative burden. For the European powers, the German prisoners' labor represented a form of reparation for the damage done to their countries by German armed forces.[50] The British and the French utilized the ambiguous status of the German prisoners to exploit them as much-needed sources of labor, both in their occupation zones and at home. The British maintained large POW labor battalions in their zone and delayed repatriation of German POWs held in camps in the United Kingdom, pending the demobilization of their own forces. Having suffered more directly at the hands of the Germans and having themselves been forced to provide labor for the Third Reich, the French were determined to exact recompense from the German prisoners under their control. They eagerly accepted the prisoners put at their disposal by the Americans, a supply that was soon cut off, however, following well-founded reports of maltreatment of German POWs in France. German prisoners continued to work in France until the winter of 1948–49.[51] The worst fate was suffered by those who fell into the hands of the Russians, either through capture or following repatriation into the Soviet zone by the other powers; they disappeared into the black hole of the Gulag, from which those fortunate enough to survive returned years later.

In early 1947, nearly two years after the cessation of hostilities, the United States had repatriated almost all of its POWs, but the British still held nearly a half million German prisoners (350,000 in England alone) and 640,000 remained in French custody. The USSR officially claimed to have 890,000 German prisoners, but the real number was much higher.[52] Since the United States's policy was mostly satisfactory and the USSR's was totally unresponsive, German efforts to secure the return of POWs in the immediate postwar years focused primarily on Britain and France. Public pressure eventually forced the British government to accelerate repatriation of its prisoners, and the French, reluctantly and slowly, began to release theirs. A survey undertaken in mid-1947 established that the bulk of unreleased German prisoners were in the East. Thereafter German demands for repatriation were directed mainly to the Soviets, and German organizations concerned with POWs concentrated on facilitating the reintegration of the growing numbers of repatriated POWs that were streaming into the Western zones from non-Soviet areas.[53]

It is difficult to make absolute generalizations about the experiences of returning veterans. The attitudes and physical and psychological states of returning POWs were shaped to a large degree by their experiences as POWs, which varied widely. For the captured Wehrmacht soldier, it is probably correct to say that the impact of the specific circumstances of the soldier's capture and imprisonment outweighed the effects of the common elements of the POW experience. Just as the character of the fighting on the eastern and western fronts differed greatly, so did the treatment of German prisoners captured by the Eastern and Western Allies. The POW's experience was also shaped by the time of his capture. Those captured at the end of the war, whose experience as POWs was only nominal, had less difficulty in adapting themselves to the postwar circumstances than those who had been captured earlier. Thus there was no homogeneous POW experience, or, more precisely, the common experiences of the German POWs were overshadowed by the specific circumstances of their time and place of capture.

POWs who were repatriated soon after the war's end found little assistance. In the immediate years following defeat, the German civilian population was too numbed, powerless, and concerned with its own survival to worry about the plight of returning soldiers. Although measures to help returning POWs emerged on the local level, the division of the country combined with Allied strictures against remilitarization, which prohibited organized activity by or on behalf of veterans, hamstrung larger-scaled efforts.[54] Unlike 1918, veterans in 1945 did not march home in closed columns but straggled back in small groups or as isolated individuals. Veterans remained an incoherent mass in a dislocated society inhabiting a devastated country.

The problems of the returning POWs and the difficulties they encountered upon their return were many. Establishing residence was often an arduous task, since cities were overcrowded and housing was scarce. In some cities the issuance of residence permits was prohibited.[55] Returning POWs often found themselves locked in frustrating "paper wars" with insensitive local officials who were unenthusiastic about the prospect of having to assimilate new, especially non-native, elements into their war-ravaged districts. Traditional arrogance combined with the real and enormous pressure of circumstances often produced a callousness that angered and demoralized the former soldiers.[56] A film designed to familiarize the public with the problems of returning veterans and to solicit financial aid was eventually withdrawn from circulation when it became clear that the main, if unintended, message was the indefensibly rude treatment of returning POWs at the hands of officials.[57]

Although there were legal guarantees to ensure that veterans would be rehired in their prewar jobs, these were of little use when former places of employment had been reduced to rubble, were in zones in which the veteran did not want to live, or were closed down. While there were desperate labor shortages in the agricultural and mining sectors of the economy, which prompted the Allies to give priority to releasing former agricultural workers and miners, the virtual stoppage of industrial production and the collapse of consumer services meant that there were few jobs for skilled blue-collar workers or former, largely middle-class, white-collar workers. The ubiquitous rubble-clearing projects provided a steady source of jobs for those in urban areas that were willing to take them; middle-class POWs, like their civilian counterparts, considered such manual labor unsuitable and took such work only as a last resort, while those who returned to rural and small-town areas undamaged by the war found no jobs awaiting them. In many cases the red tape surrounding residency permits clashed with the needs of the labor market.[58] As a consequence of these factors, many returning POWs became involved in the black market or resorted to thievery to keep alive.[59]

The socioeconomic problems of returning POWs were compounded by psychological difficulties connected with their imprisonment and the changed and unfamiliar circumstances with which they were forced to contend upon their return. Military life in general and combat at faraway fronts in particular led to a progressive disassociation and "desocialization" of soldiers from civilian society and their families. Memories of preservice life and familial experience tended to take on a fixed, idealized character. This process was intensified among POWs whose circumstances permitted them to dwell at length on idealized memories of home life and on the way things would be when they returned. Such unreal expectations of life following their release were also often tinged with feelings of shame and guilt for having been taken prisoner and for having failed to defend or being able to help their families in their time of need.[60] For the troops captured during the fighting in Germany, who had had recent contact with the conditions on the home front, the gap between postwar expectations and reality was not so great, though even here the lack of communication with families during the final stages of the fighting and the sudden, cataclysmic events accompanying the war's end often produced a postwar homecoming environment that was unexpected and difficult to adjust to. For prisoners who had been interned for a number of years, the readjustment to an alien, war-ravaged country in which personal and familial relationships had been lost, forgotten, or radically altered was difficult, and their return and reassimilation were fraught with monumental problems.

In an effort to prepare prisoners for actual conditions in Germany and to prevent overwhelming disillusionment, which, it was feared, would lead to political consequences like those in 1918, POW camp officials initiated programs designed to inform those about to be released of the problems they would face upon their return. Such efforts probably succeeded on the whole but often backfired by producing total despair.[61] The general fear and anxiety over what sort of fate awaited them upon their return was complicated for many by the fact that life in the POW camps had freed them from the responsibility of having to care for themselves. Freedom, especially in the harsh material circumstances to which they returned, was often overwhelming. Instances were reported of released prisoners who, after returning home to find their houses destroyed and their families missing or dead, returned to their POW camps.[62] There were also cases of married men who, unable to adapt to the changed circumstances or incapable of accepting the responsibilities now thrust upon them, returned to their parents and readopted the role of a dependent child.[63]

Many younger veterans had never known real independence, having spent their early years in Nazi youth organizations and their adulthood in the military. Without experience or job skills, they saw only a bleak future ahead after their release. One response was to grasp at any straw that promised continuation of a military career. These hopes were fed by constant rumors of a war between the Allies and their presumed plans for the recruitment of German volunteers.[64] According to a British intelligence report, the mayor of Bad Oeynhausen had reported that in response to the rumor that the British were recruiting Germans to fight in an imminent war with Russia, he was receiving three or four applications a day. In the mayor's view, this represented a fundamental lack of a sense of personal responsibility for the reconstruction of the country and an attempt to evade the difficult task by running away. Many veterans, discouraged at the prospect of rebuilding Germany, wanted to start afresh in the new world. Older Germans, the report concluded, were saying that

> many of these youths, trained in the Hitlerjugend and Wehrmacht, have never known a normal peacetime life, where hard work counted for more than loyalty to the Führer and obedience to military and party discipline. These youths find themselves released from POW camps into a strange and frightening world. Rather than trying to adapt themselves to such completely unfamiliar conditions, they wish to return to the military life which they know so well and in which they would be respected for their knowledge and experience of warfare.[65]

Capitalizing on this mood, the French recruited extensively and successfully for the French Foreign Legion among their German POWs. In 1946 it was rumored that nearly 60 percent of the French legion was German, of which a good number were former SS men.[66]

In contrast to 1918, German soldiers were not welcomed home as victors in 1945. This was noted by numerous postwar observers, who commented on the bedraggled, pathetic appearance of the remnants of the former Wehrmacht.[67]

After World War II the returning soldiers were not seen as heroes or as heralds of a new age. Total war had erased the boundary between the fighting and home fronts, especially in the final months of the war when Allied planes were able to bomb German cities virtually without opposition.[68] Civilians had suffered and died just as soldiers had. While occasionally welcomed with enthusiasm and sympathy, veterans were most often greeted with indifference by a numbed civilian population whose full energies were devoted to its own survival. The returning soldiers were frequently embittered by the lack of understanding and, sometimes, the open hostility exhibited toward them by the civilian population. Particularly irritating to returning veterans was the charge that they were responsible for the war's loss or, conversely, that their success had only prolonged the war and caused Germany's present difficulties.[69]

The veterans' anticipated joy at the prospect of reunion with their families was also blighted by changed emotional and material circumstances. Returning soldiers often found that their wives had entered into relationships with other men, sometimes with soldiers of the occupying army.[70] During the absence of their husbands, German women, especially mothers of small children, had been forced to become more assertive and independent. Now self-sufficient, such women were unwilling to return to the traditionally subservient role that their husbands expected.[71] The inability to find jobs—or at least jobs that provided the status and income of preservice employment—worked to diminish the esteem of returning POWs in both their own and their families' eyes. In some cases, the return of husbands and fathers, now virtual strangers, was resented because it resulted in the cutoff of welfare payments or other forms of aid.[72]

Unable or unwilling to accept the new conditions, returned POWs often sank into despair or listlessness. Interestingly, it seems that those most susceptible to such behavior more often came from captivity in the West, where their treatment had been relatively good, while those who had been in Soviet captivity showed a more positive attitude after their return. As the wife of a former POW in the British zone complained: "What does my husband do now? He sits around all day and does no work. He is always asking for food. He seems to think he can continue existing in Berlin as well as he did in captivity. He is always pestering me for cigarettes which he has become accustomed to. If I get them from Allied soldiers, he wants to know what I have done to get them. Our living conditions are bad, and half the day is spent bickering."[73] In contrast, the wife of a POW returned from the East reported that her husband was overjoyed to find that she and their children were alive and healthy and could not believe his good fortune. This man's enthusiasm may have been aided by the fact that his wife also had found a job with the British and that their house had not been destroyed; yet the report went on to contrast attitudes of Eastern and Western POWs employed by the British in work battalions. The work habits of the two groups, it was asserted, differed as greatly as their appearance. Whereas the former prisoner of the Russians, despite his poor physical condition, worked well and gratefully received his meal, the POW from the West asked for a cigarette before starting, was indifferent, and was late for work on the second day.[74]

If returning German veterans expected to receive special treatment, they were sorely disappointed. The material hardships and general indifference they encountered upon their return comprised perhaps the most universal aspect of their experience. Efforts at self-help, as well as state forms of assistance, remained fragmented and localized. The victorious powers were well aware of the disruptive role of German veterans after World War I and of the critical role played by veterans' organizations in the rise of the Nazis. The isolated POW self-help organizations that began to spring up on the local level in 1946 were treated warily by both military and German officials.[75] Organizations dedicated to easing the conditions of POWs still in captivity made some progress; by 1948, however, attention began to turn to the problems of returning POWs. Although efforts of former POWs to form organizations to represent their interests were increasingly tolerated by officials, their effectiveness was undercut by zonal and other geographical divisions as well as by the tendency of former prisoners to organize not as POWs, but as POWs from specific places of internment—for example, Russia, France, or Great Britain—which increased the movement's fragmentation.[76] There were also other divisions. Frustrated, angry, and often consumed by self-pity, many POWs turned on their compatriots; those who had returned early resented the warmer welcome and social welfare measures that "late-returners" enjoyed, while the "late-returners" were convinced that they had been irredeemably disadvantaged by their late return.[77]

By the middle years of the occupation, the punitive attitude of the Western powers toward veterans began to weaken. The feared military threat from veterans had failed to materialize, and, in the context of the emerging Cold War, the harsh treatment of German prisoners by the Soviets helped to promote a more humane policy on the part of the Western Allies. As former POWs began to stream back in increasing numbers from Western camps, organized forms of assistance began to crystallize. Such measures now found the support of the Anglo-American occupation authorities. In 1947 the Americans permitted the formation of a committee for POW affairs that soon became a part of the Länderrat, the central governing organ of the U.S. zone.

A similar committee was formed in the British zone, and networks of organizations dedicated to assisting the reintegration of POWs spread throughout the Western zones. Attempts at organizational consolidation following the creation of Bizonia failed, however, and it was only after the creation of the Federal Republic that a central office for POW affairs was established.[78]

In the war-ravaged conditions of 1945, life was difficult for all Germans. Food and shelter were scarce. Employment was hard to find. Much of one's time was spent on the move, foraging for food or scavenging material for makeshift shelter. For the sick and disabled, the situation was desperate. Those hospitals that were still standing were overcrowded, understaffed, and sometimes requisitioned by the occupying forces. Medicine was scarce or nonexistent.[79] In a society that was both literally and figuratively mobilized, those who were unable to move because of illness or disabling injuries were at an enormous disadvantage. The infrastructure that had previously made life at least bearable for the war-disabled—medical care, public transportation, public assistance—had been shattered. Of all the social groups that were adversely affected by the war and Germany's defeat, the war victims were the hardest hit.[80]

At the outbreak of the Second World War, 1.6 million Germans were receiving war-victim pensions from 1914–18. At the end of the war, 1.3 million of these were still receiving pensions, and German officials estimated that the war had produced another 4 million war victims.[81] In contrast to the First World War, there were massive numbers of air raid victims; adequate orthopedic care was a severe problem in view of the large number of arm and leg injuries. A more general problem was the youth and the lack of vocational training of the vast majority of the war-disabled, which made them unemployable or greatly limited their ability to work. Only slightly over half of the World War II war-disabled were employed.[82]

In discussing the structure of postwar war victim legislation, German experts expected to return to the "democratic principles of the old Reichsversorgungsgesetz, which had enjoyed wide support." However, in view of the unfavorable economic situation, benefits, especially for categories of war victims such as the lightly disabled (*Leichtbeschädigten*) and survivors, would have to be reduced. The new law was to avoid not only "all fascistic and militaristic viewpoints" but the "excesses . . . of recent years," that is, the expanded and inflated benefits provided by the National Socialist regime in order to maintain support for the war.[83] These speculations about the structure of future legislation for war victims, exchanged in memos between bombed-out ministries in Germany's war-ravaged capital, proved to be quite accurate. However, the form in which the law would eventually emerge and, above all, the fact that it would be five years before it even began to take shape were totally unforeseen.

German plans for the postwar restructuring of war disability benefits were thwarted, ironically, by a combination of Allied unity and disunity: political disunity, which led to the division of the conquered country, prevented the establishment of a system of uniform treatment of war victims; unity regarding the issue of veterans' benefits, however, ensured that, at least initially, the treatment of war victims would remain at levels substantially below German expectations. If the victors agreed on little else, they were united in their determination to root out nazism and militarism in Germany. According to JCS 1067, which laid down the basic guidelines for occupation policy, this included the prohibition of payment of "all military pensions, or other emoluments or benefits, except compensation for physical disability limiting the recipient's ability to work, at rates which are no higher than the lowest of those for comparable physical disability arising from non-military causes." Control Council Law 34, which repealed all German legislation regarding the legal status and privileges of military and ex-military personnel and their families, completed the Allies' systematic dismantling of the German system of war-disability benefits.[84] Pension payments were stopped, and pension offices were closed down. Disabled veterans were forced to rely on pension benefits accrued in other pension plans or, lacking these, to turn to public welfare.

No matter which principles were eventually adopted by the occupying powers, the extent of care and the level of pension payments for war victims were less than they had been before 1945. This was deliberate. The victors believed that the generous pensions and the favored (that is, separate or *gehoben*) treatment of the victims of war in Germany had served to encourage promilitary sentiment and to shield Germans from fully experiencing and comprehending the horrible consequences of war. In their view, treating the war-disabled as a favored group only worked to perpetuate the German tradition of glorifying the military and war, including its victims—a practice that had allowed the military to retain its position as a privileged and arrogant caste. As a report of the U.S. military government put it: "The objective of abolishing war pensions is to discredit the military class in Germany, to reduce their influence in society and to impress upon the public that a military career bears neither honor, profit nor security."[85] In addition to this political and unmistakably punitive goal, the occupiers were also motivated by the desire to rationalize and cut the costs of German social services, which, in a period of social dislocation and economic stagnation, presented a tremendous fiscal burden.[86]

While the Allies' unanimous desire to stamp out militarism ensured that the treatment of German war victims would be harsh, their disunity prevented them from imposing a common policy. The Soviets, not surprisingly, adopted the hardest line, followed closely by the British and Americans. The French, contrary to the standard view of their occupation policies, pursued a more lenient course.[87] In the spring of 1946 the Social Security Committee of the Allied Control Council began to discuss war victim benefits and in June agreed on a set of general guidelines mandating destruction of the existing systems of military pensions and transfer of the treatment of the war victims to existing social security systems. While Control Council Law 34 effectively demolished the old system in August 1946, however, there was still no agreement on the details of what should replace it. When it came time to supplant negative actions with positive policies, negotiations bogged down. There was general agreement that under the new system war victims should receive no more than victims of industrial accidents, a principle supported by German unions, but agreement on the details of pension levels and the way in which they were to be calculated was more difficult to achieve. As a result, the discussions of the relevant Control Council committees dragged out for over a year.[88]

Finally, in December 1947, just as the Control Council's work was coming to a de facto end, a compromise settlement was reached. The Manpower Directory's seven-point program, with a few exceptions, followed the principles laid down in the summer of the previous year. The German tradition of a separate system for war victims was rejected; war victim benefits were to be modeled on those of the industrial accident disability program and administered by existing social security agencies. Those eligible for pensions under the old system would still receive them under the new, but only if their ability to work was obviously limited. Pensions were to be scaled to those received by victims of industrial accidents and were not to be so high as to discourage the search for employment. Recipients of pensions from more than one system were allowed to keep only the highest, giving up the others. In short, the proposed policy of the Control Council essentially retained the harsh and punitive principles that were at the heart of the measures introduced at the beginning of the occupation.[89]

The laboriously achieved compromise of December 1947 was never implemented. The Manpower Directory's proposal became a victim of the Cold War and the Control Council's subsequent collapse. It was never issued as a Control Council Law. As a consequence, no comprehensive, unified system for the treatment of war victims was created to replace the one that was dismantled. From 1945 to 1950 the treatment of disabled veterans remained a zonal matter. Although war victim legislation, especially in the Anglo-

American zones, was shaped by the discussions of the Control Council, it varied, at times sharply, from one occupation zone to another.

In the Soviet zone, all pension payments were stopped, and the offices of the corresponding administrative authorities were disbanded. Benefits were limited to those who qualified for general welfare. In the fall of 1945 a unified social insurance system was erected that united the previous old-age, industrial accident disability, and miners' compensation systems. Payments under these programs were resumed in the spring of 1946. War-disability pensions as such were not resumed. Instead, state social insurance agencies were empowered to pay pensions to disabled persons who were not members of the established social insurance programs if they were unable to work. Pensions for war-disabled veterans as such were only authorized in July 1948 and then were limited to persons who were two-thirds disabled, that is, those whose vocational ability had been reduced by two-thirds as a result of their wounds. Pensions for the survivors of soldiers killed in the war were equally narrowly defined and limited.[90] Although improvements were later made in the amounts paid, the basic structure of the war-disability system in the Eastern zone remained the same after the creation of the German Democratic Republic. Thus, in eastern Germany one can speak of a fundamental and permanent discontinuity in the treatment of war-disabled veterans. In the west, things were more complex.

In the U.S. and British zones the course of events initially was similar to that in the Soviet zone.[91] War-disability pensions were stopped, the associated administrative offices were dissolved, and benefits were essentially limited to those who qualified for general welfare. Later, the payment of pensions to disabled veterans and to survivors of soldiers killed in the war was taken over by traditional social security programs. In the French zone a unified system was never established; instead each state in the zone developed its own system, based on different principles.

No matter which principles were employed, the war victims were worse off than they had been before 1945. Impelled by the dual imperatives of ideological conviction and financial necessity, Allied policies had a devastating effect. Hundreds of thousands of disabled veterans, their families, and survivors of soldiers killed in the war were reduced to poverty and made dependent on the already overburdened general welfare services. The material desperation of the war victims was matched by an equally strong sense of injustice and degradation. Public opinion supported the war victims' demands for better treatment.[92] German officials, charged with implementing the unpopular policies, urged the military governments to change them.[93] Yet the occupying powers, convinced of the rightness—and righteousness—of their cause, initially seemed either oblivious or indifferent to the effects of their actions.

Gradually, military government officials began to realize that their policies had produced genuine hardship for innocent citizens, and that in their zeal to root out militarism they had created conditions that were producing political consequences exactly the opposite of those intended. This change of viewpoint, prompted in part by the warnings of German officials, began to manifest itself in early 1946 and was summed up in a U.S. Office of Military Government report of January 1947:

> The objective of abolishing war pensions is to discredit the military class in Germany. . . . At the same time to leave a large category of disabled, aged, and survivors without any means to care for their needs [other] than public relief, especially when large numbers were unwilling draftees, would run the danger of creating a revengeful, self-conscious, under-privileged class detrimental to successful democratic development in Germany. The problem is therefore to cut off all privileges heretofore accorded for military service without creating a resentful class dangerous to democracy and without promoting obvious injustice.[94]

With such considerations in mind, military government authorities began to introduce systems of war-disability benefits in their zones that conformed to their principles of reform. In 1946 the British instituted a system of war-disability payments that was administered under the old-age disability insurance program. In early 1947, after nearly a year of negotiations with German officials, the U.S. military government approved a war-disability system that was subordinated to the industrial accident disability insurance program.[95]

French policy, motivated by more complex considerations than those of the other victors, was more diverse and, basically, more generous.[96] To begin with, unlike their Anglo-American counterparts, the French were not inherently hostile to the idea of special treatment for war victims, since their own system was based on a similar concept. Determined to prevent German reunification and to secure long-term dominance over those areas of the German Reich that had come under their control, the French sealed off their zone and sought to subordinate its economy to France's. At the same time French authorities worked to win over the hearts and minds of the Germans under their control through the implementation of progressive social programs.[97] While war victim benefits were higher in the French zone, they were not uniform, however, varying from state to state.

Although logical and justifiable in theory, incorporation of the war-disabled into the traditional social security programs raised some problems. The financial situation of these systems was already precarious as a result of the combined effects of the war, Germany's collapse, and the general economic chaos of the immediate postwar years. The inclusion of large numbers of pensioners who, due to their youth, had made few if any contributions to the social insurance programs' funds threatened to overburden them. Those entitled to pensions under the programs feared that their pensions might be cut to pay benefits to those who had contributed nothing to the programs;[98] at the same time, the war-disabled and survivors were angered because they received fewer benefits under the new systems than they had under the old.

While the new programs represented an improvement in the lot of the war victims, they were still far from generous and, at least in the eyes of the Germans, in serious need of further reform. Of the systems introduced in the Western zones, the British was the most seriously flawed. Like the Soviets, the British limited war-disability pensions to those who were at least two-thirds disabled. Moreover, the incorporation of the war-disability system into the old-age disability program, regulated according to the principles of the National Social Security Law (Reichsversicherungsordnung [RVO]), was beset with structural problems that worked to the disadvantage of the war-disabled.[99] For example, the methods of determining the percentage of disability under the RVO were different—and, in effect, more stringent—than those used under the former RVG, so that many veterans who would have been certified as two-thirds disabled under the latter were given a lower rating under the new law and, therefore, did not qualify for a pension. In addition, the health care and, above all, the vocational rehabilitation programs of the old-age disability system were structured to meet the needs of a clientele (aged pensioners) whose needs were radically different from those of the majority of disabled veterans and their families.

Many of the problems of the British system were overcome in the U.S. zone by placing the war-disabled under the industrial accident disability program, whose structure, especially in the areas of health care and vocational rehabilitation, more closely resembled that of the former RVG and therefore better met the needs of disabled veterans. Moreover, disability payments in the U.S. zone started with a disability of 40 percent, as determined by criteria similar to those of the RVG. Nonetheless, pension rates were low, largely because pensions, especially those for younger veterans, were calculated on the basis of a fictive annual income that was considerably lower than the recipient was likely to have been receiving had he been employed as a civilian instead of serving in the armed forces.[100]

While introduction of the new programs helped to ease the uncertainty and destitution that had plagued German war victims in the early stages of the occupation, benefits, especially pensions for survivors (widows, children, and dependent parents), were substantially less than they had been under the old war-disability systems. The discontent of the war victims remained great. Moved by sympathy, as well as concern over the potentially explosive consequences of further inaction, German officials repeatedly urged military government officials to liberalize their policies. At the same time, German legislators began to discuss the reform of war victim legislation in the recently formed state (*Land*) parliaments.

IN THE YEARS immediately following the war, the war victims were powerless to resist the changes imposed by the victorious Allies. For the first time since 1918, they were unorganized and without leadership. The NSKOV, insofar as it still existed, was dissolved in October 1945, and its functionaries were prohibited from engaging in public life.[101] The opportunity to form new war victims' organizations was precluded by Control Council Law 34, which prohibited all veterans' organizations, including those concerned solely with the interests of war victims.[102] Yet even as Control Council Law 34 was being proclaimed, small groups of war victims were beginning to organize on the local level to provide mutual support, defend their interests, and lobby for improvements. The leadership of the new organizations was usually provided by older men who had been active in the war victims' organizations of the Weimar Republic. World War II veterans who came of age in the Third Reich were generally unused to taking the initiative.[103] The fledgling organizations were watched closely by military government officials, who insisted that they represent all social pensioners, not just the war-disabled and their survivors. The use of "war" in the names of the new organizations was prohibited. Any attempts to resurrect war victims' organizations of the old type were, like the efforts to reestablish a separate war-disability pension system, quickly and firmly opposed by military government authorities.[104] This "demilitarization" of the war victims' movement, which paralleled the efforts to "civilianize" the war-disability pension system, was greatly resented by the war victims and their leaders. Though, ironically, the "demilitarization" of the war victims' organizations was to ensure their long-term survival, it was only reluctantly accepted.

The development of German war victims' organizations after the Second World War, as after the first, was shaped by and reflected the sociopolitical climate. There was both continuity and discontinuity. One element of continuity between the two eras was the failure to create a single, unified war victims' organization; yet the causes and nature of the post–World War II disunity reveal some of the fundamental changes that had taken place in German society between 1933 and 1945. The Weimar war victims' organizations were organized along lines that corresponded roughly to the main political/ ideological cleavages within society at large: communist, socialist, moderate, and conservative.[105] After the Second World War there were fewer divisions (two instead of four major organizations), and, more important, the main source of division was not political or ideological but geographical.

Geographic location, indigenous historical traditions, and the policies of the occupying forces all interacted to shape the development of the war victims' movement in post–World War II Germany. The division of the country into four zones that were virtually sealed off from one another re- stricted organizational activities to the zones. Within the zones themselves, past history and present occupation policy combined to influence the pace and structure of organizational development. More by chance than by design, the policies adopted by the occupying powers reinforced local political and ad- ministrative practices. Here, as in so many other areas of postwar develop- ment, the final outcome was a product not of Allied policy alone but of the interaction of Allied policy and local conditions. It was the high degree of congruence between occupation policy and local tradition, rather than mili- tary government policy itself, that was decisive.

British policy, reflecting the centralized administrative tradition of Great Britain, favored uniform, centralized administration on a zonewide basis. This fit well with the established practices of the German territories that were controlled by the British. The British zone for the most part was composed of territories that had previously been a part of Prussia. With the exception of the Hansa cities, Bremen and Hamburg, the *Länder* of the British zone did not have viable historical traditions. During the occupation, Bremen was under American control, however. Hamburg retained its special status not only as a separate state but as the seat of the Zonenbeirat. The rest of the British zone consisted of former Prussian administrative units accustomed to uniform and centralized direction from outside. It was an easy task to replace Berlin with a Bad Oeynhausen–based British military government.

The political traditions that shaped U.S. occupation policy as well as the indigenous political traditions of the area the Americans controlled were vastly different but no less congruent. U.S. policymakers, convinced that centraliza- tion was a major source of Germany's failure to democratize and that federal- ism, as practiced in the United States, was a decisive component in the growth of democratic traditions, adamantly promoted decentralized, federalistic political and administrative practices in their zone. This fit well with local custom and history, since the German states within the U.S. zone had long histories of independent self-governance.

The French, although their own political and administrative models were highly centralized, pursued a policy of decentralization in their zone out of the desire to keep Germany as dismembered and weak as possible. Though the goal was thus somewhat different than that of the Americans in their zone, the result was the same.

As a consequence of these factors and their interaction, the development of war victims' organizations in the Western zones was not uniform. When the Federal Republic was founded in 1949, there were two major war victims' organizations with different power bases and separate organizational philosophies. The formation of the Federal Republic created a uniform political environment and, eventually, a uniform system of war-disability benefits. However, the organizational division of the war victims, nurtured during the occupation period, remained. Attempts to unify the two organizations failed: but the failure was not, as in Weimar, the result of ideological or political differences. It was not so much competing *Weltanschauungen* that kept the two organizations separated as the competition for members. To be sure, differing organizational principles played a role and, later, there were some programmatic differences, but the main factor was simple organizational— and, at times, personal—egotism.

The organization, or reorganization, of war victims proceeded most rapidly in the British zone. The restructuring of the war-disability system and the ensuing hardships for pensioners quickly evoked resentment and protest among war victims and their supporters. They formed local organizations to defend their interests and made plans to create a zonewide organization. The driving force behind these efforts was the Reichsbund, which had reconstituted itself in Hamburg-Altona in April 1946. Following negotiations with British military government officials, the Reichsbund was given permission to call a conference of war victims' organizations in the British zone. The meeting took place in Hamburg in late November 1946 and produced the hoped-for fusion.[106] A provisional executive committee was elected for the new organization, now called the National League of Physically Disabled, Social Pensioners, and Survivors (Reichsbund der Körperbeschädigten, Sozialrentner, und Hinterbliebenen). In December the executive committee met to consider the organizational structure of the Reichsbund and to draft its bylaws. The Weimar Reichsbund had been organized along centralized lines, and its postwar successor was similarly organized, a development that was aided by the structure of the British zone and the proclivities of the British military government.[107] On 1 January 1947 the new charter was promulgated and the Reichsbund was formally organized as a zonewide organization composed of four state organizations (*Landesverbände*), with headquarters in Düsseldorf, Hannover, Kiel, and Hamburg. Hamburg was also the seat of the zonal leadership. Attempts to expand the organization to the U.S. and French zones were thwarted by U.S. and French military authorities, who refused to grant the necessary licenses.

In southern Germany the organization of the war victims proceeded more slowly and in a more decentralized fashion. War victims' organizations were formed in the U.S. zone during 1946–47 at the local and regional levels, but no zonewide organizations emerged. *Landesverbände* for Bavaria, Württemberg-Baden, Hesse, and Bremen were organized, but they remained separate and independent from one another. Because of the more restrictive policies of French occupation authorities, war victims' associations emerged more slowly in the French zone, and their subsequent development paralleled the decentralized pattern of the U.S. zone.[108]

The formation of the Anglo-American Bizone, designed primarily to unite the economies of the two zones, stimulated similar efforts in other areas, including social legislation. For the remaining years of the occupation, German and military government officials worked with varying success to create a unified system of war-disability benefits for Bizonia.[109] These efforts were paralleled by attempts to unite the war victims' organizations of the U.S. and British zones. The first step was taken in July 1947 when delegates of the Reichsbund and the war victims' organizations of the U.S. zone met in Kassel to discuss ways to coordinate their activity. A Working Committee (*Arbeitsgemeinschaft*) was formed with Paul Neumann of the Reichsbund as president. A presidium, based in Kassel, was established along with a sociopolitical committee whose headquarters were in Frankfurt, the seat of the Bizone's de facto government, the Economic Council (Wirtschaftsrat). In late November, at a meeting of delegates of war victims' organizations from both zones held in Goslar, it was decided to proceed further and to establish a unified organization for the Western zones. Thereafter, things moved slowly, as both sides concentrated on building up their own organizations, a process complicated by the currency reform. The concentration on organizational matters was also spurred by the desire of both groups to strengthen their position in future negotiations for the creation of a united organization.

By virtue of its earlier foundation and centralized, zonewide rather than statewide organization, the Reichsbund had the early edge. It exploited this at

Goslar and attempted to use its first congress, held in Bad Sachsa in early summer 1948, to bring about a fusion on its terms. The representatives of the southern war victims' organizations resisted these efforts; for them the focal point of unification attempts remained the Working Committee's presidium in Kassel, where the growing strength of the U.S. zone's war victims' organizations was making itself felt. On 17 June 1948 the presidium met to discuss unification plans. Meanwhile, the Reichsbund made it clear that it wanted the decisions made at Goslar to remain in force and that it expected the leadership of the Working Committee to continue to be in its hands.[110] When, instead, the leader of the Hessian state war victims' organization of the U.S. zone was elected president of the Working Committee, the Reichsbund began to lose its enthusiasm for unification under its auspices. This change was hardened when some of the Reichsbund's *Landesverbände* began to respond positively to the proposals for a united war victims' organization along federal lines that were being put forth by the war victims' organizations in the U.S. zone. Having lost its dominant position in the Working Committee, the Reichsbund sought to put the brakes on its efforts to create a united organization.[111] The next meeting of the presidium, held in Kassel on 14 August, was boycotted by the Reichsbund. The presidium's call following its August meeting for the holding of a unification conference in Stuttgart the following month was rejected by the Reichsbund. That the Reichsbund had reason to be concerned about the loyalty of its rank and file was shown when the leader of the Westphalian *Landesverband*, Heinrich Klerx, in defiance of the executive committee, attended the 14 August meeting and then announced his support for the Stuttgart conference, a move that touched off a bitter and debilitating struggle within the Reichsbund.[112]

In the absence of Reichsbund delegates, leaders of the U.S. zone *Kriegsopferverbände* voted at Stuttgart to join together in the League of War- and Civil-Disabled, Social Pensioner, and Survivor Organizations of Germany (Bund der Kriegs- und Zivilbeschädigten, Sozialrentner und Hinterbliebenenverbände Deutschlands [BdK]).[113] Although its geographic base was the U.S. zone, the Bund, a confederation of *Landesverbände*, was designed to organize war victims in all three Western zones. Thus by the end of 1948 the war victims' movement was divided into two separate organizations, one based in the north and one in the south. The events of 1948 had produced bad feelings on both sides. These increased as competition for members intensified and each began to poach on the other's territory, with Westphalia the most bitterly contested prize. Several halfhearted attempts to discuss unification were made in 1949, but they quickly collapsed, and the Federal Republic began its life with a divided war victims' movement—a legacy, like the division of the country itself, of the occupation period.

WHILE THE WAR victims' organizations sparred with one another, German officials were struggling to improve and unify the war-disability programs of the Western zones. In the Bizone some progress was made in the immediate aftermath of its creation, but thereafter efforts became stalled and the American and British systems were never completely integrated. The first and most significant move to create a uniform system of benefits came in May 1947, when the British reorganized their zonal system according to the principles employed in the U.S. zone, transferring the care of the war-disabled from the old-age disability program to the industrial accident disability program, which experience had shown was better suited to the needs of the war-disabled.[114] A number of differences in the calculation and payment of benefits in the two zones remained. Discussions to iron these out were initiated by a bizonal committee (Bizonale Arbeitsgemeinschaft für Sozialversicherung), which in turn established a special commission (Bizonale Sonderkommission zur Rechtsangleichung des Kriegsbeschädigtenrechts im Vereinigten Wirtschaftsgebiete) to draft a new system that would be uniform and provide improved benefits where necessary, especially in the area of survivors' benefits. Meetings were held throughout 1948, but progress was slow.[115] In September, at a meeting at Bad Nauheim, the special commission produced a draft, which was then submitted to the Labor Ministry (Verwaltung für Arbeit [VfA]) to be put in final form.[116] This was completed in early 1949, but the bill languished as a result of uncertainty over the Economic Council's legal competency to legislate in this area. Meanwhile, the situation was complicated by the passage of a law in the U.S. zone that improved benefits for war victims, especially survivors. In May the CDU and its Bavarian counterpart, the Christian Social Union (Christlich-Soziale Union [CSU]), introduced a bill for the standardization and improvement of benefits in the Economic Council that was closely modeled on the VfA proposal. The bill was supported by Anton Storch, the director of the VfA, but foundered on fiscal and legal considerations. Storch then submitted an abbreviated version, but this too was rejected by the Economic Council's Länderrat as a result of the states' opposition to its financial consequences. A compromise was finally worked out and passed by the Wirtschaftsrat in July 1949, only to be rejected by the military government on the grounds that legislation relating to war victims should be drafted and implemented by the soon-to-be-formed Federal Republic.[117] Following this, the states in the British zone legislated measures of their own to improve the situation of the war victims. North Rhine–Westphalia introduced changes similar to those in the U.S. zone; Hamburg and Lower Saxony introduced less far-reaching changes. Schleswig-Holstein, the poorest state in the British zone, retained the old levels.[118]

Although the level of benefits varied from state to state in the Bizone, the structure of war victim programs in both the U.S. and British zones was based, at least after May 1947, on the same conceptual foundations. In the French zone both the rates and the structure of the pension system varied from state to state. Yet, no matter which principles were employed, benefits in all states of the French zone were higher than those in the Bizone. In Baden, for example, the pre-1945 war victim benefits administration was left essentially untouched, and the RVG, shorn of its National Socialist excrescences, continued in force. As a result, war victims' pensions in Baden were the highest in Germany, a situation that soon necessitated controls to prevent a massive influx of pensioners (*Rentenmigration*).[119]

In contrast to Baden, the war victim benefit system of the newly created state of Rhineland-Palatinate was rebuilt completely from scratch.[120] The model for the new state system was the program that had been introduced in the province of Hesse-Pfalz in 1945 that combined elements of Control Council policy and Weimar practice. As a consequence, the law (Landesversorgungsgesetz) passed by the Rhineland-Palatinate Landtag in April 1948 formed a bridge between the war victim legislation of the Weimar period and that of the Federal Republic. French military authorities, much to the chagrin of their Anglo-American allies, approved the new law, which provided more generous benefits than Bizone legislation.[121]

In the remaining state of the French zone, Württemberg-Hohenzollern, the French followed a policy closer to that of the Bizone, not so much out of respect for their allies or the Control Council's policies, but for their own reasons.[122] French policy was designed to ensure the emergence of a strong, united Württemberg state once the occupation ended, since this would help to ensure a decentralized, strongly federalistic structure for the new postwar Germany. To this end the French took care not to create infrastructures within their section of Württemberg that diverged too sharply from those introduced by the Americans in theirs, fearing this would later hinder the state's reunification. The result was a system that was structured more closely along the lines adopted by the Control Council than in any other state of the French zone. Not surprisingly, developments in Württemberg-Hohenzollern found more favor with France's allies than with the state's war victims. Yet, while benefits in Württemberg-Hohenzollern were the lowest in the French zone, they were still more generous than those in the Bizone, not to mention the Soviet zone.

Thus, as the occupation period drew to a close and plans for the political fusion of the three Western zones began to be formulated, the care of war victims in Germany remained fragmented and diverse; not only did the systems vary from zone to zone, but there were variations within the zones themselves.

THERE IS A NATURAL tendency when looking at developments in Germany during the military occupation to see it as a time of clear-cut domination, a period during which the military governments simply dictated policy to the powerless Germans. In reality, the situation was much more complex. As the desire for revenge gave way to concern for overcoming the chaotic conditions in defeated Germany and the occupying powers became increasingly dependent upon German personnel for the implementation of their policies, a dialogue emerged between the victors and the vanquished.[123] To be sure, it was never a dialogue of equals, but the vanquished were not voiceless. Thus, although the occupying powers generally imposed their will, German officials were able to wage determined (if not always successful) opposition against unpopular policies, occasionally undertook important initiatives of their own, and frequently played a not insignificant role in shaping legislation implemented during the occupation.[124]

The history of the treatment of the war-disabled from 1945 to 1950 reflects such a dialogue. German officials helped to convince representatives of the military governments that their treatment of war victims was unduly harsh and not only was producing dangerous discontent among those directly affected but also could have more general, politically deleterious consequences as well.[125] At the same time, the occupying powers, with the partial exception of the French, were unyielding in their insistence that the previous system of separate—and in their eyes, privileged—treatment of war victims must be scrapped, that military and civilian casualties be treated equally, and that the best way to achieve this was to incorporate the treatment of war victims into existing civilian disability programs. Attempts by German officials to circumvent these guidelines were to no avail.[126] Occupation officials were not totally deaf to criticism, however. The meager pensions of survivors, which had been a constant source of German complaint, were gradually expanded; following the currency reform of June 1948, which further worsened the precarious economic position of the war victims, benefits were again improved. Yet, while some improvements had been achieved, German efforts to implement further reforms and, most importantly, to establish a uniform system of war-disability benefits remained unrealized as the period of occupation and military government drew to a close. On the eve of the founding of the Federal Republic, the destitution and suffering of the war victims constituted a pressing social problem that threatened to become a major political problem as well.[127]

FOUR

EARLY AND PROVISIONAL
LEGISLATION

On 14 August 1949 West Germans went to the polls to elect their first Bundestag. The results reflected the uncertainty of the electorate and the fluidity of the situation. No party received a majority. The Union parties, Christian Democrats and Christian Socialists, got the largest vote, 31 percent with 139 seats, but the Social Democrats were close behind with 29.2 percent and 131 seats. The remaining votes (40 percent) were divided among various smaller parties, of which the Free Democrats (Freie Demokratische Partei [FDP]; 11.9 percent, 52 seats), the Communists (Kommunistische Partei Deutschlands [KPD]; 5.7 percent, 15 seats), and the German Party (Deutsche Partei [DP]; 4 percent, 17 seats) were the main winners. Although the position of Konrad Adenauer, who was elected chancellor by one vote (his own) on 15 September, at first seemed precarious, it was not as weak as it appeared. Adenauer held a number of strong cards, which he played adroitly to strengthen both his own and his party's position. He could be reasonably sure of the support of the two rightist bourgeois parties, the Free Democrats and the German Party, which were offered positions in a coalition government, since they were sharply divided from the Social Democrats over the question of the economy, which had been the main issue of the campaign. The chancellor also enjoyed the tacit support of the Bavarian Party (Bayernpartei [BP]; 4.2 percent, 17 seats), which, following initial expressions of opposition to demonstrate its independence, generally supported the government on final legislative votes.[1] Judicious use of cabinet and administrative appointments was also employed to win support and weaken rivals, a tactic of "governmental embrace" that Adenauer was to develop into a fine art in future years.[2]

With semisovereignty came full responsibility for the care of war victims. Whereas earlier the shortcomings of war victim legislation could be blamed on Allied policies, the new West German government now had to demonstrate that it could improve matters.[3] The issue was fraught with potential problems. War victims were organizing and becoming more vocal in their discontent, and Bundestag deputies were sensitive to their cries. The issue was high on the social-legislative agenda, but the means for dealing with it were limited. The administrative means—a federal ministry—still had to be created, while the enormous fiscal means necessary to fund an adequate program for the nearly 4 million war-disabled and survivors had to be found within a tight budget based on a fledgling, uncertain economy burdened with the needs of other social programs as well as heavy occupation costs. Yet while war victim legislation presented the new government with a multitude of problems, at the same time it provided an opportunity to demonstrate its competence and thereby win the support of an important constituency.

The creation of a federal Labor Ministry was eased by the fact that the Verwaltung für Arbeit (VfA) of the Economic Council had developed into a well-articulated quasi-ministry; both its organization and personnel could be taken over relatively intact.[4] The actual structure of the new Labor Ministry as well as the person who would lead it were still a matter of considerable discussion and political controversy. Anton Storch, director of the VfA, was Adenauer's first choice, but his appointment was strongly opposed by the two coalition partners, as well as by conservative elements in the CDU and, in particular, the CSU.[5] The opposition to Storch was due to his close ties to the unions and, above all, to his advocacy of the need to reform the traditional social security system, including a unification of the different branches that had long been advocated by Social Democratic unions and that had been the core of Allied reform efforts.[6] Adenauer, who wanted to retain Storch precisely because of his ties to the unions, tried to resolve the dilemma by proposing the creation of two separate ministries, Labor and Social Policy. Whether it was best to create a sort of "superministry" that would perform the functions of the traditional Labor Ministry as well as handle the numerous new social problems created by the war or to divide the tasks among the Labor Ministry and a number of newly created ministries had been a matter of debate ever since it became clear that a West German state would be formed. Storch himself wanted a Labor Ministry that focused on workers' problems; in his view the best solution was a separate ministry for welfare programs, and he believed that it would be a serious mistake to assign refugee matters to the Labor Ministry. At the same time, however, he wanted to retain social security programs under the direction of the Labor Ministry and to include housing, as had been done in the VfA.[7] Adenauer, who did not see eye to eye with Storch on a number of issues, opposed the development of too powerful a Labor Ministry, fearing that it could become a citadel of the unions. Yet when it became clear that the CDU unions would insist on Storch, Adenauer, who had been considering other candidates who would be more acceptable to his coalition partners, decided to stick with him. Acceptance of Storch's appointment was secured by the creation of two new, separate ministries, one for Refugee Affairs and one for Housing, the latter of which was entrusted to an FDP minister (Eberhard Wildermuth), and by the appointment of Maximilian Sauerborn, a staunch defender of the traditional social security system, as state secretary in the Labor Ministry, a move designed to control Storch and ensure the failure of any efforts undertaken to unify and reform the social security system.[8]

As the structure of the new Labor Ministry began to take shape, demands for action by the war victims increased in intensity. The lifting of Allied restrictions on their activities and the creation of unified ministries upon which to focus lobbying efforts gave a strong impetus to the war victims to organize and expand. The new situation unleashed two contradictory movements within the war victims' movement: on the one hand, increased competition and fragmentation; on the other, renewed efforts to create a united organization. Initially, the former impulse was strongest. With the creation of the Federal Republic, the sporadic attempts at unification between the Reichsbund and the BdK came to an end.[9] In January 1950, at a meeting in Düsseldorf, the BdK reorganized itself; a more centralized (though still strongly federalistic) leadership was created, and the Bund renamed itself the German Association of War-Disabled, War Survivors, and Social Pensioners (Verband der Kriegsbeschädigten, Kriegshinterbliebenen und Sozialrentner Deutschlands [VdK]). The new organization immediately began to establish *Landesverbände* in the states of the British zone, the heartland of the Reichsbund. The resulting competition for members was frequently acrimonious and further soured relations between the two largest war victims' organizations. At the same time, a new competitor appeared, the League of German War-Disabled and Survivors (Bund Deutscher Kriegsbeschädigter und Kriegerhinterbliebener [BDKK]). In order to comply with Allied restrictions, both the Reichsbund and the BdK had accepted disabled civilians and other nonmilitary social pensioners. Although the war victims' organizations found this distasteful and resented the provision, they soon came to live with it, since the non-war-disabled members composed only a small minority of the overall membership.[10] With the creation of the Federal Republic, the need to adhere to this occupation-period restriction lapsed, but both the Reichsbund and the newly constituted VdK continued to include nonmilitary social pensioners.[11] Hoping to capitalize on the resistance of war victims to being lumped together with civilian victims, those interested in creating a "pure" war victims' organization began to organize in early 1950. These efforts culminated in July with the foundation of the BDKK. The new organization, which had close ties to the nondisabled veterans' organizations that had begun to emerge as a result of the lifting of Allied restrictions, only accepted war victims.[12] More national-ist—and less pacifist—than the Reichsbund or the VdK, the BDKK railed against the "mixed" war victims' organizations, but its appeal remained lim-ited. While at the beginning of 1951 the VdK claimed 1.1 million members and the Reichsbund 450,000, the BDKK probably had no more than 50,000.[13]

In addition to the broad-based war victims' organizations, there were also specialized war-disability organizations whose roots went back to the Weimar Republic. The oldest and most prominent was the League of War-Blinded (Bund der Kriegsblinden), originally founded in 1916. Taken over by the NSKOV in 1940, it was reconstituted in 1949. Although small (6,600), it played an important role in shaping those aspects of war-disability legislation that touched upon its constituency.[14] Another special war victims' organization with roots in the past was the League of Brain-Wounded (Bund hirnverletzter Kriegs- und Arbeitsopfer [BhK]).[15] The Bund was originally founded in 1926, later absorbed by the NSKOV, and then refounded in 1946. Like the Bund der Kriegsblinden, the BhK was an officially recognized specialist organization (*Fachorganisation*) that worked to ensure that war-disability legislation in-cluded provisions that met the special needs of its members. Recognizing that the symptoms and behavior of its members often resembled (especially to the public) those of the mentally ill and aware of the traditional lack of sympathy for the latter, the Bund worked constantly to underline, both for the public and officials, the difference between brain-damage disabilities, which were pro-duced by physiological wounds, and war-induced psychotic disorders.[16]

While the separate existence of specialist organizations was of little concern to most war victims, the continued division of the major war victims' organi-zations was. Organizational fragmentation of the war victims' movement was accepted during the occupation, when war victim legislation was a matter for the individual states; with the formation of the Federal Republic and impend-ing federal legislation to govern war victims' benefits, however, the continued division of the movement became increasingly intolerable. There was a strong feeling among the rank and file that the division must be ended and that the VdK and Reichsbund had to merge in order to exert more effective pressure on the government. The organizations' leaders were aware of the mood of their members and constantly spoke of the desirability of fusion. At its first Bundeskonferenz following the Republic's founding (January 1950), Reichs-bund leaders promised to do all they could to promote unification. The chairman of the Reichsbund, Paul Neumann, pledged support for a unified war victims' organization "with which we can more effectively press better and quicker implementation of our social-political demands and program." Helmut Bazille, a leader of the VdK who was attending the conference in his capacity as a member of the Bundestag's Twenty-sixth Committee, the Committee for War Victim and Prisoner of War Questions (26. Ausschuss für Kriegsopfer- und Kriegsgefangenenfragen), also expressed his desire for a single organization, citing the counterproductive consequences of organizational competition in a time when "our common concern must be how we are to deal with the great problems that must be solved in the coming year."[17]

Later in the month, similar thoughts were expressed at the BdK meeting in Düsseldorf. At first sight, the Düsseldorf meeting would appear to have been a setback for unification hopes, since it resulted in a fusion of the BdK's *Landesverbände* into the VdK and prepared the way for the southwest-based organization's expansion into the entire Federal Republic. At the same time, however, by strengthening the central leadership's role, the reorganization diminished the organizational differences between the VdK and the Reichsbund and facilitated negotiations between the two.[18] The Düsseldorf meeting also provided the opportunity for delegates to put pressure on the VdK's leaders to begin working for the creation of a united organization. This desire was given concrete expression at the meeting's end when an apparently spontaneous motion from the floor was passed calling for renewed talks with the Reichsbund. Erich Rossmann, former general secretary of the Länderrat of the U.S. zone, a member of the VdK, and an early organizer and leader of the Reichsbund in the Weimar Republic, was chosen to initiate talks and to serve as mediator in negotiations. In March Rossmann wrote the leaders of the Reichsbund, deploring the "civil war" between the two organizations, which only worked to the disadvantage of the war victims, especially since it was taking place at a time when one "had to fight for the formation of a new and just victim benefits system within the Republic."[19] The Reichsbund responded by inviting Rossmann to a meeting in Hamburg, where the possibility of negotiations between the two organizations could be discussed.

The meeting took place on 20 April. In his opening remarks, Rossmann stressed the fact that the continued division hampered the effective representation of war victims' interests. It allowed the Labor Ministry to play one organization against the other and opened the way for a further fragmentation of the movement, as was shown by the formation of new groups on the right, that is, the BDKK. If the VdK and Reichsbund merged, they could stand up to the bureaucracy and counter the efforts of their common enemy on the right.[20] Rossmann pointed out that the differences between the two organizations were no longer so great. The more centralized structure adopted by the

VdK narrowed organizational differences, and the two organizations were not divided by partisan political affiliations, as had been the case in the Weimar era. While this was generally true, the two organizations did have slightly different political colorations, as became clear in the following discussion. The Reichsbund was closer to the SPD, probably a reflection of its geographical base and the comparative weakness of the CDU in the area. The fact that one of the most vocal Communist deputies in the Bundestag, Heinz Renner, was affiliated with the Reichsbund also was exploited by its opponents to claim that the Reichsbund was leftist and radical. For the VdK, the situation was just the opposite. While its most prominent leaders were affiliated with the SPD, the influence of other parties was much more evident and at least one of the VdK's leaders, Max Wuttcke, had been active in a rightist war victims' organization in the Weimar period and had played a leading role in the NSKOV. Opponents of the VdK charged that it was a tool of the government parties and that it could not be relied upon to fight strenuously against governmental proposals.

In the discussion that followed Rossmann's remarks, the differences between the two organizations were analyzed. While much of the discussion was accommodating, it was clear that the wounds opened during the occupation years were still unhealed. Reichsbund speakers argued that they had constantly worked for a fusion of the two organizations and that their efforts had repeatedly been undercut by the VdK, whose leaders bore the responsibility for the continued division. The exaggerated federalism of the VDK, they claimed, as well as the cautious nature of some of its *Landesverbände*, made it impossible for the VdK to function as a true *Kampfbund*. Reichsbund leaders resented the charges that their organization was Communist, contending that what Renner said did not reflect the Bund's policy. They also challenged the VdK's claim of having more members, which it used to justify its attempts to dictate the form that talks between the two organizations should take. In spite of the occasionally heated nature of discussion, Rossmann left with an agreement to initiate negotiations on a merger. Spurred on by pressure from below and the opening of the Bundestag debate on the Federal War Victims' Benefits Law (Bundesversorgungsgesetz [BVG]), these talks began to assume concrete form in the summer of 1950.[21]

Another group of veterans for whom the creation of the Federal Republic opened the way for a concentrated lobbying effort was made up of the former POWs.[22] Like the war victims, their early activities had been hampered by zonal divisions, the lack of a central governmental agency devoted to their needs, and Allied restrictions on organizational activity. The first organizational efforts on behalf of POWs were directed toward securing the release of prisoners and improving communication with, and the conditions of, those still being held captive. By 1948, however, attention had shifted primarily to the problems of former POWs who had returned. The main thrust of organized POW activity was to secure legislation that would alleviate material needs and, above all, facilitate reintegration into the workplace. Coordination and unification remained difficult, not only because of the exogenous organizational restrictions imposed by occupation authorities but also because of the indigenous tendency of the POWs to organize on the basis of where they had been imprisoned, for example, England, France, the Mideast, and Russia, which further fragmented the movement.[23] Nonetheless, by 1949 organizations of former POWs had emerged on the state and zonal levels, and by the time of the founding of the Republic there were two main groups, the Central Association of Former Prisoners of War (Zentralverband der Heimkehrer), centered in Württemberg-Baden, and the Federal Association of Former Prisoners of War (Bundesverband der Heimkehrer), centered primarily in Bavaria and Lower Saxony.[24] Spurred by the creation of a centralized agency for POW affairs within the newly created Ministry for Refugee Affairs, by the desire to shape impending federal legislation dealing with POWs, and by the fear of losing out to better-organized rivals for social legislation, the Bundesverband and the Zentralverband merged in March 1950.[25] The resulting organization, the Association of Former Prisoners of War (Verband der Heimkehrer [VdH]), overnight became the main POW organization and immediately began to push for legislation to aid its constituents, which, in addition to returned POWs, included the families of those still imprisoned or missing.[26]

OF ALL THE GROUPS hurt by the war, the plight of the war-disabled was the most visible and heart-wrenching, and their needs were generally recognized as being most pressing.[27] All of the political parties had promised relief. In order to ensure that they would not forget, deputies entering the opening session of the Bundestag were met by picketing war victims reminding them of their campaign promises.[28] The liberal sprinkling of war victims among the Bundestag deputies and members of the relevant committees seemed to promise quick and sympathetic action.[29] Although the issue was therefore in a sense nonpartisan, it could also be used for partisan purposes. The war victims represented a substantial voting bloc, and the advocacy of their cause was quickly seized upon by the parties as a touchstone of social conscience—either to prove their own or to demonstrate their opponents' lack thereof. Nine days after the opening of the Bundestag, the Social Democrats seized the initiative by demanding that the government immediately submit a proposal for a new law governing benefits for the war-disabled and survivors.[30] Four days later, in his inaugural address, the newly elected chancellor acknowledged the importance of legislation for war victims, stating that "the guiding principle [Leitstern]" of the government's work would be to strive for "the amelioration of social misery and for social justice," and singling out the needs of the war-disabled and survivors in his remarks concerning "social policy per se."[31]

At the same time the chancellor made it clear that "the best social policy was a sound economic policy," emphasizing that the government's main priority was economic revival and expansion.[32] The emphasis on economic growth and the means adopted to promote it within the framework of Ludwig Erhard's "social market economy,"[33] the government's constant invocation of the fiscal constraints associated with social welfare policies, and the vexatious problem of German rearmament, which began to emerge at the same time that the debate over war victim legislation began, all combined to shape the debate over the BVG and related legislation.

The government's insistence on fiscal restraint coupled with the inevitable bureaucratic delays connected with the drafting of new legislation often combined to give the appearance of hardheartedness or indifference, opening it to attacks by the opposition parties and discomfiting its supporters. One week after the chancellor's address, the German Party requested that the government move to standardize and improve state-paid benefits for war victims.[34] In October, the KPD, citing proposed increases in payments to military pensioners in several states, demanded comparable improvements for the war victims.[35] The CDU countered with a proposal for a provisional law (Überbrückungsgesetz [ÜBG]) that would provide immediate interim payments until the "submission of a new [permanent] benefit program."[36]

The proposals were referred to the relevant committees, and on 4 November the Committee for War Victim and Prisoner of War Questions (Twenty-sixth Committee) returned to the Bundestag a recommendation for the drafting of an interim law along the lines suggested in the CDU proposal.[37] After outlining the history and defects of the existing system and the need to help the war victims, the committee's spokesperson urged the deputies to, as in the past, consider the issue of benefits for war victims as a nonpartisan issue and to refrain from attempts to use it as a pretext for partisan propaganda. On the whole, the deputies complied, although the Communist speaker, Renner, made it a point to link his party's demands with the proposed hikes in military pensions, arguing that "if our impoverished country [Volk] has money for this group of people, then it should also have the resources to guarantee an adequate system of benefits for the victims of war."[38] The Bundestag unanimously approved the committee's request, and the Labor Ministry began to draft an interim law designed to standardize benefits for the war victims and rectify the most grievous imbalances.[39]

On 13 December the matter was taken up by the cabinet. Storch, the newly appointed Labor Minister, argued the necessity of an interim law, presented the salient demands of the war victims' organizations, and discussed the main components, especially the cost-of-living increases (*Teuerungszuschläge*), included in the Bundestag resolution. The finance minister, Fritz Schäffer, responded that until 31 March 1950 the states were responsible for war-disabled benefits and that they were financially strapped and unable to accept further burdens. Pension increases would have to be covered by the supplementary budget of the federal government, and since this would increase the deficit, he could not agree to increases. Further discussion of the matter was postponed until after a meeting of the coalition parties scheduled for the afternoon.[40]

Meanwhile, pressure on the government was mounting in the Bundestag. In an interpellation the SPD criticized the government's failure to act on the Bundestag proposal of 27 October and asked why it did not simply implement the law that had been passed in July 1949 by the Wirtschaftsrat and vetoed by the military government.[41] Not to be outdone, the KPD accused the government of having broken its promise to the war victims and demanded that pensioners be given a bonus of an extra month's payment.[42]

At a morning meeting of the cabinet on 16 December, Storch presented a draft law that would rectify the main discrepancies in the treatment of war victims but would avoid expensive across-the-board increases. He estimated the cost at DM 20 million for a three-month period and requested permission to agree in principle to the suggested improvements at the Bundestag's next meeting, scheduled for that afternoon, in which the Social Democratic and Communist interpellations were to be discussed. The cabinet agreed.[43] In the afternoon, Labor Ministry state secretary Sauerborn presented the government's case to the Bundestag.[44] Implementation of the Wirtschaftsrat version, he argued, was not possible for three reasons: first, it had not included the French occupation zone; second, in the meantime various lands had introduced improvements of their own; finally, the financial situation of the states had worsened, and the federal government was not scheduled to take over payment until the beginning of the fiscal year, that is, 1 April 1950. The combined outlay of the states for war victim benefits, he continued, was already high (DM 2.4 billion), and they were unable to provide further funds. The Communist proposal, providing for an extra month's payment, would entail an increase of about DM 200 million, which was clearly impossible. Having rejected the proposals of the opposition parties, Sauerborn put forth the Labor Ministry proposal discussed at that morning's cabinet meeting, which was designed to improve benefits in the poorer states and bring them up to the levels recently introduced in the more prosperous ones. These changes, it was estimated, would cost DM 80 million, a sum that would be covered by the federal government in the ÜBG. Sauerborn stated that the draft of the law had been completed and that it would immediately be submitted to the legislature; he concluded by noting that work on the Bundesversorgungs-gesetz was well under way.

The floor was then opened to spokespersons of the parties sponsoring the bills under consideration. Renner, the KPD representative, began by questioning the extent of the states' fiscal problems in view of their payment of improved pensions to former military personnel, officers who, he noted, were "physically healthy people who have only become unemployed as a result of the loss, the temporary loss, of their employer, the Wehrmacht. When I say 'temporary,' you know what I mean," he added, referring to the emerging debate over German rearmament. Renner went on to argue that his party's proposal was not unfeasible, accusing the government of not really wanting to do anything for the war victims and of having cynically misled them.

Bazille, the spokesperson for the SPD, opened by saying that "flaming protests" did not help the war victims and that "polemical outbursts" would not change the deplorable circumstances caused by the government's delay in submitting a law. Although not disputing the Labor Ministry's objections to the SPD proposal, Bazille criticized the government's foot-dragging. In view of the situation outlined by Sauerborn, he argued, it seemed a waste of time to continue working on a ÜBG, since its purpose had essentially been defeated by the delay in passing it. As a consequence, he suggested that the idea of an interim law be dropped, that the DM 80 million be paid out immediately along the lines suggested by the Labor Ministry, and that work on the BVG be accelerated and completed as quickly as possible. In view of the need of the war victims, he concluded, they had to end polemical, partisan activities and get to work: "The war victims cannot be helped, Herr Kollege Renner, through great words, but only through deeds."

The CDU representative, after a swipe at Renner regarding the paucity of war victim benefits in the East, seconded Bazille's suggestion of an immediate dispersal of payments to achieve equity "even before the passage of the ÜBG." If the government would agree to this, he then moved that the discussion of the SPD and KPD proposals be closed.

Sauerborn replied that immediate prepayment was impossible. The law and its funding had to be backed by appropriate legislation. Although payments could not be made before Christmas, a particular source of anger for all of the preceding speakers, the Labor Ministry's proposal foresaw the payments beginning on 1 January. There followed a series of bitter exchanges in which Renner accused Bazille of having betrayed the members of the VdK, of which he was a leader, and the SPD of having adopted the same position on war victim legislation as the coalition parties, while speakers for the other parties accused Renner of demagoguery and taunted him again about the low benefits paid to war victims in the Eastern zone. The debate closed with the unanimous acceptance of an SPD proposal urging the government to do what was necessary to allow advance payments of the benefits foreseen in the ÜBG. No advance payments were made, but on 21 December the Labor Ministry's draft of the ÜBG was submitted to and approved by the cabinet and then sent immediately to the Twenty-sixth Committee and the Bundesrat for consideration.[45]

Following the Christmas break, the law went to the Bundestag. The purpose of the ÜBG was twofold: to standardize benefits and, in the process, to improve those in the poorer states by bringing them up to the level of those in the states that had introduced improvements during the course of 1949. The main areas of improvement were provisions for 20 percent pension increases and the expansion of benefits for widows. Health care for survivors, requested by the Bundestag, was not provided. The estimated cost of the improvements was set at DM 79.8 million annually, which was to become a source of dispute since many had assumed that the government's figure of DM 80 million, put forth in the earlier Bundestag debate, was intended to cover only the first quarter of the year, before the first fiscal year began. The Bundesrat had proposed three amendments to the government's bill. The first two, which were minor, were accepted by the cabinet, but the third, which involved a reduction in pension payments to those with less than a 50 percent disability who were employed, was rejected. To the Bundestag, Storch claimed the amendment had been rejected because the bill was supposed "to bring improvements, not reductions." In reality, the existing benefits for the lightly disabled had been retained out of the fear that if cut they would be restored at even higher levels by the Bundestag.[46]

In presenting the bill, Storch related the history of war victim benefits since 1945, which, as a result of Allied occupation and restrictions, had produced the current fragmented system. He discussed the main features of the bill, which were designed to provide uniform benefits and to remedy major inequities, and emphasized that limited economic resources were available. Storch urged the Bundestag to pass the law as quickly as possible and requested the deputies to "withhold demands for further improvements until they could be considered in connection with the final law."

In the debate that followed, the inadequacies of the provisional law were denounced by all of the parties, including those of the governing coalition.[47] As usual the most unrestrained attack came from the KPD, whose spokesperson, Renner, equated the government's war victim program with the bogus social welfare programs of the Third Reich and appealed to the war victims' organizations to unite so that they could put more effective pressure on the government. The SPD sharply criticized the bill, questioning the government's fiscal arguments and deploring its slowness and ineptitude in drafting the law. Here the SPD adopted the attitude that was to characterize its position throughout the debates concerning war victim legislation—thorough, persistent criticism, coupled with a pragmatic willingness to compromise in the face of economic reality. This won the SPD respect and praise from the bourgeois parties and reflected the parties' generally sincere and nonpartisan approach to the problem.

The coalition parties were hardly less sparing than those of the opposition in their criticisms of the proposed law and equally anxious to demonstrate their desire for improvements. Foremost among these were the creation of a separate system for war victims, provision of health care for survivors, higher pension payments, especially for widows, and the elimination of provisions that effectively reduced war victims' benefits by linking them to outside income levels and other pensions. The Bundestag heeded Storch's request to move quickly, voting to send the bill to committee, but ignored his plea to postpone requests for improvements until later by coupling their approval with promises to work for improvements while the bill was in committee.

Such promises were not empty, as the government soon realized with alarm. In committee the bill became the proverbial legislative Christmas tree, as members tacked on their favorite improvements. During the Bundestag debates all the parties had expressed surprise—real or professed—that the DM 80 million figure promised by the government was an annual figure, not a quarterly one, and the committee appeared determined to proceed as if the latter were true. Cabinet ministers anxiously monitored the bill's passage through committee and urged restraint, but to no avail. When the committee finished its deliberations, it turned out that its version would cost over DM 200 million, instead of the DM 80 million that the government claimed was available.[48] The cabinet refused to consider such an increase,[49] and on 31 January the labor and finance ministers appeared before a joint meeting of the Budget and War Victims' committees to argue their case.[50] Schäffer sketched the federal government's precarious financial situation and pointed to the threatening deficit. The government, he declared, was determined not to try to solve its problems with some sort of "experiment" that would involve unsound fiscal policies ("währungspolitische Manöver"). At the same time, it wanted to avoid the extreme deflationary policies of 1931–32, which had only contributed to unemployment and increased misery. The most that could be provided was DM 80 million. Moreover, the committee's version of the bill would certainly be rejected by the Bundesrat. Schäffer related how difficult it had been to get the state finance ministers to agree to the government's proposal; if the costs, which were to be borne primarily by the states until 1 April, were greatly increased then the states would drag out debate in the Bundesrat and postpone its implementation until the beginning of the new fiscal year, defeating the whole purpose of the ÜBG, which was to provide relief from January until April, when the BVG was scheduled to come into force.

Storch echoed the finance minister's arguments. He readily conceded that improvements had to be made but insisted that this was not the time or place to make them. What was needed now was standardization and speed, both of which were provided in the government's draft. Changes at this point would only delay things. For these reasons the changes proposed by the Bundesrat had been rejected. The necessary changes should—and would—be incorporated into the BVG. A majority of the committee—whose composition reflected that of the Bundestag—was persuaded by the ministers' arguments. In its report to the Bundestag, the committee struck out the extensive changes it had initially approved. Except for some minor changes, including the stipulation that the proposed increases would not be included in welfare means tests, the committee's version of the ÜBG was substantially the same as the government's.[51] The SPD responded by submitting an amending bill that retained the changes contained in the committee's original proposal.[52]

That bipartisan support for the bill had evaporated was made clear when it was reported out of committee by Maria Probst (CDU) instead of Bazille (SPD) as originally planned. Probst outlined the legislative background of the bill and its course through the committee, detailing the changes that had been originally proposed and the committee's last-minute decision to abandon them in the face of the arguments set forth by the finance and labor ministers in the meeting of 31 January. She closed by pointing out the improvements that the bill provided and urged the Bundestag to accept it as it was. The government's argument was put forth even more forcibly by another CDU member of the committee, Josef Arndgen. He portrayed the committee as being both sympathetic and realistic. It had made changes in response to requests of the war victims' organizations and as a result of the committee members' desire for improvements. When the extent of the additional expenses associated with the proposed changes became clear, however, the majority of the committee realized that the bill would have to return to the Bundesrat where it would be either rejected or delayed. In either case the war victims would suffer, and therefore, according to Arndgen, the present bill should be accepted, since it was better "to have a bird in the hand than two in the bush [besser . . . einen Spatz in der Hand als eine Taube auf der Dach zu haben]." One must realize that "politics was the art of the possible." To ensure that the final law would incorporate those measures that could not be included in the present bill, the committee had added a resolution binding the government to include them in the BVG.[53]

Speaking for the SPD (and the minority of the committee), Bazille did not dispute the fact that it was impossible to have everything that was desirable included in the bill but argued that much more was necessary and possible. After outlining the changes that would be retained by the SPD's proposed amendments, he concluded that the funds for the additional measures could be provided through "greater economy in the expenditure of public funds and a more just program of taxation."

In the discussion that followed, Renner of the KPD came back to his argument that the government really did not intend to give any more than DM 80 million for the war victims and that the coalition parties were more concerned with the fate of former officers than with war victims. The KPD, he announced, would vote for the SPD bill. Support for the SPD bill also came from some of the smaller parties. Gebhard Seelos of the BP, for example, argued that if priorities were to be set, the war victims must come first, and he claimed that the DM 120 million difference between the original bill and the one supported by the government could easily have been made up by eliminating superficial ministries and by having left the seat of the federal government in Frankfurt instead of making the costly move to Bonn, an argument that was picked up by other opponents of the bill. Speakers for the Center Party (Zentrumspartei) and the Bavarian Economic Reconstruction Association (Wirtschaftliche Aufbau-Vereinigung [WAV]) also supported the SPD position. Heinrich Leuchtgens, an extreme rightist deputy, who was obviously ill at ease over the political capital being acquired by the SPD through its exploitation of a traditional right-wing issue, spoke of the duty to provide the war victims with the "Dank des Vaterlandes." He attacked the government's stinginess and the committee's cowardice and moved that the committee's original proposal be accepted. Erich Mende of the FDP supported the government's arguments, and Arndgen concluded the government's case by stating that the Bundesrat, "which in great part is composed of Social Democratic ministers," had agreed to the law essentially in the form in which it was being presented and that the finance minister had told the Budget Committee (of which Arndgen was also a member) that any increases in expenditures connected with the bill would be rejected by the Bundesrat, "including those ministers who belong to the Social Democratic Party."[54]

The second reading ended tumultuously with a heated exchange between Renner and Margot Kalinke of the German Party, in which the former dredged up the latter's Nazi past. The ensuing vote was close, requiring a division; it resulted in the rejection of the SPD bill and the acceptance of the committee's final version of the government's proposal by a vote of 177 to 162.[55] The third and final reading was anticlimactic and passed with the SPD abstaining.[56]

WITH THE WAR victims taken care of, at least provisionally, attention turned to the former prisoners of war. As with war victim legislation during the occupation, legislation dealing with benefits for returned POWs had been enacted on the local and/or state level and as a result was subject to wide variation.[57] The first goal of the new federal government was to consolidate and standardize existing legislation. The problems of returning POWs were generally seen as analogous to those of the expellees and refugees. This was reflected in the placement of the office for POW affairs within the Ministry for Expellee Affairs. The connection between POWs and expellees was also manifested in the fact that POW benefits were included in early discussions of the Equalization of Burdens Law (Lastenausgleichsgesetz [LAG]). In March 1949 a special commission of the Wirtschaftsrat decided that POWs should not be included under the proposed LAG and that a separate law should be passed to deal with them. Protests by POWs failed to change the decision. After the founding of the Federal Republic, an attempt was made to include former POWs in the Emergency Assistance Law (Soforthilfegesetze) of September 1949, but this also failed.[58] By early 1950, government action and public pressure converged and the first steps were made toward the drafting of a Returned Prisoner of War Law (Heimkehrergesetz [HKG]).[59] The demands of the former POWs focused on three areas: material support to ease the transition to civilian life, assistance in finding employment, and compensation for time spent in captivity. The latter demand was justified on the grounds that the labor performed as POWs was a reparations payment for which the entire German people were liable but which in practice had been paid only by the POWs, who should now be compensated.[60]

The concerns of the former POWs were stated in a petition sent to the committee in charge of drafting the HKG by the *Heimkehrer* organizations of the U.S. zone.[61] The petition began with typical interest group rhetoric maintaining that the demands of the organizations served the interests of the state as well as those of their members. The fundamental purpose of the POW organizations, it was claimed, was to prevent the former POWs from becoming a long-term structural problem, to keep them from becoming politicized, and to stop them from being pushed into the background by other interest groups.[62] To avoid these undesirable developments, three categories of needs had to be met: immediate securing of a decent standard of living, assistance in finding employment, and recognition of and compensation for work performed as POWs. To achieve the first objective, it was argued, the former POWs should receive an adequate monetary supplement and sufficient clothing and personal goods to start a new life, be given preferential treatment in housing, and be reintegrated into the various social insurance programs in a manner that did not penalize them for the time spent in captivity. The second demand, employment, was the most pressing and the "politically most important task" that had to be met if *Heimkehrer* were not to become "a long-term disadvantaged group." A satisfactory solution, it was argued, required strict enforcement of legislation guaranteeing veterans their old jobs or preferential hiring when their old jobs were no longer available, extended unemployment benefits, and extensive vocational training programs such as those provided for the war-disabled.[63] The final goal, compensation for labor performed while a POW, was recognized as a long-term objective and did not figure prominently in the debate over the HKG.[64]

The first reading of the HKG took place on 17 March.[65] Although the debate over the HKG in many ways mirrored that over the ÜBG, with the government pressing for standardization and stressing the need for economy while the parties deplored the law's inadequacy, the discussion and accompanying negotiations were not nearly as intense or complex. This was largely because the financial stakes were not as great.[66] Storch introduced the bill, and his opening remarks indicated that the government had taken into account many of the requests of the former POWs. The proposed law included provisions for immediate assistance at the time of release, measures designed to facilitate the establishment of residency and finding employment, and special provisions to ensure reintegration into basic social programs on an equal footing.

Speakers for all of the parties expressed their sympathy for the former POWs and pledged support for legislation to ease their plight; such legislation was necessary not only for humane and moral reasons, but, as some pointed out, to win over the war generation and prevent it from becoming alienated and hostile to the new democratic state. The emotive appeal of the issue invited a certain amount of grandstanding, but discussion of the bill was generally reasoned and objective. Nonetheless, the Cold War political context of the *Heimkehrer* problem virtually assured polemical fireworks, and they were not long in coming. They were touched off by the Bavarian CSU deputy, Franz Josef Strauss, who angrily responded to criticisms of the government's delay in presenting the law, thundered that the treatment of German POWs had violated international law, and accused others of seeking to exploit the POWs for their own political ends. Strauss was followed by Renner of the KPD, who roundly criticized the law, charged the other parties with having rejected the Communist proposals to the committee to improve benefits during the drafting of the law, and returned Strauss's accusation of exploiting the former POWs for partisan political purposes. Renner's remarks were interrupted by Strauss's sarcastic call to read the comparable law in the Eastern zone, and the next speaker, Peter Tobaben of the German Party, heatedly stated that if Renner "instead of raising demagogic demands and claiming his own belief in human rights would encourage—or had earlier encouraged—his friends to honor them, then we would not have to be discussing such a law here today."

Substantive discussion revolved around two points: the low level of payments to aid reintegration (*Entlassungsgeld*) and the need to ensure that the provisions of the new law would be enforced uniformly and in a spirit of goodwill by the authorities charged with its implementation. If nothing else, the debate over the HKG demonstrated that the former POWs had made the public and its representatives aware of their anger at their arbitrary and callous treatment by unfeeling bureaucrats on their return. At the conclusion of the first reading, Storch admitted that he was not surprised at the deputies' dissatisfaction with the law, but that this might have been reduced somewhat if they had first debated the budget. Governmental revenue was DM 8.7 billion. Of this, 7.5 billion was being spent on burdens incurred as a result of the war (*Kriegsfolgelasten*): 4.5 billion to cover occupation costs and 3 billion for war victim benefits. The HKG's costs (DM 74 million) were also a part of the *Kriegsfolgelasten*. Before 1933, Storch noted, the entire Reich budget was 8 billion Reichsmark and was supported by the taxes of 70 million citizens, which meant that the total budget then, at a time when the total number of taxpayers was greater, was the same as that now being spent on *Kriegsfolgelasten* alone. While he and his colleagues were aware of shortcomings of the HKG, it was impossible to allot more than was foreseen in the proposed law.

When the amended law returned from the Twenty-sixth Committee for its second reading on 26 April, only two significant changes had been made. Both concerned the level of material support to be given former POWs on their release. The payments had been raised from DM 50 to DM 100, and the wording of the clause governing provision of clothing and necessary personal items had been changed to read "in the value of DM 250" instead of "up to the value of DM 250." The latter change was designed to curb the discretionary powers of administrative officials.[67]

The discussion was characterized by the usual polemic exchanges between Renner and members of the other parties. The Communist deputy again pointed out that his party had suggested raises in all categories of payments and that these had been rejected by the other parties, proving that the latter were not really interested in the *Heimkehrer* but only in using them for propaganda purposes. Kurt Pohle of the SPD, referring to KPD tactics in the Weimar Republic, warned that one could never win in the competition with the KPD to raise benefits since the party was not interested in helping recipients but only in embarrassing the other parties. Mende of the FDP added that he wished Renner would give his speech to former POWs who lived in areas where they did not have the good fortune to receive any sort of benefits and later described the HKG as a part of the "compensation [Wiedergutmachung] to victims of Bolshevism . . . who are now coming by the thousands into our zone." To this the KPD delegation responded with derisive cries of "Who started the war?," "Who sent them to Russia, the Nazis or us?," and "When was the last time you shouted 'Heil Hitler'?"

Debate in the second reading focused on the need to raise the *Entlassungsgeld* payment even higher. All three of the Bavarian parties (BP, CSU, and WAV) submitted proposals to increase the payment to DM 150. This was what the Bavarian state HKG provided, and the representatives of the Bavarian parties contended that they did not want to vote for a federal law that would effectively lower the benefits paid to Bavarian *Heimkehrer*. Others also supported an increase, arguing that DM 100 was too low and that it would be unfair to have a level that in practice would mean that former POWs now returning would in some cases receive less than those who had returned earlier.

Mende defended the committee's version of the bill. Many within the committee, including those in his party, the FDP, had wanted a payment of DM 150 but had taken into account the objections raised to such a large increase. The committee had unanimously agreed to DM 100, with the representatives of the BP and WAV abstaining. He noted that although DM 150 was indeed paid in Bavaria, the sum for the provision of goods (*Übergangshilfe*) was less. The committee's bill, by paying an *Entlassungsgeld* of DM 100 and setting the *Übergangshilfe* at DM 250, with payment in cash possible, provided a total of DM 350 for former POWs. If the *Entlassungsgeld* were set at DM 150, then it would be likely that the *Übergangshilfe*, which was determined according to need, would generally be cut, hurting those who needed it most. Mende was obviously angered at the actions of the Bavarian parties, especially the CSU, which, he complained, had "nullified the agreement made in the committee." He noted that the SPD, which as an opposition party had more to gain by such a maneuver, had stuck responsibly to the agreement. Arndgen (FDP) suggested that the Bavarian parties' proposals were part of a scheme by the Bavarian government to shift more of the costs connected with former POW aid to the federal government.[68]

In spite of the efforts of the coalition parties to hold the line, it was clear that there was strong support for a further increase to DM 150 and that many deputies of the coalition parties, either out of conviction or fear, were prepared to vote for it. A motion to have a roll call vote on the BP's proposal was narrowly defeated, indicating the reluctance of opponents to make their opposition public and the likelihood that some members of the coalition parties intended to vote for the bill and hoped to conceal their break with party discipline. The final vote produced a clear majority in support of the increase, whereupon the FDP, invoking a procedural rule, obtained a delay of one day before the third and final reading of the bill.

When the deputies assembled the next day, they found a new proposal for change introduced by the CSU and supported by the CDU. The ensuing debate revealed cracks in the governmental coalition and again raised questions about the character of the bureaucracy.[69] The proposal retained the DM 150 *Entlassungsgeld* but restored the words "up to DM 250" in the section regulating the *Übergangshilfe*. The BP quickly labeled the new bill a trick (*Kunstgriff*) that would subject the legitimate claims of former POWs to bureaucratic arbitrariness. The Center Party charged that the revision simply took away with one hand what it gave with the other. Hans Löfflad of the WAV sarcastically remarked that in the previous day's vote the CSU had proven itself to be both Christian and social, but now things appeared quite different. "We can assume," he continued, "that Herr Minister Schäffer has exercised a certain pressure on the CSU."

The CSU was indeed in an awkward position, caught between the need to compete with its Bavarian rivals and the requirements of coalition discipline on the federal level.[70] The former necessitated the CSU's earlier proposal for raising the supplement to DM 150. The latter required support of the new proposal, which clearly reflected the Finance Ministry's desire to offset increased monetary supplement costs through closer control of outlays for the provision of goods.[71] The CSU's embarrassment was reflected in the defensive and belligerent response of Strauss, who contended that the change was insignificant and at the same time insisted that it was necessary in order to assure passage in the Bundesrat, where earlier proposed increases in *Heim-*

kehrer aid had been rejected by the states—including, he was careful to note, employing a favorite stick of the bourgeois parties to beat the SPD, states governed by Social Democrats. Anyone really concerned about bureaucratic arbitrariness, Strauss argued, should have tried to remove all forms of means tests in the bill.

Pohle, speaking for the SPD, said that his party's members had tried to do just that in the committee and they had only agreed to leave them in after Storch had assured them that it would be Labor Ministry officials who reviewed claims, not welfare officials. He noted that it had been the Social Democratic members of the committee who had insisted on striking out the words "up to" in the original proposal and who had insisted on the provision making it possible for recipients to receive the DM 250 in cash. The Social Democrats therefore considered the CSU proposal superficial and declared that they would vote against it.

Mende, speaking for the FDP, made it clear that he felt that the SPD had acted more responsibly in the matter than his party's nominal coalition partner. He confirmed Pohle's account and asserted that the proposals for change that had been submitted following the committee's compromise agreement had only worsened things. In view of what had happened, the FDP (and the DP, for whom he also was speaking) no longer felt bound by the committee's agreement and would support the increase to DM 150. With regard to the proposal to restore the original wording of the *Übergangshilfe* provision, Mende felt it was dangerous to place additional authority in the hands of officials, though he cited different reasons than the SPD. In a characteristic argument of the FDP, which had steadfastly opposed postwar reform of the bureaucracy, he stated that his position was the result not of any "mistrust of the bureaucracy as such . . . but out of mistrust of what the bureaucracy has become since 1945 as a result of the undermining of the principle of a professional bureaucracy." Because of this, the FDP would not support the CSU's amendment.

Schäffer, speaking briefly, disclaimed any responsibility for the latter's proposal and tried to reassure the house that there were no evil intentions behind the original wording of the HKG. Since the *Übergangshilfe* dealt with goods, he maintained, one could only set approximate values with DM 250 marking the highest limit. The point, he continued, was not DM 50 more or less, but the more fundamental question of political and fiscal responsibility. The Bundestag committees, in making hard decisions, were correctly trying to see the whole picture, considering the various proposals not in a vacuum but in relation to the general need. Deputies had the responsibility to represent the interests not only of those covered by a particular piece of legislation but of the entire population, above all the taxpayers. If the Bundestag routinely increased the costs of the bills presented by the government, then the government would be unable to calculate costs rationally and it would no longer be able to make proposals that were designed to include the maximum possible benefits. For these reasons, Schäffer claimed, he opposed the changes that had been made in the committee's version of the HKG.

In spite of the finance minister's protests, the changes were retained. CDU spokespersons, after weakly trying to defend the CSU/CDU proposal, withdrew it. The version adopted after the second reading was passed in the third reading, and the law went into effect in this form.

THE HKG PROVIDED welcome relief for former POWs, but the Verband der Heimkehrer saw it as only a first step in meeting the problems of its members. The law itself was branded as imperfect, and a campaign to increase its benefits began immediately.[72] Most importantly, the HKG had failed to deal with the third major demand that had been articulated by the VdH— compensation for the labor performed by POWs that had been exacted as reparations payments by the victors. The issue naturally attracted the support of former POWs and offered the VdH an excellent opportunity to expand its membership and solidify its position as the primary interest group of former POWs. Thus, while the VdH continued to press for improvements in the HKG, its central demand in the coming years was the need for a law compensating POWs for the labor they had performed in captivity.[73]

The war victims were even more disappointed by the ÜBG. Derisively labeling it the "Sparrow Proposal," the Verband der Kriegsbeschädigten's organ *Die Fackel* criticized the new law for being too little and too late.[74] The government, it claimed, had not proven its case for the low level of benefits provided for in the new law, a situation that would be remedied by the provision of accurate statistical evidence by the war victims themselves. Uppermost in the minds of the war victims' organizations were not the provisions of the ÜBG itself but the fear that with its passage the pressure for the drafting and passage of permanent war-disability legislation would abate. In view of the protracted debate over the ÜBG and the fact that the date promised originally for the enactment of permanent legislation (1 April 1950) clearly would not be met, this concern was not unfounded. Consequently the war victims' organizations focused their attention not so much upon criticism of the ÜBG, but instead upon pressuring the government to begin moving on the promised Bundesversorgungsgesetz, citing the growing and explosive nature of discontent within the war victim community and threatening massive demonstrations unless the government began to take action to honor its promises.[75]

Dissatisfaction with the ÜBG also helped to stimulate and strengthen calls for a unification of the war victims' organizations. A united organization, by exercising increased pressure on the government and Bundestag, could, it was argued, ensure that the BVG included better benefits and prevent the sort of foot-dragging that had so far characterized the government's attitude toward war victim legislation. The efforts of Rossmann to initiate negotiations between the Reichsbund and the VdK, goaded by anger about the ÜBG and the upcoming debate over the BVG, began to bear fruit. A joint committee was formed to explore the merger of the two organizations.[76] It held its first meeting in July, and by the fall, when the BVG began to move through the Bundestag, the chances for unification of the two largest war victims' organizations appeared promising.

FIVE

THE FEDERAL WAR
VICTIMS' BENEFITS LAW

The Federal War Victims' Benefits Law (Bundesversorgungsgesetz [BVG]), promulgated in December 1950, was the first major piece of social legislation enacted in the Federal Republic. Over 4 million West German war victims were covered under the law; directly or indirectly, its provisions affected a fifth of the population. The expenditures associated with it were larger than those of any other social program and second only to the occupation costs borne by the Republic.[1] The BVG was—and was perceived as—a clear repudiation of the war-disability systems imposed by the Allies on the Germans during the occupation.[2] Since it was closely modeled on the Reichsversorgungsgesetz (RVG) of the Weimar Republic, the BVG can also in a sense be considered an element of a post-1945 "restoration."[3] This is only partially true, however, for the framers of the new law neither wanted nor were able to return in toto to the RVG. While the elements of continuity may have been dominant, both change and continuity were embodied in the new law. The BVG was shaped not only by the lessons learned from the past but also by the straitened fiscal circumstances of the Federal Republic's early years. The blend of change and continuity was evident in other ways as well. The drafting and legislation of the BVG represented a revival of the mixture of bureaucratic, interest group, and parliamentary politics that had emerged in the Weimar Republic and that was to reemerge even more strongly in the post–World War II era. In contrast to Weimar, however, the parliamentary component was stronger and the legitimizing function was far more successful. Although contemporary critics now accuse it of having produced stasis, in its early stages during the formative years of the Federal Republic, the process of corporate decision making greatly expedited the passage of social legislation as well as the sociopolitical integration of the groups involved.[4]

THE GOVERNMENT was well aware of the war victims' dissatisfaction with the Überbrückungsgesetz (ÜBG).[5] Responding to the storm of anger and criticism that accompanied its passage, the Labor Ministry invited leaders of the war victims' organizations to meet with government officials concerned with the drafting of the BVG on 3 March.[6] The initial meeting, which involved representatives of the four main war victims' organizations, officials of the Labor Ministry, and representatives from the Finance and Housing ministries, was followed up by two further meetings on 7 and 8 March.[7] The discussions revealed a general consensus on the overall shape and nature of the new law, though there was disagreement on the specific structure of pension payments and, as was to be expected, differences between the war victims' organizations and the government over the fiscal boundaries within which the new law would have to operate. Attempts by the representatives of the *Kriegsopferverbände* to persuade ministerial officials to reveal how much the government planned to allocate and to commit themselves to a figure were repeatedly evaded by the government officials.

Representatives of the war victims' organizations made it clear that their model for the structure of the new system of benefits was the system that had existed during the Weimar Republic. They were unanimous in requesting that an Advisory Council (Beirat) be established that corresponded to the earlier Reichsausschuss der Kriegsbeschädigten- und Kriegshinterbliebenenfürsorge and in their insistence that war victim benefits be separated from other social programs. The Labor Ministry representatives promised to examine the question of creating an Advisory Council and assured the *Kriegsopferverbände* that the war victim benefits would be administered by an independent and equal department within the Labor Ministry. There was general agreement among the war victims' representatives and their ministerial counterparts on a number of specific questions: that welfare measures for former prisoners of war and their families should not be covered under the BVG but under a separate law administered by the Ministry for Expellee Affairs, that all war widows be entitled to pensions, and that aid to the parents of disabled and deceased veterans be limited.[8]

The war victims' organizations were also united in their insistence that all disabled persons, both those classified as "lightly disabled" (less than 50 percent) and those considered "severely disabled" (more than 50 percent), receive pensions, and that pension reductions mandated as a result of the receipt of outside income, other pensions, and the like be kept to a minimum. There was only one point of serious disagreement among the war victims' organizations—the form of the pension payment. The VdK supported a two-tier structure similar to that which had existed in the Weimar Republic under the

RVG: an inalienable base pension determined by the degree of physical disability supplemented by a compensatory pension tailored to meet the specific economic needs of the individual. This two-tier system was clearly favored by the Labor Ministry. The Reichsbund insisted on a single pension based on the degree of physical disability alone, a scheme that would require higher base pensions.[9]

Following the talks with the *Kriegsopferverbände*, representatives of the federal and state ministries concerned with war victim legislation and members of the Bundestag committee responsible for the BVG met together on 23 and 24 March to clarify and coordinate action on the state and federal levels and to discuss the requests of the war victims.[10] The Labor Ministry spokesperson who chaired the meeting began by describing the fiscal foundation of the ÜBG, which presumably would also be the model for the BVG.[11] He stressed the desperate financial situation of the Republic, while again refusing to give specific figures on how much the government intended to provide for war victim legislation. Discussion then turned to the points raised by the war victims' organizations at the earlier meetings. There was general agreement concerning their requests for a separate system modeled along the lines of the RVG and the creation of an Advisory Council. Debate then turned to the more thorny question of pension structure. The state representatives were united in their support of a two-level pension system, consisting of a fixed base allowance supplemented by a variable compensation allowance based on need. The question of pensions for the lightly disabled was discussed in great detail. The main problem was that the proportion of severely disabled to lightly disabled was much higher after 1945 than it had been after 1918.[12] Thus, more veterans were entitled to higher pensions, a problem compounded by the greater economic destruction of the Second World War, which further limited employment opportunities for the severely disabled and made them more dependent on government assistance. In the view of some state officials, the only way out of the dilemma was to disallow (or temporarily suspend) pension payments to the lightly disabled so that the more pressing needs of the severely disabled could be better met. The Bundesrat's version of the ÜBG had cut pensions for the lightly disabled; although the government had later restored these cuts, it was clear that the Labor Ministry had not ruled out a possible temporary suspension of payments to lightly disabled veterans if dictated by financial constraints.[13] The *Kriegsopferverbände* had steadfastly opposed the elimination of pensions for the lightly disabled, claiming that it was a "dangerous experiment" and "politically impossible."[14] The state representatives unanimously supported the view that the lightly disabled should be included in the new law in order to compensate them for the extra expenses they faced compared to nondisabled persons and with the awareness that ending their pensions would hit the elderly, lightly disabled veterans of the First World War especially hard. Thus, while the extent of pensions for the lightly disabled was left unclear, the war victims' organizations' demand that they be included in the law was approved.[15] With regard to the question of ending the linkage of pension levels to outside income, including other pension payments, the war victims' organizations were less successful. Both the state and the Bundestag representatives felt that, in view of the critical financial situation, a complete renunciation of some sort of means tests for outside sources of income was impossible.

Having sounded out representatives of the *Kriegsopferverbände*, the state labor ministries, and the Bundestag committee responsible for war victim legislation, federal Labor Ministry officials withdrew to the sanctity of their ministry, where a small committee of experts, using the RVG as a model, began work on a preliminary draft of the new law. On 17 May the draft was sent by Labor Minister Anton Storch to the other ministers for their scrutiny, and an interministerial meeting to discuss the draft proposal was scheduled for 23 May.[16] The meeting was opened by a Labor Ministry representative who had recently attended meetings of the statewide war victims' organizations of Bavaria and Württemberg. The situation, he reported, was "extraordinarily tense." The demands of the *Kriegsopferverbände* went far beyond what the government's draft proposed, and, he claimed, "it was clear that strong Communist forces were exploiting the difficulties of the war victims for political ends."[17]

The Labor Ministry's draft found general approval. All of the ministerial officials agreed on the need to create a uniform law that was independent from the social security system and modeled "as closely as possible on the old Reichsversorgungsgesetz." There was general support for the income threshold provisions of the Labor Ministry's draft and its proposed exclusion of war victim benefits from the outside income provisions (*Ruhenvorschriften*) of the Social Security Law (Reichsversicherungsordnung [RVO]). The cost of the Labor Ministry's draft was a little over DM 3 billion, some DM 500 million over the amount that had been allocated. Not surprisingly, the main opposition to the draft came from the Finance Ministry. Its representative argued that the financial consequences of excluding war victims' pensions from the RVO income threshold provisions needed to be checked more closely; he also proposed that pension payments for the lightly disabled be suspended for one or two years and that pensions for young, childless widows be dropped altogether. The latter two proposals were overridden by the other ministerial representatives as being impossible on political, legal, and other grounds. Two other measures designed to cut costs were supported by the assembled officials, however: geographic cost-of-living differentials (*Ortsklassen*) were retained, and it was agreed that payments under the law should commence only after it was promulgated and not be retroactive to 1 April, the originally promised date of enactment.[18]

Meanwhile, pressure for action was mounting. The lead article of the April issue of the VdK's *Die Fackel* blasted the slowness of the Labor Ministry; referring to the famed "Hunger March" of U.S. veterans in the 1930s, it threatened that if a new proposal was not introduced soon, there would be mass demonstrations by the war-disabled ("Krücken auf der Strasse sind eine ernste Gefahr!"). In the May edition, a "Final Warning" was published condemning the government for failing to fulfill its promises and threatening that unless the new proposal was ready in eight weeks, the VdK would call upon its 1 million members to engage in mass demonstrations in order "to fight for their rights with the final democratic means at their disposal," a threat that was repeated in the June issue.[19]

Officials were not immune to this threat and sought to defuse the situation by acceding to the war victims' organizations' demand for the creation of an Advisory Council that would provide them input into the drafting of the new law.[20] On 26 April the Labor Ministry announced its intention to create an Advisory Council and invited the war victims' organizations to send representatives to a meeting scheduled for late May.[21] The council, composed of representatives of the war victims' organizations, state officials, and various experts concerned with war victim legislation, was formally constituted on 25 May. In the following weeks, it met four times to discuss the Labor Ministry's preliminary draft of the BVG.[22]

The first question addressed by the Advisory Council was the total sum that was to be budgeted for war victim legislation. The Finance Ministry's representative claimed that the original sum allocated, DM 2.6 billion, was the absolute maximum and that the sole possibility for obtaining additional funds was a cut in the occupation costs paid by the Germans. If the occupying powers would agree to such cuts, then the money saved would go primarily ("in erster Linie") to the war victims. If occupation costs remained unchanged, certain benefits included in the proposed BVG would need to be temporarily suspended. By honoring the war victims' requests that the new law be completely independent from the social security system and that payments under the BVG be exempted from the income and external pension threshold provisions of the former, thus ensuring that war victim pensioners would receive all the social security benefits to which they were entitled, the Labor Ministry's draft had added considerably to the BVG's cost. According to the Finance Ministry's calculations, the exclusion of war-disability pensions from the *Ruhenvorschriften* of the social security system would cost the government DM 350 million. This would further limit the amount of money available for social services; the DM 2.6 billion allocated for the BVG was, therefore, the absolute maximum. Moreover, if all of the provisions of the draft law were to be accepted, this limit would be exceeded. In order to stay within the BVG's budget, the Finance Ministry proposed that the scheduled payments for the lightly disabled and childless widows under fifty be temporarily suspended. In response to complaints of the council members that the present budget was burdened by what were essentially onetime start-up costs and that to accept these constraints as permanent would produce a poor piece of legislation, the Finance Ministry's representative replied that, on the contrary, one would have to expect substantial retropayments in the coming years.[23] Thus, from the start the lines were drawn, and the meetings proceeded in an atmosphere of tension and uncertainty.

For the most part the draft met the approval of the council, and its suggestions were readily accepted by the Labor Ministry's representatives. The sections of the law dealing with eligibility, medical care, and social welfare were discussed and revised with relatively little disagreement. As was to be expected, however, the sections dealing with the extent and level of pension payments quickly became the source of bitter conflict between the representatives of the Finance Ministry and the war victims' organizations and, to a lesser degree, the Labor Ministry, which was caught between sympathy for many of the demands of the war victims, on the one hand, and the need to maintain governmental solidarity, on the other.

At the beginning of the second meeting on 6–7 June, the representatives of the war victims' organizations not only supported the payment of pensions to the lightly disabled but also proposed an across-the-board increase. Starting from the premise that a total pension of at least DM 180 per month was necessary for the survival of an unemployed disabled person and that DM 80 of that should be provided by the base allowance, the VdK's spokesperson, Max Wuttcke, suggested a table of base allowances that raised the proposed rates from 20 to 50 percent and urged the abolition of cost-of-living differentials. While Wuttcke and the VdK accepted the proposal's division of payments into two parts, a base allowance and a compensatory allowance, they urged that the latter be calculated solely on the basis of economic loss, not on the basis of social position or profession, and that the income thresholds connected with the compensatory allowance be raised so as not to stifle "the desire to work." The Reichsbund seconded the removal of cost-of-living differentials, repeated its opposition to the two-tier pension system in favor of a higher base allowance, and argued against a differentiated compensatory allowance since it would discriminate against young disabled veterans who had not had the opportunity to find or develop a profession. The blind veterans' representative supported the Reichsbund's opposition to the divided pension structure, agreed that cost-of-living differentials be abolished, and argued against any income limitations for the severely disabled, which included all blind veterans. Further debate failed to produce any change in the organizations' positions on the structure of pension payments, and, after a proposal to create a subcommittee to investigate the matter was voted down, the council voted overwhelmingly to support the two-tier system embodied in the Labor Ministry's proposal, although the provision for extra compensation for those who had been in professions that involved "considerable knowledge and training and a high degree of achievement and responsibility" was dropped.

At its next meeting on 14–15 June, the council continued to expand the law's benefits. After declaring its support in principle of pensions for all widows, the council did, however, indicate its willingness to support a temporary suspension of pensions for childless widows under fifty if the payment of such pensions would result in cuts in the benefits of other widows. A subcommittee, formed at the conclusion of the previous meeting, recommended pensions for all widows except those under forty who were childless and employable. The report was accepted by the council, prompting the Finance Ministry's representative to announce that the council's recommendations had now raised the cost of the BVG to DM 3.8 billion, an impossible sum. A heated exchange broke out between council members and the Finance Ministry's representative; the latter repeated his argument that there was no extra money to be had unless the occupying powers agreed to a cut in occupation costs, while the former argued that their purpose was to ensure that the BVG was the best possible law for the war victims. The chairman, trying to get discussion back to the proposal, urged that the council continue to make suggestions for improvement and then calculate the costs. The point-by-point discussion resumed. At the end of the meeting, when the entire proposal had been dealt with, the chairman returned to the question of how the discrepancy between the costs associated with the original and the amended proposals should be resolved. It was agreed that the Finance Ministry should provide an itemized account of each of the improvements and that the council should draw up a list of priorities. These materials would then form the basis for another meeting to take place within two weeks.

That meeting, which was held on 27 June, was brief and stormy. Following a review of the changes made by the council and their costs, the Finance Ministry's representative read a prepared statement that expressed the Finance

Minister's sympathy with the war victims but reiterated his position that there were no funds to cover the council's suggested improvements, which exceeded the DM 2.6 billion allocation by DM 500 million.[24] While the finance minister would "probably agree to the law out of social-political grounds," he also would have to insist that various benefits be suspended until there were sufficient funds to cover them. Among others, this would mean a temporary suspension of payments to the lightly disabled and a postponement of the lifting of the *Ruhenvorschriften* of the social security system. It appeared, commented one council member ruefully, that they were "back where they had started." Angry, the representatives of the war victims' organizations declared that they would not agree to any limitations that did not have fixed time limits and that they would stick with the changes they had introduced. Above all, they opposed the retention of social security threshold provisions for disability pensions and the cutting of benefits for the lightly disabled. The chairman tried to put a good face on things by stating that the council had discharged its obligation to improve the law, that some of its suggestions had been accepted, and that others could be incorporated later when conditions had improved. Asked whether it wished to continue discussion of the proposal and if it wished to draw up a list of priorities, the council voted to discontinue discussion of individual points of the proposal and unanimously refused to draw up a list of priorities.

While the Beirat deliberated, the war victims' organizations intensified their campaign against the government's delay in introducing the bill and demanded action. Letters from local branches to the Chancellor's Office warned of the growing unrest and radicalization of their memberships, gave dark hints of the adverse effect continued inaction would have on the growth of democracy in the fledgling Republic, and argued, following the lead article of the June issue of *Die Fackel*, that the purported policy of "denigrating war through the denigration of its victims" was not only unjust but dangerous.[25] By the end of the month, protest demonstrations were being held by groups of war victims in Stuttgart, Düsseldorf, and Wiesbaden, and Bundestag deputies were urging the government to act more quickly in order to cut the ground from under the war victims' organizations, whose propaganda against the government and the Bundestag, according to one deputy, "was at least as destructive as the propaganda of the Communists and Bolshevists."[26]

A MONTH AFTER the Beirat's last meeting, the Labor Ministry sent its draft of the BVG to the Chancellor's Office.[27] In key areas—coverage of the lightly disabled, base allowance levels, widows' pensions, removal of cost-of-living differentials, and income thresholds—the Labor Ministry's new draft incorporated the suggestions of the Beirat.[28] As a result, its projected annual cost was just over DM 3 billion. While Schäffer, the finance minister, supported the law in principle, he continued to maintain that the earlier limit of DM 2.6 billion could not be exceeded during the current fiscal year.[29] Storch, defending his ministry's bill, argued that the increased pension payments would be balanced out by reductions in welfare payments, of which the federal government paid 75 percent, which would result when war-disabled pensioners began to receive the higher pensions. Although it was noted that some crucial points, for example, the date that the law would go into effect, were left open and that some details were likely to be changed during the legislative process, the cabinet was urged to act quickly on the law because of its "especially pressing nature."[30]

On 25 July the cabinet met to discuss the draft.[31] Labor Ministry state secretary Maximilian Sauerborn outlined the existing system of war victim benefits and developed the main features of the new law. The main concern in drafting the law had been to give as much as possible to the severely disabled, the most needy, while reducing the benefits of the less needy, the lightly disabled, to what was essentially a "token payment [Anerkennungsgebühr]." There was extensive debate over the costs of the law and how they would be covered in the budget, which still only allocated DM 2.6 billion for war victim legislation. If the original demands of the war victims' organizations were all met, it was argued, the law would cost DM 6–7 billion. The Labor Ministry's draft foresaw an outlay of DM 3.034 billion, and, according to Storch, much of the funding of the new law would be covered by the savings realized in welfare pensions that would be made unnecessary by the increased pensions paid under the BVG. This fact, however, had been deliberately left vague in order to prevent demands for further raises in pensions.[32] The removal of cost-of-living differentials, which increased the cost of the law, was defended on the grounds that it would end migration into the cities by disabled veterans seeking higher pensions and encourage pensioners to move out of the cities. Schäffer was skeptical of the figures produced by the labor minister and complained that the latter's proposal failed to uphold four points that the two ministers had earlier agreed upon, namely, the retention of cost-of-living differentials, the setting of the base rate of widows' pensions at DM 20 (instead of DM 40), suspension of the payment of pensions to widows under fifty (instead of forty) years of age, and a normative minimum pension of DM 160 per month (instead of DM 180). All these changes, he maintained, involved increased costs that could not be met.

Storch replied that the changes were necessary since they were the product of long and intensive negotiations with representatives of the war victims' organizations and unions, that is, the Beirat. All of the parties involved, he claimed, had given their approval to the benefit levels contained in the draft, and therefore one could safely assume that the Bundestag and its committees would not demand more. Not only the war victims' organizations, he contended, but individual war victims were satisfied with the new legislation. This was a "significant success." The promises made to the war victims that they would be removed from the welfare system had to be honored. The labor minister concluded by arguing that the Finance Ministry underestimated the savings projected by the Labor Ministry; he was confident that the changes would not exceed the DM 3.034 billion figure and suggested that if the finance minister still felt additional means were necessary to cover the expenses of the new law, they could consider raising the states' contribution from 15 to 25 percent.

The labor minister was strongly supported by Vice Chancellor Franz Blücher, who was convinced by Storch's arguments and pushed for the acceptance of the law as it stood. The passage of the law without changes in the pension levels, he believed, was necessary on political and ethical grounds and "was of great value for the government's prestige [Ansehen]." The labor and finance ministers retired to discuss ways of resolving their differences, and at the next cabinet meeting, on 28 July, the Labor Ministry's draft was passed with the following new provisions: pensions were not to be paid to those with a monthly income of DM 800 or more, the law would go into effect on the first of the month in which it was passed, and the states' share of the BVG would be raised from 15 to 25 percent.[33]

This final provision, not surprisingly, was met by opposition in the Bundesrat, to which the government's draft was now sent for discussion and approval. The states had already chafed under their 15 percent contribution to the ÜBG and were in no mood to accept an increased contribution to the new law, the costs of which were greater and permanent.[34] In mid-August the Finance and Social Policy committees of the Bundesrat discussed the Labor Ministry's proposal. In general, the Social Policy Committee was sympathetic to the proposal, while the Finance Committee raised strenuous objections to its costs. Under the pressure of persistent questioning by members of the Finance Committee, the precarious united front of the federal Labor and Finance ministries collapsed. Representatives from the latter abandoned their Labor Ministry counterparts and tacitly supported the heavy cuts proposed by the Bundesrat Finance Committee.[35] Despite the Labor Ministry's spirited defense of its draft, the committee stuck with its demands for a severe pruning of benefits.[36] The main point of attack was the proposal to increase the states' contribution from 15 to 25 percent, which was opposed on constitutional and financial grounds.[37] Meanwhile, the Social Policy Committee showed itself to be much more receptive to the Labor Ministry's proposal.[38] It supported two of the changes demanded by the Finance Committee—the lowering of the outside income threshold to DM 400 instead of DM 800 and the striking of the provision to raise the percentage of state support—but supported the basic pension levels proposed by the Labor Ministry. A joint meeting of the two committees on 17 August failed to reconcile the differences, and the Bundesrat, which met on the next day, was presented with two sets of recommendations. Support for the Social Policy Committee's version of the bill was virtually unanimous; after a clause-by-clause discussion, it was accepted with only minor changes.[39]

On 19 August the amended bill was returned to the cabinet. In addition to a number of minor alterations, the Bundesrat version contained three major changes: the lowering of the threshold of outside income from DM 800 to DM 400, provisions for the inclusion of West Berlin in the new law, and rejection of the provisions raising the states' share from 15 to 25 percent. On 26 August the Chancellor's Office's state secretary of interior sent the revised law to the labor minister for his comments, noting in his covering letter that the Bundesrat's change of the outside income threshold to DM 400 had to be rejected. In his reply, which later formed the basis for the government's official position on the Bundesrat's proposed changes, the labor minister agreed, arguing that the change was politically impossible, since the war victims' organizations were threatening demonstrations and that the savings to be gained (DM 6–7 million annually) would not outweigh the "political costs."[40] When the cabinet met on 12 September to discuss the law before the next step in the legislative process—its submission to the Bundestag—the labor minister's arguments easily won the day. Storch urged quick action, since the "passage of the proposal was for political reasons extremely pressing."[41] The minor, mostly editorial changes proposed by the Bundesrat were accepted, but its lowering of outside income thresholds was rejected. Although it was eventually agreed that there were no constitutional reasons for rejecting the Bundesrat's inclusion of Berlin, the proposal was rejected on financial grounds. The major concession made by the cabinet was to agree to the Bundesrat's refusal to have the states' contribution raised by 10 percent. Although the finance minister had previously insisted that there was no way of covering the anticipated costs of the BVG without this increase, on 5 September he agreed to withdraw his objections to the states' insistence that the level of their contribution be retained at 15 percent.[42]

On 13 September the bill came up for its first reading in the Bundestag. The speakers generally focused on questions of principle and substance, and the pattern of debate was much the same as that over the ÜBG: the government claimed that it had done all that was possible given existing financial constraints; the coalition parties supported the bill in principle but promised improvements; and the opposition parties attacked the bill and urged more substantive changes. As with the debate over the ÜBG, the BVG debate also occasioned a series of polemical exchanges.

Storch presented the bill, apologizing for the long delay in bringing it to the Bundestag. He assured his listeners that the delay was not the result of "bad intentions or an attempt to stall [böse Absichten oder Verschleppungstaktiken]" but of the need to think things through thoroughly. He sketched the course of war victim legislation since 1945, emphasizing the inadequate and negative aspects of occupation policies, and boasted that the new law represented a decisive break with the principles employed during the occupation and a return to earlier practices. With the passage of the new law, war victims would again be treated under a separate, independent system, which assured modern health care, extensive social welfare provisions—especially in areas of job retraining and placement—and higher pensions. The new law was structured along the lines of the RVG and had been expanded to include "victims of the bombing war on the home front." In order to keep within the available means, Storch argued, it had been necessary to adopt a two-level system of pension payments, but he quickly noted that the new law provided for a 33 percent increase over what had been spent for war victim legislation the previous year and that the BVG comprised the second-largest item in the budget, surpassed only by occupation costs. He concluded by pointing out the many demands of the war victims that had been met and by stressing that the government had done all that it could to ensure that the law was adequately discussed, including the creation of the Beirat, "which had provided a very decisive and valuable service in the drafting of the law." He urged that the law be passed as quickly as possible so that "the justified wishes of the war victims must not have to remain unfulfilled any longer."[43]

Storch was followed by Maria Probst, spokesperson for the CDU and the party's leading member of the Bundestag's Twenty-sixth Committee, the Committee for War Victim and Prisoner of War Questions. Noting with pride that the BVG was the first major piece of social legislation to be submitted by the government and to be debated by the Bundestag (which demonstrated that all parties "recognized the priority of war victim legislation"), she castigated the structure of the system imposed by the Allies, especially its attempt to merge war victim benefits with other social programs. War victim legislation, she argued, is a problem that is unique and incomparable. The enormous sacrifice made for the greater community, the permanent loss of strength, of health, of a loved one, provides the grounds for a legal claim, justified on moral, indeed, on natural rights, to sufficient care and support by the community for which the sacrifice was made. This sacrifice has nothing to do with a chance accident, whose monetary recompense can be provided by actuarially calculated insurance premiums. We decisively reject settlement and simple compensation according to social security principles for war victim benefits. The foundations for the new legislation are entitlement: to sufficient care, on the one hand, and the obligation of the state for support, on the other. The proposed new law—and here we support it completely—makes a sharp break with the inappropriate use of social security principles for war victim benefits.

Probst supported the two-tier division and the general levels of the pensions, as well as the inclusion of the lightly disabled in the bill. She rejected outright income level thresholds in connection with base allowances (as provided for in the Bundesrat version); thresholds associated with the compensatory allowance were accepted in principle but, Probst promised, would be closely scrutinized since the purpose of the new law "was to promote and to reward the desire to work and to produce, which is especially strong among the war-disabled. . . . The declared wish of the war victims is to be integrated into the work process. They do not want to become wards of the state." Provisions of the law that worked against these principles were to be changed. The "postulate of integration into the work process" was to "be filled in every way." To this end, Probst welcomed the new law's provisions for vocational training for orphans. Not only sociopolitical but political goals were met therein, since "the circumstances in which these 1.33 million war orphans grow up are of extraordinary importance for the democratic state—whether as young people who support the democratic state because of their experience of fair treatment or whether as angry and disillusioned children, who, denied sufficient training, grow up rejecting it." The main areas in which Probst foresaw changes were in survivor benefits, especially the temporary suspension of pensions for childless widows under forty, which could "not be justified." On the whole, she concluded, the new law could be considered as a well-laid foundation that could be built upon in the future.[44]

Probst was followed by Bruno Leddin, spokesperson for the SPD and chairman of the Twenty-sixth Committee.[45] Leddin wasted no time in attacking the government's slowness in producing the BVG. Noting that the SPD had proposed the drafting of a law for war victims nearly a year earlier, he claimed there was no excuse for the delay, which had generated justified bitterness and outrage among the war victims. Now, after the government's own foot-dragging, it was asking the Bundestag and the Twenty-sixth Committee to debate the law "on the double [im Schnellzugtempo]" or, more likely, "to rubberstamp it." But if this was the government's intent, then it had failed, for the SPD intended to examine the law minutely and critically. Admitting that the present bill was an improvement over earlier proposals, Leddin rejected the exaggerated claims made by the government and went on to criticize the low pension rates for the lightly disabled, the "too strongly anchored principle of need" in the law, and the inappropriate income thresholds. In addition, Leddin declared, the SPD "would under no conditions" accept the government's attempt to move back the date of the law's becoming effective: "The government has repeatedly declared that this law is to be in effect as of 1 April 1950. The Social Democratic delegation will see to it that here once again a given promise of the government is not broken and thereby the prestige [Ansehen] of democratic institutions still more discredited."

With regard to the funding of the law, Leddin argued that DM 3 billion was not enough and that at least DM 3.6 billion was necessary, adding:

> Neither we nor the war victims have forgotten that with the tax proposal the government made a gift of one billion to the rich. In view of the recent discussion of the problem of remilitarization, it is perhaps justified to ask whether the otherwise so frugal finance minister also will not have the necessary means for this. We are certain that for this matter the financial means will be quickly forthcoming, even at the cost of higher taxes. This is certainly not the first time in history that the enthusiasm of certain circles and parties has been stronger for the acceptance of a military budget than for the passage of social legislation.

The willingness of the Social Democratic delegation to work out a compromise on "this great social-political work," Leddin concluded, presupposed that improvements along the lines contained in its proposals were made.[46]

Speakers from the center-right and rightist splinter parties used the debate to express their sympathy with the war victims and to suggest improvements. On the whole, however, they accepted the government's argument that the law provided what was possible under current economic conditions. Thea Arnold of the Center Party, for example, conceded that all wishes could not be granted because "our country is a gigantic poorhouse," but her party strongly believed that "before the state votes one penny for the remilitarization of Germany, the money for adequate care of the war-disabled and survivors from both world wars—1914 and 1939—must be provided." This view was echoed by Hans Löfflad of the WAV, who argued: "An economy that was able to finance two world wars must also be able to finance the compensation of the victims of these two wars. . . . Today, since one is again speaking of remilitarization and rearmament, . . . I believe it is justified to demand that first the victims of these two world wars receive a humane and socially acceptable pension system [Rentenversorgung]." Ludwig Volkholz of the Bavarian Party argued that the struggle for a just system of war victim legislation was "the struggle of a generation which had to pay for the political errors of the Nazi period and the people of 1933 with their blood and health." The National Socialist state had compelled its soldiers to fight, and even though the present state rested on different political principles, it was "obligated to care sufficiently for the victims. It would be the greatest shame for a people to let its brave, previously much celebrated soldiers go out with a hand organ and beg. The soldier cannot be made the scapegoat of politics."[47]

The real polemics began with the speeches of the Communist spokesperson, Rudolf Kohl, and Erich Mende of the FDP. Kohl claimed that the government was only interested in helping the rich and the warmongers. Although the finance minister claimed there was no more money for the war victims, he and the government were willing to pay DM 4.5 billion in occupation costs; moreover, they had asked for additional military support from the occupying powers, which would cost a great deal of money, and were ready to provide the means necessary for the creation of a new German army. According to Kohl, at least DM 3.6 billion was necessary to provide adequate care for the war victims.

As for the law itself, Kohl opposed the two-level pension system, which, he claimed, only helped "the severely disabled at the cost of the lightly disabled." The inadequate treatment of the lightly disabled, he claimed, would lead to a "wave of [medical] investigations, which we know from the past as the so-called pension wringer [Nachuntersuchungswelle, die wir aus der Vergangenheit als sogenannte Rentenquetsche kennen]." He also criticized the structure of compensatory allowances and the low thresholds on outside income. In addition, the KPD demanded a minimum *Vollrente* of DM 180 and that the law's effective date of implementation be 1 April. Kohl claimed that the law was a "rotten deal [fauler Wechsel auf die Zukunft]" that incorporated "the National Socialist idea that the war-disabled who are employed have no right to worthwhile pensions." Kohl ended his speech with the threat that "the march of the disabled on Bonn has not been abandoned but only postponed. It will come!"[48]

Mende excoriated the war victim legislation under the occupation and charged that those on the left, now posing as friends of the war victims, were in large part responsible, since they had helped the occupiers to dismantle the old system in 1946. Although agreeing that the original proposals of the BVG were unsatisfactory, Mende claimed that the draft now before the Bundestag was structurally sound and a model. While individual provisions of the French law might be more generous, he argued, if the French, like the Germans, had 4 million war victims instead of only 100,000, their laws would not be so magnanimous. Although he opposed the income thresholds of the BVG since they weakened the will to work and hindered efforts to mobilize the war victims for the economy, Mende generally approved the law. He was especially pleased by the Bundesrat's striking of the provision that had excluded Waffen-SS veterans, since, he argued, the Waffen-SS was simply a part of the Wehr-macht. To exclude Waffen-SS veterans was a blow against equality and gave support to the principle of collective guilt, which, he asserted, was "thank God not a part of German law." To apply it in the case of Waffen-SS veterans was not only "morally and ethically unsupportable" but also "politically dan-gerous," since it would "create a *Kampfgruppe* against democracy." With regard to article 8 of the BVG, which denied eligibility to those who had been convicted of political crimes, Mende was less happy, arguing that it repre-sented "a prolongation of denazification."[49] Mende ended by blasting Kohl for stirring up the war victims and accused the war victims' organizations of having gotten into a *Rivalitätskampf* in which each tried to outbid the other. They would, he stated, have the opportunity to make their wishes known to the committee.[50]

At the end of the session, Josef Arndgen of the CDU urged bipartisan cooperation to ensure the passage of the bill, claiming that the rank and file of the SPD did not support the arguments presented by its spokesperson, Led-din. Erwin Schoettle of the SPD replied that the government should not be so touchy when improvements were suggested, noting that there were signs that many members of the coalition parties shared the SPD's misgivings. If the law was indeed as good as it was claimed to be and the government parties were united, then there was no need to worry about cooperation. With this, the first reading of the bill ended, and the Bundestag, against one vote, voted to send the government's draft to committee.[51]

When the Twenty-sixth Committee met to begin its deliberations, it was well informed of the war victims' desires. Throughout the drafting of the law, the war victims' organizations had sent proposals, petitions, and position papers to Bundestag deputies in general and members of the Twenty-sixth Committee in particular.[52] One week after the BVG's first reading, *Kriegsopfer-verbände* representatives met with the committee.[53] The Reichsbund alone continued to wage a spirited campaign in favor of a unitary pension. Although some of the smaller organizations continued to favor the unified pension in principle, they had resigned themselves to the two-level pension envisioned in the draft and focused their attention on securing specific benefits for their specialized constituencies; for example, the brain-damaged pushed for equal treatment with the blind, who automatically received certain increased benefits. In contrast to the other groups, the VdK strongly supported the two-level system, claiming that the keystone of the pension system was the guarantee of a pension of DM 180 for an unemployed, severely disabled veteran and that to ensure this in a unitary system would cost over DM 5 billion, which was impossible under the current circumstances; a unitary system, given available resources, would mean the exclusion of pensions for those with a disability up to 60 percent.[54] Although divided on the question of a unitary or divided pension structure, the war victims' organizations were united in their desire to retain, and if possible improve, pensions for the lightly disabled and for younger widows and were vehemently opposed to the various clauses of the law that tied pension levels to outside income.

After the war victims had aired their views and departed, ministerial representatives presented their cases. The Labor Ministry representative referred to Storch's comments at the first reading of the BVG, extolled the virtues of the law, and claimed that it embodied all that could be done. The proposed law, he promised, contained no "tactical reservations [taktischen Vorbehalte]," and, he maintained, the government had gone to the "outermost limits of the Republic's financial ability." These points were picked up by the finance minister, Schäffer, who appeared personally to plead for restraint on the part of the committee when amending the law.

According to Schäffer, he and Storch had from the beginning decided to offer all that was possible. Moreover, their decision had been made before recent developments (the decision to rearm Germany) had made it clear "that a certain change was taking place in the world that will bring new, heavy burdens to the German national economy." He assured the committee that neither the government nor the Finance Ministry were unfeeling calculating machines and that they wanted to do all that could be done for the war victims. Yet they could not adopt measures that would damage the economy and make it impossible to meet the needs of not only the war victims but other needy groups as well. New social burdens would soon be added, for example, the costs of the *Lastenausgleich* and the impending reform (*Sanierung*) of the social security system, and increased tax revenues could not be counted upon to meet costs. The point, repeatedly stressed, was that the costs connected with the existing draft of the BVG could, with difficulty, be covered, but that costly amendments could not be accepted. Schäffer ended by reiterating the government's goodwill toward the war victims, noting that their representatives had participated in the drafting of the law and expressing the hope that the government and the committee could work together to create a law "that will utilize all available economic resources to provide benefits for German war victims and at the same time be economically sound."[55]

When Schäffer had finished, Kurt Pohle (SPD) asked if, given what the finance minister had just said, the task of the committee and the Bundestag was simply to rubberstamp the government's proposal. Schäffer answered testily that the law was a common work of the government and the parliament. The government made a proposal, and it was the job of the parliament to modify it, but, he continued, "I cannot hide the fact that if you make changes in the law, then you only have two alternatives if they produce increased expenditures: either equivalent cuts will be made in other parts of the law, or other new sources of revenue must be found and pointed out to the taxpayers. These are your two choices."[56] This led to a discussion of article 113 of the Basic Law, which Schäffer had mentioned earlier and which he claimed would have to be invoked if the BVG exceeded the money currently budgeted for it. According to article 113, a decision of the Bundestag or Bundesrat that raised expenditures beyond the sums provided in the budget (which was proposed by the government) required approval by the cabinet. The article, designed to ensure a balanced budget, gave the government a de facto suspensive veto and a club to hold over the head of the legislature. Inquiries by committee members about possible reserves and tax revenues were brushed aside by the finance minister, who again referred to upcoming defense costs and repeated his conviction that all that could be done had been done and that the war victims were on the whole satisfied; then, in what was to become a refrain of the coalition parties, he pleaded for nonpartisan unity.[57]

The committee members continued to ask questions. Asked about the date the law would become effective, Schäffer somewhat disingenuously claimed he hoped it would be as soon as possible, while at the same time stating that a retroactive date of 1 April was "totally impossible." When asked if he could in any way provide more funds for war victim legislation, the finance minister said he could not.[58] The committee then adjourned. Realizing that the bill would be controversial, the committee requested that stenographic recordings be made of its future meetings. This stipulation, coupled with the subsequent publication of the minutes, was unusual, if not unprecedented; its purpose was to allow the committee to cover itself, while at the same time publicly pinning down ministerial representatives on positions that would be unpopular as well as on any promises they might make regarding the implementation of the law that would not show up in the law itself.

IN A SERIES of ten meetings, lasting from 26 September to 12 October, the Twenty-sixth Committee exhaustively discussed the proposed law.[59] The main points of debate and substantive revision revolved around the level and extent of benefit payments for the disabled, war widows' pensions, thresholds for outside income, and the date on which the law would go into effect.

After considering and decisively rejecting the Reichsbund's proposal for a unitary pension structure, the committee turned to the proposed base allowances provided for in article 30.[60] The discussion focused almost exclusively on the lightly disabled, whose inclusion in war victim legislation, as we have seen, had been a matter of debate throughout the postwar era. The preliminary proposal submitted by the Labor Ministry to the Beirat had included base allowances for those who were 30 and 40 percent disabled that were acknowledged to be nominal. Suggestions that pensions for the lightly disabled either be abolished or temporarily suspended had been strongly rejected by the Beirat; the Labor Ministry's final proposal not only had retained payments to the lightly disabled but had raised them, in accordance with the Beirat's wishes, from DM 7.5 to DM 10 for the 30 percent disabled and from DM 12.5 to DM 15 for the 40 percent disabled. These increases had been removed by the Bundesrat, but the cabinet had restored them.

There were several reasons why the issue was controversial. On the one hand, most of the lightly disabled were employed or employable and did not depend on pensions for survival. Those in favor of striking or temporarily suspending pensions for the lightly disabled argued that those who were capable of getting by without them should make sacrifices for those who could not, namely the severely disabled, who were less unemployable and often dependent on their pensions for survival. Proponents of pensions for the lightly disabled countered that this entailed a *Lastensausgleich* among the war victims that was unjust and immoral. They pointed out that the wounds of the "so-called" lightly disabled were not insignificant—the lightly disabled included those who, for example, had lost a hand, a foot, or an eye. What made the question of pensions for the lightly disabled a hot social and, ultimately, political issue were the numbers involved. There were 474,000 persons designated as 30 percent disabled and 187,000 as 40 percent disabled. Together they comprised nearly half (46 percent) of the war-disabled. Seen through the eyes of the Finance Ministry, any increases in the pensions of the lightly disabled threatened to burst the fiscal bounds of the law. Seen through the eyes of the politicians and the leaders of the *Kriegsopferverbände*, the lightly disabled represented a highly visible and potent constituency, a substantial repository of votes for the former and the organizational backbone of the latter.

Although the government's draft provided base allowances for the lightly disabled, it had no provisions for granting them compensation pensions (*Ausgleichrenten*). These were limited to those with a disability of 50 percent or more. At the committee's second meeting, the chairman, Bruno Leddin (SPD), noted that the question of compensation pensions for the lightly disabled was still open but that, in view of the finance minister's remarks, he doubted if the government would offer them on its own. Helmut Bazille, a Social Democratic member of the committee and, like Leddin, a prominent leader of the VdK, asserted that the "completely falsely designated" lightly disabled should be eligible to receive compensatory pensions of DM 20 and 30.[61] The debate then developed along essentially partisan lines, with the SPD representatives seeking to ensure that no lightly disabled person would fall through the cracks and be forced to draw upon welfare for subsistence, while the Finance Ministry's representative and the CDU representatives argued that expansion of pensions for the lightly disabled was impossible or undesirable. The Finance Ministry's representative pointed out that the U.S. zone's Länderrat, the Bizone's Wirtschaftsrat, and the Bundesrat had all excluded the lightly disabled. The government's draft had included them, but in view of the numbers involved, no further increases in benefits were possible. Josef Arndgen of the CDU argued that since the compensation pension would be dependent on salary and most of the lightly disabled worked, it would not come into effect and therefore was unnecessary.

Although it was agreed to postpone further discussion of expanded benefits for the lightly disabled until all the other provisions of the law had been discussed, the issue continued to surface and to prompt heated, as well as partisan, debate. When at one point Leddin threatened to have his party bring up proposals for increased benefits for the lightly disabled during the Bundestag's later readings of the bill, Maria Probst of the CDU exasperatedly retorted that "we have reached the point where we must stop. Anyone who wants to indulge in partisan propaganda will find it a boomerang, since the people know what the situation is and will understand that such efforts will only work to delay a law which is essentially strong."[62] Members of the opposition parties saw things differently. Thea Arnold of the Center Party repeated the argument she had presented at the law's first reading, claiming that sufficient funds could be achieved by limiting expenditures for remilitarization and expansion of the police.[63] Kurt Pohle of the SPD argued that the real political danger would be to do nothing, since people would wonder if the committee's work was necessary if no positive results were visible; the war victims would find it hard to understand why, after weeks of discussion, all that came out of the committee was an unchanged version of the government's proposal. Moreover, even if the improvements were only nominal, their symbolic value was great. If the committee could unanimously agree to the improvements, it would have a calming political effect since it would take the wind from the sails of the radical right elements who were claiming that "the honor of the soldiers was being trampled in the dust."[64]

When it came time for the decisive vote on increased benefits for the lightly disabled, the lines were largely unchanged. SPD members pushed for an increase in base allowances, from DM 10 to DM 15 for the 30 percent disabled and DM 15 to DM 20 for the 40 percent disabled.[65] CDU spokespersons continued to express opposition, claiming that the needs of the lightly disabled who really required help could be met better through other measures and that the increases only threatened the passage of the law. The latter argument was reinforced by the representative of the Finance Ministry, who claimed that the DM 44 million in increased expenditures produced by the changes could not be covered by the present budget, which would mean the implementation of article 113 and new taxes. CDU opponents were unable to convince either their coalition partners or (apparently) some members of their own party of the necessity of rejecting what was bound to be a politically popular revision. The measure passed with a large majority.[66]

Another controversial section of the BVG was that regulating pensions for war widows. The provisions for widows in the Labor Ministry's draft were an improvement over those that had been in force during the occupation period, but they were still limited by financial constraints. According to article 39, all widows were given the legal right to a base allowance pension; those that qualified were also eligible for compensatory allowances (article 40). Recipients of the base allowance were divided into two categories: widows who were unable to work, who had children at home, or who were over forty years of age were to receive DM 40 per month; employable widows under forty who were childless (or whose children were grown) were to receive DM 20. Not only did the latter category receive half of the former's pension, but, according to article 64, payment of the DM 20 pension was to be indefinitely suspended. Most of the debate on widows' pensions revolved around the justness of creating two classes of widows and the problems of equity that arose from determining eligibility for benefits on the basis of age rather than social and economic criteria.

The discussions of widows' benefits were strongly shaped by the female members of the committee, who clearly were perceived as the "natural" spokespersons for this group.[67] In the first session, discussion centered on the difficulties faced by working widows with children. The traditional role of the German mother as the partner responsible for the raising of children was accepted and defended by all of the women, regardless of party. Thus, while it was agreed to ease the plight of working widows by raising the amount of outside income that would not be considered in calculating the compensatory allowance (from one-quarter to two-sevenths, later raised to three-tenths), concern was also expressed that if such changes were too favorable they would provide an incentive for women to leave their children alone at home in order to join the work force.[68]

Although there were logical grounds and practical fiscal reasons for discriminating against younger widows who were childless and could work, committee members were concerned about the legal and moral consequences of establishing a two-tier base allowance. The Labor Ministry's representative noted that although childless widows under forty would not receive a pension, they would still receive the fixed death benefit (*Witwenabfindung*) of DM 1,200. To pay the DM 20 pension would mean an additional outlay of DM 20 million.[69] When Mende, defending the two-tier allowance structure in the law, likened it to the division between lightly and severely disabled war victims, Bazille responded by saying that the claims of the war-disabled and widows could not be compared, since the war-disabled suffered physical disability that diminished the victim's capacity to work, while a widow's claim was based on the need for support created by the death of the family's breadwinner. To compare diminished vocational ability used in war-disability pensions with age criteria embodied in the BVG's provisions for widows was to compare apples with oranges.[70] Still, Bazille made it clear that he did not like the formulation of article 39 since it was not legally consistent. The Finance Ministry's representative agreed in principle but reiterated that distinctions had to be drawn in order to keep within the existing fiscal boundaries. One had to help those most in need. In general, the committee agreed that younger widows were less needy than older ones, primarily since they were more employable. Also, it was well known that many widows, because of the extraordinary circumstances of the Third Reich and the war, were not widows in the traditional sense but rather partners in spur-of-the-moment weddings ("Ehe auf den Helmen"), whose husbands had soon afterward been killed; these women had never established a true marital relationship. Some had even been married by proxy (*Ferntrauung*) and had never even lived with their husbands before they were killed.[71] Many of these women had either never left the labor market or could easily reenter it. While they were legally widows, their position was much different from that of women who had been married for years, had lost whatever vocational skills they might have possessed, and were now thrown, unprepared, into the labor market. The problem, as Bazille was later to express it, was how to find a just balance between "legal rights, social needs, and financial capabilities."[72] It was a vexatious problem, and the committee's deliberations were interrupted several times to enable members to consult with their parties' Bundestag delegations regarding the question.

After one such break, Margarete Hütter of the FDP proposed that the law be changed so that all widows would receive the DM 40 base allowance, since "in the struggle for existence" widows were always "at a disadvantage vis-à-vis men." Widows, she continued, were "at a disadvantage in all aspects of life. Certainly widows under forty could and should seek work, but to reduce their legal claims as extensively as provided for in the proposed law would not be right."[73] Several members agreed with the goal of achieving legal consistency by removing age as a determinant in fixing the pension level. Kurt Pohle returned to the problem of providing pensions to widows who had not actually led a married life, and Elinor Hubert, another SPD member of the committee, proposed linking eligibility to the length of marriage. Probst opposed this since it created problems by making eligibility a matter of chance, dependent on when the husband was killed in war, not the fact that he had been killed.[74] Pohle also felt it was unfair to favor a woman who had been married by proxy over one who was unmarried, or, as he later noted, over one whose fiancé had been killed. Hütter argued that the use of length of marriage to determine eligibility deviated from the essence of the law. It was important not to change the structure of the law and to ensure that any such changes that were made "were not once again made at the expense of women [nicht wieder einmal auf dem Ruecken der Frauen ausgetragen werde]." The Finance Ministry's representative argued that the suspension of payments to childless widows under forty prevented a budgetary overrun and pointed out that in the future, when the legislature moved to lift the suspension, it would be easier to accomplish if the sum involved was DM 20 instead of DM 40. Hütter blasted this "German preoccupation with working out every detail of the future"; one should not consider everything on the basis of what might be done in four to five years, she maintained, since that meant "not recognizing the realities of the present."[75] The pros and cons of the various proposals were discussed, and the meeting adjourned to permit members to consult with their parties before the decisive vote, which was scheduled for the next day.

At the next meeting, most of the proposed amendments to the articles dealing with widows' benefits were voted down. While the legal consistency of Hütter's proposal for uniform benefits was recognized, many members were uneasy with the fact that it would provide benefits for some who were felt to be undeserving. Speaking for the retention of the government's draft, Mende admitted that some of his colleagues would say that there was no such thing as "half or full widows," but he argued that in the Third Reich there were different kinds of marriages—for example, the misuse of proxy marriage— that had "completely contradicted our entire ethical and legal mores." Different circumstances justified different judgments. The division in the government's draft was justified, especially when one considered the fact that widows were not equal in any case when judged on the basis of need.[76] In rejecting the proposed amendments, Margot Kalinke of the German Party also referred to the experience of the Third Reich, citing the confusion and rancor generated by the wide-ranging, uneven nature of the benefits provided to the wives of soldiers.[77] To avoid such problems, she argued, the law must be consistent, but she conceded that there was a considerable difference between the situation of a twenty-year-old widow and that of a forty-year-old widow in regard to employability. While realizing that such a stance could make her unpopular, she nonetheless would support the government's version of the law.[78] In a long speech, Bazille elaborated on the difficulty of finding a fair balance between legal rights, social need, and financial means. With regard to the claims of widows against the state, one could not employ the principle that justice is that which benefits the state. Without question, the institution of marriage had been brought into crisis by the Third Reich, yet the fact remained that it was still a legal act and that a partner had a legal claim on the state for compensation when a spouse was killed as a result of an act of state. In determining social need, it was necessary to consider many factors, such as age, number of children, and ability to work. The SPD was convinced that length of marriage was a better criterion than age for evaluating a widow's need for a pension.

The vote on Hütter's proposal for uniform benefits produced a deadlock and was defeated. A proposal to permit payments to widows under forty who had been married eight or more years was dropped. An earlier proposal, to allow payments to widows who were employable but were unemployed through no fault of their own, was discussed, only to be rejected as impracticable.[79] Committee members remained troubled by the problem, however. In a lengthy debate, the Labor Ministry representative was grilled about what types of public support existed for such widows, and the committee discussed various remedies. When a male member of the committee, apparently wearied by the discussion, suggested that the female members hold a caucus and report on their findings the next day, he was curtly told that "the male members should not be allowed to escape their responsibility and that a common solution must be achieved."[80] A provision was eventually added permitting pension payments to widows under forty who were unemployed through no fault of their own, but it was dropped in the final report, which retained the position of the original draft.[81]

Although the government was successful in convincing the committee of the necessity of temporarily suspending pension payments to young childless widows, it failed completely in its efforts to suspend base allowances for disabled veterans who enjoyed high levels of outside income. The number of widows affected by the suspension of benefits (article 64, clause 3) was relatively small, and, as we have seen, even those who opposed their suspension had reservations.[82] This was not the case with those affected by clause 2 of the article, which suspended the base allowances of disabled veterans with a monthly salary over DM 800. Here the number involved was large and the issue hot. Besides the creation of a separate benefit system for war victims and pensions for the lightly disabled, the limitation of outside income was probably the issue that aroused the most active lobbying effort on the part of the war victims. Supporters of the abolishment of income thresholds could rely on one of the most powerful arguments in German society—the work ethic.

The cabinet, recognizing the strong feelings on the issue, had firmly overridden the Bundesrat's attempt to lower the limit to DM 400, arguing that the political cost did not justify the savings involved.[83] Yet the government proposal's DM 800 threshold was scarcely more popular with the war victims. They lobbied for the removal of all thresholds applied to base allowances on the ground that the cutting off of base allowances (as opposed to compensatory allowances) violated the fundamental principle of the law, which was based on the recognition of and compensation for injury incurred in defense of the state. The most widely used, and probably the most effective, argument in favor of abolishing income thresholds was that they would lessen the war-disabled's desire to work, which was to be avoided on personal and moral grounds as well as in consideration of the national interest. More negatively, it was argued that thresholds would promote cheating and that the costs of tracking down fraud would entail more expense than the savings realized by their imposition. The committee members were apparently swayed by these arguments as well as by the awareness that the issue was highly visible and that much political capital could be gained by meeting the wishes of the war victims. Clause 2 of article 64 was struck out of the law with virtually no debate.[84] Similarly, the cabinet's reservations regarding the inclusion of West Berlin were overruled, and it was incorporated into the BVG.

On the whole, the committee's debates had proceeded harmoniously with little overt partisan conflict. As the committee neared the end of its deliberations, however, an issue emerged that split it sharply along partisan lines—the question of when the law was to go into effect. During the debate over the ÜBG, government spokespersons had promised that the BVG would be in place by 1 April 1950, which continued to be the nominal date after which benefits would be paid. As the legislative process dragged on, however, it was clear that the government was stalling. Its willingness to make concessions was increasingly tied to a later date for the law's implementation. Although the finance minister had assured the Twenty-sixth Committee at its first meeting that he wanted to see the law passed as soon as possible, there is evidence that he hoped and expected the law to go into effect around the first of the coming year.[85] Throughout the committee's deliberations, the ministry's representatives made it clear that they had abandoned the 1 April date and would oppose any attempts to make payments retroactive to the originally promised date of implementation. Each quarter-year of retroactive coverage, they argued, represented an additional outlay of DM 100 million, an impossible fiscal burden that would necessitate the invocation of article 113 of the Basic Law.[86] The war victims, of course, wanted payments retroactive to the original date, and the Reichsbund had made it a prominent demand. For the SPD, support of the original date of 1 April was irresistible, since it simultaneously provided an opportunity to woo the war victims and to embarrass the government.

The government was well aware that the issue was becoming a tricky political question. On 3 October Heinrich Karsch, a member of the CDU's Committee on War Victims and of the executive committee of the VdK, discussed the matter with Ernst Wirmer, state secretary in the Chancellor's Office.[87] Karsch pointed out that the question had a "highly political character." As virtually every war victim knew, the labor minister had repeatedly stated that 1 April would be the effective date. Now, however, the finance minister claimed that the law could not be retroactive because of fiscal limitations. According to Karsch, the SPD was preparing to make political capital out of the issue by demanding that the law go into effect on 1 July. The VdK was now in a bind. It had agreed to accept 1 October, and the finance minister had finally concurred.[88] The earlier date demanded by the SPD would undoubtedly be supported by the "strongly leftist" Reichsbund, leaving the VdK, including the moderates, no other choice but to also demand 1 July. Karsch was of the opinion that the government would lose the political gains connected with the law if it stuck to the 1 October date. It would give "the SPD and the radical elements among the war victims the opportunity to stir up discontent . . . and promote the [movement's] radical wing."

Things turned out even worse than Karsch had expected. Instead of proposing 1 July, the SPD stuck to the 1 April date, and its proposal was supported by a majority of the Twenty-sixth Committee at a preliminary vote on 11 October.[89] When the issue came up for a final vote at the committee's last meeting before the bill was to go back to the Bundestag for its second and third readings, the Finance Ministry's representative again repeated the government's arguments, noting that the proposal already included increases, pointing out the enormous costs connected with making the law retroactive, and reiterating that upcoming expenses associated with rearmament would add further fiscal burdens in the future. This was capped with the spurious argument that resources should be reserved for other "social" measures such as the *Jugendhilfswerk* and the development of the Emsland.[90] The committee's Social Democratic members remained unmoved. The coalition parties argued for 1 October, which, given the legislative schedule, represented a compromise. Bazille argued that the government could not blame the SPD or parliament for the 1 April date, since it had set that date itself. "The government," he argued, "either had irresponsibly aroused expectations which later could not be realized, or it had failed to take the measures necessary to make them realizable." In either case it was culpable. For the opposition, it was "a political question not to allow the government to escape its responsibilities."[91] Spokespersons for the CDU, realizing they were representing an unpopular position, tried to bring the SPD members of the committee around by invoking convoluted, self-serving appeals for unanimity.[92]

Representatives from the smaller parties were divided. None were totally convinced by the Finance Ministry representative's arguments, but not all were prepared to support the SPD amendment. The vote on the amendment produced a tie, and it was thus defeated.[93] The committee then rejected a compromise measure proposing 1 July and accepted the coalition amendment stipulation that 1 October be the date for the law's implementation.

OFFICIALS IN THE Chancellor's Office had been closely monitoring the deliberations of the Twenty-sixth Committee. The cabinet was kept informed of the changes being made in the government's proposal and the increased expenditures connected with each change.[94] The committee's report was issued on 13 October,[95] and on the next day, a Saturday, Schäffer sent a telegram to the head of the CDU parliamentary delegation, Heinrich von Brentano, that described the situation as "very serious." The committee's version entailed additional expenditures of approximately a quarter billion DM, which could not be covered. If the committee's version was to be approved, the finance minister declared, then a "supplementary budget proposal [Deckungsvorschlag] must be introduced immediately and the Bundestag delegation [Fraktion] must commit itself to support it." Brentano was urged to arrange as soon as possible a meeting of the CDU members of the Twenty-sixth Committee, the labor minister, leaders of the coalition's other parties, and, if possible, Adenauer.[96] The meeting took place on the following Monday; Schäffer, State Secretary Sauerborn of the Labor Ministry, Arndgen, Probst, and Paul Lücke of the Twenty-sixth Committee, and the chancellor attended. It was agreed that the finance minister would make a statement after the second reading explaining the need to invoke article 113. The Budgetary Committee would be asked to meet and respond before the third reading. The CDU parliamentary leaders hoped to arrange a united vote of the coalition parties and the SPD in favor of the Twenty-sixth Committee's report and thereby prepare the way for the government's statement.[97] On the following day, the cabinet met to discuss the situation. The finance minister noted that the cabinet, as a result of "the pressure of the coalition parties," had gone as far as it could and that he had explained to the Twenty-sixth Committee that further expenditures could not be covered without finding new revenues. Nonetheless, the committee had voted increases and, "since it was virtually impossible to reject the improvements," he had to introduce a supplementary budget bill. Schäffer believed the increased expenditures could be covered by raising the gasoline tax, and he felt that the government should inform the Bundestag between the second and third readings that the cabinet would only be able to give its approval to the amended version of the BVG if the Bundestag approved the supplementary budget along with the BVG. Adenauer felt it was not wise to make approval dependent on the proposed tax increase, since it would entail a delay in the passing of the BVG, which would have "undesirable consequences." He urged that the labor and finance ministers immediately begin to negotiate with the coalition parties. The cabinet decided to try to postpone the second and third readings for a week in order to allow the groundwork to be laid. A possible solution, it was agreed, was to have the original proposal approved and then to present the committee's version, coupled with the supplementary budget bill, as an amendment. If these efforts failed, then the finance minister would have to declare after the second reading that the cabinet, on constitutional grounds, could not approve the BVG until the question of funding had been clarified.[98]

The cabinet's hopes of obtaining a postponement of debate on the BVG were not realized. On 19 October the Bundestag began the second reading.[99] A delegation of war victim dignitaries listened via radio to the debate from a ship anchored in the Rhine across from the Bundestag building. The deputies were clearly anxious to pass the bill. The widespread, nonpartisan support enjoyed by the bill was demonstrated at the outset when it was read out of committee by a Social Democratic member, Kurt Pohle. Pohle described and defended the changes made by the committee, which he said had acted responsibly and done what was feasible. The committee, he stated, had taken into account both the budgetary considerations raised by the finance minister and its "comradely ties" with the war victims, and he urged acceptance of the bill. A tiresome series of proposed amendments by the KPD were quickly voted down. The only serious partisan challenge came when the SPD, as expected, introduced an amendment to article 83, changing the law's effective date from 1 October to 1 April. In the ensuing vote the coalition parties held fast, however, and the proposed amendment was rejected.

Since the second reading produced no changes in the committee's draft, it was possible to proceed immediately to the third and final reading. Before this occurred, the finance minister, as planned, read the government's declaration to the Bundestag that since the version of the bill just approved mandated additional expenditures beyond those provided for in the current budget, the cabinet was required to approve the law before it could go into effect. This approval would not come until the Bundestag approved a supplementary finance bill that covered the difference. An immediate coupling of bills was not demanded, however. Schäffer did not indicate what measures the government intended to take to solve the problem and ended on a conciliatory note, pledging that it would do all that it could so as not to endanger or delay the enactment of the BVG. The final reading of the bill was opened by Leddin of the SPD, who declared that the law, as amended by the committee, contained much that was good (in large part because of the work of the committee's Social Democratic members) and that his party would honor the decisions that had gone against its wishes. While the SPD did not accept the arguments of the finance minister, it would, in accordance with the clearly expressed wish of the war victims' organizations, vote for the law. The other parties, with the exception of the KPD, similarly expressed their support, and the Federal War Victims' Benefits Law was passed unanimously.

How the amendments to the law were to be funded was still not settled, however. On the same day the law was passed, Schäffer prepared a draft for a supplementary budget bill to cover the deficit. It proposed raising the needed revenue by increasing the gasoline tax and imposing an Autobahn user's fee. At the cabinet meeting on the following day (20 October), Schäffer described his actions at the previous day's Bundestag meeting and presented his proposals for generating the funds needed to cover the BVG.[100] None of the cabinet members wanted to delay approval of the law, but the minister of transportation was opposed to the fiscal remedies proposed by the finance minister, arguing that the BVG was a general measure that should be funded by a general tax, not one that would be borne by a specific segment of society.

To this point of principle he added the practical consideration that taxing the Autobahns would result in an "extremely undesirable" transfer of traffic to side roads, and then, obviously grasping at straws, he closed his case with the somewhat specious argument that user's tax windshield stickers would pose a traffic danger by obscuring the vision of drivers. In place of the taxes proposed by the finance minister, he urged raising the sales tax. Schäffer replied that the raising of the sales tax had to be held in reserve for "future budgetary burdens [Mehrbelastungen]," presumably those connected with defense, and that the imposition of user's fees was the most feasible solution in view of the general financial situation, since it did not harm the economy as a whole and essentially only affected the more wealthy elements of society. Against the opposition of the minister of transportation, the cabinet accepted the finance minister's proposed tax bill.

Two weeks later little progress had been made and the pressure for action was mounting. A report to the chancellor, prepared on 3 November and transmitted to him by his personal aide, Hans Globke, noted that withholding approval of the BVG until after the passage of the supplementary budget bill would "apparently not be politically possible."[101] One solution proposed by Schäffer was to negotiate an agreement with the coalition parties. If they would promise to vote for the bill when it came before the Bundestag, then the cabinet would approve the BVG. According to the report, the present situation was "regrettable, since the opposition has managed to garner a considerable share of the political success connected with the BVG through its handling of the government's proposal in committee and in the Bundestag, while it is to be feared that it will not share with the government and the coalition parties the burden of the supplementary budget bill."[102]

As feared, the opposition did make capital of the government's having to link the BVG with the passage of a supplementary budgetary bill. Although at a cabinet meeting of 7 November the minister for the Marshall Plan claimed that there was not a connection since the budget bill simply served to cover a general budgetary overrun and was not specifically linked to the BVG as such, he also argued that the continued failure to resolve the issue of the BVG was "politically undesirable [politisch nicht für tragbar]" and pressed for a settlement of the issue as soon as possible.[103] The situation was complicated further when the Transportation Committee of the Bundesrat rejected the finance minister's proposal for raising the gasoline tax and imposing user's fees on the Autobahns.[104] Schäffer immediately began to work on an alternative scheme, and a week later he appeared before the cabinet with a new proposal to cover the deficit based on an increase in the petroleum tax.[105] The new proposal, which was more likely to find approval, also promised greater revenue. The transportation minister supported the new measure and urged that the earlier proposals be withdrawn. The economics and Marshall Plan ministers opposed this, arguing that the original proposals be retained since "sooner or later" the taxes proposed in them would have to be levied. Adenauer argued that it would signify a loss of authority for the government if it withdrew the bills and added that one should keep the big picture in mind, "including the additional burdens that would be incurred through the strengthening of the defense forces." Against the opposition of the minister of transportation, the cabinet approved Schäffer's proposal.

Three days later the finance minister reported to his colleagues that the Bundesrat was prepared to accept a raise in the petroleum tax but that the raise in the gasoline tax and the imposition of an Autobahn user's fee were considered unacceptable.[106] Schäffer was still reluctant to approve the BVG before its funding was covered. When on 21 November Storch pressed for approval, the finance minister continued to voice his reservations, since support for the budget bill still had not been nailed down.[107] In order to prevent further delay, however, the BVG was sent to the Allied High Commission on 24 November.[108] In early December preparations for submission of the supplementary budget bill to the Bundestag were completed. On 6 December the finance minister reported that the economic adviser of the Allied High Commission had informed him that the increased defense contribution would add DM 650 million to the occupation costs for the coming year. This sum could only be raised through loans; new taxes were impossible during the present fiscal year. Until then it was all the more important to bring the present budget into order. Raising the petroleum tax would cover the costs of the BVG as well as several other programs. After some discussion, the new tax proposal was accepted unchanged by the cabinet, and on 14 December it received its first reading in the Bundestag.[109]

On the following day the Allied High Commission approved the BVG. The cabinet was scheduled to discuss the issue, but by now the outcome was a foregone conclusion.[110] At the cabinet meeting of 19 December, the finance minister agreed to give his approval to the acceptance of the BVG if it could be guaranteed that the coalition parties would support the petroleum tax increase. The cabinet's view was that the parties would support the tax increase, and on the following day the BVG was formally promulgated.[111]

THE Bundesversorgungsgesetz was the Federal Republic's first piece of major social legislation. Its passage represented an affirmation of past German practices and the overturn of an unpopular system imposed by the victorious

Allies; as such, the BVG was perceived not only as a major legislative act but also as an assertion of the young Republic's growing sovereignty. The drafting of the BVG also represents a classic example of the postwar neocorporate decision-making process in the Federal Republic. The removal of Allied restrictions on veterans' organizations, followed by the formation of federally organized war victims' organizations, took place at the same time that the new federal ministries charged with social legislation were being forged. Overwhelmed by the complexity of war victim legislation and under pressure to act quickly, the newly formed ministries and the legislative committees charged with the drafting of war victim legislation were receptive to the input offered by the emerging interest groups. The result was a corporate, consensual decision-making process that simultaneously strengthened the position of the interest groups and the legislative and administrative institutions of the fledgling Republic.

Because of their numbers and the visible, highly graphic manifestations of their plight, especially that of the war-disabled, there was widespread sympathy for the needs of the war victims, and the BVG was universally supported. The same could not be said for the next group of veterans for whom legislation was being considered—the former professional officers.

SIX

THE 131 LAW

Like demilitarization, reform of the German bureaucracy was high on the Allied agenda. The realization that the bureaucracy had played a significant role in the collapse of the Weimar Republic and in helping the Third Reich to carry out its hideous policies destroyed the generally favorable reputation enjoyed by the German civil service before the Second World War.[1] In the Soviet zone the old system was summarily abolished in September 1945.[2] In the Western zones the military governments tried to solve the problem through a combination of purges and structural reform.[3] The Anglo-Americans in particular worked to restructure the German bureaucracy so that it would conform more closely to their civil services, which they considered more democratic and better suited to support a democratic political system.[4]

Guidelines reflecting Allied views were imposed on the German occupation states (*Länder*), but the main reform efforts were mounted with the creation of the Bizone, which, it was realized, would form the model for any further German state.[5] The Allied efforts to reform German bureaucratic practices enjoyed considerable support within the Social Democratic Party and the unions. The Economic Council (Wirtschaftsrat) was controlled by bourgeois parties, however, which were dead set against reform, in part because they saw the bureaucracy as an "unpolitical" bulwark against an expected surge of the left.[6]

During the final years of the occupation, a prolonged tug-of-war ensued that ended with German opponents of reform successfully resisting Allied reform efforts. While the Wirtschaftsrat and military government battled to a standstill, the Parliamentary Council (Parlamentarischer Rat), which was drawing up the constitution of the Federal Republic, adopted a position that was flatly opposed to reform. It inserted a provision in the Basic Law (Grundgesetz) that ensured that the traditional prerogatives of the German bureaucracy would be maintained.[7] In retaliation, the Allies issued an order (Military Government Law Number 15) in February 1949, which put the Anglo-American reform guidelines in effect until the Germans passed their own law and made the latter subject to Allied approval.[8]

The victory of Adenauer's coalition of bourgeois parties in August 1949 ensured that German resistance to Allied plans for reform of the bureaucracy would continue under the Republic. Opponents of reform skillfully used the Grundgesetz as an effective tool to oppose Allied pressure for change, arguing that it was now the law of the land and that it guaranteed the continuation of established practices. Allied efforts were undercut further by the fact that earlier German support for reform was ebbing. As the Bundestag dragged out its deliberations, the Allied position steadily weakened; the British began to lose interest, and the revision of the Occupation Statute in March 1951 decisively shifted the balance of power in favor of the Germans. The Civil Service Law (Beamtenrecht), finally passed in 1953, essentially restored established German practices.

The question of the bureaucracy's place in the new Republic also had a social component. This was connected with article 131 of the Grundgesetz, which charged the federal government with the regulation of the legal position of former members of the civil service who had lost their positions following Germany's defeat. Although designed to deal primarily with civil servants from areas that had been annexed by the Soviets and Poles, the article 131 legislation also was to cover other groups, including certain categories of denazified officials. Originally the government did not plan to include former professional soldiers in this legislation. Eventually, however, government officials decided that, in the absence of better alternatives, former professional soldiers should be included in the 131 Law.

Social legislation for the "131er" enjoyed considerable support. Although the Social Democratic Party opposed restitution for certain—in its view, overly compromised—categories of former officials, it generally favored efforts to provide financial benefits to displaced civil servants, including former officers of the Wehrmacht. Opposition to the Allied assignment of "collective guilt" and the Third Reich's socially liberal recruitment practices for military officers, especially noncommissioned officers, combined to blunt traditional Social Democratic hostility to officers' benefits.[9] As a result, the government and Bundestag worked together to enact legislation, and in May 1951 the Law for the Regulation of the Legal Position of Persons Falling under Article 131 of the Basic Law was passed.[10] The law established pensions for eligible civil servants, including professional soldiers, who had lost their positions; it also provided guidelines for the reemployment of those who had lost their previous jobs but did not yet qualify for a pension.

THE FUTURE SHAPE of legislation for military pensions, like much else, was still unclear in the summer and fall of 1949. In July the military governments turned the question over to the states.[11] Officers eligible for pensions claimed that this nullified Control Council Law 34 and demanded the restoration of prewar benefits or, failing this, increased Maintenance Grants. Pressure was put on the states to act, but the *Länder* governments stalled, hoping to shift the burden to the soon-to-be-formed federal government. As a consequence, when the Federal Republic was founded in September, not only the scope but the eventual legal basis of future military service pension legislation remained open. The former officers of the Hansen-Kreis moved quickly to fill the void. A lobbying headquarters was established in Bonn, and a press campaign was inaugurated. On 20 September Admiral Gottfried Hansen wrote the newly appointed finance minister, Fritz Schäffer, expounding the former officers' case and requesting that his organization's experts be given a voice in the drafting of future legislation. The admiral also provided a draft proposal for a new pension law, which, according to Hansen, "was based on the WFVG, but took account of the changed circumstances."[12] In fact, there was little sign of concessions due to "changed circumstances" in the bombastic demands that were initially raised by the former officers. Again and again they insisted that they were legally entitled to the benefits provided by prewar legislation. When their claims that the lifting of Control Council Law 34 had restored the WFVG/WEFVG were ignored, they contended that any new laws must include the old entitlements. Although these maximalist demands were retained for tactical purposes, they gradually began to be accompanied by a fallback position based on the contingency that future military pensions would be included in the legislation connected with article 131 of the Basic Law. The position contained two demands: the first was that former officers be treated equally with the expelled civil servants; the second was that those covered by the 131 Law receive the same benefits as *einheimisch* civil servants, that is, those currently employed or receiving pensions in the Federal Republic. These demands were grounded in the former officers' conviction that they had been discriminated against vis-à-vis civilian state employees during the occupation, when the military officers had lost their pensions but the civilians had not, and in the fear that they now—along with the expelled civil servants—faced the prospect of second-class treatment since the pensions envisioned for those covered by the 131 Law were to be less than those received by *einheimisch* civil servants.

In early October 1949 the finance minister received a delegation of representatives of the Hansen-Kreis, headed by General Fritz Koch from the Bonn office. Koch opened by reiterating the misery being experienced by former officers. According to the general, the number of suicides involving former officers and their families had now reached two hundred. The main purpose of Koch's delegation was to persuade the finance minister to put pressure on the states to heed the military government's decree of July and to enact uniform and adequate legislation. The draft for such a law, as well as Hansen's earlier proposal for a future federal law, were presented to the finance minister. Koch then produced the usual list of demands and complaints, defending the right of former officers to their pensions and expressing the anger of the former soldiers over the preferred treatment of civilian state employees. The former officers insisted that they did not want "special privileges, but only to be dealt with in accordance with the civil service law, in the same way [nach gleichem Recht] as all other state servants."[13] Requests for equal, not special, treatment were of course the standard currency of virtually every interest group in the early years of the Republic and easily became the rhetorical starting point for much more extensive claims.[14]

The finance minister expressed his sympathy with the delegation's requests and promised to do what he could to help. In Schäffer's view a long-term solution based on federal legislation was preferable to short-term assistance. For the moment, however, the problem was a matter for the states; it would only become a federal matter in April 1950, with the beginning of the Republic's first fiscal year, and following the passage of appropriate legislation. With regard to the latter, Schäffer welcomed the offer of assistance and promised to forward Hansen's proposal to those in his ministry working on the law. While he lacked the authority to send the admiral's directives for state laws to the state finance ministers, he promised to ask them to act as quickly and as generously as possible on the military government's decree of July.[15]

In a letter to Schäffer of 30 November 1949, Koch thanked him for having urged the states to take action but complained about the states' continued refusal to act.[16] While the victims of the unjust pension cutoffs now had hope and had placed their trust in the federal government, he stated, they were "deeply disappointed and extremely painfully surprised" to see that German authorities and state parliaments continued to enforce the unjust regulations of the occupation period. Former soldiers—indeed even participants in the resistance—were denied their rights, while bureaucrats, many of them convicted Nazis, received their full pensions. It was intolerable, Koch complained, that after the occupiers had ended their policy of "economic euthanasia," it was being continued by Germans, who were now carrying out "this policy of *Sippenhaftung*, family destruction, and collective punishment against innocent [freigesprochene, nicht betroffene, nicht angeklagte, nicht verteidigte, nicht verurteilte] Germans." The real danger, Koch concluded, was the effect of these policies on the children of those concerned:

> The sons and daughters of the parents who have been robbed of their economic means of existence [Existenzgrundlagen] see themselves being deprived of the position in life that was expected, in view of their back-ground, through the loss of proper professional training; it is to be feared that they will never forget such a *Deklassierung*. Bitterness will grow in the hearts and minds of these innocent and unfairly destroyed youths and this will prevent the development of reasonable and tolerant political views [der einsichtsvollen Vernunft und der verträglichen Gesinnung auch im politischen Denken den Weg versperren]. This, as past experience shows, promotes a radicalization which will grow all the stronger with each month, semester, and school year that the opportunity for an appropriate education is lost.

Unless the pensions of their parents were restored, in short, these middle-class youths of the Federal Republic would go the same way their Weimar counter-parts had gone.

The unlikelihood of immediate relief for former officers and their families was resignedly acknowledged in a report prepared by the Hansen group's chief lobbyist, General Kurt Linde, following a five-hour meeting with Fi-nance Ministry officials held on 4 November in Bad Homburg.[17] The first official with whom he spoke stressed the difficult fiscal circumstances of the fledgling Republic and cautioned against too strong an emphasis by the former soldiers and civil servants on legal rights—that is, the restoration of prewar benefits—since it would add fuel to the SPD's frequently discussed plans to transfer civil service pensions to the white-collar social insurance program. A conversation with the official in charge of drafting legislation connected with military pensions, Minister-Rat Hans Meyer, revealed that the state governments intended to turn the matter over to the federal government and that therefore nothing could be done on the basis of the military govern-ment decree of July. Settlement would only come with the passage of federal legislation, which would probably be connected with article 131 of the Grund-gesetz. Linde protested that this would mean a continuation of the existing state of "suffering and injustice" for one and a half to two years.[18]

The remainder of the conversation also provided little comfort. Meyer rejected the idea that the Federal Republic was the legal successor of the Third Reich, which meant it was not bound to honor the legal claims of former soldiers. In any case, prewar pension benefits would not be reinstated. A new law had to be created. Moreover, as Adenauer himself had stressed in his inaugural address, the promotion question needed to be examined, since even those who were disposed to generosity could not overlook the problematic effects of providing inflated pensions to officers who had experienced meteoric rises under the Nazis.[19] With regard to the administration of the law, however, Meyer was sympathetic to the soldiers' dislike of being lumped together with the war victims and having their pensions administered by social security offices. He promised that the new system would not be administered by the Labor Ministry but probably by the Ministry of Interior, which would be in charge of drafting the new law.[20]

Linde came away from the meeting convinced that the former officers were in for a hard fight and that the most promising course was to link their cause with the law for expelled civil servants. In early 1950 this linkage was made official. In January the interministerial debate over which provision of the Basic Law would serve as the basis for expelled civil servant benefits was settled in favor of article 131 and in February it was decided to include former professional soldiers in this legislation.[21] By March the bureaucratic and legislative machinery was in place and the laborious work of drafting the Law for the Regulation of the Legal Position of Persons Falling under Article 131 of the Basic Law had begun.

ON 14–15 MARCH the Bundestag's Twenty-fifth Committee, the Committee for Civil Service Law (25. Ausschuss. Beamtenrecht), invited representatives of concerned interest groups, including those of former professional soldiers, to present their cases. On the eve of the hearings, a South German leader of Hansen's fledgling League of Pension-Entitled Wehrmacht Personnel and Their Survivors (Bund versorgungsberechtigter ehemaliger Wehrmachtsangehöriger und deren Hinterbliebenen [BvW]) spoke informally with State Secretary Alfred Hartmann of the Finance Ministry at the home of a mutual acquaintance about the situation.[22] According to Hartmann, the question had become "a purely political one," and he urged the former officers to abandon their strictly legalistic position; the federal government would in no case allow itself to be considered the legal successor of the Reich, since the debts of the Reich were "so monstrously high" that the Federal Republic could never assume them. In addition, the state secretary strongly advised the former professional soldiers to work on having their petitions to the government and its representatives signed by fewer generals and more persons from lower ranks. On the whole, the BvW representative concluded, the conversation was "distressing and has, unfortunately, made it clear that not legal, but political and economic considerations will be decisive in the settlement of our pensions."

Whether Linde, who was scheduled to meet with the committee on 14 March, was aware of the state secretary's views is uncertain, but it is unlikely that he would have heeded them in any case. Responding later to Hartmann's remarks, Linde asserted that the question was political only for those who for financial reasons were unwilling to recognize the soldiers' legitimate claims, namely "representatives of the Finance Ministry." According to Linde, those in the Ministry of Interior who were drafting the law accepted the legalistic interpretation, and the chairman of the Legal Committee, he claimed, "has told me repeatedly: 'Do not give up one iota of your legal claims; in a year the situation may have changed completely. Whoever voluntarily gives up their rights then has no grounds for complaint.'"[23]

In his presentation to the committee, Linde followed this advice fully, making it clear that he did not intend to surrender any of the legal claims of his constituency.[24] He argued that Control Council Law 34, whose "political goal was the defamation and economic destruction of members of the Wehrmacht and their families," had not removed but had only temporarily suspended existing pension rights. Moreover, he contended, its successor, the Allied High Commission Law 16 of December 1949, had rescinded Control Council Law 34, which meant that the High Commission no longer opposed the payment of pensions; pensions, therefore, should be restored on the basis of existing laws, that is, those in force before 1945. The rights under those laws, according to the general, were still legally binding and could not be revoked. The legal situation was independent of the Republic's financial problems and must be handled as such. If cuts had to be made, the only defensible legal position was that all civil servants must share the burden equally; former soldiers would willingly accept such restrictions, but only if they affected all civil servants.

Linde's arguments were repeated and backed up with further legal details by his fellow lobbyist, General George Tzschirner.[25] According to Tzschirner, if, as was rumored, the state did not have enough money to meet the demands of the former professional soldiers, then there could be none for the remaining civil servants either. Since both groups' legal rights were equally binding, by paying pensions to one group and not to the other, the state would be violating the provisions of the Basic Law that guaranteed its citizens equal treatment before the law. Both benefits and burdens had to be equalized.

Tzschirner referred angrily to the cries of outrage from the *einheimisch* civil servants that had followed the finance minister's proposal that part of the costs for 131er benefits be covered by a levy on the salaries of currently employed civil servants.[26] The civil servants had claimed that the proposed levy (*Abgabe*) constituted a special tax that was unconstitutional because it would make one group more liable than others for the war's costs, which were to be borne by the entire population. The protests of those fortunate enough to have jobs and pensions only fed the resentment of those who had neither, and the former general stoically declared that these dispossessed civil servants would pay any price and bear any burden to regain their rights—as long as the burden was shared by all, including those fortunate enough to still have positions. According to Tzschirner, "Our claims must be balanced by an equalization of burdens within the entire public service and its pensioners by means of salary reductions. We are willing to submit to such a measure. All public servants have to bear the burden of the lost war, not just those covered by article 131 of the Basic Law. . . . It is disgraceful how little comradely spirit some public servants reveal when they oppose this more than justified equalization within their ranks."

In discussing the specific demands of former professional soldiers, Linde and Tzschirner reiterated the main features of pre-1945 legislation and demanded their restoration: pensions after ten years' service for officers and after eighteen for noncommissioned officers and positions in the civil service for retired officers and for noncommissioned officers with twelve years' service. The two spokespersons devoted considerable attention to the issue of promotions, insisting that they all be recognized. The reason for this was simple: rank at time of retirement, whether voluntary or forced by the war's end, determined pension levels. Former officers maintained that they should be able to count all promotions received before 1945. Because numerous officers had had meteoric careers either as a result of the opportunities offered by the rapid expansion of the Wehrmacht and wartime conditions or, more ominously, as a result of favoritism by the National Socialist regime, there was widespread resistance to this demand. For both political and fiscal reasons, most legislators felt there should be a cap on the number of promotions counted after 1933. Like the representatives of most interest groups, however, Linde and Tzschirner refused to recognize exceptional factors that favored their constituency, arguing that the number of promotions had not been inordinate and that justice required their recognition.

Although in their presentations both Linde and Tzschirner sought to be objective, hard-nosed, and legalistic, neither could resist the opportunity to try to win the sympathy of committee members. Both mentioned suicides of former officers and their wives who had been driven to desperation, and Linde related examples of the hardships endured by old officers who had been deprived of their pensions and pushed to the edge of existence. He concluded his remarks by stating:

> As difficult as these fates might be, they will be bearable if justice prevails and all burdens are borne equally. The former professional soldiers fully understand the misery of all those who likewise have been hurt by the war, since in most cases they themselves are war victims, expellees, victims of nazism, or have had their homes bombed out. If, however, need is compared to need, then one should never forget that the former professional soldier since his early youth has devoted his life to the people and now is refused entrance to another profession because he is accused of being a militarist or presumably lacks the requisite training. That gives his present existence a special tragedy.[27]

The committee's hearings began in an atmosphere of steadily mounting pressure to act on behalf of the 131ers. It came not only from outside the government but from within the CDU's ranks as well.[28] At a 17 March meeting, the cabinet decided to have the Finance, Interior, and Expellee ministries draft a common proposal.[29] On 28 March Adenauer wrote the three ministers involved, reminding them of the cabinet's decision and emphasizing that "it is necessary to draft the proposal *quickly*." Previous delays were understandable, since the budget had not been settled, but now that it had been settled (at the 17 March meeting), further delay was "no longer justified." The chancellor stated that he was being flooded daily with petitions from all sorts of organizations and individuals. The growing public interest in the subject, he noted, was reflected in its increased discussion in the press. The Bundestag was also raising the matter in interpellations, questions, proposals, and so forth. "Under these circumstances," Adenauer concluded, "I believe it is desirable that the government submit its proposal to the legislative bodies before the Bundestag makes [its own] decisions."[30]

Another reason for intensified action on the matter was the upcoming state elections scheduled for June in North Rhine–Westphalia and July in Schleswig-Holstein. According to the minister of interior, Gustav Heinemann, the government had to seek a solution "that meets the justified demands of the voters and is shaped so that it does not produce undesirable results in the upcoming elections."[31] To forestall problems with the military beneficiaries of 131er legislation, the Chancellor's Office was keeping channels open. For some time a meeting of the chancellor with a delegation of former professional soldiers had been planned, but Adenauer had been unable to fit the meeting into his schedule. Instead, the former soldiers met with officials of the Bundeskanzleramt on 19 June.[32] Meanwhile, events in Schleswig-Holstein had shown the potential explosiveness of the former officers' discontent and the way in which it could be exploited by the opposition. There, on the eve of the scheduled elections, the content of the government's draft of the 131 Law had leaked out and become an issue. According to a Bundeskanzleramt report, this had produced "constant protest demonstrations by former officers and noncommissioned officers," and "the DGB [German Federation of Trade Unions (Deutscher Gewerkschaftsbund)] had begun to take up the issue, claiming that the government was not responsive to the needs of the former soldiers and that the proper representatives for their interests were the unions." Heinemann had been informed immediately of these developments. The report went on to advise that the requests of former professional soldiers should be transmitted to the chancellor and that a response to their demands be drafted.[33] Shortly thereafter State Secretary Hans Globke, Adenauer's personal aide, circulated a list of the officers' demands to various ministries for their comments.[34]

The frustration of the former soldiers with the slow pace of progress was manifested at a meeting of BvW *Landesverband* leaders held in Bonn in mid-July, at which Linde reported on the state of negotiations with government officials.[35] The most difficult question, he claimed, was that of promotions, for which the ministers had no understanding whatsoever. There was also dissatisfaction with the lack of hiring provisions for former officers. Lobbying efforts aimed at Bundestag deputies were discussed, as was the initiation of a press campaign and the possible use of street demonstrations ("democratic means of the street"). The main demand, it was concluded, had to remain "equal rights with the civil servants." With regard to future activity, it was decided that it would be worthwhile to work with the leader of the expellees, Linus Kather, who was leading a vigorous campaign on behalf of the expelled civil servants.[36]

When the government's draft proposal was made public in late July, there was a storm of protest from the expelled civil servants and former soldiers.[37] To assuage the latter, a meeting was set up between the chancellor and a delegation of former professional soldiers for 25 August. In the preceding days, government officials worked out their response to the soldiers' demands.[38] The soldiers continued to advance their maximalist position, claiming that they were entitled to the benefits provided under the WFVG of 1938. With regard to the 131 Law, the main complaint of the former soldiers was that civil servants covered by the law received lower benefits than *einheimisch* officials, and that, of the various groups covered by the law, former soldiers received the least. Further complaints about the 131 Law reproached the limited provisions for providing civil service positions for former professional officers (*Unterbringung*), the 8 May 1935–45 dates of entitlement,[39] and the two-promotion restriction. The government's position was that its difficult fiscal situation made it impossible to honor old laws and that the 131 Law was an attempt to create a new, uniform resolution of the problem that took into account the Republic's fiscal limits. Government spokespersons claimed that the new law was constitutionally sound and that recognizing special rights for soldiers would lead to demands for special treatment by all groups covered by the law. The government's position was repeated to the BvW delegation at a meeting in the Chancellor's Office the day before the scheduled meeting with Adenauer. Ministerialrat Karl Gumbel, who was in charge of coordinating the drafting of the 131 Law, stressed that a restoration of the WFVG was impossible and that limited finances made a new regulation necessary. Moreover, he maintained that the former soldiers were being treated equally with the other groups covered by the law. Following the meeting, Gumbel summed up his impressions of the mood of the former soldiers: he expected that the BvW functionaries would drop their demand that the old laws be honored and that they would accept the 131 Law in principle at their meeting with the chancellor; at the same time, he expected that they would continue to claim that there were a number of inequalities in the draft, that they would insist on changes, and that they would request that the changes they considered to be "absolutely necessary" be made before the draft was submitted to the Bundestag.[40]

Gumbel's predictions proved to be accurate. At its meeting with the chancellor the next day, the BvW delegation declared that it rejected the 131 Law in its present form since it did not treat those covered by it equally with *einheimisch* civil servants and, in addition, did not treat soldiers equally with expelled civil servants. Former officers would agree to be included in the law if "complete equality with expelled civil servants was actually achieved" and the "special circumstances of former soldiers were taken into account." In addition, the delegation demanded that the "de facto boycott against the hiring of former professional soldiers in both the civil service and private economy be ended." Adenauer spoke out against the "still existing defamation of German soldiers" and promised a thorough review of the points raised by the delegation.[41]

Although the main pressure for action on the 131 Law was generated by expelled civil servants, the demands of the former officers had begun to take on more urgency as a result of Adenauer's initiatives in the rearmament question, which was resolved in principle in late September.[42] Fearing that there would be "much unpleasantness" unless the bill was introduced immediately, the Chancellor's Office decided to forgo introducing any changes at the time, since this would produce unacceptable delays. To meet the demands of the soldiers, however, it was decided that they should be informed that the government agreed to "certain changes in the law." These changes would be approved by the cabinet, and the ministerial representatives in the Bundestag committees would be instructed to work for "change in the agreed-upon sense."[43]

On Adenauer's instructions, two meetings between ministry officials and BvW representatives were held in September to discuss possible changes. The first took place on 9 September in the Finance Ministry and was chaired by Schäffer. The second meeting was held on 18 September in the Interior Ministry. In a report at the end of the month, Heinemann related the progress of the two meetings.[44] The main demands of the former professional soldiers had concerned better opportunities for the hiring of officers with more than ten years of service and noncommissioned officers with ten to twelve years, removal or change of the 8 May 1935 entitlement date (*Stichtag*), inclusion of POW time after 8 May 1945 in calculating pensions, recognition of all promotions, provision of pensions to noncommissioned officers with twelve to eighteen years of service, inclusion of professional soldiers transferred from the Wehrmacht to the Waffen-SS in the legislation, and a general hardship provision (*Härtevorschrift*). The government's draft originally gave officers with more than ten years of service pensions but made no provisions for mandatory *Unterbringung*. This, according to Heinemann, was not the result of discrimination, but because the officers in question lacked the proper training. Few would qualify, and their inclusion would only be a form of "window dressing." In any case, there were so many groups already covered by mandatory hiring regulations (for example, lower-level bureaucrats and noncommissioned officers with over twelve years of service) that enforcement had become a difficult problem; to increase the numbers of those eligible would only make things worse. The new proposal, worked out in the recent discussions, took a middle ground, allowing officers with over ten years' service who were hired to be counted as part of the employing agency's hiring quota (*Unterbringungspflicht*); this enhanced the chances of qualified ex-officers in finding employment without mandating it. While these provisions were fully justified, Heinemann concluded, the government "for political reasons" would not oppose the Bundestag's making provisions for the mandatory hiring of eligible officers. Noncommissioned officers did not fare so well. The request to include those with ten to twelve years' service was rejected as impossible due to the numbers involved. The minister of interior was willing to loosen the provisions somewhat, however, by allowing those noncommissioned officers with ten to twelve years' service who were employed by state agencies to be counted as a part of the mandatory hiring quotas.[45]

The BvW's other requests received little encouragement. The 1935 *Stichtag* was retained, and the argument that it discriminated against soldiers was rejected.[46] The two-promotion limit was also retained. According to Heine-mann, two promotions was an average number and even the July 1944 peace plan of the Wehrmacht had envisioned a scale of six promotions within twenty-nine years of service. The allowance of two promotions was, in his view, actually quite generous, considering that some of the state delegations in the Bundesrat wanted even stricter limitations. Providing pensions for non-commissioned officers with less than eighteen years of service was rejected because it deviated from accepted practice, because it would give the recipients more than they had been entitled to before, and because it would open the door to increased demands by other groups. A general hardship provision was also rejected on the grounds that those who needed extraordinary assistance were provided for by existing individual clauses of the law. The inclusion of time spent in captivity as a POW was accepted in the calculation of pension levels but not in the establishment of pension rights. Heinemann urged the cabinet to make a decision on which changes to allow at its next meeting and suggested that governmental representatives in the Bundestag committees then be instructed to support the agreed-upon changes. On 6 October the cabinet met and voted to accept his proposal.[47]

Summarizing the discussions, an Interior Ministry representative con-cluded that "as the results show, the negotiations were not very successful for the professional soldiers."[48] The soldiers agreed. Linde's summary of the negotiations, while noting the "more receptive and constructive" atmosphere of the talks, conceded that the soldiers had received less than they had hoped for.[49] At both meetings, the BvW representatives had repeated their funda-mental position that the old laws were still valid. While this position had been nominally acknowledged by officials, Linde complained that at the second meeting they had done it in a "smirking manner [schmunzelnder Weise]," probably because the former officers' claims had experienced "almost unan-imous rejection" during the draft's first reading in the Bundestag, which had taken place a few days earlier.[50]

As a result of the discussions, Linde was strengthened in his conviction that "a separate legislative proposal for former professional soldiers outside the framework of the 131 Law would promise even less success than a common front [Zusammengehen] with the other 131er." Ministry officials had stressed the difficulty they had encountered in getting the soldiers included in the law at all and in overriding the Bundesrat's original position of not recognizing any promotions granted after 30 January 1933. While a decisive change in the former officers' favor might come about as a result of "the political situation," that is, the rearmament decision, one had to adjust to the circumstances. In response to criticism that a harder line should have been taken, Linde defended the position taken by the BvW delegation. The decision to accept the 131 framework, instead of uncompromisingly demanding a Wehrmacht Pension Law outside the 131 Law, was correct, he contended, since "detachment from the 131er circle most likely would not bring a betterment in material and financial provisions, but only introduce further delay." If such a hard-line position had been taken, he claimed, the 9 September meeting would have lasted only five minutes and the second meeting would have never taken place. The "outspoken willingness to negotiate that was now evident among government officials," Linde argued, demonstrated that the correct path had been taken. Concessions had been obtained and the government had promised to have its representatives introduce changes during the committee discussions.[51]

Meanwhile, the government was also taking steps to assist former professional soldiers in finding employment. For years the latter had complained that they were victims of a boycott by state officials and, above all, by the industrial factory councils (*Betriebsräte*).[52] Although Hansen and the BvW had systematically cultivated relations with the SPD, the issue of an *Arbeitsboykott* continued to trouble the relationship. In private meetings and in public statements, Kurt Schumacher, the SPD's leader, was receptive to the former officers and supportive of their demands.[53] Cooperation offered benefits to both sides: the Wehrmacht officers gained legislative support for their pension demands, and by supporting their demands, Schumacher demonstrated his "national" policy and hoped to gain their support for his campaign against German rearmament.[54] The views of Schumacher and other leading SPD leaders did not always trickle down to lower layers of the party and to rank-and-file workers, however.

During the occupation, the issue of officer benefits, which was left to the state parliaments, often collided and became intertwined with other political issues. Differing priorities regarding allocation of scarce resources was the main source of friction. SPD legislators continually weighed the former officers' demands against those of others and invariably subordinated them to the needs of the victims of fascism, a position that officers were unable to comprehend.[55] The narrow, selfish attitude of officers and the frequent insensitive outbursts of their representatives riled Social Democrats and reactivated old resentments. These resentments, combined with a tight labor market, produced hostility on the part of factory councils toward former officers. Thus, while officially relations between the SPD and the officers' organizations were cordial, especially at the top, there was often tension at the state and grass roots level.[56]

At a meeting with the labor minister on 1 August, Hansen had complained about the *Betriebsräte*'s alleged boycott and demanded that the government persuade the DGB to bring about its end.[57] The demand had been raised again at the 25 August meeting with Adenauer, and the chancellor, undoubtedly pleased with the opportunity to curry favor with the former officers by putting pressure on the unions, responded quickly. On 15 September, Herbert Blankenhorn, the chancellor's personal adviser, wrote to the state secretary in the Economics Ministry that for a variety of reasons, including the "change in attitude toward these persons [*Kreisen*, that is, former officers] that is beginning to manifest itself both at home and abroad," it had become "advisable to undertake measures to provide employment for those former professional soldiers who until now have not found jobs and who will not be entitled to pensions." The chancellor, Blankenhorn continued, would "especially welcome it" if the Economic Ministry, along with the Labor and Agricultural ministries, would undertake the appropriate steps with the relevant economic organizations ("Industrie- und Handelskammern, Handwerkskammern, Wirtschaftsverbänden") and the BvW to achieve this objective. Guidelines, according to Blankenhorn, had been worked out in a meeting of the economic minister, General Linde, and Gerhard Graf von Schwerin, "the representative of the Bundeskanzler in this matter," that had taken place in the Chancellor's Office on 5 September. The necessary contacts with the unions would be made by the Chancellor's Office. The state secretary concluded that it would also be a good idea to acquaint the public at large with the need to hire former Wehrmacht personnel who were not provided for in the pension law "in order to remove as far as possible remaining hardships and resentments."[58]

On 25 October a meeting of Schwerin, Linde, and representatives of the DGB and the SPD took place at Bad Orb. According to the Chancellor's Office report, the meeting was held in a "candidly open atmosphere in which both sides demonstrated a serious desire to achieve practical means for the improvement of the lot of former soldiers." Labor representatives freely admitted the existence of a boycott against former professional soldiers, which was manifested especially at the lower levels. The reasons for this could be traced in part "to unpleasant personal experiences during military service, in part to unpleasant experiences following the First World War, and finally also to the fact that the workers perceived the industrious, ambitious soldiers as an unwelcome competition." Further points of conflict were the lack of appropriate training on the part of former officers and an "unfair salary policy for white-collar workers," which unduly favored the former officers who were hired.[59] Additional talks were scheduled among the interested parties, and it was agreed that measures on the local level ("auf der Linie Betrieb-Kreisverband des BvW") should be undertaken to increase the hiring of former professional soldiers.[60]

MEANWHILE, the 131 Law had been introduced into the Bundestag by the government and had had its first reading. "No one," Heinemann declared when he presented the government's draft, "is happy with this bill." Although the interior minister was aware of and sympathetic to the discontent of those affected, at the same time he deplored the form and nature in which they had expressed their dissatisfaction and found it "deeply troubling."[61] The anger of those affected by the law should not be directed against the Federal Republic, Heinemann maintained, since it was not the cause of their difficulties, but against Adolf Hitler. Heinemann then outlined the main features of the government's proposal. It was impossible, he maintained, for the Republic to assume the full burden of the obligations contracted by its predecessor. Thus it had been necessary to create a completely new piece of legislation, one that solved problems as fairly as possible given the existing strapped circumstances. The law would cover 265,000 persons, of which one-third were former professional soldiers.[62] Two provisions of the bill affected former professional soldiers in particular: the requirement of ten years' service for entitlement and the limit of two promotions between 1933 and 1945. Both, according to Heinemann, represented a return to established procedures that had been violated by the Nazis.[63]

Once debate began, it quickly became clear that two key provisions of the government's proposal would be challenged by all the parties. The plan to cut benefits of displaced civil servants vis-à-vis those currently employed in the Federal Republic was rejected, and equal treatment was demanded. In addition, the provision to generate DM 120 million to help fund support of displaced civil servants by means of a 3 percent cut in the salaries and pensions of *einheimisch* civil servants was roundly criticized, though one speaker, himself a displaced civil servant, deplored the selfishness of those who had the luxury and security of jobs. Most deputies spoke of the unfairness of the provision and of the hardships already suffered by civil servants, and some pointed to the danger of their becoming radicalized if their salaries were not raised. The large degree of support for civil servants was not surprising, given the high level of organization of civil servant interest groups and the fact that bureaucrats, both displaced and employed, were well represented in the Bundestag and its committees.[64] The former Wehrmacht officers were less well represented, and their demands found less support.[65]

As was to be expected, the strongest support for the former officers came from the splinter parties on the right. The spokesperson of the German Party rejected the bill because it was "budget-driven" instead of being based on legal rights. According to Franz Richter, who was later active in the outlawed Socialist Reich Party (under his real name, Fritz Rössler), the law only continued the "open intention of the 'former' enemies" to defame the German Wehrmacht. The WAV spokesperson claimed that the law discriminated against soldiers and would perpetuate such discrimination, which was intolerable. In view of the present "total political situation," that is, the discussion of German rearmament, it was the duty of the government and the Bundestag to restore the honor of the former soldiers before the German people and the world at large, and the proposed bill had "the exact opposite effect." The speaker for the German Reich Party, Adolf von Thadden, supported the argument that the Federal Republic was the legal successor (*Rechtsnachfolger*) of the Third Reich and reiterated the resentment-laden view of rearmament that was held by many former officers and widely propagated on the right, namely, that while the country was planning to ask the former soldiers to again risk their lives, they continued to be defamed, and therefore rearmament should be rejected. The major parties generally accepted the government proposal's provisions regarding former soldiers, although the SPD announced its intention to improve the provisions for noncommissioned officers and those who had been interned as POWs for a long period after the war. Following its first reading, the bill was referred to the Committee for Civil Service Law for further discussion and amendment.

On 20 November the committee discussed articles 48 and 49 of the law, which dealt with former professional soldiers.[66] The concerns raised by the petitions of former officers that had been submitted to the committee were enumerated, and the committee's chairman, Josef Kleindinst (CDU), dutifully brought up the changes that the government had agreed to sponsor following its meetings with representatives of the former professional soldiers. The proposal to include officers in the mandatory hiring provisions of the law found little support and was rejected. The discussion of the handling of former Wehrmacht personnel who had been transferred to the Waffen-SS sparked a heated debate, revealing the lingering effects of the committee members' experience in the Third Reich. An FDP member supported the inclusion of these Waffen-SS veterans, arguing that "one must make a distinction between the so-called political SS and the Waffen-SS, which had been a part of the German Wehrmacht." An SPD member then recounted his personal observation of atrocities carried out by "young SS people" at the war's end and concluded, "When one has seen these sort of things, one loses all desire to have any sympathy with these people." He was backed up by a CSU member who had witnessed similar atrocities and wanted to exclude those who had committed crimes from coverage. Franz-Josef Wuermeling of the CDU opposed his two colleagues' negative views, arguing that such experiences should not be the starting point of the committee's deliberations since they only lent support to the Allies' charges of collective guilt against the German people. Valentin Baur of the SPD in turn rejected Wuermeling's argument, stating that it was necessary to find a way of ensuring that those guilty of crimes would be excluded from the law's benefits. He cited cases of officers blowing up bridges at the end of the war, who thereby had "conducted war against the German people, not the French or Americans." While he concluded that one must "strive for a genuine reconciliation with those who had remained decent," one also had to avoid "rewarding the real scoundrels and dogs [eigentlichen Gauner und Hunde]."[67]

On the whole, former officers received little as a result of the committee's deliberations. Those who were hired still were to be considered as part of the employer's quota, but officers were not brought into the regulations for mandatory hiring; the 1935 *Stichtag* and the two-promotion limit were retained.[68] Former noncommissioned officers fared somewhat better, though their main demand, to be placed on more equal footing with officers regarding pensions, was not met, in spite of strong support by the SPD. The wide disparity between commissioned and noncommissioned officers in the number of years of service needed to qualify for a pension (ten versus eighteen) had been the source of a large number of complaints submitted to the committee. Proposals to award pensions to noncommissioned officers after twelve years of service were supported by the SPD and the smaller parties represented in the committee, but they were steadfastly opposed on legal and fiscal grounds by members of the coalition parties and ministerial representatives. The issue was hotly debated and not resolved until the final discussion of the clause on 9 March 1951.[69] While the lowering of the amount of service time for noncommissioned officers' pension entitlement was blocked, the government did honor the promises made to them in September. Noncommissioned officers hired with between ten and twelve years of service were to be counted in hiring quotas, and, to further ease their situation, those with over twelve years of service who had not found employment were given three months' financial support.[70] The committee's proposals were forwarded to the Bundestag, and the second reading of the 131 Law, as amended by the committee, took place on 5–6 April 1951.[71]

The second reading was prefaced by a dramatic appearance by Adenauer. For months, former officers had been pressing him to make a public statement against the purported continuing "defamation" of the Wehrmacht. The chancellor had repeatedly put it off, however. In the fall of 1950 he felt the time had come. His rearmament policy had generated a storm of controversy, and Heinemann, the interior minister, had resigned over the issue. The chancellor was now prepared to appease the former members of the Wehrmacht since he needed their support. Sensing that their position had been strengthened, the former officers had increased their pressure on the government for concessions. Since few of their material demands had been met, Adenauer may have felt that the long-desired public statement would serve as a useful and relatively inexpensive sop.

The chancellor began by noting the recent release of German officers charged with war crimes by the Belgian government. He maintained that his government was doing all that it could on behalf of officers imprisoned for war crimes and intimated that further releases would soon take place. While the government would not intervene on behalf of those who were guilty of crimes, the chancellor claimed that "the percentage of those who were actually guilty is so extraordinarily narrow [gering] and so extraordinarily small that . . . their actions have not stained the honor of the Wehrmacht." Adenauer concluded with "a word to the members of the former Wehrmacht." The 131 Law, he claimed, clearly demonstrated the fact that there was no discrimination against them vis-à-vis other civil servants and pensioners. He continued:

> The feeling of such discrimination coupled with financial need has previously played a psychologically unhealthy role. This is especially true for the professional soldiers of the former Wehrmacht, who in the period following the collapse were affected by special measures such as Control Council Law 34 and were, completely unjustly, made collectively responsible for the lost war, although they for the most part had only fulfilled their duty. No one can fault the professional soldiers on account of their earlier actions or, insofar as they are to be brought into public service, discriminate against them when they have equal personal and professional capabilities. The time of collective guilt of the militarists along with that of the activists and the beneficiaries of the National Socialist regime must be ended once and for all.[72]

The second and third readings of the bill produced few changes in the provisions dealing with benefits for former officers. The tone was set by Kleindinst, who reported the bill out and explained the committee's changes. While sympathetic to the demands of the former professional soldiers, he contended that the committee and the government had gone as far as possible. Former professional soldiers naturally wished to reinstate the WFVG, but this was impossible. Kleindinst noted that the law had been promulgated between the *Anschluss* and the outbreak of war and claimed that "even at that time [it] exceeded the financial capacity of the Reich." Five and a half years of war made it even more impossible to implement the law since there had been an enormous increase in the number of persons covered and since the law's provisions, such as the reserving of large numbers of places in the bureaucracy for former Wehrmacht members and the agricultural settlement of veterans "particularly in the border areas," had been "completely superseded by the catastrophe of 1945." For these reasons it was necessary when formulating the principles governing hiring practices and pension levels to create "new provisions that are financially acceptable and that can be carried out in view of the present circumstances."[73]

The ensuing Bundestag debate brought few changes in the law as amended by the committee. The two-promotion limit was retained, although a coalition-sponsored provision was added stating that "documented promotions for personal bravery in the face of the enemy" were to be taken into account. The main attempts at substantive change came from the SPD, which again tried to improve the position of noncommissioned officers by providing pensions after twelve years of service and to expand benefits for late-returning POWs. The coalition parties evaded taking a stand on the latter issue by claiming that it could not be settled until the Beamtengesetz was passed; accordingly, they voted to refer the issue to the committee working on the civil service law, which, as an SPD deputy remarked, amounted to a "first-class burial." To counter the SPD proposal to grant pensions to noncommissioned officers with twelve years of service, the government brought out its big guns, including the finance minister. Referring to his meetings with former officers in late 1949 and early 1950, "when the mood toward the word Wehrmacht was different than it is today," Schäffer maintained he was one of the first to recognize and sympathize with the plight of former professional soldiers. Yet he also had to represent the interests of the taxpayers. The current bill, he argued, provided noncommissioned officers benefits that were legitimate under normal conditions, which had not been the case when the WFVG was created. "I cannot," he concluded, "take as a standard a law promulgated in 1938 by Adolf Hitler whose fulfillment was predicated on a total military victory for the creation of the territory and resources necessary to meet the law's provisions."[74] The SPD proposal was voted down, and an attempt to revive it in the bill's third reading was again rejected.

The rush by party spokespersons to emulate Schäffer's declaration of support for former soldiers while sticking to the committee's version of the bill prompted Carlo Schmid of the SPD to note that he doubted "that this competition for the honor of being the first to have defended the honor of the German soldier will someday enhance the reputation of this house." Schmid then articulated what appeared to be the dominant opinion in the Bundestag regarding the treatment of the former professional soldiers. After castigating the Allied doctrine of collective guilt, he went on to say that "as bad and false as the lesson of collective guilt was, we should not want to create a myth of collective nonguilt." Moreover, he continued, "when one speaks of the honor of the German soldier, one should not only speak of it when discussing professional soldiers, but should also include all those who have bravely [opfermütig] and honorably fought for their fatherland, and this was done by professional and nonprofessional soldiers." It was right and proper for the state to provide for those who had served it, but anyone who received a pension had reciprocal responsibilities. These had not always been observed. "After the First World War," Schmid declared, "those who received pensions did not always fulfill their duty toward the state that provided them." Indeed, "many among those who were pensioned made it their lifelong task to undermine the Weimar Republic. I hope that this will not be repeated this time."[75]

Schmid's remarks found wide support, and he concluded by expressing what was clearly the majority sentiment of the deputies: "There are a great, great number of responsible men among the old professional soldiers who are loyal to this state and who are prepared and determined to participate in the building of German democracy. I direct an appeal to them: the honor of the German soldier is not something exclusively concerned with past activity; this honor is also a matter to be realized today by entering into that loyal relationship to the present state, in its time of need [in seinem Leide wirkend], to which he—justifiably—directs his claims."[76]

Many former professional soldiers were prepared to heed Schmid's words. Although they might have been dissatisfied with the level of benefits provided by the 131 Law, they now had a firm legal basis for their claims and materially they were far better off than before. The new state had rectified many of the inequities of the occupation period and had thereby earned respect and gratitude, though these were often offered only grudgingly. Whereas after the First World War former officers had perceived the Weimar Republic as a threat, after a half decade of uncertainty and deprivation following the Second World War, the Federal Republic appeared as a savior. Like the Bundesversorgungsgesetz before it, the 131 Law helped to legitimize the Republic and the new political order it represented in the eyes of its beneficiaries. By overturning unpopular legislation imposed by the occupying powers, the Bundestag again asserted the growing sovereignty of the new West German state. As the president of the Bundestag stated exultantly following the passage of the 131 Law, "Through this law the intolerable consequences of the lack of German sovereignty have to a large degree been rectified by the German Bundestag."[77] By demonstrating both its willingness and capacity to meet the needs of former officers, the young Republic did much to facilitate their integration into the new postwar order.

SEVEN

THE PRICE OF SUCCESS:
THE SEARCH FOR NEW MISSIONS

Passage of the 131 Law marked the end of the first, and most important, wave of postwar veterans' legislation. The attention of the public and of legislators then turned to the Equalization of Burdens Law (Lastenausgleichsgesetz [LAG]), which provided compensation for those who had suffered material damage as a result of war.[1] Veterans' interest groups naturally complained of the inadequacy of existing legislation and pushed for improvements. Many of these were obtained in a second wave of legislation that began in 1952.[2] With the substantive realization of their original legislative goals, the veterans' organizations, like other interest groups, were confronted with a potential existential crisis.

In a pioneering work written in 1955, Rupert Breitling constructed a typology of interest groups in the Federal Republic. Among these he included what he called the citizens' association (*Staatsbürgerverband*), a type of organization that fell between those that were either more political or more social in nature. These organizations, Breitling contended, had a symbiotic relationship to the state in that their members were organized as citizens and their actions were directed toward the state. Most of these organizations, Breitling observed, in fact owed their existence to a negative sense of citizenship since their members were organized out of the conviction that they had for no reason of their own been put at a disadvantage, "because as a citizen of the state [Zwangsmitglied des Staatsverbandes] they had been made to suffer by the state for the state."[3] The citizens' associations, therefore, were composed of persons who held the state responsible for the injury that they had suffered and sought recompense from the state for their suffering. This negative sense of citizenship could constitute a danger to the state, since it could lead to the repudiation of the state, or it could be converted into a positive sense of citizenship, if the state recognized the injury and provided compensation.[4]

The interest groups representing the various categories of veterans that we have investigated in this study—the war-disabled, former prisoners of war, and former professional soldiers—all belong to the type of citizens' association described by Breitling. As their demands were met and they became anchored in the elaborate neocorporate institutional fabric of the Federal Republic, their potential as a negative factor in the Republic's social and political life declined.[5] In varying degrees they were coopted and became state-supporting elements.

With the realization of their original legislative goals, veterans' organizations, like other interest groups, were faced—to a greater or lesser degree—with the need to justify their further existence.[6] For a variety of reasons the war victims' organizations—the Reichsbund and the Verband der Kriegsbeschädigten—were able to continue to focus primarily on their original goals, but both the Verband der Heimkehrer and the Bund versorgungsberechtigter ehemaliger Wehrmachtsangehöriger undertook substantial efforts to redefine and expand their missions. For the former, the impetus was primarily internal and structural in nature; for the latter, it was more the result of external forces.

AS WE HAVE SEEN, anger with the Überbrückungsgesetz and concern over the impending Bundesversorgungsgesetz gave new impetus to the stalled efforts to unify the two major war victims' organizations.[7] Continued division, it was feared, would weaken the case of the war victims and bring defeat in its wake. The government would be able to play the two organizations off against each other, and the parties would be able to discount their demands, claiming that they were exaggerated in order to win the competition for new members. The continued division between the two major organizations also opened the way for new groups, whose presence would only further divide the war victims' movement and weaken the existing organizations. The recently founded Bund Deutscher Kriegsbeschädigter und Kriegerhinterbliebener, for example, was claiming—among other things—that neither the VdK nor the Reichsbund could be effective since their leadership was dominated by SPD members who, because their party was in opposition, would not have the ear of the government.[8] Most importantly the rank and file of both organizations were demanding that they unite in order to be a more effective force in shaping the BVG, which began to be drafted in the early summer of 1950.

In response to this pressure, negotiations for unification had been initiated under the leadership of Erich Rossmann.[9] The first meeting of the unification committee met in Stuttgart in mid-July. It was composed of six members from each organization. Continuity was reflected in the fact that the starting point was to be the 1949 Kassel proposal of the Reichsbund, while hopes for a fresh start were manifested in the decision that delegates should be younger persons who had not been involved in the earlier negotiations.[10] That this would suffice to remove entirely the rancor between the two organizations was quickly shown to be unrealistic, since the representatives immediately began to jab at one another over the deficiencies of the other's organizational structure and to complain of purported unwarranted attacks. Such wrangling became a discordant *Leitmotiv* throughout the negotiations, providing an unsettling counterpart to the constant professions of support for unity.

The desire for unity prevailed, however, and a subcommittee was formed to begin work on a set of bylaws that was acceptable to both organizations. Six general propositions provided the basis, among which were the continued acceptance of civilian disabled members, political and religious neutrality, and the renunciation of war as a means of resolving political differences.[11] Debate over the substantial issues of the structure of the new organization and of the BVG were consciously postponed.[12] Rossmann worked to keep the focus on points of agreement before going on to the more divisive issues. At the conclusion of the meeting, he was asked to write a letter to the executive committees of both the Reichsbund and the VdK requesting them to direct their members at all levels to cease attacks upon their rivals for the duration of the negotiations. Past experience had shown that without such a truce (*Burgfrieden*) negotiations were likely to be torpedoed.

The bylaw commission held its first meeting two weeks later in Altena.[13] It began with a number of complaints about violations of the *Burgfrieden*. Rossmann tried to exclude discussion of infractions and was again instructed to inform the leaders of the respective organizations of the need to hold to the *Burgfrieden* during the negotiations. The committee succeeded in producing a detailed draft of bylaws regulating nonessential matters but still left open the critical issues of the organizational structure of the united war victims' organization and its specific demands regarding the structure of the BVG.

By late summer the question of the structure of the BVG had become an important issue. Discussions with Labor Ministry officials had revealed that while the Reichsbund and VdK were united on most features of the newly drafted BVG, they differed on the question of the proposed structuring of the pensions for the war-disabled. The VdK supported the two-level structure favored by the Labor Ministry and the government, while the Reichsbund insisted on a unitary pension.[14] The unitary structure backed by the Reichsbund promised higher pensions for the average recipient, and in view of the mounting anger and unrest of the war victims, which had begun to manifest itself in protest demonstrations by members of both organizations, the issue offered an irresistible club to the Reichsbund with which to beat the VdK. The smaller organization hoped to use the VdK's support of the two-tier system as a means of detaching discontented members from the VdK and attracting them, as well as previously unorganized war victims, to its ranks. Negotiations in the following months were dominated by the twin issues of social policy and parity. The Reichsbund sought to use social policy to discredit the VdK and demanded parity as a means to offset its numerical inferiority. The VdK sought either to exclude the social policy issue or, preferably, to pin the Reichsbund down in support of the two-tier system; while it was willing to grant parity in the composition of the committees involved in the unification negotiations, it adamantly refused to consider granting parity in electing delegates to the proposed general meeting in which the unification process was to culminate and at which unresolved issues would be decided.

The second meeting of the bylaw committee took place on the day following the BVG's introduction in the Bundestag. "Continuation of the discussion on the bylaws," Rossmann noted, "was not possible at this meeting." The reason for this was a heated debate over the problem of the two organizations' differing positions regarding the proposed BVG that had publicly come to light during the previous day's Bundestag debate. The VdK's leadership wanted to settle the question once and for all. As far as Rossmann was concerned, the differences that had emerged were not all that serious, but, he acknowledged, "they played a large role in the position of the Reichsbund and often became the source of propagandistic outbursts that caused substantial conflicts between the two organizations."[15] The point was that the VdK, although expressing reservations, had given its support to the draft's two-level pension structure while the Reichsbund had rejected the law because of it. Fearful that the Reichsbund would be able to capitalize on its hard-nosed opposition, the VdK sought to postpone debate on the issue and to smother it under the *Burgfrieden*. A social policy committee was established, composed of experts from the two organizations who had been summoned to the meeting, to draw up a general statement. The committee's report essentially tried to evade the issue by stressing points of agreement and concluding that "aside from the . . . question of the unitary or divided pension there are no fundamental differences of opinion."[16] In Rossmann's view, they had agreed to disagree and had left the question open in the hopes that it could be resolved in further discussions. The main thing was that the unification committee's work had not been scuttled over the issue.

In spite of Rossmann's hopes, the situation continued to deteriorate. The next meeting of the bylaw committee was set for October in Bremen and was to be arranged by the Reichsbund. The latter rather heavy-handedly tried to dictate the agenda of the meeting and to influence the selection of VdK representatives, a move that infuriated the VdK and exasperated Rossmann. When the meeting, rescheduled for Hamburg, was finally held on 20 October, most of the VdK representatives remained in Bonn, presumably in order to participate in meetings that had been occasioned by the recent passage of the BVG. It was now the turn of the Reichsbund to be angered, and the Hamburg meeting, Rossmann noted, took place under "an unfavorable star." Although the passage of the BVG to a large degree nullified earlier arguments about the need for unity to force its passage, neither side could publicly abandon the talks, especially since the rank and file continued to press for the unification of the two war victims' organizations.[17] Accordingly, a new meeting of the unification committee (as well as other important representatives of the two organizations) was scheduled for Wiesbaden in January.

At the Wiesbaden meeting, the differences dividing the two organizations were again thrashed out. Speakers for the VdK claimed that the passage of the BVG with near unanimous support had made the question of the pension structure a nonissue. The Reichsbund responded by arguing that the interests of the war victims could only be effectively represented by a unified and centralized organization. Each side continued to stress the need for unity but tried to ensure that it would come on its own terms. Resolutions were introduced by both organizations expressing their willingness to unite, while at the same time trying to push the other into a corner and forcing it to accept the onus for the collapse of the talks. Finally, the unification committee drafted a compromise resolution that left open as many questions as it addressed. At the meeting's end, a rather vague press communique, under the hopeful heading "On the Path to Unity [Auf dem Wege zur Einheit]," was issued stating that the leaders of the two organizations had concluded that there were "no fundamental, unbridgeable obstacles to unification . . . which could not be resolved through negotiations." Accordingly, the bylaw committee had been charged to continue its work on a new charter; this was to be accompanied by efforts to develop a common social policy that would then be placed, along with the new charter, before a general meeting of the two organizations.[18]

The bylaw committee dutifully met in Bad Sachsa 2–4 March and worked out an elaborate set of bylaws. While the minutiae of unification were being painstakingly delineated, the larger process had begun to unravel irreversibly, however. The Reichsbund insisted that there be parity at the proposed general meeting. This, naturally, was opposed by the VdK. Meanwhile, charges and countercharges of violations of the *Burgfrieden* escalated. The Reichsbund was accused of using the VdK's support of the BVG to woo away discontented members, while the VdK was charged with reviving the old smear tactic that the Reichsbund was tainted with Communist influences. Rossmann, though apparently not sharing the VdK's hard-line opposition on the question of parity, began to lose patience with the Reichsbund, feeling that it was primarily responsible for the violations of the *Burgfrieden*. The Reichsbund in turn accused Rossmann of having ceased to be impartial and of favoring his own organization. The downward spiral continued. Both sides appeared to be going out of their way to find reasons to justify breaking off negotiations. The faltering attempts to keep the unification talks going finally broke down in a storm of mutual acrimony.[19]

In the end, Rossmann placed the major responsibility for the failure on the Reichsbund, an opinion later shared by Breitling.[20] Yet he acknowledged, as he had throughout the negotiations, that there were a good number of persons in both organizations, including many in high leadership positions, who had been opposed to unification and who had worked against it from the start.[21]

Thus, as with the earlier attempts at unification, the latest round of negotiations not only failed to overcome the divisions within the war victims' movement but also hardened them. A variety of factors contributed to the continued division of the war victims' organizations. Plain organizational egotism undoubtedly topped the list. By the time the Federal Republic was founded, both the Reichsbund and the VdK had become well established in their respective zones. The falling of the zonal lines and the creation of an enlarged arena of organizational activity touched off a competitive struggle that created ill will and lessened the willingness to compromise.

The continued division was abetted by other factors as well. The long-term, structural nature of the war victim problem and the immensity of the affected constituency permitted the luxury of division and encouraged competition. The very fact that the BVG had been passed in spite of the divisions among the war victims' organizations lessened the immediate pressure for unification; at the same time, the law's inadequacies, coupled with its provisional character—that is, the fact that many aspects of it were linked to the state's fiscal and economic growth—assured the war victims' organizations' future role as interest groups and encouraged continued competition among them as each sought to convince the war victims that it was the most effective representative of their interests. Another factor that tended to harden the divisions was that the existing groups were organizationally anchored in the administrative structure of the BVG: on the federal level, as members of the national Advisory Council; on the local level, as advocates, administrative advisers, and facilitators for war victims seeking assistance in receiving benefits.[22] All these considerations worked to undergird existing divisions.

Most interest groups claim to be more than an organization for the representation of their members' material interests. To this end, they commonly ascribe social and moral attributes to their work. The achievement of an organization's original goals produces an organizational imperative to expand its mission, to find new goals that will justify its further existence. As we will see, this development was most clearly manifested in the cases of the Verband der Heimkehrer and the Bund versorgungsberechtigter ehemaliger Wehrmachtsangehöriger. The war victims' organizations were no exception to these general rules of interest group behavior. Like the others, the war victims' organizations stressed their role in promoting and preserving comradeship. In addition to lobbying, they provided other services for members, for example, housing and sports programs.[23] Like other interest groups, they claimed that their efforts worked to prevent the radicalization of their constituents and that their existence helped to support democracy and its institutions.[24] To a greater or lesser degree, veterans' organizations claimed the role of surrogate family. This was especially true of the war victims' organizations, and while at first sight this claim may appear to be just one more example of organizational hyperbole, it had a real basis.[25] The social and familial aspects of the war victims' organizations were more genuine, natural, and unforced than those of other interest groups, and this decreased their need to develop the more extensive organizational missions that characterized the development of other veterans' organizations. This sense of family was rooted in the fact that the war-disabled were permanently marked by war and were set off from the rest of society by their disability. While the other organizations represented *former* POWs and *former* professional soldiers, there were no *former* war victims, only war victims. Unlike the others, the disabled could never be completely compensated or completely reintegrated into society through pensions and/or jobs. Through their disfigured bodies and broken health, they remained a permanent "community of fate [Schicksalsgemeinschaft]." The disabled remained outsiders in a society of nondisabled, and this promoted a sense of family among them. They shared and understood each others' problems in a way that the rest of society could not.

A poignant example of this was the discussion in the pages of *Die Fackel* on the gender-specific problems faced by war victims that took place under the rubric "The Disabled Veteran and Women [Der Versehrte und die Frauen]." It was initiated with the reprint of an article from a women's magazine that detailed the problems of the war-disabled veteran. The article began with a general analysis of the psychological problems of the war-disabled—the feelings of inadequacy and lack of self-esteem that accompanied physical disability and the way in which these feelings often produced self-pity and anger. Such feelings naturally complicated the relationship of the war-disabled veteran to his spouse or potential spouse. One of the main purposes of the article was to warn women of the danger of either callously disregarding the special difficulties of a disabled partner or of babying them ("zum Baby zu machen"). *Die Fackel*'s editors drew their readers' attention in particular to the concluding section of the article in which the war-disabled veteran was described as "the prototype of the present day German male. He has been robbed of the qualities that appeal to the esteem of women. He is not impressive [repräsentabel], chivalrous, or especially 'tender.' He is physically and spiritually sick, tortured, and irritable, filled with numb resignation or smoldering, blind feelings of hatred, which can be directed against everything and everyone."[26]

The article amply fulfilled the editors' intention to promote discussion. In the following months, it generated a steady stream of letters. The first responses came from disabled veterans protesting the negative generalizations contained in the article and maintaining that the majority had adapted to their circumstances and led productive lives.[27] Later letters expanded the discussion in a manner that threw a revealing light on the problem of disability and gender relations in post–World War II Germany. A male reader wrote of the difficulty the war-disabled faced in working up the courage to approach women and their fear that if one agreed to marry them it was "only because she had no other offers."[28] Another spoke of the loneliness and isolation felt by the disabled, surrounded by those who were healthy and indifferent to their difficulties. "I often," he admitted, "long secretly for the time [when I was] in the hospital, where one was among 'one's own' and where one could count on the support of one's fellow sufferers."[29] That it was not men alone who were affected was shown by a letter from a disabled woman, who noted that while the problems of disabled men were justifiably a focus of attention, one should not overlook those of women who had been disabled. As a consequence of bombing attacks, women had been injured and suffered the same wounds that soldiers had; yet society tended to ignore them "perhaps because it is a more unaesthetic picture to see a pretty young woman on crutches than a man, which in today's circumstances is hardly uncommon." When it came to finding a mate, she continued, disabled women were more disadvantaged than men since "most men still consider a woman's looks first. She should be beautiful, well-formed and have excellent legs" (the writer had had a leg amputated). Moreover, a disabled woman was suspect as a future wife, since it was feared that she would not be up to the demands of housework. A man who had lost a leg, on the other hand, had no difficulty in finding a woman to marry him. The writer ended her letter with the plea that society consider not only the plight of disabled men but of disabled women as well.[30] The loneliness of the disabled was echoed by a (nonwar) disabled woman ("zivilbeschädigtes Mädel"), who noted how much more at ease the disabled were with others who shared their fate and suggested that *Die Fackel* initiate a correspondence section in which VdK members could make contact with others. "Perhaps," she concluded, through such a service "two lonely people could find a life partner."[31] Her suggestion sparked further discussion and found considerable support. Letters followed debating the pros and cons of marriage between war victims, and in December *Die Fackel* began to run personal advertisements for members who were seeking spouses.[32]

For all their auxiliary activities, however, the war victims' organizations' main role remained their lobbying to improve legislative benefits. These efforts were rewarded by a series of improvements of the BVG in the 1950s, the passage of a new law for the severely disabled (Schwerbeschädigtengesetz) in 1953, and the far-reaching reforms of the Federal Republic's pension systems in the 1960s and 1970s.[33] The main general issue of the time that affected the war victims' organizations was rearmament. Their position on the issue was colored by their desire to remain "politically neutral," their inherent pacifist tendencies, and their self-interests. Eventually they supported rearmament as a necessary evil, but they coupled their support with the demand that the government must take care of the victims of the last war before it began to divert resources to a new remilitarization.[34]

Unlike the VdH and BvW—who, once they had achieved their primary legislative objectives, chose or were forced to expand their goals—the Reichsbund and VdK could remain for the most part focused on their original objectives. The size and the nature of their constituency postponed and to a large degree obviated the need, which soon confronted other veterans' organizations, to seek new missions. When structural demographic changes did finally begin to erode their initial bases of support—the war-disabled and the survivors of those killed in the war—the war victims' organizations were, ironically, saved by the initially unwelcome strictures imposed by the Allies that they accept and represent the interests of the civilian-disabled as well as the war-disabled.

FOR THE representatives of former prisoners of war, the main problem was not unity, since this had been achieved with the founding of the VdH in March 1950, but the need to redefine and expand their organization's goals once its original demands had been met. Like all interest groups, the VdH responded to legislation directed to the needs of its members in a schizophrenic fashion: taking credit for it on the one hand, and on the other decrying its inadequacy, which, of course, justified further lobbying efforts. The Heim-kehrergesetz was criticized by the VdH, and the law's failures were used as evidence of the need for the further existence of an organization that would press the interests of former POWs.[35] In the following years, the VdH suc-cessfully worked for an expansion of the HKG's provisions.[36] As we have seen, the law's primary purpose was to provide assistance for the reintegration of former POWs into society. Since the problem of returning POWs had discrete structural limits, the urgency of the problem began to decline as the years progressed and the German economy began to improve. Leaders of the VdH had to face the fact that the very success of their organization threatened its future. In order to justify its further existence, the legislative agenda had to be expanded. In fact, this had been realized from the start. Even before the foundation of the VdH, POW organizations had raised the issue not only of assistance for reintegration but also of compensation for the time and hardship of captivity. The labor performed as POWs, it was argued, represented a form of reparations; since reparations were to be paid by the entire German nation, but had in fact only been rendered by the POWs, the POWs were entitled to compensation by the remainder of the German people. Initially, it was ex-pected that these claims would be handled under the legislation dealing with the equalization of burdens (*Lastenausgleich*), but when it became clear that that POWs would be excluded from the Equalization of Burdens Law, the VdH began to push with increasing insistence for a separate piece of legisla-tion that would provide compensation to former POWs.

The VdH's campaign for a POW Compensation Law provides a classic example of interest group politics.[37] The campaign attracted new members, since the law promised material benefits to virtually all POWs, including those who had already received help from the HKG as well as those who had been successfully reintegrated without needing assistance from the HKG. Once the VdH began to push for the Compensation Law, its membership soared.[38] The decline of the VdH that had followed the achievement of its original goal was arrested; at the same time, the swelling ranks of the organization increased its chances of achieving its new objective. The campaign thus set in motion a cycle of positive feedback. By making new demands on the state, the VdH's leadership simultaneously created a renewed need for the organization, which helped to secure its survival; this, not incidentally, also ensured continued employment for the organization's largely middle-class functionaries who otherwise would have had difficulty finding socially acceptable forms of em-ployment.[39] The growing membership of the VdH increased its political clout, which in turn enhanced its prospects of success, and since the secret of success is success, this worked to increase its odds of survival.

The VdH doggedly reiterated its claim that former POWs were just as entitled to compensation as other groups who had received it, for example, expellees and political victims of the Third Reich.[40] While the government remained cool to such claims, Bundestag deputies were more vulnerable to the VdH's pressure. In the fall of 1952, the issue became a subject of debate in the Bundestag, and in late November it passed a resolution requesting the government to present the Bundestag with the proposal for a law that would recognize the sacrifices of the POWs and provide them with "suitable compensation and necessary assistance."[41]

Already burdened with the enormous outlays for war victims, LAG recipients, and beneficiaries of other social legislation, the government dragged its feet, hoping to keep payments to *Heimkehrer* limited to those who were in need and to avoid expensive across-the-board compensatory legislation. Although some desultory efforts to draft a bill were made, the proposal remained unfinished and was never submitted to the Bundestag. After six months' inaction, accompanied by growing pressure from the rapidly expanding VdH, the Bundestag again took up the issue. Partisan political considerations were not absent in the timing of the Bundestag's renewed interest. The first legislative period was coming to an end, and deputies wanted to be able to go to the electorate in the upcoming election campaign saying they had passed a law that recognized the sacrifice of the *Heimkehrer*. This put the CDU/CSU deputies in a bind, since the finance minister, and the cabinet, made it clear that there was no money to fund such a law. The coalition parties tried to finesse the issue by introducing a bill for an expanded HKG, for which funds existed.[42] The SPD (supported by several of the smaller parties) responded by submitting a proposal for a Compensation Law along the lines demanded by the VdH.[43] The government's supporters in the Committee for War Victim and Prisoner of War Questions tried to block discussion of the SPD proposal, or at least to postpone it until the CDU bill had been dealt with, but in a close vote the committee agreed to draft a law based on the SPD proposal, which was dutifully submitted to the Bundestag in June.[44] The impending elections (set for early September) made the outcome inevitable. Few deputies were willing to go on record as opposing the law, and it passed easily. The cabinet gave its approval but, invoking article 113 of the Basic Law, made the law's implementation contingent on funding, which delayed it indefinitely.[45]

The VdH was outraged. The delay was portrayed as a defeat for democracy ("verlorene Schlacht der Demokratie"), and massive street demonstrations were threatened unless the law was immediately implemented.[46] The issue remained unresolved until January 1954, when the law was finally funded and promulgated.[47] This, according to the VdH, represented a "victory for democracy," and it expressed its relief that it had not had to call its members into the streets, asserting that if this had been necessary it would have been done with a heavy heart. Seeking to dispel the notion that the organization was simply following selfish interests, the VdH further maintained that the driving force behind the demonstrations, had they taken place, would not have been "material demands, but the ethical value of this law and the desire to defend a decision of the Bundestag, the supreme constitutional body of our young democracy."[48]

While the VdH could rightfully celebrate the passage of the Prisoner of War Compensation Law (Kriegsgefangenenentschädigungsgesetz [KgfEG]) as a victory and as a proof of its prowess, the law's passage presented the organization with a dilemma. Although the KgfEG secured a limited future role for the VdH by anchoring it, like the war victims' organizations, in the law's administrative apparatus,[49] POW legislation, unlike that for war victims, did not involve long-term pensions but essentially onetime payments. This meant that, unlike the war victims' organizations, which could justify their further existence on the need to fight for improved pensions, the VdH's fight for the material interests of former POWs had now largely come to an end. The problem was compounded by the fact that by 1954 most German POWs had returned, and the organization's role as an agent to effect repatriation and to facilitate reintegration had become superfluous.[50] Thus the VdH's greatest triumph was followed by the strongest threat to its existence it had yet experienced.

With the successful achievement of legislation to secure the reintegration and compensation of the *Heimkehrer*, the homogeneous collective needs of former POWs, which provided a common bond for membership in the VdH, began to dissolve. Although material demands continued to be made, it was clear that the organization's further existence hinged upon the development of new missions. Like other interest groups, the VdH had from the beginning played upon the sympathies of the general population, while at the same time asserting that its members did not want pity but desired only justice. In the course of time, again like the other veterans' interest organizations, it developed a series of rationales to support its claims for material assistance, and these arguments eventually evolved into an organizational ideology (*Verbandsideologie*). While the ideologies of the different organizations naturally varied in their particulars, they all underlined the special character of the social group involved, extolled its positive virtues, and stressed the desirability of harnessing these virtues in support of the new political order. At the same time, the negative consequences of the state's failing to win the support of the affected constituency were painted in the darkest possible colors.

According to the propagandists of the VdH, the POW camps, especially those in the East, where the majority of the *Heimkehrer* had been interned, had forged a group of men who were immune to the virus of communism as well as that of national socialism. Their harsh and inhuman treatment at the hands of the Soviets had revealed the true nature of the Soviet system and ensured that they would not heed the call of Communist pied pipers. It was also claimed, though somewhat less convincingly, that the experience of the war and the horror and humiliation of their experiences as POWs had made the *Heimkehrer* aware of the destructive consequences of national socialism and the falseness of its doctrines.[51] Steeled by their adversity and stripped of all false illusions, the *Heimkehrer* were portrayed as ideal supporters of the new democratic state. Like the war victims, and to a lesser degree the former professional soldiers, the *Heimkehrer* were transformed into a "community of experience [Erlebnisgemeinschaft]" whose negative experience was now given a positive evaluation.[52]

Here we encounter one of the most interesting and fundamental departures from the post–World War I political environment: after 1945 it was not the heroes of the war, the front fighters, but the war's victims that were to provide the political role models for the postwar state.[53] The support of the new state by the *Heimkehrer* did not come without cost, however. Like that of the war victims and the former professional soldiers, it had to be purchased by meeting their "just" and "moderate" demands. The leaders of the VdH, like those of the other organizations, found themselves in the rather ambiguous position of extolling the democratic potential of their members, on the one hand, while warning of the dangers of their possible radicalization, on the other.[54]

Following the passage of the KgfEG and the return of the last groups of POWs, the VdH began to stress and to develop its pedagogic-ideological role. The development of this new focus, of course, was closely tied to its leaders' desire to ensure the organization's (as well as their own) survival. Yet, as a perceptive observer of the VdH's evolution has noted, it would be unfair to characterize the change as being entirely due to cynical manipulation from above. Instead, what had previously been a secondary aspect of the organization's activity became primary, as its original purpose increasingly declined in importance.[55]

The increased emphasis and articulation of the VdH's *Verbandsideologie* helped to create a more sharply profiled self-image and to bind members to the organization at a time when the earlier bonds of material self-interest were beginning to unravel. *Heimkehrer* were portrayed as "bearers of experience [Erlebnisträger]," whose task was to convey the knowledge and strength gained from the POW experience to society as a whole. As the theme was developed, a certain contradiction became evident between the claims made by the VdH leaders about the group's constituency and the actions of the former POWs themselves: on the one hand, the *Heimkehrer* were presumed to be possessed by the need to pass on the lessons of their experience, while, on the other, the VdH's leadership was obviously having to expend considerable energy in its effort to convince members of this need and to arouse their enthusiasm over the new mission.[56]

At the VdH's third congress in 1955, its bylaws were expanded in order to signal and institutionalize the organization's transformation from a "simple community of interest [reine Zweckgemeinschaft]" into a "community of fate [Schicksalsgemeinschaft]." The change was preceded by a debate over the VdH's fundamental principles whose purpose was to construct an updated program. In the end the leadership's efforts to transform the VdH's goals were successful, but it was not achieved without resistance, and the establishment of a new mission unrelated to material interests failed to stem the loss of members.[57]

The VdH's emergence as an agent of civic education was accompanied by a subtle but significant change in its relationship to the government. Whereas earlier, as a pure interest group, it had represented the material interests of its members *against* the government, it now found itself increasingly functioning as an interest group *for* the political system vis-à-vis its members. In its new capacity, the VdH worked to integrate its members politically and ideologically into the new political order by "overcoming their reservations" and inculcating them with the "spirit of constitutional [rechtsstaatlicher] democracy."[58] The so-called Mehlem Discussion Weeks that were inaugurated in 1954 reflected the new symbiotic relationship. On the one hand, they provided an opportunity to advertise the organization's mission of civic education and to demonstrate its desire to contribute to the stabilization of the Federal Republic; on the other, they offered a ready forum for the Republic's political and institutional leaders.[59]

Two of the larger political questions that the VdH felt compelled to address were rearmament and anticommunism. Building on the fact that many of its members had suffered firsthand the cruelties of communism, the VdH billed itself as a "bulwark against communism," a solid bloc of citizens who had been immunized against Communist infiltration and contagion. Although the VdH at first waffled and initially linked its support of rearmament to demands for the release of all remaining war prisoners, including those imprisoned as war criminals, as both an "anti-Communist" and "state-supporting" organization it steadily moved toward support of the government's policy. As the debate over rearmament developed, the VdH also began to claim a role as the representative of the "war generation" and to insist that it be given a voice in the shaping of the new Bundeswehr.[60] In its self-proclaimed role as a bridge between the old and the new army, the VdH sought not only to carve out a new institutional niche but also to tap a new, potentially self-perpetuating and endless reservoir of future members.[61] These ambitions quickly brought it into competition with other veterans' organizations that had emerged on the scene and that had staked out for their own expansion the same territory that the VdH was now seeking to occupy.

IF IN 1950–51 the major institutional issue for the war victims' organizations was unity and that for the VdH was the search for new missions, the BvW found itself confronted with both. Just as the passage of its legislative agenda created an institutional crisis within the VdH, so success in the legislative arena produced a certain malaise in the BvW. With the passage of the 131 Law, its fight for the restoration of pensions for former professional soldiers largely came to an end. Even though the BvW had serious complaints about the law, it was recognized as a fact of life, and the leadership on the whole realized that the basic framework of the pension system had been created with its passage.[62] To be sure, the law was immediately decried as being inadequate, and the fight for the rectification of its flaws and the expansion of benefits associated with it ensured the future of the BvW as an interest group. In this regard the BvW's situation was more similar to that of the war victims' organizations than to that of the VdH, since the structure of the 131 Law, like that of the BVG, openly invited continued and sustained pressure for improvement.[63] Nonetheless, the law's passage was followed by a drop-off in membership and produced an institutional crisis.[64] The BvW's leaders could and did claim that the fight against the defamation of the Wehrmacht must be continued, but since they themselves had made the restoration of pensions the centerpiece of their campaign against defamation, the passage of the 131 Law robbed such arguments of much of their force. Moreover the urgency of the continued fight for the release of military leaders imprisoned as war criminals declined with the ongoing return of imprisoned officers, either through the completion of their sentences or the granting of amnesties.[65] Thus, the passage of the 131 Law both ensured and limited the further existence of the BvW.

External developments soon offered new opportunities for the BvW, however. As the 131 Law was wending its way through the legislative labyrinth, a new issue emerged that, in the view of the Bund's leadership, opened promising possibilities for future activity. The debate over rearmament, which reached new intensity after the outbreak of the Korean War in June 1950, unleashed a flurry of activity within the Federal Republic's heretofore largely dormant "military subculture," and the BvW, as its most visible representative, moved to place itself as the leader and mouthpiece of a united war generation, whose voice, it was claimed, must now be heard.[66]

The possibility of West German rearmament had been raised even before the founding of the Federal Republic. By 1950 the issue occupied not only the victors but also the new chancellor, Konrad Adenauer, who hoped to use the issue as a means to pry concessions from the Allies.[67] The explosiveness of the issue, coupled with significant differences among the Western Allies, initially prevented any concrete action. The outbreak of the Korean War, however, marked a watershed in the approach to the problem, both in Germany and in the Allied nations.[68] In August Adenauer made it known that the Federal Republic was willing to make a military contribution to the defense of Europe; at the September 1950 meeting of the Allied foreign ministers in New York, the United States, the foremost proponent of West German rearmament, was able to gain acceptance of the policy, at least in principle. With China's entry into the Korean conflict in December 1950, the pressure for West German rearmament mounted and became a heated topic of debate both within and outside the Federal Republic.[69]

Adenauer had planted the seed of a future Defense Ministry even before the outbreak of the Korean War. In May 1950 he named Gerhard Graf von Schwerin as his personal military adviser. Schwerin's office, originally little more than a secret hole in the wall, was expanded in August and renamed the Center for Home Service (Zentrale für Heimatdienst). Though expanded, its role was still kept secret since its activity was technically illegal. The Zentrale was not the only place where Germany's military future was being debated and planned. Groups of former officers throughout the Federal Republic gathered to discuss the issue, and their ideas, whether solicited or not, were passed on to the chancellor and to the press.[70] There were divisions over what form the German "contribution" should take and especially over the question of preconditions, that is, what concessions were to be made in return by the former victors. The first issue was mostly technical in nature and to a large extent was taken out of German hands by external developments. The second was more political and occasioned wider and more bitter discussion. Both were discussed at the Himmerod meeting of military experts held in October 1950.[71] Here general agreement was reached on strictly military questions and the need for substantive reforms to be introduced in the future German military establishment. With regard to preconditions, however, the Himmerod meeting did not close but further widened the divide between those who were willing to rearm quickly on the basis of moderate concessions and good-faith promises for the future and those who were determined to confront the German and Allied governments with opposition and boycott unless their far-reaching demands were met.[72]

Although the divisions among the former officers, including Adenauer's own military advisers, may have complicated the issue for the chancellor, they were probably not entirely unwelcome since they allowed him to play one faction off against the other in order to better achieve his own objectives. He, too, was determined to trade rearmament for concessions, and his demands in many cases were identical or similar to those of the more pragmatic and moderate elements of the former Wehrmacht officers. In the summer and fall of 1950, Adenauer moved to make contact with these elements and to mend his fences with them. As we have seen, a meeting was arranged between the chancellor and representatives of the BvW in August, followed by a meeting, chaired by Schwerin, between representatives of the former officers and labor leaders to resolve the alleged boycott of the factory councils against former officers.[73] While on balance Adenauer remained leery of the veterans' organizations and probably would have preferred not to have to deal with them, he and his supporters were aware of the potential utility of their support. On the one hand, the *Soldatenbünde* could be used as a counterweight to the prevailing *ohne mich* attitude within German society and, in addition, as a means to win the support of former officers who would be needed to staff the new German army. On the other hand, they could be used to reinforce the government's demands on the Allies. Thus, the government was not averse to veterans' organizations as such, providing that they were reasonably compliant. Throughout 1951 both the Chancellor's Office and Schwerin's Zentrale encouraged efforts to create a single, unified veterans' organization that would speak for all veterans and would support the government's policy of rearmament.

These developments had an enormous impact on veterans, especially former officers. Adenauer's plans were not popular with the public as a whole and met a mixed reaction among those most immediately affected by them. To the surprise of the Allies, especially the Americans, the supposedly incorrigibly militaristic Germans refused to heed the siren call of rearmament. Instead there was widespread resistance and apathy. The scars of Germany's defeat were still very visible, and the outlay of limited state resources for military spending, when so much remained to be done to overcome the country's material and human destruction from the previous war, was widely resisted. Even former officers were divided on the issue. While some, especially those who hoped to continue their careers, found the issue of burning concern, others, who had found a place in postwar civilian society, were indifferent.

Many former officers shared the *ohne mich* sentiments of the population at large—some from the conviction that war was futile, others out of resentment for the way they had been treated after the war. Aside from the pacifists and those on the antidemocratic right, who refused to do anything to help either the Allies or the new democratic government in Bonn, most former officers supported rearmament, even while voicing opinions that often sounded little different from those that came from the hard-core *ohne mich* camp on the right. Their reluctance to endorse the government's policy was generally more opportunistic than principled. They did not dispute the need to rearm but differed over the price that should be paid for their support and participation.[74] An end to the "defamation" of the army was the universal demand. This encompassed demands for the release of soldiers imprisoned for war crimes, for assurances that the new German army would enjoy full equality—that is, that German forces would not be used as "cannon fodder" or as "Hiwis"[75]— and for public statements by both the government of the Federal Republic and the Allies restoring the "honor" of the Wehrmacht. Positions of the veterans' organizations on rearmament in late 1950 reflected a combination of resentment, *Schadenfreude*, and the hope of gaining concessions. In October 1950, for example, the executive committee of the BvW sent a resolution to Adenauer stating that it considered the discussions of "measures for the security of the Federal Republic to be a vital question for the German people and Western civilization" and that making the decision on the question was "exclusively the task of the government [der politischen Führung]." The BvW felt it could justifiably state that former professional soldiers "would not evade an appeal, in the case of pressing need, to defend Germany and Europe." But, it continued,

> we are also convinced that only a person with a healthy feeling of honor can be a good soldier. For this reason we feel compelled to note with great seriousness that the ending of the German soldier's defamation is the prerequisite for the revival of a solid army [Soldatentum] that is supported by the trust of the people. . . .
>
> The elimination of defamation includes the recognition and fulfillment of the legal claims of all former professional soldiers and their survivors.
>
> Moreover, in the recognition that an honorable German soldier cannot be expected to bear arms so long as comrades, who in the view of soldiers did nothing more than carry out their duty, remain imprisoned, we request, Mr. Chancellor, that you and the government exert your influence most strongly with the High Commission so that these soldiers [that is, those still imprisoned for war crimes] regain their freedom and honor.[76]

Even such tepid "support" caused difficulties. It was attacked by many in the Bund as being too "unconditional," and the BvW's leadership was accused of having sold out by the more radical elements of the legion of self-proclaimed spokespersons of the "war generation" that began to emerge in the wake of the rearmament controversy.

Another issue that divided veterans, especially former officers, was the question of honoring the Twentieth of July 1944. Seeking to find a usable past, the leaders of the Federal Republic had seized upon the conspirators of the abortive assassination plot against Hitler as the prime, symbolic examples of the "other" Germany, the Germany of opposition, which was to provide the moral and ideological foundations for the new Republic.[77] This had a twofold impact on former members of the Wehrmacht. On the one hand, the fact that many of the most active conspirators were military officers reinforced the myth of the army as an institution untainted by nazism, a bastion of resistance, which had functioned as a haven for opponents of national socialism during the Third Reich.[78] On the other hand, it called into question the actions of the vast majority of soldiers who had continued to honor their oath to Hitler and had remained loyal to the regime during and after the unsuccessful assassination attempt. Whether out of conviction or a sense of guilt for their opportunism and failure to act, many officers denounced the conspirators as traitors who had betrayed the nation by perpetrating another "stab in the back." In their view the glorification of the officers of the Twentieth of July constituted a new "defamation" of the army, one that was all the more despicable because it was pursued by Germans. Even among those who recognized the honorable intentions of the would-be assassins, it was generally felt that their actions had weakened the war effort and created the circumstances that had led to Germany's unconditional surrender, a view apparently shared by the majority of Germans.[79] The voices of the opponents of the Twentieth of July and their counterarguments celebrating the virtues of discipline and obedience and the necessity for loyalty to oaths grew in intensity as the fear that one's position on the Twentieth of July might become a litmus test in the selection of officers for the new German army.[80]

As the debate over rearmament gathered momentum, the dispute over the meaning of the Twentieth of July also became more volatile. Admiral Hansen, the BvW's leader, was willing to honor the conspirators, recognizing that their martyrdom had helped to rehabilitate the military; yet he was well aware of the divisiveness of the issue. He moved to defuse it by issuing a statement that recognized the honorable intentions of both the supporters and opponents of the assassination attempt.[81] Although this compromise preserved peace in the BvW, it was a fragile peace that was subjected to increasing pressure as new organizations appeared on the scene whose leaders, emboldened by the prospects of rearmament, fanned the flames of resentment of those who had remained loyal to their oaths and now feared that their wartime actions would prejudice their chances for a postwar military career.[82]

The situation created by the debate over German rearmament produced a dilemma for the BvW. If it could become the representative of German veterans, who were now being courted by both the Adenauer government and Germany's presumptive allies, its role would be enhanced and its future secured. At the same time, however, the new tolerance toward veterans produced competitors who threatened to usurp the leadership role coveted by the BvW. The year 1951 witnessed a seemingly endless proliferation of veterans' organizations in the Federal Republic. Even the Stahlhelm was revived, proclaiming itself, as in 1918, to be the political home for the front generation.[83] Waffen-SS veterans, whose officers were still excluded from the pension benefits of the 131 Law, were emboldened by the new climate and began to discuss the formation of a group of their own.[84] Regimental, service-branch, and unit-tradition organizations (*Waffengemeinschaften/Traditionsverbände*) were founded, representing, among others, former paratroopers, members of the Afrikakorps, fighter pilots, and members of the Grossdeutschland Panzer Division. Even former female Wehrmacht auxiliaries (*Wehrmachthelferinnen*), which included canteen personnel and female signal corps workers, the so-called *Blitzmädel*, formed a group.[85] Many of the leaders of these organizations were extremely popular, and some, such as Hasso von Manteuffel, the head of the Grossdeutschland Panzer Division *Traditionsverband*, combined charisma with considerable political ambition. For many of these veterans, especially the leaders, 1951 marked the long-delayed return of former soldiers to the political arena.

The BvW looked upon these developments with unease. Its own hopes of assuming the leadership of the revived German veterans' movement were threatened by the emergence of the new, more dynamic and broadly based organizations and their politically ambitious leaders. The main threat came not from the new associations, however, but from an old quarter. At the time of the formation of the *Notgemeinschaften* in 1949–50, Hansen's supporters in Bavaria had been challenged almost from the beginning by a competing organization, the League of Former Pension-Entitled Soldiers and Survivors (Bund der ehemaligen versorgungsberechtigten Soldaten und Hinterbliebenen), which had been founded by a former sergeant named Eugen Eisenschink.[86] When, in the summer of 1950, Hansen united the state-based *Notgemeinschaften* into the BvW, he tried to persuade Eisenschink to join, but he refused.[87] Eisenschink's organization soon adopted a more nationalist and populist course, renaming itself the League for the Defense of Former German Soldiers (Schutzbund ehemaliger Deutscher Soldaten [BDS]) and opening its ranks to all veterans, not just former professional soldiers. In the process, Eisenschink was pushed aside by more radical elements, some of whom had dubious political pasts, who opened membership in the Schutzbund to former Waffen-SS men, a move that Eisenschink apparently opposed.[88] In the fall of 1950 Schwerin's office endeavored to negotiate a fusion of the competing Bavarian *Soldatenbünde*, but to no avail.[89] In early 1951 the Schutzbund, now led by General August Krakau, launched an aggressive program of recruitment and expansion, breaking out of its Bavarian base and initiating the publication of a national newspaper, the *Deutsche Soldaten Zeitung* (DSZ).[90] In April 1951 Hansen and Krakau tried to work out a modus vivendi between their two organizations. Although Hansen remained dubious about the acceptance of former Waffen-SS members, he was willing to discuss the possibility of a common program; while he was open on the question of programmatic goals, he was adamant in his insistence that the BDS must cease its recruitment activities in the north. For his part, Krakau demanded parity.[91] Hansen was willing to consider concessions in Bavaria (despite the numerical superiority of his organization there) but not elsewhere. In a move that reflected both his concern about the threat of the BDS and his view of his relationship to the government, Hansen sought help from Bonn to pressure Krakau into accepting his terms.[92] An uneasy truce was worked out at a meeting of the two men in Kiel, but it soon broke down when the BDS resumed its aggressive recruitment campaign in the north.[93] The breakdown of relations with the BDS and the fervid activity of the *Traditionsverbände* convinced Hansen that the BvW needed to expand its goals if it were to avoid being pushed aside. At a delegates' meeting held in May, he advanced a series of resolutions designed to convert the BvW into a general veterans' organization, which the admiral and his supporters hoped would emerge as the core of a united veterans' movement.

In 1951 the BvW was thus presented with both challenges and opportunities. It had several strong cards to play in meeting the former and in seizing the latter. It had built up a solid organizational structure, and it represented those whose support the government was most interested in winning—former professional soldiers whose expertise and moral support were felt to be indispensable for the rearmament effort.[94] The BvW's leaders were convinced that their organization was the logical foundation for the unification of German veterans, and if this could be achieved, they reasoned, they would have a powerful lever with which to extract concessions from the government.

The relationship between the government and Hansen's organization was far from smooth. While both sides expected to gain from the formation of a united veterans' organization pledged to rearmament, each remained wary of the other. Each was determined to retain its independence. Too close or obvious a relationship with the government would result in a decline of credibility for the BvW and cost it the support of those who wanted a more adversarial relationship with both the government and the Allies. For the government's part, both domestic and foreign political considerations made too close a connection dangerous. While the government welcomed the support of veterans for its rearmament plans, the policy itself was not popular, and the country's past experiences with organized veterans had made many Germans, including those who supported the government, suspicious of politicized veterans. Memories of their role in the fall of Weimar as well as of the sycophancy and militarism of the official veterans' organizations in the Third Reich were fresh. Any sign of undue concessions on the part of the government to what remained a suspect group in order to gain its support for an unpopular policy had to be avoided at all costs.[95] Foreign opinion also remained suspicious of a revival of German militarism. Not only the French but also others who had felt the weight of German conquest were fearful; even in the United States, whose government most strongly favored German rearmament, public opinion remained skeptical.[96] To add to the problem, intemperate remarks made by overly exuberant spokespersons of the newly founded veterans' associations embarrassingly revived memories of the country's chauvinistic, aggressive activities in the past and renewed doubts about the wisdom of German rearmament.

Thus, while the Adenauer government desired the formation of a single, united veterans' association, it was careful not to become too closely linked or involved—at least publicly.[97] From the start, deniability was maintained as far as was possible, a fact that greatly complicates the task of the historian.[98] The government pursued a policy of cautious encouragement, while at the same time attempting to avoid picking sides and immediately pulling back whenever its activity became public. Schwerin, who was the original contact man, was forced to resign in late October 1951 as a result of public remarks that revealed too much of the government's plans for rearmament.[99] His successors in the Dienststelle Blank, the forerunner of the West German Defense Ministry, were more circumspect.[100]

The relation of the veterans' organizations to the government was equally ambivalent. Their leaders wanted to bargain for concessions, but they also wanted to avoid dependence. They, too, had unfavorable memories of the Third Reich, namely the *Gleichschaltung* of the veterans' movement. Moreover, they could not appear to be too closely linked to Bonn for fear of attacks by the many and vocal opponents of rearmament within their own ranks, as well as those who argued that an independent group would be better able to exert pressure on the government for increased benefits.[101] This *Eiertanz* of the government and the veterans' organizations continued throughout 1951 until it ended in disappointment for both.

EIGHT

THE VERBAND
DEUTSCHER SOLDATEN

The first general meeting (*Vertreterversammlung*) of the BvW was held in late May 1951, on the heels of the passage of the 131 Law. At this meeting, the Bund's leaders took stock and debated the organization's future course.[1] Admiral Hansen opened the meeting by recounting the organization's history and stressing the necessity of expanding its goals. He was followed by General Linde, who made it clear that the 131 Law would form the basis of future action and discussed strategies for the realization of the BvW's legislative goals.

Linde devoted considerable time to defending his office against attacks that it had not adequately represented the interests of the Bund's constituency.[2] Things were different in Bonn, he argued. One had to take into consideration the fact that the government and the Bundestag had to satisfy the demands of other groups, such as those covered by the Equalization of Burdens Law and war victims, as well as those of the former professional soldiers; the government had to finance all of these benefit programs and justify the expenditure to the taxpayers. Thus, "our demand, as justified as it is, cannot be 100 percent fulfilled."

To complaints that the BvW and its representatives had not been forceful enough, had not at least "banged on the table," Linde replied that he could only make demands if he had power behind him, that is, a ministry that was directly responsive to the needs of former officers; since there was no longer a Wehrmacht, there was no Defense Ministry, and, thus, such a ministerial advocate and conduit was lacking. This meant they were "on their own" and that "we can not simply bull our way through but must constantly adapt ourselves correspondingly to the situation." In defense of what he and his colleagues had obtained, Linde noted that the government's original proposal for coverage of the 131 Law had been for DM 350 million and that the final law foresaw an outlay of DM 750 million. The former officers' struggle to regain their rights, he claimed, "has reached a new stage with the passage of the 131 Law." While the law's passage was only the first step, it provided "the platform for our continued fight." Linde dismissed the idea of trying to realize some of their demands through the LAG but noted that there were plans to resolve some of the issues that they considered vital through legal action.

The latter point was developed by the next speaker, who had been instructed by Hansen to check into the possibility of filing a suit on behalf of the former professional soldiers. A legal expert had advised against filing any suits until the Beamtenrecht was settled, however, since it would regulate many issues, such as eligibility, promotions, and the calculation of POW time. Once the legal situation had been clarified, then they could consider a lawsuit. The legal adviser was also of the opinion that it was better "for political reasons [auch aus optischen Gründen]" not to file a suit against the Republic, since

> among the war victims and LAG beneficiaries there is unrest and anger toward those receiving 131 benefits because of the low level of war-disability benefits. We may have been "state servants," but the war victims are "state cripples [Staatskrüppel]," for whom the state has the same moral duty to care for as for us. If in this atmosphere we were to make immediate legal demands . . . public opinion would not support us. In fact, one could imagine that on the part of some groups, for example, the war victims, their unrest would be deliberately [künstlich durch Schlag-worte] aroused.[3]

The decisions not to push its demands through the LAG and to postpone a lawsuit showed that the BvW had come to terms with the 131 Law in so far as it recognized the law as the basis for future action.[4] This confirmed the Bund's future role as an interest group. But would this be enough? Was it necessary or desirable to do more?

In his opening remarks at the *Vertreterversammlung*, Hansen declared that "the fight for the recognition of our soldierly honor has essentially come to an end," while acknowledging that the struggle to achieve their "rights" would require additional time. But, he continued, "What will happen then? Should we disband our organization or should we maintain it by widening its goals and membership?" For Hansen the answer was obvious: it would be irresponsible to dissolve an organization that had become a "repository and guardian [Pflegestätte] of all the old soldierly virtues." It was necessary to carry its work further; to do this it needed the younger war generation. These men would not be attracted to the Bund, however, if it remained "an organization of pensioners, an organization with a limited goal." Other groups were now emerging that were seeking to attract this younger war generation. The overwhelming mass of former professional soldiers belonged to the BvW. Was it not, the admiral asked, "our duty to preserve and transmit their tradition?" At the very least they had to work with the new organizations in order to prevent a fragmentation of the veterans' movement, since "peace and freedom are endangered."[5]

Hansen's ideas were given further support in a lengthy presentation later in the day by "Comrade" Schmoeckel entitled "Integration into Society."[6] According to Schmoeckel, the former officers had been fighting for honor and justice, but that should not become a goal in itself. The Bund's charter stated two goals: equality of former professional soldiers with other state servants and the complete integration of former professional soldiers into society at large. Schmoeckel's purpose was to elaborate on the second goal. Integration, he argued, must not be thought of only in individual terms but also in collective terms, which presented the BvW with "an important political task."

To illustrate his point, Schmoeckel began with a negative example, a sketch of veterans' organizations in the Weimar Republic. He noted the divisions within the officer corps (the NDO and DOB) and between the officers' organizations and the *Frontkämpfer* organizations of the younger veterans, which, Schmoeckel claimed, "affected a heroic pose with their uniformed marches and parades and felt themselves superior to their more moderate brothers." Political groups appeared that became "increasingly radicalized" and called for a "strong" man who would extricate the Fatherland from its "purported morass and democratic disorder." When the strong man did appear, he accused the officers of being "hopeless reactionaries," and the Reichswehr, isolated, was unable to resist the "revolutionary nationalist right." The result was disaster for Germany.

Schmoeckel urged that they learn from the past and not repeat the errors of the 1920s. There were many among them "who, after all they have experienced in recent years, have not been able to come to terms with our new state here in the west." They had to realize that the new state was only now beginning to gain its freedom and "that every nation is inclined to seek scapegoats for a lost war." Those who simply wanted to withdraw, to sulk, grumble, scorn, and revile, were, according to Schmoeckel, unwise. They wanted to distance themselves, to keep out of "the muck of politics [Drecklinie der Politik]," to stand on the sidelines and carp and, on the whole, wash their hands of all that happened. Should the BvW do this, Schmoeckel asked; was it really the wisest course? That, he claimed, "was more or less what the majority of the professional soldiers' organizations had done after the First World War. They looked on with grim satisfaction as the state's authority was increasingly undermined, until it was too late and they too were dissolved. Do we believe that the state in which we live is not our state and that its fate is not ours? To be sure, we could have a better state, but we—precisely we professional soldiers—can also do more to improve it. If we want to enjoy rights, then we must also recognize responsibilities." This included a willingness to defend the state and to oppose "the *ohne mich* position," which was "worse than desertion."[7]

Not all of the Bund's members were convinced of the need or wisdom of expanding the Bund's program. Yet the admiral and his supporters felt such expansion was imperative if the Bund was to survive. When later in the day a leader of the Bavarian state organization expressed reservations about expanding goals in a "political manner," Hansen responded that if they did not, they would be overrun. Other organizations would seize the initiative. If the BvW became a larger, stronger organization, it would be able to represent the cause of soldiers more effectively.[8]

The second day of the meeting dealt with business affairs; the issue of expanding the Bund's program was submerged. The decisive debate on the issue took place on the third and final day. Some of the delegates were concerned about leaving the debate until the end of the meeting, fearing that things would be "railroaded through in the final minutes."[9] In fact, if the minutes can be trusted, the final discussion was rather anticlimactic.[10] The issue was incorporated into a proposal of the organizational committee to create two main divisions (*Hauptsachgebiete*) within the executive committee, one to deal with benefits and the other to encompass "all other questions dealing with soldiers." The proposal, according to a committee spokesperson, embodied the central question that had been the basis for calling the meeting. For his part Hansen declared, "If you do not clip my wings in the pursuit of this task, then I believe we will make progress; we will unite German veterans and then be able to devote ourselves to the tasks that fate demands of us."

The proposal was widely supported. Opposition came only from the southern *Landesverbände*, whose leaders felt that the time was not yet ripe to expand the Bund's mission. Skeptical about becoming involved in political activity and dubious whether the move would win over younger veterans as intended, they argued that the Bund should be certain the benefit question was settled before moving on to other tasks. A younger member supported the change, arguing that if the Bund remained limited to the question of benefits, the younger members would be unsatisfied. Pensions, he pointed out, were less important to them since they could not live solely on their pensions. It was impossible "not to become involved with genuine political questions [die echte Politik]. If we are true citizens, then we must involve ourselves with such questions. We are at a turning point that demands that we expand our goals."[11]

The ensuing vote was 10 to 2 in favor of expanding the BvW's goals. Only

Bavaria and Württemberg-Baden opposed, arguing that the idea was not necessarily wrong but that its time had not yet come. Hansen countered by repeating that they had to move quickly in order to forestall others from seizing the initiative. Most of the *Landesverband* leaders agreed. Hansen and his supporters had prevailed. The manner of implementing the new course and its timing was left largely to the admiral.[12]

Spurred on by the continuing efforts of the BDS to expand its influence in the north and the proliferation of newly founded *Traditionsverbände*, Hansen moved to carry out the decisions made at the May meeting. The BvW's new goals were publicly announced, a name for the new expanded organization was selected, Der Deutsche Soldatenbund (DDSB), and a meeting of the executive committee was scheduled for late July in order to discuss and confirm the decisions of the May meeting.[13]

MEANWHILE THE government was also moving to gain a measure of control over the mushrooming *Soldatenbünde*.[14] On 23 June representatives of the Dienststelle Blank and prominent military personalities met in the small Rhine town of Hattenheim near Wiesbaden. The meeting was officially sponsored by a private organization, the Wirtschaftspolitische Gesellschaft von 1947, located in Frankfurt, and was chaired by Otto Klepper, a former Prussian finance minister, and General Erich Dethleffsen.[15] After an introductory speech by Klepper on economic matters, which was clearly intended as window dressing, the assembled guests got down to the real purpose of the meeting—the creation of a united veterans' organization.[16] The Dienststelle Blank was represented by Graf Kielmansegg, Hans Speidel, and Adolf Heusinger. Other prominent military figures were Hasso von Manteuffel, Johannes Friessner, Heinrich von Vietinghoff, and Gotthard Heinrichi. The BvW was represented—albeit unofficially—by a confidant of Hansen, Johannes Sapauschke.[17] The need for a general veterans' organization was quickly agreed upon by those present. The recent decision of the BvW to expand its membership was studiously ignored, at least initially. This was soon remedied by Sapauschke, who, at least in his opinion, was able to convince the assembled guests that the BvW was the logical vehicle for the project. Speidel and Heusinger appeared supportive, and Klepper assured Sapauschke that the BvW's plans "would be welcomed by the Americans." When Sapauschke noted that Hansen did not plan to head the expanded organization and was looking for someone younger to take his place, a spirited discussion followed over possible choices. Eventually, Friessner, a compromise candidate, was chosen. Although hardly a charismatic personality, he had proven himself as a troop leader, and, above all, he was "unburdened" either with regard to the events of 20 July 1944 or his prewar career. The meeting ended, according to Sapauschke, with the decision that a general veterans' organization should be created with the BvW as its core.

The following week, BvW leaders met in Kiel to discuss the recent course of events.[18] Once again the need to take action and to change the character of the BvW were examined. According to Sapauschke, the problem was that veterans saw the *Traditionsverbände* as the idealistic embodiment of their soldierly front comradeship, even if they only met once a year or less, while they considered the BvW an organization for the representation of material interests. Hansen reiterated his determination to change the Bund's role and image. According to Erich Röhlke, the BvW's treasurer in Bonn, members of the Dienststelle Blank and Otto Lenz, state secretary in the Chancellor's Office, had given the green light for the BvW's new course.[19] Sapauschke gave an account of the Hattenheim meeting, and the arguments that had led to Friessner's selection as head of the expanded BvW were rehashed. Hansen, on the whole, supported the choice.[20] He promised that he would contact Friessner soon.

True to his word, Hansen wrote the general on 2 July. While seeking Friessner's cooperation, it was clear that the admiral had no intention of surrendering the initiative. He explained that the decision at the Hattenheim meeting conformed to the plans of the BvW adopted in May and informed Friessner of the upcoming meeting of the BvW's executive committee. He concluded his letter with a rather convoluted and guarded request for Friessner's participation in achieving "the great goal."[21] Following his overture to Friessner, Hansen set out on a whirlwind trip to Bonn and Düsseldorf to pave the way for the executive committee's meeting. His haste was not unwarranted. Considerable activity was being manifested among the *Soldatenbünde* and those who felt called upon to lead the war generation. One of the most prominent of these was Hasso von Manteuffel, leader of the recently founded *Traditionsverband* of the Grossdeutschland Panzer Division. According to Manteuffel, who was also corresponding with Friessner, he had been approached by a number of people asking him to form a unified veterans' organization.[22]

More ominous were the efforts of Gert Spindler, a wealthy manufacturer, who was deeply involved in conservative, nationalist causes and linked to a number of neo-Nazi personalities and enterprises.[23] During the summer of 1951, Spindler hosted a series of meetings at his estate in Altenberg to discuss the question of German rearmament and the formation of a mass-based veterans' organization. The first meeting, held on 2–3 June, was rather small. Most who attended were former officers. The Dienststelle Blank was represented by

Graf Kielmansegg. The main topics of discussion were the role of German border guards in the remilitarization of the Federal Republic, the problem of military war criminals, the plot of 20 July, and the nature of a future West German army.[24] On 21–22 July, a second meeting with a much larger guest list gathered to discuss, in addition to the general problems of rearmament, the foundation of a veterans' association that would give former soldiers a voice in decisions regarding Germany's rearmament. Among those who were present were General Hermann Ramcke, the former leader of the airborne troops who had recently returned from French imprisonment, and Generals Paul Hausser and Herbert Gille of the Waffen-SS. The BvW was represented by Karl Koller, a leader of the Bavarian *Landesverband*. Both Dethleffsen and Friessner also attended. Lieutenant Colonel Ulrich de Maiziere represented the Dienststelle Blank. On the question of rearmament, the meeting divided between attentists, who insisted that all their demands be met before they would agree to participate, and pragmatists, such as Dethleffsen and representatives of the Dienststelle Blank, who were opposed to the not-so-subtle efforts at blackmail urged by the attentists; they considered the Russian threat to be too great to permit indulgence in maximalist fantasies. In the end, the pragmatists won out. It was agreed that the soldiers' demands should be made forcefully but that their fulfillment should not be an absolute prerequisite to their support of rearmament. Agreement on the desirability of a unified veterans' organization was reached more easily, as was the decision that the *Notgemeinschaften*, that is, Hansen's organization, should take the lead in the formation of the new veterans' group.[25] Differences over the structure and purpose of the new organization remained, but these were concealed by the general enthusiasm for the project and vague generalizations about its goals.[26]

Meanwhile, Hansen continued to lay the groundwork for the expansion of the BvW. During his trip south in early July, he had been scheduled to see not only a number of military personalities but also Kurt Schumacher, the leader of the SPD, Christian Fette of the DGB, and, if possible, Lenz. Hansen had also been prepared to see Adenauer if necessary.[27] It is unclear how many of the political figures he actually contacted during the trip. However, two meetings with prominent personalities who were involved in the burgeoning veterans' movement were held in Düsseldorf on the weekend before the scheduled meeting of the BvW executive committee in Bonn.

Hansen had arranged the first of these meetings, which took place on 23 July and was dominated by Hansen and representatives of the BvW. Among those invited by Hansen were Friessner, Hausser, Gille, Manteuffel, and a representative of the recently revived Stahlhelm.[28] Hansen opened the meeting by recounting the history of the BvW and explaining the decision to broaden its goals. He made it clear that for him the defense of the West German state and support of the government's efforts to achieve this end were essential. It was not true, as some maintained, that pension questions could be separated from the question of support for rearmament. Pensions, he declared, were meaningless without freedom. Veterans must support the government's rearmament efforts; otherwise, it was quite likely that the Americans would withdraw from Europe, leaving the Germans at the mercy of the Soviets.

Friessner, who followed Hansen with a long presentation of his own, seconded the admiral's call to action but adopted a more attentist position. Soldiers, he argued, had to raise their voices and become actively involved. An enlarged, centralized veterans' organization would increase their influence and would be the best means with which to fight for their rights, including the rights of those who were still in prison. Former members of the Waffen-SS must also be included in the new organization. It was necessary to overcome the previous apathy of veterans and to attract the younger generation, from whose ranks the future leaders of the state would come. Friessner mentioned the Altenberg meeting and noted that there was much interest in the formation of a united veterans' organization, not only among Germans but in the High Commission. With an organization of a million members it would be possible to exert a "completely different" type of pressure on the representatives of the occupying powers, the government, and the parliament; this would ensure that the former soldiers would not be overlooked or steamrollered.

Manteuffel followed with a short talk, agreeing with Friessner and supporting the plans for the creation of a united veterans' organization. Former soldiers needed to establish a link to the state. It was their task to make it a desirable one. He stressed the need to move carefully, however, and to ensure the support (*Einverständniss*) of Adenauer, Schumacher, Fette, Blank, and the High Commission. Hausser, speaking for the former Waffen-SS veterans, also supported the enterprise, agreeing to join the new organization if it would work for their rights.

The second meeting, held the following day (24 July), had been arranged by Manteuffel. Most of the participants of the previous day's meeting were present, but only Hansen and Sapauschke were invited from the BvW.[29] In addition, a representative of the Bavarian-based BDS and several members of the FDP, to which Manteuffel belonged, attended. The BvW was in the minority and was put on the defensive. Again the talk was of the need for a united veterans' organization. Manteuffel proposed an umbrella organization (*Dachorganisation*), which would ensure greater independence for the *Traditionsverbände*, such as his own. The desirability of a fusion of the BvW and the

BDS, which Friessner had agreed to mediate at the previous day's meeting, was reaffirmed, but the BDS representative insisted on parity, which, of course, was anathema to the BvW. Once again the positive political effects of a united organization were stressed. These were outlined in some detail by Dethleffsen, who argued that the new organization would contribute to political stability, help to promote soldiers' rights, and "disabuse the public of the notion that the soldier has *no* interests whatsoever." According to Dethleffsen, "the generation of the Second World War will hold the fate of Germany in its hand in 1960. Thereby the soldier is predestined to shape international and internal relations in the age of supranational union. Because he is unburdened [by the past], he will be able to more easily adapt himself to the new age than others who are still burdened with the baggage of the past and he will be most able to attract the younger generation's support."[30]

One of the FDP representatives saw the political role of the veterans in a considerably less idealistic light. He saw a united, mass-based veterans' organization as a necessary counterweight to the trade unions, which, he argued, were the dominant political force in the Republic and whose leaders, he claimed, had largely been on the side of Germany's enemies during the war.[31] Such overtly partisan objectives did not find favor with all those present, including Hansen.[32] At the end of the meeting, it was agreed to form a working committee (*Arbeitsstab*), which was to work out a merger of the BvW and BDS and to prepare the foundation of the new veterans' organization.

The two meetings in Düsseldorf had to all appearances created a consensus. Both had unanimously endorsed the need and desirability of a single, united veterans' organization. At both it was agreed that efforts to form such an organization should be begun immediately and that the first step in the process should be a merger of the BvW and the BDS. But when it came time to go beyond general declarations of support, to discuss exactly how the new organization was to be formed and what its nature and the structure of its leadership were to be, sharp differences emerged. Underneath the outward harmony, there were deep antagonisms that soon surfaced.

One of the major points of contention was the relationship between the BvW and the BDS. While all concerned agreed on the necessity of a merger, the leaders of the two organizations had totally different ideas of how this was to be done. The BDS demanded parity throughout the Federal Republic, claiming that the organization's paper, the *Deutsche Soldaten Zeitung*, compensated for its numerical weakness in the north. Hansen was willing to concede parity where it existed—that is, Bavaria—but not elsewhere, and he insisted that once the fusion was completed, the BDS must cease to recruit as a separate organization. Leaders of the BvW's southern *Landesverbände* were considerably less enthusiastic about the admiral's willingness to concede parity in their bailiwicks, and the issue produced considerable tension within the ranks of the BvW.

There were also differences over the nature of the larger organization. Manteuffel's proposal for a *Dachorganisation* found little support from Hansen and his supporters, who envisioned the BvW as the core of the new organization, not just one of several columns. They hoped to expand the BvW through the DDSB, absorb the BDS, and require the members of the remaining veterans' organizations to join the DDSB as corporate members. The presidium of the new organization would include the leaders of the *Traditionsverbände*, but it would be dominated by the BvW/DDSB's *Landesverbände* leaders. The independent *Arbeitsstab* proposed by Manteuffel at the second meeting considerably reduced—as was intended—the role of the BvW. Hansen, although he agreed to participate, made it clear that continued work within the framework proposed by Manteuffel would have to be ratified by the BvW's executive committee at its upcoming meeting. He intended his organization to play a leading role in the future and had no intention of surrendering the initiative.

Hansen opened the following week's meeting of the BvW's executive committee (28 July) by reassuring those who felt that the new course would lead to a deemphasizing of the fight for pension rights.[33] He related briefly what had happened at Hattenheim, Altenberg, and Düsseldorf and sketched out his plans for expanding the BvW. Through the proposed measures, he argued, the BvW would develop into a large *Soldatenbund*, which "eventually would encompass all veterans." He went on to discuss in some detail the fact that Friessner had spoken in the same vein at the various meetings and had declared his willingness to cooperate extensively in the project. According to Hansen, Friessner had made a very favorable impression. He also reported that Hausser was prepared to have his Waffen-SS veterans join the new organization if it would forcefully represent their demands. Hansen concluded by reading the text of a proposed programmatic declaration that would be made public "as soon as political preconditions [Voraussetzungen] had been created through discussions [Fühlungnahme] with the government, the opposition, unions, and the High Commission."

The debate that followed was spirited. Support for the admiral's plans divided along geographical lines. Representatives from the southern states were hesitant, believing that the organization should continue to concentrate on benefits. The northern leaders agreed that the 131 Law was inadequate and that its improvement must remain a major objective of the new organization but in general endorsed Hansen's view that the Bund needed to expand its sphere of activity.

Admiral Raul Mewis, the leader of the Hamburg *Landesverband*, expressed surprise that any doubt over the need for expansion still existed. The Berlin representative declared that the fight for benefits no longer sufficed and that the proposed expansion of goals could no longer be postponed. This view was seconded by leaders of the North Rhine–Westphalian, Schleswig-Holstein, and Hessian *Landesverbände*. The leaders of the southern *Landesverbände* remained skeptical, arguing that the time was not yet ripe, that the fight had to remain focused on benefits, and that the entry into the political arena not only would not have the desired effects but might even threaten what had already been achieved. They rejected the conditions demanded by the BDS and opposed the acceptance of former Waffen-SS members into the BvW.

Hansen countered these arguments by stressing that the new group would be fully independent from the parties and the government and that it would continue to fight for benefits. He repeated his Düsseldorf argument that if there was too great an opposition to the military contribution in Germany, the danger existed that, among other things, the Americans could pull out of Europe and then all "benefit questions would become irrelevant [sowieso hinfällig]."[34]

At the end of the first day's session of the executive committee's meeting, differences remained unresolved. Consequently, Hansen proposed a compromise in the form of a general statement that was to serve as the basis for discussion the following day. It expressed the executive committee's support of the unification of German veterans in a single organization "whose main pillar would be the BvW in its present form" and reiterated that "the primary task of the BvW remains the fight for benefits." The name of the new organization was to be Der Deutsche Soldatenbund.[35]

Hansen's attempt at reconciliation failed. On the following day no agreement could be reached on the compromise solution. The northern groups were especially displeased with it, feeling that it "did not guarantee sufficient opportunity for action and initiative." The southern groups still felt that it went too far and feared that in an enlarged organization the original membership would be overwhelmed and lose its influence. To break the deadlock, Hansen appointed a committee to work out a proposal that was acceptable to all.

The new proposal, though vague, clearly reflected the position of the northern *Landesverbände* more than that of those from the south and left

Hansen a free hand. The ensuing debate focused on the name of the new organization and the critical question of the BvW's place in it. By a vote of 14 to 4 with 2 abstaining, the name originally proposed, Der Deutsche Soldaten-bund, was approved. The central question of whether the BvW should remain as a separate organization in the new Bund or whether it should reconstitute itself as the DDSB was then rehashed. The committee's proposal favored the latter. Attempts by opponents to change it failed. The committee's proposal, with the change in name and some minor alterations to emphasize that the new group was open to all ranks, was brought to a vote and approved 13 to 5 with 2 abstentions.[36] Hansen and the northern *Landesverbände* had won out, but at the cost of dividing their organization.

Hansen was quick to inform government officials of the executive commit-tee's decision. On 30 July he met with Lenz, and on 3 August he sent the state secretary a copy "of the memorandum that you requested on the Deutsche Soldatenbund." The memorandum described Hansen's reasons for founding the new organization, among which was the need "to prevent with all means the radicalization of former soldiers," of which "the most dangerous example was the *ohne mich* campaign." Copies of the materials sent to Lenz were distributed to the *Landesverbände* of the BvW/DDSB and members of its executive committee. In his covering letter, Hansen took care to show that officials in Bonn supported the Bund's recent decisions, a move undoubtedly designed to assuage the fears of those who felt the new course could lead to difficulties with the government.[37]

Three days later Hansen wrote Speidel at the Dienststelle Blank, reporting on the events of the past two weeks and noting that as a result of the decision of the BvW's executive committee, rifts had emerged among himself, Friess-ner, and Manteuffel. At the second meeting in Düsseldorf, he explained, the BvW had been "more or less pushed to the wall." There he had agreed to participate in the *Arbeitsstab* proposed by Manteuffel, which was to prepare the way for the formation of a *Dachorganisation*. The subsequent decision of the BvW's executive committee to go ahead with the DDSB, the admiral noted, "diverged from the 'decision' of the Manteuffel meeting." In his defense he argued that he had accepted the decisions of the 24 July meeting only as "suggestions or proposals [Anregungen oder Empfehlungen]" and they had subsequently been rejected by the executive committee. The resolution adopted by the latter, Hansen claimed, had been necessary "to prevent the breakup of the BvW which otherwise was to be feared." He continued, "I remain aware that this decision does not agree completely with that made at the Manteuffel meeting of 24 July. I am convinced, however, that the goal that we are all pursuing—the unification of German veterans—is more likely to be achieved through this decision than in any other way."[38]

ON 30 JULY Hansen had written Friessner reporting the decision of the BvW's executive committee and expressing the hope that Friessner would be able to bring about a fusion of the BDS with the newly created DDSB.[39] Hansen's rather bland goodwill failed to propitiate Friessner, who quickly registered his dissatisfaction with the admiral's actions in a letter of 1 August. Friessner accused Hansen of having gone back on his word and claimed that the founding of the DDSB had created enormous difficulties.[40] According to Friessner, it had been agreed at Düsseldorf that the BvW and BDS were to be fused before any new organization was formed and that it was the *Arbeitsstab* that was to spearhead its creation. Now things had taken "a completely different course," and a "completely new situation" had been created. The actions of the BvW had disillusioned and angered the other participants in the project, especially the BDS, and had created considerable public confusion. If the "further cooperation of neutral personalities of the veterans' movement was desired," Friessner continued, the *Arbeitsstab* demanded that the following conditions be met: the merger of the BDS and BvW was to be effected on the basis of parity; the official organ of the new organization was to be the *Deutsche Soldaten Zeitung*; contact with government officials, political parties, and the High Commission was to be made only through the *Arbeitsstab*, which was to prepare all public announcements; the executive committee of the working committee was to be composed of one representative from the BvW, one from the BDS, and a neutral representative, who was to be the leader of the committee; and, finally, there were to be two business offices, one in Bonn and one in Munich. Friessner urged Hansen to consider the proposals and to agree to them, which would "save our common cause." Otherwise, he concluded, "I see no alternative but to resign."

In a long letter of 4 August Hansen rejected Friessner's demands.[41] He began by stating that they would have been better off "if the second meeting in Düsseldorf under Manteuffel's leadership had never taken place." Hansen claimed that he had had severe reservations about attending and had only done so after being assured that Manteuffel did not intend to propose a different path than the BvW was following. Hansen found the attempt by Manteuffel to raise the smaller and geographically limited BDS to an equal partner especially distressing. Moreover, Hansen charged, its leaders had refused to honor the clear and definite agreement between the two organizations concluded in April. Hansen repeated that he was only able to accept the decisions made at the second meeting as suggestions to be proposed to the BvW's executive committee. The committee's rejection of the suggestions and decision to expand the BvW into the DDSB were the result of the democratic process. In any case, the decision, according to Hansen, had furthered the cause "for which we both are striving." The BvW could not surrender its leading role, and its transformation into the DDSB had created the firm core of German soldierdom (*Soldatentum*), to which the other veterans' groups could join. With regard to the specific demands raised in Friessner's letter, with the exception of agreeing that the *DSZ* should be the official publication of the new organization, Hansen refused to budge. The measures to diminish the role of the BvW/DDSB were rejected, since their fulfillment "would lead to the collapse of the present DDSB." In addition, Hansen claimed, as the head of a democratic organization, he did not have the authority to agree to such "far-reaching demands" without the consent of a general meeting. In a postscript, which he added after "sleeping on it," Hansen spelled out his scenario in more positive terms, justifying the claims of the DDSB, stressing that he had no personal ambitions, and expressing the hope that they would be able to work together in order to succeed.[42]

The exchange revealed much of what was at stake. The goals of the two men and their respective supporters were similar in many ways, but there were also significant differences. Both wanted to create a single veterans' organization that would attract younger, nonprofessional soldiers. Both sides saw such an organization as a means to allow them to shape decisions that were to be made concerning rearmament. However, the two groups differed on how the organization was to be constructed and, to a lesser degree, what its policy and relationship should be regarding the government. Hansen wanted the BvW/DDSB to form the core of the new organization. This was in part, of course, a simple manifestation of organizational egotism, but it was balanced by a genuine conviction that the BvW had been the first postwar veterans' organization, that it had performed a valuable role, and that it could easily be converted into a vehicle for larger purposes by opening its ranks to younger veterans. Hansen's larger goals were relatively conservative in that he wanted to combat the widespread *ohne mich* attitude and rally support for the government's rearmament policies. Genuinely concerned about the radicalization of the war generation, he saw the new organization as a means of preventing it. Finally, he saw the new organization as a lever to exact more benefits from the government.

Friessner and his backers wanted to create a completely new organization, one more dynamic and political in character.[43] While they did not reject the BvW's claims of having rendered an important service (after all, many of them received pensions as a result of the 131 Law), they felt it had served its purpose and that giving it, or the DDSB, a prominent role in the new organization would discourage young veterans, who were not interested in pension questions, from joining. Thus, they were determined to undercut Hansen and his efforts to make the BvW/DDSB its core.[44] Though more radical than Hansen, the group around Friessner did not share the view of the more extremist elements, such as those associated with Spindler. They wanted to form a solid block composed of members of the war generation and to use it as a political force, though not, as some feared, as a battering ram to destroy the Federal Republic. Their main purpose was to stand up to—and get back at—the Allies, to end the defamation of the Wehrmacht, with all that this entailed, and to have a voice in shaping the new Bundeswehr, in which many expected to serve.

The conflict over the role of the BDS revealed the different strategies and goals of the two groups. To Hansen and the BvW, the BDS was an unwelcome competitor, and the relations between the two groups had been soured by a year of mutual recrimination. To those in the BvW, the BDS had not only weakened the united front in the fight for benefits, but, in addition, it represented precisely the sort of radicalization of the war generation that they hoped to forestall. As a result, Hansen and the BvW, especially its southern *Landesverbände*, which were in direct competition with it, disliked and distrusted the BDS and were unwilling to make what they felt were unwarranted and risky concessions.

Friessner and his colleagues, on the other hand, saw the BDS as a model to be emulated.[45] It had attracted younger veterans, including former Waffen-SS members, and it had a successful newspaper, the *Deutsche Soldaten Zeitung*, that appealed to a much wider readership than any publication connected with the BvW could ever hope to reach.[46] As Hansen quickly realized, the plans of Friessner, Manteuffel, and their supporters would, if realized, work to enhance the position of the BDS at his—and the BvW's—expense. Thus the failure to resolve the relationship of the BvW and the BDS reflected a number of larger unresolved problems that eventually contributed to the failure of the effort to create a unified veterans' movement.

During August it appeared that the more serious disagreements between Friessner and Hansen had been smoothed over. Meetings between Hansen's representatives and Friessner and, later, between the two men themselves helped to resolve some of their differences, and on 22 August Hansen issued an invitation to prominent military personalities to meet in early September for the purpose of constituting a united veterans' organization.[47] Cooperation was far from total, however, and both sides used the weeks leading up to the

September meeting to strengthen their respective positions. The not unexpected breakdown of merger attempts between the BDS and the BvW/DDSB thwarted Hansen's plans to neutralize and, if possible, absorb the BDS. While he was still determined to secure a leading role for the newly founded DDSB, Hansen appears to have resigned himself to a somewhat reduced role for his organization within the context of the sort of *Dachorganisation* earlier proposed by Manteuffel.[48] For his part Friessner still hoped to create a completely new organization. As he unwittingly revealed in a letter to Hansen in late August, "If I had things my way, all the existing veterans' organizations would be thrown into a pot, stirred together, and then run through a sieve whereby it would be determined who wanted to stick with the old and who wanted to join the new venture."[49] Friessner and his supporters continued to fear that Hansen's DDSB would have the upper hand at the September meeting, and in any organization that was likely to emerge from it, because of its already existing organizational base. They worked to offset Hansen's advantage in this area by expanding the numbers of representatives from other veterans' organizations to be invited.[50]

On the eve of the meeting, Friessner and his allies were confident that they were gaining control.[51] Hansen's failure to merge the BDS and BvW on his terms had weakened his bargaining position, and the admiral found himself fighting a two-front war: against Friessner and his backers, on the one hand, and against the BvW's southern *Landesverbände*, on the other. While the former wanted to sidestep the BvW/DDSB, the latter continued to oppose the expansion of the BvW's role.[52]

A memorandum drawn up by the Baden-Württemberg *Landesverband* at the end of July cataloged its complaints and provides an accurate reflection of the position of the southern groups.[53] While the *Landesverband*'s membership was 2 to 1 in favor of the idea of an expansion of goals, the memo noted, one-half of those who approved felt it was premature (*verfrüht*). The main concern should remain benefits. Already dissatisfied with the provisions of the 131 Law, members feared that premature action might well destroy what little they had managed to gain. There was considerable distrust regarding the Allies and any associated strategy that banked too heavily on playing the presumed trump card of support for rearmament. If the great powers should come to an agreement that Germany should not be rearmed, then those groups that had expressed a willingness to rearm (*Wehrwillen*) could, "as experience has shown [erfahrungsgemäss]," find themselves in a difficult position, that is, they could be banned on the basis of Allied High Commission Law 16. This concern, a *Leitmotiv* of the southern *Landesverbände*'s opposition to expanding the BvW's mission, may well have been a residue of the comparative harshness of demilitarization measures undertaken in the U.S. and French zones of occupation, an experience that had scarred them more than the northern *Landesverbände*, who had suffered less at the hands of the British.[54] Similarly, the unconditional acceptance of former Waffen-SS members was opposed, since the government could use their presence as a pretext to ban the BvW.

The main concern, however, was that the implementation of the new goals would divide the organization and weaken its effectiveness in securing improved benefits. The 600,000 expected new members, unconcerned about benefits, would overwhelm the existing membership and politicize the organization. This would then drive out many of the original members, especially the noncommissioned officers and widows, which would only exacerbate the problem. Finally, "the political questions which we have until now consciously avoided in order to retain a united front in the benefits question, for example, remilitarization, the Twentieth of July, . . . SS, etc., will bring into our ranks, in which all parties are represented, the most severe conflicts of opinion, with all the attendant consequences." In the minds of the southern *Landesverbände*, the risks associated with expansion far outweighed the potential benefits.

The conflicts within the BvW/DDSB were still unresolved as the delegates gathered in Bonn for the 8 September meeting. Hansen scheduled a meeting of the BvW/DDSB *Landesverband* leaders for 7 September in the hopes of uniting the organization and getting them to agree to a common line before the general meeting. In response, Koller arranged a gathering of the southern *Landesverband* leaders on 6 September. According to the Bavarian leader, at all of the previous meetings in Bonn the southern states had found themselves confronted by a united northern block that had already arranged things among themselves; the southern groups were then presented with faits accomplis and steamrollered. In order to prevent this from happening again, the southern leaders pledged to work together and to vote as a block. They agreed to support the formation of a larger organization, but only if it took the form of a *Dachorganisation* that ensured the full independence of its member groups. Moreover, the negotiations for the new organization had to proceed in a measured, unprecipitous manner.[55] Thus united, the southern leaders prepared to take on their northern adversaries.

Hansen's attempts to forge a consensus the following day failed miserably.[56] To begin with, he invited Friessner to attend, a move that angered the southern leaders, who had requested that the meeting be closed. Friessner's presentation, which lasted forty minutes, left his critics unmoved. They felt it was too theatrical (as well as being given in a Saxon dialect), and that he had vacillated between promising to work for benefits and declaring the need to take up other tasks; moreover, he had left unclear whether the new organization was to be unitary (*Einheitsverband*) or confederative (*Dachverband*). In the discussion that followed, the old differences between the northern and southern *Landesverbände* reemerged, with the former supporting a centralized organization that would be open to ex-Waffen-SS members and the latter opposed to both positions.

After two hours of debate, the fronts remained unchanged. Following a break for lunch, the meeting resumed without Friessner. The two sides were torn between the fear of being politicized and radicalized, which could weaken the Bund's effectiveness in the struggle for benefits, and of being outstripped by radical competitors. Those favoring an expanded organization stressed that if they did not form one, someone else would. When it came to a vote, the northern groups again prevailed, though the idea of a unitary organization was abandoned in favor of a *Dachorganisation* in which the DDSB would retain its independence. The vote was 14 to 6 in favor, dividing along geographical lines.[57] The vote for the leader (Geschäftsführender Vorsitzender) of the new organization, who would also head the DDSB, was even closer. Koller and others expressed reservations about Friessner, and he was endorsed only by a very slim margin, 11 to 9. Hansen and his supporters in the north had managed to get their way, but the rift in the ranks of the BvW/DDSB had been deepened.

The meeting on 8 September was well attended.[58] There were over fifty delegates, as well as a number of unofficial observers. The *Traditionsverbände* were well represented, but the meeting was dominated numerically by representatives of the DDSB.[59] After a few brief introductory remarks, Hansen turned the meeting over to Friessner, who gave a lengthy presentation on the need for a united veterans' organization, its structure, and the goals for which it would strive.[60] Friessner asserted that the meeting was a gathering of soldiers of all ranks, "not a meeting of generals." He then repeated his remarks of the previous day about the need to create a model for the younger war generation and that this was the last chance for the older generation to prove itself. This had not been possible in the first veterans' organizations founded after the war (that is, the BvW and BDS), Friessner noted, since they had been formed "when most of us were still in prison." Former soldiers now had to have a voice in political matters, though not, of course, in "day-to-day politics." The purpose of the meeting, Friessner declared, was to create a united soldiers' league: "Today all the barriers must fall. We are not striving for a confederation of individual leagues, but for the larger goal—the unification of all German veterans in a large, single association." Such an organization, he maintained, would help overcome distressing "signs of the times," such as disunity, egotism, and selfishness. History, he intoned, had repeatedly proved "how the renewal and revitalizion of peoples had arisen from their soldiers. This is what I envision."

Following these ego-stroking platitudes, Friessner went on to outline the real purpose of the new organization. On the one hand, they could not avoid the fact that "we lost the war and are now completely dependent. If we do not go along with the Western states, then the feed bag [Brotkorb] will be taken away and we will be unable to survive." He insisted that this had to be said and that the eyes of those who refused to recognize it must be opened. On the other hand, Friessner continued, "it is impossible for us to take up weapons before all prisons in which 'war criminals' sit are opened." The soldiers had to fight for justice, but, Friessner maintained, he could not carry out the fight "vis-à-vis the government and the occupiers as the leader of a small club. I can only be effective if I can come and say I have behind me a powerful force of two, three, or four million men who will not let themselves be run over, who want to know how things will be done, what will happen if they join up, whether gallows will be erected again, etc." These were questions that could only be influenced by a body that had a high profile. For those who feared that the new area of activity would weaken the emphasis on benefits or that it might endanger previous gains, Friessner argued that the opposite would be the case—that the pressure for improved benefits would be intensified and expanded "if great masses stood behind it."

Friessner wound up his presentation by emphasizing the need for a new, united organization and claiming that Bonn supported the undertaking. There was "no doubt that the best solution, both in terms of domestic and foreign considerations, was to unite German veterans in a large, single association." This was what the government wanted; the establishment of a *Dachorganisation* was merely a fallback solution. In the course of many discussions and meetings, it had become increasingly clear, Friessner argued, that a large, united organization "is the correct solution—the other is only a half-solution." At today's meeting, Friessner concluded, they must achieve three goals: decide whether or not to form a united organization, which he suggested should be called the Association of German Soldiers (Verband deutscher Soldaten [VdS]); form a provisional or working committee to lay the foundations for its creation; and choose a person who would be empowered to initiate and direct these efforts. Friessner ended by declaring dramatically, "I ask the question: who is against the constitution of an association of all German veterans?"[61]

No one, of course, was willing to say they were against the founding of a united organization. While many of the delegates pressed for an immediate affirmative decision, arguing that "the form" of the new organization could be decided later, Hansen, who had a great stake in the resolution of precisely this question, equivocated. He was torn between his desire to unite German veterans and his fear that in the process his organization would be shunted aside or, worse, displaced by the BDS. Aware that he or his supporters would be unlikely to dominate the working staff proposed by Friessner and that Friessner and his supporters had little sympathy for Hansen's plans to make the DDSB the core of the new organization, the admiral worked to secure pride of place for the DDSB before things got out of control or, failing that, to slow down the pace of events.

After a brief pause, BvW leaders pressed Friessner to elaborate in more concrete terms what his plans entailed. To the question of whether the creation of the VdS would mean "the dissolution of all already-existing organizations and their merger into the newly created association," Friessner responded evasively that the *Traditionsverbände* and the *Waffengemeinschaften* would retain their independence. When pressed further as to whether the more general veterans' organizations, such as the BDS and DDSB, "would have to dissolve themselves," he replied, "So far as necessary, yes." This prompted a further question, "Where does necessity begin?," that remained unanswered.[62] Assured of their own independence, the leaders of the *Traditionsverbände* and *Waffengemeinschaften* (Ramcke and Heinz Guderian, in particular) pushed for a vote. Hansen asked if the delegates were willing to agree to the principle of unification while leaving the question of form open to further discussion. Agreement was unanimous, and the delegates took a break.[63]

During the pause, Hansen met with the BvW/DDSB leaders. He was urged not to surrender the Bund's independence since all the other groups were demanding theirs.[64] When the meeting resumed, Hansen worked to ensure that the declining fortunes of the DDSB were not capitalized on by the BDS. He began by asking the representatives of the BDS and the Stahlhelm where they stood on the question of fusion.[65] The BDS delegate, Joachim Ruoff, replied that his group supported the creation of a single organization, but that such an organization could only succeed if there were no differences regarding its goals. A program had to be worked out "which all could unconditionally acknowledge, one in which no essential questions of a comprehensive military policy [Wehrpolitik], including the oath question, were circumvented or omitted. . . . Obviously, unification cannot take place when there is disagreement on essential questions." The working committee must create a program that would deal clearly with those issues, and each group would have to decide whether or not to support it. Yes would signify the willingness to merge, no the opposite. Ruoff then pointed out how important it was for the new organization to have leaders that were popular with the war generation, men who could win over young veterans. Such a consideration worked against Hansen and his organization, as Ruoff obviously intended. In addition, the BvW had always worked to avoid controversial issues in the interest of maintaining a united front in the fight for benefits. Hansen had studiously waffled on the oath question, eventually formulating a compromise that allowed peace to be maintained in the ranks of the BvW but that was unacceptable to more radical elements such as Ruoff.[66] While the political line of the BDS was undoubtedly shared by many in attendance, its recalcitrance opened it to attack. Hansen pounced on the conditions demanded by the BDS, claiming that they indicated that it was unwilling to agree to a fusion and shifting the onus for the failure of unification to it. The admiral then painted the Stahlhelm into a similar corner.[67]

Meanwhile, the pressure for action increased. Dethleffsen declared that they had to form a united, centralized organization. It was, he claimed, what the war generation wanted. Moreover, it was conceivable that in the coming months negotiations on Germany's military contribution would take place and the chancellor would "be able to represent German interests more effectively if a large association existed to back up his demands." They needed a new organization that would attract the younger war generation, and, he concluded, they needed to decide on the creation of the organization now.[68]

Kurt Student, a former pro-Nazi air force general, also stressed the need to attract the young war generation. "We must realize," he stated, "that the existing organizations only comprise at the most 5 percent of veterans. The remaining 95 percent are either indifferent, engaged in the daily struggle for existence, or mistrustful of the leagues and associations." Student urged caution, warning against becoming too dependent on Bonn or appearing to act at the bidding of the Allies.[69]

Admiral Hellmut Heye, who later became a CDU Bundestag deputy and was active in military policy, suggested that they utilize the structure of the DDSB "as it stands now. . . . Take the shell [Schneckenhaus] and fill it with a new content." They needed to unite now and to build a large organization—not "an old boys' club"—which would attract the war generation, that is, veterans thirty to forty years of age. He cautioned against bringing political matters into the debate and stressed the necessity of acting immediately. "The Allies and the government," he asserted, "are not interested in a thousand small organizations or a pension club." Only an organization that included all veterans could be a "significant factor."[70]

Manteuffel also joined in the push for the immediate creation of a united organization. If they wanted to have any weight, then they must attract the younger generation and give them a voice. The younger generation, he claimed, were waiting to hear from men whom they trusted. "We must create a partnership of trust and transform it into a partnership of responsibility."[71] General Guderian, who, like Manteuffel, had been working actively behind the scenes for the formation of a new veterans' organization, joined in to say that Hansen had "unknowingly and unwillingly" created an obstacle by bringing up the question of fusion. He urged the delegates to found the new organization first and to worry about its structure later. If they did not act today, he threatened, then he would form his own organization.[72] General Ramcke and others supported Guderian's motion, and Gille followed Guderian's threat with one of his own: if a new association was not created at today's meeting, then he would found a separate organization for Waffen-SS veterans, a move that he had previously rejected.[73]

At this point the meeting had been going on for over two hours with no concrete results. Friessner and his supporters began to press the assembly to take action. Dethleffsen offered a "technical proposal" that incorporated the three steps outlined by Friessner in his opening statement.[74] This found general support. Hansen agreed to the proposal but expressed concern about continued competition between the BvW and BDS in Bavaria, insisting that once the new organization was formed this must stop. Brushing aside Koller's concern about moving too fast and Ruoff's claim that he did not have the authority to dissolve the BDS and merge it into the new organization, Friessner moved on and appointed a committee to draw up a program that was to be presented for discussion later in the afternoon.[75]

When the committee presented its seven-point program, there was little debate; the new organization's goals were sufficiently vague and platitudinous to prevent conflict. The main discussion centered on its name and the position of the DDSB and BDS within it. Friessner had proposed the name Verband deutscher Soldaten, but the committee had dropped this in favor of Allgemeiner Deutscher Soldatenbund, a suggestion that found little support. Heye again suggested that they take over the organizational structure of the DDSB and leave the name intact. Friessner asked if the DDSB was willing to agree to this, and Hansen replied that it was. When the admiral asked the *Landesverband* leaders if they would support such a move, those from the north quickly agreed; those from the south hesitated but were outnumbered and easily outvoted. Finally, a compromise of sorts was worked out with Bavaria, Württemberg-Baden, Württemberg-Hohenzollern, and Rhineland-Pfalz agreeing to give "provisional acceptance [vorbehaltliche Zustimmung]," subject to the approval of their members.[76]

Further debate now revealed dissatisfaction with the name Der Deutsche Soldatenbund, primarily on the part of the *Traditionsverbände*. The DDSB's leaders doggedly fought for its retention, arguing that to change the name would only confuse the public and that to completely dissolve the DDSB and then build a new organization was "to carry the church to the village." Friessner and Guderian, who were now in control of the meeting, sided with those who wanted a new name.[77] Friessner proposed the name he had originally suggested, Verband deutscher Soldaten. Presumably the DDSB would continue to exist as a separate organization, while at the same time putting its organizational framework at the disposal of the new organization. Hansen, exasperated at the course of events, complained that the DDSB was making all the sacrifices and claimed that the "entire problem would be solved if the BDS and DDSB were to merge." Why could that not be done? After further discussion, Hansen finally exclaimed that there was only "one solution." The Verband deutscher Soldaten would be built. Its core would be the DDSB and the BDS. Once the Verband was formed, however, competition between the two organizations had to cease and they were eventually to merge. The *Traditionsverbände* and the *Waffengemeinschaften* would join with the DDSB and the BDS to form the Verband deutscher Soldaten.[78]

Brushing aside protests within his own ranks that the admiral's proposal went beyond what the delegates were empowered to agree to, Hansen seized the opportunity to put the BDS on the defensive, pointedly observing that while one of the organizations involved—his—had proved willing to make sacrifices for the common good, the other continued to drag its heels. Dethleffsen joined in, declaring that "the one that does not want to go along, excludes itself." When Ruoff protested that he did not have the authority to commit his organization, Guderian brusquely ordered him to call his superiors and get permission. Otherwise, he threatened, the BDS would be left out of the public appeal to veterans that would be issued announcing the formation of the VdS.[79]

Ruoff left the room to telephone Munich, while the delegates turned to the business of electing a provisional president. Hansen, who had announced that he would not run and, furthermore, that he planned to resign as head of the DDSB, nominated Friessner. The latter agreed to accept, provided he were given an "absolutely free hand . . . naturally, within the framework of a democratic organization." Following Friessner's election, an executive committee (*Präsidium*) was chosen.[80] As this was being done, Ruoff dramatically reappeared, announcing that he had just received permission from the BDS's president, Krakau, to join the new organization. This was greeted with applause, and Krakau was added to the executive committee. The latter was charged with forming a working committee (*Arbeitsstab*), which was to carry out the organizational buildup of the new association and "ensure the cooperation of the younger war generation." The final shape of the VdS, as well as the election of permanent officials, including the president, was to be determined at a general meeting to be held in November.[81]

Friessner expressed his joy "that today we have succeeded in coming to a positive conclusion which proves to all that the meeting has not been in vain." He praised Hansen as the instigator of the enterprise ("Vorkämpfer dieser ganzen Dinge") and thanked him for the sacrifice that he and his organization had made for the cause.[82]

Friessner's praise notwithstanding, Hansen left the meeting with mixed feelings. Although the goal of a unified veterans' organization appeared to have been realized, his own hopes of creating a nearly monopolistic position for the DDSB within the new organization had been thwarted. Also, while the larger ambitions of the BDS may have been checked, the unwelcome competitor had not been eliminated or totally neutralized. Although the admiral could take solace in the founding of the VdS, it was clear that he had been outmaneuvered by Friessner and his supporters.[83]

At a meeting of the BvW/DDSB's leaders on the following day, Hansen appeared listless, and the confusion within the ranks of the organization was manifest.[84] The admiral confessed that he had been disappointed with the course of events and, according to one observer, gave "a sort of farewell speech." Hansen reaffirmed his intent to resign and stated that after that he believed the BvW would cease to exist. Otto Mosbach, his deputy, took over the meeting but was unable to clarify the situation since he swung between support of the VdS and the need to retain the BvW. The *Landesverband* leaders finally decided on a resolution that nominally recognized the previous day's decision but in fact only revealed the doubt and confusion in the ranks of the DDSB. As one of the southern leaders put it, not without a certain amount of *Schadenfreude*: in legal terms the VdS was still nonexistent and remained a castle in the air (*Luftgebilde*); the BvW still existed legally, but had no president; meanwhile, the BDS both continued to exist and had a president capable of action. In short, the previous day had been an unmitigated disaster. Events in the coming weeks were to further reinforce this view on the part of the southern leaders.

In contrast, the mood in the camp of Friessner and his supporters was one of triumph tinged with smugness. This was reflected in an exchange of letters between Manteuffel and Friessner immediately after the Bonn meeting. Manteuffel offered his congratulations to Friessner and apologized for leaving early, claiming he did so because he "did not want to listen any more to the twaddle [dumme Gerede] of the people around Hansen."[85] Friessner replied, thanking Manteuffel for his good wishes. He noted the importance of his upcoming meetings with President Heuss and the chancellor, which he recognized as a "true historical event given the present foreign political situation." More than ever, it was necessary to intensify the work to build and consolidate the VdS. "I know that there will be many difficulties connected with this," he acknowledged, "but we must not let this deter us. We are sitting in the saddle now and we will ride." With words that were much more prophetic than he realized at the time, Friessner concluded: "Now it is a matter of handling the job of construction with political sensitivity and tact [mit gutem politischem Fingerspitzengefühl und Takt]. Any mistake [Entgleisung] will hurt the cause."[86]

THE FORMATION of the VdS had emboldened the soldiers, and, not for the first—or last—time, they overestimated their power. The resentment and desire for revenge of the more radical elements among the group's founders were strong and were shared by many of its leaders. Although most rejected the neo-Nazi or reactionary political views of the extremists, they hoped now to get even for their earlier treatment at the hands of the occupying powers, especially the United States, and to give comeuppance to those who they felt had inadequately defended them. Although they did not support the larger, more extremist political ambitions of Spindler, many of the VdS's leaders shared a number of the resentments expressed in Spindler's letter of congratulation to Friessner.[87] According to Spindler, the VdS should avoid becoming a veterans' organization of the old type (Kriegerverein). It had to become a "political factor in both domestic and foreign policy, somewhat in the sense of a soldiers' union." It should work to inculcate soldierly values in public life and once again make them the measure of conduct in all spheres of activity. Spindler urged Friessner to downplay benefit questions, "since they only affect a small number of veterans." He went on to contend that the war generation rejected the current parties, "since they represented a restoration of the unmourned [unrühmlich zugrunde gegangen] Weimar Republic." It was also unhappy with "the increasingly prevalent Americanism," which was perceived as an "unnatural irritant in our domestic development." It was imperative, Spindler warned, that the VdS remain completely independent from both the government and the Americans. The members of the executive committee should not belong to political parties. Moreover, the headquarters of the VdS had to be moved from Bonn, and negotiations with government officials must be handled in such a way that "they cannot be perceived as Loyalitätserklärungen to Bonn or the Americans." Spindler concluded by stressing the need to complete the VdS's organizational buildup so that it could make its voice heard in matters that concerned former soldiers, such as the rumors that only those who supported the 20 July assassination attempt would find positions in the new army and the necessity of ensuring that the military orders of the Third Reich would be worn in their original form, that is, with the swastika intact.[88] Friessner replied that he agreed fully with Spindler's views. With the exception of the orders question, Dethleffsen also concurred.[89]

Given the combination of such views, the euphoria and the exaggerated sense of importance that followed the founding of the VdS, and Friessner's political inexperience, Friessner was an accident waiting to happen. According to his account, the meetings with Heuss and Adenauer went well, as did a conversation with Schumacher a few days later. There were signs, however, that he had rubbed the chancellor the wrong way.[90] Two weeks after his election as head of the VdS, the explosion occurred. On 21 September Friessner held a press conference before the foreign press corps in Bonn. A more inauspicious start could hardly have been imagined. Although he later claimed that he had spoken in a simple, candid, "soldierly" manner, Friessner managed to press virtually every button that could alarm the foreign press and embarrass the Federal Republic's government. In the question period that followed his address, Friessner poured out a series of resentment-laden and ill-considered statements that may have sounded commonplace, indeed even moderate, within his normal milieu but that caused a sensation when expressed publicly. First, he emphasized the "demands" the VdS expected in return for its support of rearmament, rather than giving the unconditional support that the Adenauer government expected. He went on to argue that the Second World War had been started by Poland and that the German army had saved Europe from bolshevism; this was followed by praise for the Waffen-SS. To top things off, the VdS's newly elected leader stated that those involved in the 20 July plot were essentially cowardly traitors.[91] Further fuel was added to the fire barely two weeks later when Colonel Ludwig Gümbel, a former Waffen-SS officer and head of the Bavarian *Landesverband* of the BDS, stated in an interview that while some of the Twentieth of July conspirators may have acted out of honorable convictions, they should not be given positions in the new army since "their return would necessarily endanger the military spirit without which any kind of military contribution is unthinkable."[92]

Not surprisingly, the remarks of the two men unleashed a barrage of criticism both abroad and within the Federal Republic.[93] The foreign press was filled with stories about the return of the militarists in Germany, and Bonn quickly distanced itself from the VdS. Friessner's fiasco also brought the tensions within the VdS to a head. Some of the *Traditionsverbände* and *Waffengemeinschaften*, already seeking a pretext to slow the fusion of their organizations with the VdS, also drew back.[94] The southern *Landesverbände* of the DDSB, seeing their fears confirmed, immediately demanded Friessner's ouster. The attack was led by Koller, whose mistrust of Friessner's political goals was deepened by personal antipathy.[95] Leaders of the dissident groups blasted the VdS president and the "political generals" around him both privately and publicly.[96] As calls for Friessner's resignation increased, the leadership of the VdS vainly sought to exercise damage control.

The majority of the members of the VdS, including many of Friessner's critics, were convinced that he had been victimized by the press. At the same time, they were well aware of the deleterious effects of his remarks, especially in view of the weak and fluid state of the VdS's organizational structure.[97] The VdS executive committee met in Königswinter on 14 October to discuss the situation.[98] The meeting was chaired by Manteuffel. Leaders of the southern *Landesverbände* boycotted the meeting. Friessner, not surprisingly, was furious with the southern groups and wanted to eject Koller from the organization. He rejected their demand that he resign, saying that he had been chosen to head the organization until the first general meeting and had no intention of stepping down before then. Many of the other participants, including those critical of Friessner's faux pas, were also displeased with the actions of the southern leaders, especially the fact that they had washed the organization's dirty laundry in public. Gümbel and Krakau, as expected, fully supported Friessner. Hansen agreed to go to Stuttgart to meet with the dissidents in order to see if he could patch things up.

Hansen himself adamantly opposed Friessner's resignation, since it would betray weakness. The final decision, he insisted, would be made at the upcoming general meeting scheduled for November. Although it appears that privately he already did not expect Friessner to be (re)elected then, the admiral continued to defend him publicly.[99] Hansen supported Friessner at Königswinter, though he indirectly rebuked him by noting that one had to exercise the "greatest discretion" with political questions and that in the future they should "only speak when spoken to." In a slap at Gümbel, Hansen declared that the military honor of the men of 20 July could not be denied and that in his view, "these men are among the most noble figures in the development of the VdS."[100] Hansen praised the progress that had been made in forging the VdS and reiterated the need for unity. He admitted that some mistakes had been made in the south and said he would try to reconcile the southern leaders at his meeting with them in the coming week, claiming that "no stone would remain unturned in the attempt to effect unity."

Friessner, especially after he had received Hansen's support, took the Königswinter meeting as a vote of confidence. He claimed that the press conference had taught him a lesson, and that everything would have been different if he had had sufficient time and personnel to prepare. After taking full responsibility for the episode, however, Friessner then went on to make further excuses, claiming, among other things, that he had been overworked and that he had cleared what he had said about the military contribution with Generals Speidel and Heusinger of the Dienststelle Blank.[101] The meeting closed with a vote to postpone the general meeting from November to January and not to make any drastic moves regarding the southern *Landesverbände* until Hansen had talked with their leaders.

Hansen's reception in Stuttgart the following week was cool, and the meeting with the southern dissidents was stormy.[102] Once again he reiterated the arguments for expanding the organization's goals. Hansen conceded that Friessner had made mistakes, for which he had been strongly criticized at the Königswinter meeting, and admitted that much damage had been done. The question was how best to remedy the situation. "Harassment, slander, and attempts to force Friessner out," he complained, "accomplish nothing." The southern groups had acted inexcusably. The final decision on Friessner should be made at the general meeting, which had been postponed in order to allow things to cool down.

Hansen's audience wanted no part of the admiral's arguments. They complained about their treatment at the Bonn meeting by Friessner and his cohorts and maintained that the professional soldiers needed to retain an organization of their own. They supported the VdS, but as a *Dachorganisation* in which the BvW would be a separate column. According to Koller, the BDS was "the old brown-black company" and Friessner wanted to deal only with it. Several participants challenged the constitutionality of the decision made by Hansen in Bonn and threatened to form a new BvW.

The meeting broke up for dinner at eight with nothing resolved. When it resumed, Hansen was not present.[103] In his absence two resolutions were passed that underlined the failure of the admiral's mission: General Gustav Keim, the head of the Hessian *Landesverband*, was to go to Bonn with a new demand for Friessner's resignation; if that failed, a coalition (*Arbeitsgemein-schaft*) of the opposition BvW organizations was to be formed. Friessner's refusal to resign ensured the creation of the *Arbeitsgemeinschaft*. Instead of resolving the differences within his organization, Hansen's attempt at mediation had only hardened them.[104]

One reason that the admiral had been willing to stick with Friessner was his belief that the uproar over his faux pas would not have negative repercussions on benefit legislation. In early October he maintained that, with regard to "our pension claims and their achievement, the Friessner case will have hardly any impact."[105] By the middle of the month, it was becoming clear that such equanimity was misplaced. Embarrassed by the reaction, especially abroad, to Friessner's remarks, the government belatedly launched a concerted press campaign against him.[106] Critical voices were also being raised in the Bundestag— in ways that were ominous for the former professional soldiers. On 16 October, during a debate on a law to modify civil servant pay scales, Paul Bausch of the CDU spoke about the dangers posed by those who received pensions under the 131 Law "but had no scruples about running around the country attacking the state which pays their pensions and provides their support." Among these, he continued, "are a number of generals who have made unspeakably stupid statements, so stupid that as a result of them we Germans have been made to look ridiculous to the entire world." Bausch demanded that the minister of interior enforce the legislative safeguards that existed to prevent situations in which "enemies of the state would continue to be paid by the state."[107] Three weeks later, Heinrich von Brentano, the head of the CDU Bundestag delega- tion, submitted an interpellation criticizing "open and covert attacks against the existing state order" by "members of the executive committee of the VdS and persons close to them." The interpellation charged that these actions had "upset the efforts of a responsible state leadership, which is working tenaciously and patiently for the reintegration of Germany into the circle of free nations," and asked what the government planned to do defend itself and to ensure that the justified concerns of former soldiers were not misused by an unrepresenta- tive minority "for treasonous ends."[108]

The extent to which Friessner's and others' oratorical derailments were threatening the Bundestag's support for military pensions was laid out to Hansen in a series of letters by Heinrich Claes, one of the BvW/VdS's parlia- mentary liaisons in Bonn.[109] Claes reported on 19 October that the Bundestag members to whom he had talked were sympathetic to Friessner's admission that he had been in over his head and had been worked over by experienced and prejudiced journalists. Yet they felt it was "unforgivable" that at his press conference Friessner had violated his recently given assurance to the chancel- lor that he would not become involved in politics. He had instead "de facto intervened in a highly charged foreign policy issue in a manner that was extremely painful for the Bundeskanzler and which had had disturbing conse- quences for his ongoing negotiations with the High Commission." When Claes had asked if it was possible that Friessner could again be "accredited [akkreditiert]" with the chancellor, he received "a flat 'no'" in reply. Claes concluded, "After all this it is impossible for Generaloberst Friessner to be able to represent effectively the pension interests of former military men and their survivors or that we can successfully negotiate . . . through an organization that is led by him." Claes ended his letter by painting in dark colors the dangers that they faced: "The dissatisfaction of the Bundestag is already so great that voices have been raised in support of the reduction or removal of officers' pensions. The more effective representation of our interests through a larger organization than the BvW that was repeatedly promised has proven to be exactly the opposite, and this at a time when the debate on the Civil Service Law [the provisions of which would affect the pensions of former officers] is about to begin!"

A week later Claes reported on the damage that had been done by an article in the *Deutsche Soldaten Zeitung*, which he claimed was widely perceived as the official organ of the VdS even though officially it still was not. The article had blasted both the coalition and the opposition parties and had demanded the chancellor's resignation as well. According to Claes, members of the governing coalition expected "a clean break, especially on the part of the BvW." Claes reminded Hansen of his earlier warnings, asserting that the "defense of the pension rights of our 80,000 members who have entrusted us with this task is seriously endangered, since in the end it is the Bundestag that has the final say on legislation."

On 30 October Claes specified the negative effects of the Bundestag's angry mood on benefit legislation. He gave some examples, including a report of Bausch's comments, and then continued:

Through two years of exhaustive work we managed through calm, directed efforts of enlightenment to prevent such attacks even when the 131 Law was being debated. . . . The trust which the BvW had won and which alone enabled it to work *convincingly* in the parliamentary arena has been totally destroyed in all parties . . . by the VdS under its present leadership. The consequences affect us not only materially in our fight for our pension rights. . . . The reputation of the German soldier is on the razor's edge. . . . The slowly rebuilt trust is again disappearing and with this the hard core opponents of the . . . values of the military profession are gaining ground. And this at a historical moment when Germans are being called upon to provide a military contribution and to fight side by side with their cultural allies for Europe's freedom, culture, and peace. One cannot cling to leaders who make such mistakes. If we exclude ourselves and close the doors previously opened to us by anger-producing actions, then we only promote the efforts of those forces, which—already not without success—are at work to limit the influence of military experts of the highest leadership quality and, in particular, to exclude them completely in the selection of leaders [for the new army].

Claes concluded that an immediate public break with the VdS's executive committee or the committee's resignation was "imperative and cannot be postponed if we do not want to experience in the next weeks further serious setbacks in the form of an official 'defamation of the generals [Diffamierung der Generalität].' That would be the end!"

In a fourth (and apparently final) letter to Hansen on 3 November, Claes again emphasized the need to retain the goodwill of the Bundestag and to restore public trust. With regard to the admiral's call for support for Friessner and the VdS's leadership, Claes responded: "As a result of my experience I can unfortunately only recognize an obligation for loyalty [Treupflicht] in the form of a member's loyalty to the leader of his organization *conditionally*. Did not even a Reich President and General Field Marshall err, when in 1933 he installed our Stahlhelm leader in Hitler's government and solemnly exhorted us: 'Support this government of mine!'"

In spite—or, probably, because—of the growing criticism, Hansen stubbornly stuck to his guns. In a memo to the heads of the state organizations on 14 November, he outlined and then refuted the main arguments of the dissidents.[110] He repeated his belief that the founding of the VdS had not been too hasty and complained that "a minority had not accepted in good faith either the decision of the delegate meeting of 19–21 May or that of the executive committee of July. They continue to oppose these decisions in disregard of the democratic process." At the meeting of 8 September, the desire for unity had been unanimous. The debate on how to achieve the goal had been long and vigorous. From the debate, "the majority came to the conclusion that the originally planned *Dachorganisation* would not achieve the desired goal. A fusion of the DDSB (previously the BvW) and the BDS was unavoidable if the danger of a new competitive struggle was to be avoided, a struggle which would produce extremely unpleasant consequences." The heads of the *Landesverbände* of the DDSB had met on 9 September and had, according to Hansen, agreed to implement the decisions made at the previous day's meeting; they— or at least some of them—had not honored their obligation, with the result that the fusion with the BDS had not been pursued with sufficient vigor. "It contradicts the spirit of the decisions of the 8th and 9th of September," he continued, "when now it is maintained that according to the text of the bylaws this fusion is impossible. In my view we must not allow ourselves to become slaves of bylaws that do not correspond to changed conditions and new demands."

Hansen admitted that Friessner's press conference had caused problems. But, he claimed, these had been discussed at the executive committee's meeting in Königswinter, which included the DDSB *Landesverband* leaders (with the exception of those from the south, who had boycotted the meeting, however), and all but one speaker had asked Friessner to stay on. "Giving in to a press campaign demanding Friessner's immediate resignation," Hansen maintained, "would not serve the cause of German veterans in the long run. The basis of trust which the leadership requires would be destroyed for all time." Alluding to Claes's reports, Hansen conceded that the mood in the Bundestag was hostile but claimed that the VdS still had the government's support and concluded: "That—as some fear—this mood could adversely affect factual and legal considerations connected with benefits is a concern that undoubtedly evaluates the mood in parliament too negatively."

At end of his memo, Hansen pleaded for unity, but his own exasperation with the southerners came through when he lamented that "it is impossible for me to understand why what is taking place in the north in the building of the VdS cannot also take place in the south." He was aware that there were still "legal difficulties connected with the dissolution of the BvW that must be overcome." But, he concluded, they could be overcome if the spirit of the meeting of 8 September and, in particular, the spirit of the "*unanimous* agreement" of the DDSB representatives at the meeting of 9 September was honored.

As Hansen was preparing this memo to stave off the threat of internal dissolution, an external threat to the VdS was emerging. On 10–11 November, representatives of a number of veterans' organizations had met in the resort town of Goslar and formed a loose union that was to be the basis for a competing general veterans' association. The undertaking apparently had the support of government officials and members of the coalition parties who had become disillusioned with the VdS. The guiding spirit behind the enterprise was Freiherr Leo Geyr von Schweppenburg, who had been exploring the possibility of founding a veterans' organization throughout the summer and whose efforts had in part spurred on those of Hansen. Geyr's ambition was to create an organization that would attract the common soldier (that is, former enlisted men), be more "social" (that is, include former POWs and disabled veterans), and have connections with veterans' organizations in other countries. Arguing that a new veterans' organization had to be built from the ground up, rather than from the top down, he had publicly boycotted the Bonn meeting on the grounds that it was dominated by former generals.[111] Geyr intended to hold an organizational meeting of his own in late October, but it had been preempted by the VdS's September meeting; the initial reaction of Geyr and his supporters was that the founding of the VdS had made the realization of their own plans unlikely.[112] Friessner's fiasco had reopened the door, however, and in cooperation with Werner Noack, a prominent leader of the Verband der Heimkehrer, and sympathetic elements in Bonn, he convened the Goslar meeting.[113]

The meeting was well attended. There were representatives and observers from a number of the *Traditionsverbände*, including some who were nominally associated with the VdS. The president of the Bund Deutscher Kriegsbeschädigter und Kriegerhinterbliebener was present, as was General Keim, who headed the *Arbeitsgemeinschaft* of the dissident BvW groups.[114] The speakers at Goslar blasted the VdS and its leadership. They stressed the need for an organization that was nonpolitical and formed on a federative basis, that is, a *Dachorganisation* that would preserve the independence of member organizations.[115] Ernst Farke, a German Party Bundestag deputy who was active in veterans' affairs,[116] painted a bleak picture of how the VdS's actions had compromised the interests of veterans in Bonn. According to him, the coalition parties had provided more generous benefits to former professional soldiers than could have been expected; as a result, in view of the grave fiscal situation, this had put them into "a defensive position [Verteidigungsstellung], which has been greatly weakened by the politically unwise conduct of the VdS." The political statements of the VdS had had deleterious effects on the government's negotiations with the Allies and had damaged its image abroad. As a consequence, the government had declared that it no longer considered the VdS a negotiating partner (*Verhandlungspartner*). This in turn had essentially neutralized the BvW, since it had melded its leadership with the VdS. According to Farke, the High Commission had demanded that Adenauer ban the VdS. The chancellor had refused but at the same time felt that he would be forced by both domestic and foreign considerations to take action against the VdS "if the soldiers did not act quickly themselves." Farke claimed that the SPD had drawn up a proposal that among other things foresaw the removal of pensions from VdS members as a result of disciplinary proceedings based on charges of treasonous activity. He also mentioned Brentano's interpellation on behalf of the CDU and predicted that if the SPD proposal came up for discussion, it would be passed by an "overwhelming majority." He concluded by saying that he hoped the soldiers would settle the matter themselves, because if they did not, the government would, and if it did not, the High Commission would crack down using Allied High Commission Law 16.

At the end of the meeting, a resolution was adopted stating that while "cooperation was necessary," the VdS, as it had developed, did not provide the foundation for "the building of a social, comradely, and state-supporting association that guarantees the independence of its member organizations." Those assembled at Goslar distanced themselves from the statements of the VdS leadership, which had "damaged the German cause," and denied its right to speak for all German soldiers. In the debate over what was to be done, it was concluded that the VdS was beyond saving. A new organization needed to be formed. A working committee was set up to draft a program and organizational framework "for the foundation of a true *Dachorganisation* of all veterans' organizations that was organizationally sound [ohne organisatorischen Wasserkopf], with a minimal number of leaders, and with fewer generals in its executive committee than the VdS." A follow-up meeting was set for December.

Observers of the meeting noted that it had been well organized. One remarked that statements regarding the VdS were generally on target, though many of the consequences that had been predicted as a result of its actions were "perhaps a bit exaggerated." It was agreed that Noack, the proposed leader of the new organization, was impressive. Schwerin, in a report to the Dienststelle Blank, concluded that the meeting was to be seen as "a serious attempt of the well-intentioned elements of German veterans' organizations to distance themselves from the destructive position of the Friessner-Guderian clique." He urged that the efforts of its leaders be given "full moral backing and forceful practical support from the side of the government, the Bundestag, and the High Commission."

Geyr also sent a report to the Dienststelle, claiming that the meeting had been a success and confidently predicting the demise of the VdS.[117] In Geyr's view, any possibility of reforming the VdS had been ruled out by its "completely inept course of action, its lingering brown character, and its disastrous effects both abroad and at home." The Friessner group, Geyr noted with considerable *Schadenfreude*, had managed within a few short weeks to earn the repudiation not only of the entire international community but of all the parties in the Bundestag, including those who were favorably disposed to the legitimate demands of veterans. According to Geyr, the VdS had become "a totally hopeless enterprise." It had no prospect of obtaining legal confirmation under the provisions of the Allied High Commission Law 16, and the government had severed its relation as a result of its leaders' actions.

For some of the VdS's supporters, the latter consideration was more of an asset than a liability. Spindler's *Der Fortschritt* continued to support the VdS and its embattled leader, claiming that the attacks against them were motivated by the fact that "Bonn was annoyed above all because the VdS would not allow the parties and the government to have unlimited influence in the organization and setting of goals of the *Soldatenbund*. . . . An independent VdS could threaten the privileged position that the victors bequeathed to the parties." The Goslar meeting was nothing more than a effort to set up a new *Soldatenbund* in case the efforts to topple Friessner and to replace the executive committee with "men who are accustomed to dance to other people's tunes" should fail. "Should this not succeed," the author concluded, "then it is planned to create a counterorganization, which would signify the rebirth of the Reichsbanner."[118]

In spite of the support of the radicals—indeed, in large part because of it—Friessner's fate became increasingly tenuous. A report of the Dienststelle Blank on the situation within the VdS that was compiled in late November detailed the problems that had beset the organization and concluded that in the final analysis success would depend on whether the planned constituent assembly could be carried out and on whether an executive committee could be elected that would be capable of appealing to the younger generation of veterans, which was still holding back, and that would be able to restore reasonable ties to the government and the coalition parties without destroying the existing good relations with the opposition. "It seems expedient," the report concluded, "that Generaloberst Friessner not stand for election but give way to someone younger."[119]

Others, including Hansen, had come to the same conclusion. The attacks in the Bundestag, with their threat of pension cutbacks, the loss of the tie with the government, and, finally, the Goslar undertaking had convinced even the admiral that Friessner had to go. Three days after his memo to the *Landesverbände* supporting Friessner, Hansen wrote to him. After thanking him for his recently received birthday greetings and discussing a number of organizational matters, Hansen mentioned somewhat offhandedly that Hans Jürgen Stumpff, the leader of the Schleswig-Holstein DDSB/VdS, had called a meeting of the northern *Landesverbände* in Hannover for 21 November. Hansen did not mention the purpose of the meeting but a bit later in the letter suddenly suggested, "Would it not be in the interest of the cause if you would now say that you do not intend to stand for election on the 5th of January?" As quickly as he had raised the subject, he dropped it and, as if nothing important had been said, returned to the organizational situation in Bavaria and ended with renewed thanks for Friessner's birthday greetings.[120]

The meeting in Hannover began with a discussion of the general situation.[121] With regard to the organizational fusion of the BvW and the BDS, it was reported that there had been no substantial change either positively or negatively. However, it was noted, there was "increasing unrest among the members over the danger of damaging pension interests and the measures taken by the government (Goslar)." There was general agreement that "the most important thing is to ascertain whether the VdS still has the ear of the government. If that is not the case, then the VdS cannot be maintained." At this point representatives of the dissident *Arbeitsgemeinschaft* appeared and presented a list of demands upon which they made their return dependent. These included the immediate resignation of Friessner and other politically objectionable members of the executive committee and the convocation of a general meeting of the BvW by 16 December.

A debate followed in which a compromise was worked out. The North German leaders agreed to ask Friessner not to run in the scheduled presidential election and to publish the decision at a time that he deemed suitable. They refused to demand his immediate resignation. In addition, it was agreed that the executive committee would cease to meet and be allowed "to slowly fade out [einschlafen] without informing the public of the decision." Finally, a *Vertreterversammlung* of the BvW was to be called for 5 January in Hannover, at which the future of the BvW would be discussed and decided.

Pressure on the hapless Friessner continued to mount. Even his staunchest supporters, including Manteuffel, dropped him.[122] Meetings of VdS leaders with government spokespersons confirmed the fact that as long as Friessner was its head, the VdS would be non grata in Bonn.[123] On 10 December Friessner finally gave way and resigned.[124] Although he had hardly distinguished himself as a paragon of perception during his brief reign as acting president of the VdS, after his resignation Friessner accurately summed up the situation when he ruefully concluded:

> After the experiences of the past months I have come to the conclusion that because of the completely heterogeneous views within the former German officer corps in particular and among veterans in general, the creation of a united veterans' organization with a unified point of view on veterans' questions, such as we had imagined, cannot be accomplished at this point. At best it may be possible to have a loose alliance [Nebeneinander] of different "interest groups," such as "professional soldiers," "former prisoners of war," "VdK," "war-disabled," "Kyffhäusser," "tradition associations," and so forth. I am uncertain at this point if an "umbrella [organization]" is necessary for this or not. What purpose and what kind of powers should it have?[125]

FRIESSNER'S resignation solved the immediate crisis of the VdS but not its long-term problems. Hansen managed to patch together the ruptured BvW and to salvage the VdS in name, but the organization remained divided. After intense debate, a compromise was worked out between the warring factions. At the January meeting in Hannover, the VdS was fused with the BvW, creating the VdS/BvW, and the *Landesverbände* were allowed to choose the name (and emphasis) that best corresponded to local circumstances. Not surprisingly, in the northern states the VdS component of the new hybrid organization was emphasized, while in the south the opposite occurred. Splinter organizations emerged in a number of states, and in Hesse the VdS/BvW split into two independent and mutually hostile organizations. The divided state of the VdS/BvW was also reflected in the election of its president. Although Hansen was elected, he was not unopposed. General Keim, the head of the Hessian branch of the BvW and the leader of the dissident BvW *Arbeitsgemeinschaft*, found considerable support and finished a strong second, receiving a third of the vote.[126] Relief that the organization had been saved was tempered with frustration. As *Der Notweg* complained, "Was it all necessary? We are again exactly where we were in May 1951!!"[127] In spite of these difficulties, progress was made. In March 1952 the Bavarian-based BDS joined the VdS/BvW, thereby ending the protracted feud that had dogged the BvW and undermined Hansen's attempts to unify veterans under its leadership.[128] Yet the closing of this fissure continued to be offset by the confusion and wounds associated with the founding of the VdS and the flap over Friessner that had followed. Many of the *Traditionsverbände* that had joined—or were prepared to join—the VdS in September dropped out or distanced themselves.[129] The organizational consolidation and stabilization of the VdS/BvW required several years.

During this time, the VdS/BvW was plagued not only by vertical, geographical divisions but by horizontal, social ones as well. From its inception, the BvW had been perceived as an old boys' club, one that catered to the needs of higher-ranking officers. In spite of its claim to represent the interests of all former professional officers, noncommissioned officers played a clearly subordinate role. The BDS had successfully exploited this source of discontent, and its success in large part was a result of its appeal to the younger generation, in general, and former noncommissioned officers, in particular.[130] Hansen had sought to improve the image of the BvW by appointing Otto Mosbach, a former noncommissioned officer and official of the earlier Reichstreubund ehemaliger Berufssoldaten, as his deputy. In the months leading up to the founding of the VdS, Hansen and Friessner (as well as others) had repeatedly discussed the need to involve noncommissioned officers more visibly in the project. The Bonn meeting remained dominated by senior officers, however, and the pathetic scramble at its end to belatedly bring noncommissioned officers into the executive committee did little to dispel the impression that the VdS was dominated by generals.[131] Former noncommissioned officers made demands for a greater role in the organization at the Hannover meeting, and, in response, the representation of noncommissioned officers on the executive committee was enlarged.[132] This mitigated but did not solve the problem. Continued dissatisfaction with the VdS and the subsequent merger of the BDS with the VdS/BvW left many former noncommissioned officers feeling alienated and without an organizational home. Voices began to be raised, both outside and within the VdS/BvW, calling for the creation of a separate organization for noncommissioned officers. Mosbach strenuously opposed these efforts, claiming that although the military precept of marching divided and striking united had made sense after the First World War, it no longer did. The common defamation and destitution of all former professional officers after 1945, he argued, meant that they had to work together in defense of their common rights.[133] Mosbach eventually prevailed, but the threat of a breakaway by noncommissioned officers continued to dog the VdS/BvW in its early years.

The manifold difficulties that beset the VdS/BvW following the Friessner fiasco did not, as many expected, redound to the advantage of its potential rivals. The leaders of the Goslar initiative were unable to capitalize on the VdS's self-destruction, and the plans developed at the Goslar meeting remained stillborn. A follow-up meeting held in Wiesbaden in February fizzled.[134] Once burned, the leaders of the *Soldatenbünde* were wary about becoming involved in a new venture: some remained loyal to the VdS; others chose to shun any activity that threatened to politicize the veterans' movement—either out of fear of creating friction with the government or, conversely, fear that it would bring veterans into too close a dependence on it.[135] Although initially there was official interest in the Goslar scheme, it soon cooled and the government steadily distanced itself from the activities of the *Soldatenbünde*. On the one hand, the paralysis of the VdS removed it as a potential threat to—or a vehicle for—governmental goals; on the other hand, its continued existence meant that sponsoring a rival organization would only have the effect of splitting the veterans' movement, something the government did not want.[136] The only lasting consequence of the Goslar initiative was, ironically, to provide a launching pad for the revival of the Kyffhäuserbund.

The Kyffhäuserbund had first reappeared on the scene in the spring of 1951. Although in part a reflection of the general founding frenzy of veterans' organizations at this time, the ambitions of the Bund's aged former leader, General Wilhelm Reinhard, were initially modest. His primary goal was to regain control of the Bund's assets, which had been placed in trust by the Nazi government following the Kyffhäuserbund's dissolution in 1943 and then frozen by the Allied occupation governments. Reinhard planned to use the recovered funds and property to create a welfare foundation (Sozialwerk des

Kyffhäuserbundes) for destitute veterans, and he turned first to the BvW and then to the VdS for help. The Sozialwerk was to be incorporated into the VdS, and VdS leaders, sensing its value as a recruitment tool, willingly lent their support to the Kyffhäuser project. Although he was not present at the founding meeting of the VdS, the former leader of the Kyffhäuserbund was elected to the VdS executive committee. Following the Friessner debacle, when it appeared that association with the VdS might become more a liability than an asset in the recovery of his organization's assets, Reinhard pulled back. Moreover, as he began to perceive in what ways the balance of power had shifted and to realize the possibilities that were opened to him and his organization by the VdS's demise, Reinhard began to entertain more far-reaching ambitions. These were fed by those who hoped to found a progovernment veterans' organization as a counterweight to the discredited VdS. The rising fortunes of the Kyffhäuserbund received further impetus with the collapse of the Goslar scheme in February. Although ostensibly attending the Wiesbaden meeting as an observer, Reinhard apparently had more than observation in mind. At the end of the meeting, when it became clear that the original plans to create a new veterans' *Dachorganisation* along the lines discussed at Goslar would not succeed, the idea of using a revived Kyffhäuserbund as the vehicle for the enterprise was suggested. Reinhard readily agreed, to the chagrin of the proponents of the embattled VdS. In the following months, the Kyffhäuserbund was officially refounded, and an aggressive recruitment campaign was inaugurated.[137] The return of the Bund's blocked assets considerably aided the undertaking. Its past was sanitized, and the Kyffhäuserbund, supported by the foes of the VdS, including Geyr and Schwerin, entered the struggle to win the hearts and minds of the war generation.[138]

The increasingly troubled waters of postwar German veterans' politics were muddied even further by the emergence in late 1951 of a separate organization for former Waffen-SS soldiers, innocuously named the Mutual Aid Society of Former Waffen-SS Soldiers (Hilfsgemeinschaften auf Gegenseitigkeit der ehemaligen Angehörigen der Waffen-SS [HIAG]).[139] Encouraged by the courtship of German veterans following the decision for rearmament, Waffen-SS veterans now emerged from the shadows. Their representatives claimed (falsely) that the Waffen-SS had been simply the "fourth arm of the Wehrmacht" and argued (even more outrageously) that it had been the precursor of the North Atlantic Treaty Organization since it had been a multinational force directed against the spread of bolshevism. More to the point, the founders of the HIAG demanded that Waffen-SS officers be granted the same pension rights as other former military officers. The Waffen-SS veterans had long been a hot potato, and they now became an even hotter one not only for the government and the parties but for the veterans' movement as well. The rightist parties, not surprisingly, supported the demands of the Waffen-SS veterans; so, somewhat more surprisingly, did the leader of the SPD, Kurt Schumacher. The government, fearful of international reaction and domestic ramifications, remained more circumspect.[140] The leaders of other veterans' organizations were divided on the issue. Some opposed any involvement with the pariah Waffen-SS, fearing it would endanger their own pension rights; cooperation was also impeded by lingering resentment generated by the wartime rivalry of the Wehrmacht and the Waffen-SS. Others felt that it was a point of honor to support the "defamed" Waffen-SS veterans. Originally opposed to the acceptance of former Waffen-SS members, Hansen had changed his mind when the decision was made to expand the role of the BvW. The VdS's leaders welcomed former Waffen-SS members, in part to increase its attractiveness to the younger war generation and in part to forestall the formation of a separate organization of Waffen-SS veterans.[141] The collapse of the VdS ended these hopes. The HIAG became involved in the increasingly crowded field of veterans politics, and the former Waffen-SS veterans became an object of courtship for both the VdS and the Kyffhäuserbund.

Despite its initial success, the latter was unable to vanquish its rival. By 1954 the VdS/BvW had recovered. In 1953 the Hessian VdS was given an ultimatum and brought to heel; in 1954 the second half of the unwieldy name adopted in January 1952 was finally dropped. The insurrection of noncommissioned officers was stymied. In 1953 government officials began to attend the VdS's meetings, officially certifying its *Salonfähigkeit*, and the featured speaker at the 1954 annual meeting was the noted historian, Gerhard Ritter, who spoke on "The Problem of Militarism in Germany."[142] The reports of the VdS's demise that had been widely circulated following its meeting in Hannover in January 1952 proved to be premature.

As a result, a stalemate emerged. Both the VdS and the Kyffhäuserbund tried to expand their influence and outflank their opponent by concluding agreements with other veterans' organizations, but these alliances remained fragile and ineffective. In 1953 negotiations were initiated between the two rivals in the hope of reaching an understanding. The talks dragged on for years with little sign of goodwill. *Burgfrieden* were repeatedly declared, only to be broken and followed by mutual denunciations. In late 1954 it appeared that an agreement had finally been reached, but it soon broke down, a victim of mistrust, organizational egotism, and renewed competition following the creation of the Bundeswehr, whose members were coveted not only by the VdS and the Kyffhäuserbund, but by the VdH as well.[143]

Five years after the founding of the VdS, there was still no united veterans' organization that could claim to be the representative of German veterans. The hopes of the proponents of such an organization—as well as the fears of its opponents—remained unfulfilled. The VdS had become a respectable interest group that was well integrated into the neocorporate political culture of the Federal Republic, but it was no more than that. Having successfully steered the VdS through the crisis, Hansen stepped down as president in 1956. He had saved the organization, but at the cost of sacrificing the more grandiose plans that had accompanied its foundation. At that time the leaders of the revived veterans' organizations were confident that their time had come, that the heretofore silent war generation could be united into a solid block capable of exerting major influence in the fledgling Federal Republic. While many outside observers watched the revival and consolidation of German veterans with alarm, others, including a significant number of high-ranking government officials, looked upon these developments more favorably. They recognized the potential utility of a well-organized, unified—and properly channeled—veterans' organization as a means of overcoming resistance to West German rearmament, on the one hand, and, on the other, as a form of "national opposition" that could be used to pry further concessions from Germany's victors. Regardless of their objectives, the hopes of the proponents of a unified veterans' movement remained unfulfilled. The majority of veterans refused to become involved, and those who did were divided.[144] Yet, although the divided loyalties of German veterans precluded the rise of a powerful veterans' movement, they ultimately facilitated the successful integration of veterans into postwar German society.

CONCLUSION

For Germany, the outcome of the Second World War was the same as that of the first—defeat. The circumstances that preceded, accompanied, and followed the defeat were, however, vastly different. In 1945 veterans did not return home as heroes "undefeated in the field." Unlike 1918, there was no comforting *Dolchstosslegende*. The obliteration of the distinction between the home and the fighting fronts also destroyed the mystique of the front—and of the front fighter. Veterans did not return to a homeland unmarked by war in which they could appear as political prophets. Moreover, in post–World War II Germany, traditional war victims—disabled veterans and survivors—found that they were now only one species in a nation of war victims created by the manifold disasters of the war and the regime that had unleashed it. Finally, in 1945 veterans returned not to a united, sovereign nation but to one that was occupied and divided. The postwar environments for veterans' politics after the two wars were as different as the wars themselves.

In 1918 it was easy for Germans to imagine that they were still undefeated. World War I ended with German troops in foreign lands, there had been no fighting in Germany, and official propaganda proclaiming victory on all fronts was not substantially undermined by counterdata from outside the country. While at the Paris Peace Conference the matter of guilt or responsibility revolved around the question of who had started the war, in Germany the reality of defeat itself was denied and the question of guilt revolved not around who had started the war but who had caused it to be lost.

Although the Treaty of Versailles, especially article 231, created a rare unity among the German people—with moderates as well as extremists from both ends of the political spectrum rejecting it—the defeat symbolized by the treaty bitterly divided them. The issue was complicated and confused by the incomplete revolution that followed Germany's defeat, a revolution that changed Germany's political structure but left its social structure intact. Strong enough to traumatize Germany's traditional elites and to turn them resolutely against the Republic, the revolution was not strong enough to break their power. In the end, those who had led the nation to disaster were able to transfer their own responsibility for having lost the war to the democratic forces who had the misfortune to inherit the consequences of the defeat.[1]

Unlike 1918, few Germans in 1945 could deny defeat. Years of aerial bombardment had foreshadowed it, and the bitter fighting on German soil, which culminated in the destruction of Germany's armed forces before the eyes of its civilian population, confirmed it. Defeat began to be sensed after Stalingrad, and when it finally came, it was not unexpected.[2] As the war ground to an end, the prevalent view was "better an end to the suffering than suffering without end." In 1945 defeat was welcomed not with disbelief but relief.[3] The acceptance of defeat was also made easier by the fact that in 1939 the German populace had not gone to war enthusiastically; unlike the First World War, the second was not seen as a transcendent, liberating force, something that would solve the nation's—and one's personal—problems.[4] Enthusiasm at the outbreak of the Second World War was strongly tempered by the experience of the first.[5] Begun with lower expectations, the war's loss produced less disillusionment.

Another contrast to 1918 was the fact that many, perhaps most, Germans were willing to agree with the victorious Allies on the question of responsibility for the war's outbreak. Both sides—though for different reasons—agreed that it had been Hitler's war and were happy, as A. J. P. Taylor has put it, to load the blame onto the "uncomplaining shoulders" of Hitler.[6] This time there was little debate in Germany over who was responsible for the defeat; except for a few diehards, there was little talk of a "stab in the back" in 1945.[7] The scapegoats of 1918, the Jews and the Marxists, had either been eliminated or repressed. There were no large-scale manifestations of opposition to the regime, even in the war's final stages, that could be blamed for the defeat. As an elderly foreman pointed out, "It is being said: 'In the last war the army was said to have done its duty and the people had failed. This time the Wehrmacht has again done its duty. The homeland does all that the leadership demands of it. If things go wrong this time whose fault is it?' "[8]

What talk there was of betrayal indicted not the left but the traditional right. Nazi true believers, searching for the betrayers of their cause, turned their wrath upon the conspirators of 20 July 1944 or on the army. Hitler, too, blamed the army. There was, of course, a certain irony in this attempt by Hitler, a prime proponent of the *Dolchstoss* legend of 1918, to invert the legend in order to escape his responsibility for the disaster of 1945.[9] Yet most Germans after the Second World War found it hard to accept the charge that the army had either been stabbed in the back or had failed. Most believed that the

Wehrmacht had been defeated by the material superiority of its enemies and remained proud of its achievements; some even complained that it had done too well, thus prolonging the war and increasing the destruction suffered by the country.[10] Since there was no revolution to confuse events in 1945, most Germans readily accepted the fact that the nation's defeat was the responsibility of the Nazi regime—even if not necessarily of Hitler himself, who for many remained a Teflon-Führer long after his death.[11]

In 1918, the victors, like many Germans, felt that the changes introduced by the November Revolution had righted the wrongs of German history and that Germany and the Germans could soon, if not immediately, be welcomed into the society of civilized Western democracies. After the horrors of the Third Reich had been revealed, the victors of 1945 were convinced that more fundamental changes were necessary to make the world safe from the apparently incorrigible Germans, who, while willing to admit defeat, showed little contrition for the crimes of the Third Reich.[12] Institutions had to be reformed, pernicious traditions rooted out, and the people reeducated to understand and appreciate democracy.

While the efforts of the Western Allies to reeducate Germans undoubtedly did affect postwar political developments in Germany after World War II, the effects of these efforts are easily overrated and are a matter of dispute. Anglo-American observers have generally tended to adopt a self-congratulatory position, claiming credit for having solved the "German Problem" at long last, what one might call the "forced to be free" syndrome.[13] Critics have argued that the policies of the Western Allies did not so much reform German society as aid a restoration of old, often illiberal elites and institutions.[14] Both sides overestimate the degree to which the slate was wiped clean in 1945 and the power the occupying forces had to affect developments. The nature and circumstances of defeat did as much to change German attitudes as the overt efforts of the victors. It must also be kept in mind that one of the most effective agents of denazification was the experience and failure of the Third Reich.

When we compare the immediate postwar years in Germany following the defeats of 1918 and 1945, we see that the benefits of occupation after 1945 were real but more often indirect than direct. The main importance of the military governments of the occupying powers was not their role as direct instigators of change so much as their function as a shield and lightning rod for German leaders who were building and running the new democratic institutions. In 1918 the new leaders of the Weimar Republic were forced to liquidate the war and to confront the massive and unprecedented problems created by the war and Germany's defeat. They were unprepared for and eventually overwhelmed by the task. Their failures discredited them and the new system they represented. German leaders and the fledgling democratic institutions created after 1945 were spared these rigors. On the one hand, post-1945 German leaders, who had had no power during the war and lacked sovereignty immediately after it, could not be blamed for the misery that resulted from the war and the sacrifices required for the reconstruction of the country.[15] Postwar problems caused by the war and defeat could be blamed on national socialism or, more conveniently, on the occupying powers.[16] On the other hand, German politicians, by their denunciation of unpopular measures and occasional successes in getting the Allies to abandon or modify unpopular policies, were able to convince their constituents that they were sincere and effective representatives of their interests.[17] In the process, they gained valuable political capital for the future, a commodity that Germany's new leaders in 1918 were sadly lacking.[18]

The "zero hour [Stunde Null]" of 1945 did not create a tabula rasa, nor were policies thereafter simply dictated from above by all-powerful victors to a supine and powerless population. Instead, there was a constant dialogue between the victors and the vanquished. Attempts to dictate policy unilaterally and rigidly often failed or backfired.[19] As a result of the dialogue between the victors and the vanquished, much of what emerged in postwar Germany was old and much that appeared new was not really so new.

Yet things were different. While many of the proposed reforms failed and old elites and institutions reemerged, the parallelogram of social, political, and economic forces was altered in ways that favored the development of parliamentary democracy. Members of the old, antidemocratic political elite remained visible, often embarrassingly so, but the balance of power shifted decisively to political veterans of Weimar's democratic parties. The Ruhr steel and coal complex remained in private hands and big business regained its traditionally strong voice in German political life, but its autonomy was reduced and its power was checked by the strengthened position of the unions.[20] Similarly, the old bureaucracy was largely restored, but it was more dependent and more compliant than it had been after 1918. Battered by the Nazis and seriously threatened by the reform plans of the occupation governments, the professional bureaucracy found a savior in the new Federal Republic. The German army was also rebuilt, but only after the new political system had been given firm foundations. Far from being—or feeling—threatened by the new state, both the bureaucracy and the Bundeswehr owed their existence to it. This engendered loyalty, and neither the bureaucracy nor the army became oppositional states within the state.[21] This was in marked contrast to the situation after the First World War.

Another contrast was that in 1945, unlike 1918, returning veterans were not seen as political heralds. Returning to a physically intact country, World War I veterans could not help but feel that their sacrifice had been greater than that of the civilian population, and civilians generally shared this view.[22] In 1945 veterans did not return *from* a no man's land, but *to* one—a moonscape of skeleton cities and massive destruction. After World War II German civilians could rightly argue that they had suffered as much as the soldiers, and veterans, returning to the rubble of 1945, were generally willing to agree. During the Second World War the civilian population not only experienced the war but also relived, perhaps even more intensely than the soldiers, the liminal, troglodyte existence of the First World War's combatants. Veterans no longer were considered to be invested with a special wisdom. Any secrets they might have were considered either irrelevant or best kept secret.[23] The barriers to understanding and the myths that developed after 1918 did not reemerge in 1945. In short, the romantic militarism that had fed nazism after the First World War did not survive the second. The effects of a regime imbued with "soldierly virtues" had been experienced firsthand—with disastrous consequences. Civilians and soldiers alike were engaged in the struggle to survive in the harsh postwar environment and to rebuild their shattered country. The commonality of experience of soldiers and civilians both during the war itself and in the *Notgemeinschaft* of postwar Germany helped to build bridges between the two groups. The pacifist-militarist bifurcation that had poisoned German society in the 1920s did not reappear; instead there emerged a consensus that war was futile.[24]

After the Second World War a potent, unifying myth that gave meaning to the war did not emerge. The mystique of the front and the front fighter was gone. The war experience remained unpoliticized. Veterans never became a significant political force as they had in the 1920s.[25] Friessner's complaint that the creation of a united veterans' organization had been thwarted by "the completely heterogeneous views within the former officer corps in particular and among veterans in general" revealed both his frustration with the VdS's failure to unite veterans into a political force and the persistence of the post–World War I myth of a unified front experience. His lament betrayed a nostalgia for a unity that in fact had never existed. The front generation of the First World War had been as divided as that of the Second World War. The division into different "interest groups" such as former professional soldiers, POWs, and war-disabled that so dismayed Friessner was as rampant in the 1920s as in the 1950s. Even the former officers were divided—except in their hatred of the Republic. Yet the war experience had been monopolized by the right and fashioned into a powerful political weapon to be turned upon the Republic and the political principles it represented. Conflicting interpretations were drowned out, and the Front Ideology espoused by the rightist veterans' organizations and combat leagues was accepted by large segments of the German population, veteran and nonveteran alike, for a variety of reasons, including nostalgia, anger, resentment, guilt, fear, and rejection of the present.

There are a number of reasons why a similarly potent myth did not emerge after the Second World War. Disillusionment with the militarized life of the Third Reich and the shared war experience of soldiers and civilians described above are two of them. Another was that those voices protesting the dominant myth, which had been increasingly smothered in the 1920s and silenced in the 1930s, could now be heard again. Here, too, the parallelogram of forces had changed. Veterans, let alone a small minority of them on the right, never gained a monopoly on the explanation and interpretation of Germany's second "war experience." While the postwar environment of the First World War had nourished veterans' politics, that following the Second World War did not. Allied strictures against organized veteran activity and the difficult material circumstances following the war combined to prevent the formation of a specifically veteran subculture. In 1918 veterans returned to a relatively intact society as alienated outsiders.[26] They joined together immediately after the war when the collective veteran consciousness was strong, and in later years veterans' organizations helped to sustain a separate veteran identity that became highly politicized. Activity as veterans (often paramilitary in nature) thus preceded social reintegration and retarded psychological demobilization. After 1945 veterans' organizations were banned during the occupation, and in the years of hard economic struggle that followed the war—a struggle intensified by the low level or lack of veterans' benefits—veterans were forced to form new economic and social ties. These ties worked to reintegrate them into society as individuals. Social reintegration therefore preceded activity in veterans' organizations, which helped to foster pragmatic policies by the veterans' groups when they were again permitted. Unlike after the First World War, veterans after the second were psychologically demobilized before they became politically active. The paucity of benefits during the occupation and the lack of broadly based veterans' organizations not only helped to prevent the growth of a general, romanticized version of the war experience but also reinforced differences among veterans. Just as the feeling of being a member of a specific "community of fate [Schicksalsgemeinschaft]" cut across class lines and helped to focus the political activity of large segments of the society as a whole on interest group politics,[27] veterans tended to remain tied to a specific subcommunity within the veteran population as a whole. This reinforced an interest group mentality and prevented any one group from emerging as *the* interpreter of the war experience.

After the Second World War, unlike after the first, the discourse was not between soldiers and civilians or about who had been heroes and who had not but about who had been most victimized by the war. On one level this was simply a means of forgetting the past and evading the coming to terms with the past (*Vergangenheitsbewältigung*) demanded by the victors. Confronted with the suffering caused by Germany's actions, Germans pointed to their ruined cities and the millions of German expellees driven from former German lands and insisted that they had suffered as much as their enemies.[28] Troops and civilians alike vividly remembered their suffering while repressing that of Germany's victims. The war was a painful memory, but only of one's own suffering. The war, as Omer Bartov has put it, became a vehicle that "served postwar German society to suppress its crimes by lamenting its own fate. The war had made the Wehrmacht into Hitler's army, the Germans into Hitler's people. Defeat converted them all into victims. If Austria was Hitler's first victim, Germany was his last. And victims cannot be called to account."[29] In postwar Germany victimology became an art and then a dizzying science run amok, with pension-less officers comparing their plight to that of Jews in the Third Reich.[30] On one level, however, the postwar German preoccupation with establishing one's status as a victim had a salutary effect in that it helped to moderate veterans' politics. If organized veterans after the First World War were obsessed with suppressing putative "internal enemies" and waging a war of revenge, veterans' organizations after the Second World War were obsessed with proving not who had been the bravest but who had suffered the most—and was therefore most deserving of a pension. In post–World War II Germany, monuments honored victims, not warriors. As one writer has observed, while the monuments of the First World War referred to the war experience itself, those of the Second World War called attention to the consequences of war.[31]

The hiatus of organizational activity during the occupation combined with the lack of benefits worked to promote pragmatic, moderate policies on the part of veterans once they were again allowed to organize. The dominant veterans' groups in the Federal Republic represented specific interests and focused on benefits: war victims, former POWs, and former professional soldiers. After 1945 the latter, without the luxury of the automatic pensions they had enjoyed in the Weimar Republic, were more cautious. When some, under the banner of the VdS, again tried to claim a monopoly on the leadership of the war generation and to politicize the veterans' movement, they failed. Within their own ranks they were reined in by those who, either out of tactical considerations or the genuine realization of the way in which their past actions had contributed to Germany's disaster, opposed politicization.[32]

The realization that the old prescriptions were unsuited for the present was clearly articulated in the views of Hermann Müller-Brandenburg, a former leader of the Stahlhelm who worked as a BvW liaison in Bonn until late 1951, when he resigned in the wake of the Friessner fiasco and became a backer of the Goslar initiative.[33] Müller-Brandenburg refused to have anything to do with the revived Stahlhelm, claiming that its revival was "totally misguided," since "today we find ourselves in a position that has nothing in common with that of 1920. The conditions are completely different and the means must also be completely different."[34] For one thing, the moral and legal considerations that had justified opposition to the Treaty of Versailles were lacking, and "this must be recognized by every German. . . . The Hitler government was *not* forced into war, but clearly *wanted* war and *rejected all warnings against it*. The German people now have to bear the consequences, just as any people have to bear the consequences of what its leaders do or do not do."[35] In the present circumstances, the role of the former soldiers was not to fight the state but to help it. "The Federal Republic that has developed here in the west has obtained certain rights and freedoms for us from the occupying powers." More had to be done, but it had to be done within the existing system, since it was "indisputable that the overwhelming majority of the German people passionately reject any form of authoritarian government." The same was true of the fight for veterans' rights: "If we join together as soldiers to fight for our rights as soldiers, to help one another as comrades, and to look after the interests of the survivors, we have the duty to do this within the existing state order . . . ; we must exclude those who are so stupidly servile as to desire a new form of dictatorship." The VdS as it had developed under Friessner and his supporters was not only mistaken but a danger:

> A general veterans' organization in the form of the VdS, as a unitary organization, is a technical impossibility, since the interests of the various components of veterans, BvW, *Traditionsverbände*, POWs, war-disabled . . . are completely different. The purpose of constituting the VdS in its present form is based on the desire to create a force [Macht] that can impose its will on the people and the state. Such a power factor [Macht-gestaltung] can only be created by imposing an authoritarian will on the majority of veterans. Such an organization is, however, a foreign body [Fremdkörper] in the state and I can assure you . . . that the state will not tolerate the creation of such a force [Machtbildung]—for its leadership would have at its disposal the opportunity at any time to misuse veterans for its own purpose and to dictate things to the state and the people that neither desires.[36]

The political officers' claim to speak for the war generation as a whole was immediately challenged by other veterans. In an angry eight-page letter to

Gert Spindler, whose newspaper had characterized him as a "civilian," Werner Noack, a prominent VdH leader involved in the Goslar project, argued that in the present circumstances all Germans were civilians and disputed the right of former officers to speak for all veterans. He repeatedly underlined the fact that in the last war POWs in Russia had fought a battle that was "no less difficult" than those who had continued to fight at the front and added that with the development of total war, bravery and the risking of one's life for the nation were no longer limited to soldiers, since "workers in the munitions factories and women in the bombed cities had shown examples of bravery and courage that were the equal of those of the soldiers." Indeed, Noack argued, the man on the front, with a weapon in his hand for defense, was freer and more in control of his fate than those who helplessly had to undergo bombing attacks. "Today," Noack continued, "the professional soldier only represents a part of the veteran population." To be a professional soldier no longer conferred privilege and the a priori right of leadership as it had earlier. "The majority of the Wehrmacht veterans," Noack contended, "refuse to acknowledge the claim that former professional soldiers are predestined to lead the debate over questions that concern us all." In response to derogatory remarks in Spindler's paper regarding the so-called "license parties" of the Federal Republic (*Lizenzparteien*), those parties that had been authorized by the occupation forces, Noack retorted, "I believe that we had enough of political soldiers or soldierly politicians from 1933 to 1945; we have seen that the consequence of their actions was to lead Germany into the greatest catastrophe of its history. Our current situation is not the consequence of the policies of the Federal Republic and the license parties, but of the policies that led to 1945 and the subsequent policies of the occupying powers." The new order needed to be defended, not attacked:

> The collective defamation of all of the representatives of the Federal Republic as licensees [Lizenzträger], American lackeys [Amerikahörige], etc., appears to me to be totally unsuited to promote the domestic peace that we need. . . . We have, my very honored Mr. Spindler, brought back with us from the Soviet Union very precise ideas about the concept of democracy . . . and those of us with the double experience of the years before 1945 and those after 1945 in the Soviet Union are of the view that human dignity and freedom are always and most effectively maintained in a democratic state.[37]

In contrast to the years after the First World War, a large, ideologically centered veterans' organization never emerged. The post-1945 attempts to revive the Stahlhelm failed miserably.[38] What had appeared modern and dynamic in the 1920s appeared hopelessly outdated in the 1950s. The fire-eating editorials that appeared in the HIAG's paper, *Der Freiwillige*, or in the *Deutsche Soldaten Zeitung* received little attention from the vast majority of veterans, whose nostalgia for the war years, if it existed at all, was quenched by the relatively benign pulp novels (*Landser-Hefte*) sold at newspaper kiosks.[39] *Traditionsverbände*, with their *gemütlich* reunions, flourished while the VdS languished. Although their leaders were subject to occasional oratorical derailments, especially in the early years, the *Traditionsverbände* never became politicized. Their main goal was to provide a forum for comradeship, not for attacks on democracy.[40] While the actions of their leaders were often an embarrassment to the Republic, they were not a threat to its existence. Endorsements of the new order were often qualified but were nonetheless real. As Hasso von Manteuffel, the leader of the Grossdeutschland Panzer Division's *Traditionsverband*, put it in a 1951 article: "Learning from past experience, we want veterans to have a *positive attitude* toward our state, even if we today still cannot regard it . . . as an ideal model. On one thing, however, there can be no doubt: the still weak seedling of Bonn is the *only* seedling from which we can raise a tree under which we will eventually find protection and from which we will someday harvest benefits."[41] Even the organization of former Waffen-SS veterans, the HIAG, eventually became a *Traditionsverband* cum interest group, whose main goal was pensions, not a restoration of the Third Reich.[42]

The Second World War, much more than the first, had democratized the military. Here, as in other areas, the experience of the Third Reich had, albeit unwittingly, helped to prepare the way for democracy following its collapse.[43] Like postwar German society as a whole, the veterans' community was pluralistic. Because there was no single veteran's experience and because the different experiences were clearly articulated and represented organizationally, attempts to impose either a single view of the war or to create a unified veterans' organization were problematical at best. The leaders of the VdS were slow to realize this. They only became fully aware of how divided veterans were when they tried to unite them. Not only were there a myriad of groups, with different constituencies and different aims, as Friessner belatedly realized, but the rank and file of veterans refused to exercise the deference that was expected. To make things worse, the former officers were themselves divided.[44] The issue of rearmament, which they planned to shape according to their views and needs, created additional divisions in their ranks, which produced frustration and political impotence.

The formation of the Bundeswehr, unlike that of the Reichswehr, was closely supervised by civilians; the role of the old officer corps, much to the chagrin of the VdS, was strictly limited. Unlike in 1918, the government had strong cards and played them adroitly.[45] In part this was possible because West German rearmament took place under the aegis of the Cold War, which produced new, previously unrealizable alignments. Neither of the maximalist positions of the 1920s—pacifism or a renewed war of national revenge—was feasible in the 1950s. Compromises were made. Liberals and (somewhat more belatedly) Social Democrats accepted the need of military defense, while the military establishment accepted the need for democratic control.[46] Under the pressure of the Cold War, a consensus eventually emerged that in large part removed, or at least blurred, the old promilitary/antimilitary dichotomy that had divided German society since the foundation of the German Empire. Although a consensus was reached, it was not unanimous and it took some time to achieve. In the meantime, veterans, like West German society as a whole, remained divided on the issue. Such political divisions, loyalty to specific veteran subcultures, and the existing organizational emphasis on interest politics combined to make impossible the united veterans' movement envisioned by the VdS's leaders; at the same time, these impediments to unity facilitated the integration of veterans into postwar German society by encouraging limited and pragmatic activity.[47]

THE DEVELOPMENT of the German veterans' movement after 1945 revealed how, as in other areas, the parallelogram of sociopolitical forces had shifted in Germany after the Second World War. The successful reintegration of veterans was also symptomatic of a larger process of integration and accommodation that worked to stabilize Germany's second experiment in democracy and to assure its success. In the Federal Republic's early years, large numbers of the new state's citizens were in desperate material circumstances and in need of support. The most obvious were those who had been directly affected by the destructive consequences of the war and Germany's defeat: the expellees, the war victims, those whose homes and businesses had been bombed out, and the hundreds of thousands of late-returning prisoners of war. To these one also must add the elderly and infirm, whose survival was threatened by the severe postwar conditions and the curtailment of German social insurance benefits.[48] Social problems were among the most pressing of the multitude of difficulties facing the new Republic, constituting what one author has characterized as a "founding crisis" or *Gründungskrise*.[49] All of these groups, as another author has said of the expellees, were like ticking time bombs planted in the foundations of the Republic.[50]

The pressing need for social legislation was acknowledged by Adenauer in his inaugural address to the Bundestag on 20 September 1949, when he declared that "the guiding principle [Leitstern] of the government's work" would be the "effort to alleviate need" and to achieve "social justice."[51] He went on to mention specifically the expellees, the war victims, the prisoners of war, the homeless, and the civil servants who had lost their positions following the war. Each group's problems were recognized, and help was promised. On the whole, these promises were kept. As one author dealing with the early history of the Federal Republic has put it, social legislation helped to integrate the vast number of socially dislocated citizens into West German society and to stabilize the new democratic order by "overcoming the misery left by the war and . . . not allowing the formation of any compact group of persons in obvious need."[52] While true, this represents a somewhat simplistic and mechanistic equation: social legislation plus benefits equals integration. Such a formulation is suitable as a sort of shorthand, but it overlooks the components and dynamics of the process.

More social legislation was passed in the first legislative period (1949–53) than in any other in the history of the Federal Republic.[53] Veterans' benefits formed a crucial component of this legislation. The Federal Republic's first major piece of social legislation was the Bundesversorgungsgesetz, which provided health care, vocational training, and pensions for the war-disabled— both military and civilian—and survivors of those killed in the war. By 1952 the BVG directly covered nearly 4.5 million citizens—close to one-fifth of the Federal Republic's population if we count those indirectly affected. The Heimkehrergesetz of June 1950 assisted late-returning prisoners of war by providing financial assistance, social insurance coverage, vocational training, and preferential treatment in housing and hiring. In May 1951 the 131 Law was passed, restoring pensions to former professional soldiers. The capstone of the Republic's early social legislation was the Lastenausgleichsgesetz, which provided compensation, vocational training, and pensions for those who had experienced material losses as a result of the war.[54]

To focus simply on the passage of the laws themselves, however, overlooks a crucial aspect of German postwar history that contributed greatly to the effectiveness of social legislation and its role in stabilizing the Federal Republic. As the history of the Weimar Republic demonstrates, progressive social legislation does not guarantee democratic stability. In order to understand why social legislation played such a positive role in the success of the second German republic, one must look at the period that preceded it, the years of military occupation. This is especially true for legislation concerning veterans, who were a specific target of discrimination during this period.

The semisovereignty of the new Federal Republic brought with it full responsibility for the care of war victims. Whereas earlier the shortcomings of benefits could be blamed on the Allies' policies, the new government now had to demonstrate that it could improve matters. This was not easy, since the enormous fiscal means necessary to fund an adequate program for over 4 million war victims had to be found within a tight budget based on a fledgling, uncertain economy burdened by the needs of other social programs as well as occupation costs. Because of these fiscal constraints, the pension levels of the BVG, passed in 1950, were lower than those the war victims had hoped for and quickly became the target of attacks by the war victims and their organizations. Nevertheless, the BVG was unquestionably a success for several reasons. First, although benefits were attacked as being inadequate, they were uniform and, with few exceptions, better than those provided during the occupation. Second, the BVG was German, closely modeled on the Reichsversorgungsgesetz of 1920. Like the RVG, the BVG established an independent system for the treatment of war victims, thus fulfilling a major demand of the war victims and their organizations.

Like the Federal Republic's reorganized but largely unreformed social security system[55] and the Beamtenrecht of 1953, the BVG thus represented a restoration—a rejection of Allied reform attempts and a return to German practices. However, this did not entail a relapse into authoritarian ways but rather an affirmation and strengthening of the democratic process. The passage of the BVG helped to establish the Federal Republic's legitimacy in two ways. First, it demonstrated the Republic's willingness and ability to provide social services that were considered indispensable. Second, by overturning unpopular legislation imposed by the occupying powers, it demonstrated the Republic's growing sovereignty. This was also true for the 131 Law.

There is more to the BVG and the 131 Law than the benefits they provided. Like the social insurance programs and the Beamtenrecht, they represented acts of successful resistance, of the assertion of German wishes. Those who resisted Allied reform attempts during the occupation and later legislated the new laws earned credibility as effective representatives of the German people. The Republic's early social legislation provided Germans with a growing and much-needed sense of being in control of their own destiny. The numerous and grave social problems facing the Federal Republic at its inception may well have represented a *Gründungskrise*, but they also provided the new Republic with opportunities to demonstrate its competency and to win the support of important constituencies.

Thus, it was not just what the laws did but what they represented that made them important. Similarly, it was not just the benefits provided by the laws that helped to integrate their beneficiaries but also the very process of creating the legislation itself. The statement attributed to Bismarck that anyone who likes either sausages or laws should never watch them being made does not apply here. The social legislation of the Republic's early years was accompanied by organizational, political, and psychological developments that facilitated social and political integration and the building of consensus, which in turn strengthened the new Republic and its institutions.

An important element in this process was the emergence of interest groups. During the occupation, many of the social groups that were to be the main beneficiaries of postwar legislation were denied the right to organize: all veterans' organizations, including those representing disabled veterans, were prohibited; similarly, organizations representing the expellees were banned. In the final years of the occupation, the military governments loosened their controls somewhat, but the activity of interest groups continued to be hedged by restrictions and weakened by zonal divisions. With the formation of the Republic, the restrictions were lifted, and centralized organizations quickly emerged. Their input into the decision-making process was facilitated by the simultaneous creation of centralized federal ministries. It may be that the social policy of the Adenauer era succeeded because "it did not allow the formation of any compact group of persons in obvious need," but an important step in getting to that point was precisely the opportunity to form "compact group[s] of persons in obvious need." The first year of the Republic's existence was accompanied by a prolific growth of interest groups, including the Verband der Heimkehrer, the Bund versorgungsberechtigter ehemaliger Wehrmachtsangehöriger, and the two major organizations of war victims, the Verband der Kriegsbeschädigten and the Reichsbund der Kriegsbeschädigten. By providing a field of activity for these organized interests, the Republic could not help but to appear in a positive light compared with the occupation period or, for that matter, the Third Reich. Overwhelmed by the complexity of the issues they faced and under pressure to act quickly, the newly formed ministries and the Bundestag committees in charge of drafting social legislation were receptive to the wishes of the emerging interest groups. Civil servants and legislators welcomed the expert assistance that could be provided by interest group representatives, many of whom had had extensive experience with the Weimar legislation that formed the basis for post–World War II social legislation. Conscious of the fact that the straitened financial circumstances of the Republic would dictate lower benefits than many of the potential recipients expected, officials hoped to bind their interest groups to the legislation by giving them a share in its drafting. As a result, interest group representatives were regularly invited to discuss their needs with ministerial representatives and parliamentary committees.

Input into the decision-making process was also manifested and made visible by the presence of representatives of the various social interests within the parties of the Bundestag and, even more importantly, by their presence in the parliamentary committees charged with the drafting of social legislation.[56] While the beneficiaries and their interest groups could—and did—complain about the need for further improvements, they could not claim that they were not getting a fair hearing. The parties in the Bundestag (both those of the opposition and those belonging to the government coalition) exercised constant pressure on the government to introduce bills, and the parliamentary committees repeatedly expanded and improved government drafts.

The even balance of political forces in the Republic's first legislative period, the fluidity of the system, and the desire of its fledgling politicians to make it work all increased the pressure on the parties to bid for the support of disadvantaged social groups. At the same time the awareness that all groups now had virtually equal *Startchancen*, combined with the knowledge that other interests were organizing, increased the pressure on the affected social groups to organize and move toward the state, rather than—as was so often the case in Weimar, especially with regard to veterans—against it.

The debates that accompanied the passage of social legislation in the early years of the Republic reflected important changes in the nature of German political discourse and did much to legitimate the new political order. While partisan polemical exchanges did not entirely disappear, especially in questions of foreign policy, in the debates over social policy partisan attacks were muted and more the exception than the rule. The concern of legislators for the victims was genuine, all the more so since if they themselves were not affected, someone in their family was sure to be. All classes of Germans had experienced the disastrous social consequences of the Third Reich and the Second World War. After 1945 social legislation cut across class lines as never before; it was not, as it tended to be in the empire and the Weimar Republic, class-specific.[57] The willingness of the parties to cooperate and compromise was repeatedly manifested in the debates on social legislation—the SPD often sided with the CDU and at times with parties on the right.[58] Debates on social legislation repeatedly reflected and reinforced the "double consensus" of the post–World War II era, the rejection of extremist solutions from both the right and the left.[59] Those charged with the rebuilding of social programs and the drafting of legislation to repair the destruction wrought by national socialism were well aware that the Nazis had played fast and loose with the welfare of the German people; similarly, developments in the German Democratic Republic quickly deflated enthusiasm for Communist solutions.

In the context of the debates over social legislation, even "Commiebashing" had a certain positive integrative function.[60] Such instances were usually touched off by statements or proposals by Communist Party deputies that were long on propagandistic intent but short on practicality; both Social Democratic and middle-class party spokespersons followed by denouncing the empty, unrealistic nature of the Communist proposals. At the same time they invariably pointed out the lack of adequate support for comparable disadvantaged social groups in the German Democratic Republic.[61] These exchanges had a double effect: within the Bundestag, internal signals were sent that facilitated cooperation between the SPD and the bourgeois parties—thus while the CDU's election posters might say that all Marxist paths led to Moscow, this was repudiated by everyday experience; the exchanges also sent an important signal outside the Bundestag to those who were affected by the laws being debated—namely, that things could be worse.

Knowing that things could be worse provides an important key for understanding the significance of postwar West German social legislation and its contribution to the success of the Federal Republic. In the 1950s, memories of the late 1940s were still fresh. Most Germans recalled the occupation period as a time not of "reeducation" but of deprivation and suffering, much of which was caused by the cutback of social benefits that followed Allied reform attempts. Full appreciation of the German "social safety-net" came only with its loss—or threatened loss. The dogged defense of traditional German programs during the occupation and their large-scale restoration in the early years of the Federal Republic did much to establish the credibility of West Germany's new leaders and to legitimate the new democratic state. The legislative process associated with the drafting of the new laws integrated the leaders of disadvantaged groups into the new political order. The ensuing benefits bound their members to it. Beneficiaries of the legislation often complained that they deserved more, but they were acutely aware that things could indeed be much worse and that the way to get improvements was to work through the system. This process was furthered by the "economic miracle," which permitted a steady expansion of benefits, and reinforced by the Adenauer government's practice of providing social legislative "election gifts [*Wahlgeschenke*]."[62] The significance of the social legislation of the early years of the Federal Republic went far beyond the benefits it provided, however. The laws represented an assertion of pride and independence—they were made in Germany, by Germans, according to German traditions. Even more importantly, they proved that parliamentary government in general and, in particular, the new state framed by the Grundgesetz could function effectively in meeting the needs of its citizens.

NOTES

Abbreviations

In addition to the abbreviations used in the text, the following abbreviations are used in the notes.

AdsD/FES	Archiv der sozialen Demokratie/Friedrich-Ebert-Stiftung, Bonn/Bad Godesberg
BAF	Bundesarchiv-Militärarchiv, Freiburg im Breisgau
BAK	Bundesarchiv, Koblenz
DBDr	*Deutscher Bundestag. Anlagen zu den stenographischen Berichten. Drucksache*
DKOV	*Deutsche Kriegsopferversorgung*
IfZ	Institut für Zeitgeschichte, Munich
NARS	National Archives and Records Service, Washington, D.C.
OMGUS	Office of Military Government, United States
PAB	Parlamentsarchiv, Bonn
PRO	Public Record Office, Kew, England
VDB	*Verhandlungen des Deutschen Bundestags. I. Wahlperiode 1949. Stenographische Berichte*

Chapter 1

1. The unification of the state organizations in the Kyffhäuserbund followed the building of a monument celebrating German unification that had been sponsored by the veterans' organizations. The monument, a classic example of the bombastic style of Wilhelmine public monuments, was built on the Kyffhäuser, a mountain in central Germany. According to German legend, the Hohenstaufen Emperor Frederick Barbarossa resided in the mountain, from which he would come to rescue Germany in time of crisis. On the early history of German veterans' organizations and the formation of the Kyffhäuserbund, see Alfred Westphal, "Die Kriegervereine," in *Deutschland als Weltmacht. Vierzig Jahre Deutsches Reich*, herausgegeben vom Kaiser-Wilhelm-Dank

(Berlin, 1911), and Wilhelm Reinhard, "Der N.S.-Reichskriegerbund," in *Das Dritte Reich im Aufbau*, Band 3 (Berlin, 1939). Also cf. Christopher James Elliott, "The Kriegervereine and the Weimar Republic," *Journal of Contemporary History* 10/1 (January 1975): 1–2.

2. Eckart Kehr, "Zur Genesis des Königlich Preussischen Reserveoffiziers," in *Der Primat der Innenpolitik. Gesammelte Aufsätze zur preussisch-deutschen Sozialgeschichte im 19. und 20. Jahrhundert*, herausgegeben und eingeleitet von Hans-Ulrich Wehler (Berlin, 1965). On the conversion of the veterans' organizations into a "bulwark against Social Democracy," see Klaus Saul, "Der 'Deutsche Kriegerbund.' Zur innenpolitischen Funktion eines 'nationalen' Verbandes im kaiserlichen Deutschland," *Militärgeschichtliche Mitteilungen*, 1969/1. See also Reinhard Höhn, *Sozialismus und Heer*, Band 3 (Bad Harzburg, 1969), and Martin Kitchen, *The German Officer Corps, 1890–1914* (London, 1968), chapters 6–7.

3. Westphal, "Die Kriegervereine," p. 762.

4. On the pacifist subculture and its relation to the dominant culture, see Roger Chickering, *Imperial Germany and a World without War: The Peace Movement and German Society, 1892–1914* (Princeton, 1975). In addition to the *Kriegervereine*, there were other organizations that propagated antisocialist, antipacifist, and promilitary values. Two of the main ones were the German Army League (Deutscher Wehrverein) and the Young Germany League (Jungdeutschlandbund). On the former, see Marilyn S. Coetzee, *The German Army League: Popular Nationalism in Wilhelmine Germany* (Oxford, 1990). On the latter see Klaus Saul, "Der Kampf um die Jugend zwischen Volksschule und Kaserne. Ein Beitrag zur 'Jungendpflege' im Wilhelminischen Reich, 1890–1914," *Militärgeschichtliche Mitteilungen*, 1971/1, and Derek S. Linton, *Who Has the Youth Has the Future: The Campaign to Save Young Workers in Imperial Germany* (Cambridge, 1991).

5. Kyffhäuser-Bund der Deutschen Landeskriegerverbände, Sitzung des Vorstandes vom 30. und 31. Oktober 1915, NSDAP Hauptarchiv, folder 913. Most of the materials of the NSDAP Hauptarchiv are currently in the Bundesarchiv in Koblenz, Germany (Bestand NS26). The material is also available on microfilm as part of the Hoover Institution Microfilm Collection in Stanford, California. See Grete Heinz and Agnes F. Peterson, eds., *NSDAP Hauptarchiv: Guides to the Hoover Institution Microfilm Collection* (Stanford, 1964). For a detailed account of the Kyffhäuserbund's activity during the war based on these materials, see James M. Diehl, "The Organization of German Veterans, 1917–1919," *Archiv für Sozialgeschichte*, 11 (1971).

6. The terms "forces of movement" and "forces of order," as well as the general analytical framework for their interplay during the war, are taken from Arno J. Mayer, *Political Origins of the New Diplomacy, 1917–1918* (New York, 1970). On the founding of the Fatherland Party, see Dirk Stegemann, "Zwischen Repression und Manipulation. Konservative Machteliten und Arbeiter- und Angestelltenbewegung, 1910–1918," *Archiv für Sozialgeschichte* 12 (1972).

7. Robert W. Whalen, *Bitter Wounds: German Victims of the Great War, 1914–1939*

(Ithaca, N.Y., 1984), chapters 6–7. For a contemporary comparative survey, see Edward T. Devine, *Disabled Soldiers and Sailors Pensions and Training* (New York, 1919).

8. For a concrete and crucial example of the importance of soldiers and the efforts of contending political factions to win their allegiance in Russia, see Alexander Rabinowitch, "The Petrograd Garrison and the Bolshevik Seizure of Power," in *Revolution and Politics in Russia: Essays in Memory of B. I. Nicolaevsky*, edited by Alexander Rabinowitch and Janet Rabinowitch (Bloomington, 1972). For a comparative overview, see Stephen R. Ward, ed., *The War Generation: Veterans of the First World War* (Port Washington, N.Y., 1975).

9. Although elections to Germany's national parliamentary body, the Reichstag, were based on universal suffrage, those to the Prussian diet, the Landtag, were still held on the basis of an antiquated and undemocratic three-class suffrage system that had been introduced during the wave of reaction that followed the abortive revolution of 1848. Based on the principle that representation should be proportional to the amount of direct taxes paid to the state, the Prussian three-class system gave enormous power to the wealthy while virtually disenfranchising the poorer members of society. In the 1898 elections to the Prussian Landtag, for example, two-thirds of the representatives were elected by less than 15 percent of the population. In 1913, although they polled nearly 30 percent of the vote, the Social Democrats won only 10 seats, while the Conservatives, who polled less than 15 percent, won 143. The manifest inequity of the three-class system was further compounded by indirect and public voting procedures as well as extensive gerrymandering.

10. On Kuttner, see Whalen, *Bitter Wounds*, pp. 121–24, 191.

11. *Vorwärts*, 31 December 1916.

12. Ibid., 3 April 1917. *Bericht des Bundesvorstandes mit Protokoll der Verhandlungen des 2. Reichsbundestages, Würzburg, 11.–15. Mai*, herausgegeben vom Reichsbund der Kriegsbeschädigten, Kriegsteilnehmer, und Kriegshinterbliebenen (Berlin, [1920]), p. 18. See also Whalen, *Bitter Wounds*, pp. 119–21.

13. *Vorwärts*, 4 June 1917.

14. For details, see Diehl, "Organization," and "Germany: Veterans' Politics under Three Flags," in *The War Generation: Veterans of the First World War*, edited by Stephen R. Ward (Port Washington, N.Y., 1975).

15. In this regard, it is interesting to note that shortly before the end of the war Westphal and other leaders of the Kyffhäuserbund were taken for a tour by the Supreme Command through the recently conquered areas in the Baltic and Ukraine. Diehl, "Organization," p. 171.

16. The percentage of nondisabled veterans in the Reichsbund was only slightly over 12 percent; the increased emphasis on the problems of the survivors of those killed in the war was made evident when shortly after the end of the war the organization's name was changed to the National League of War-Disabled, War Veterans, and Survivors (Reichsbund der Kriegsbeschädigten, Kriegsteilnehmer, und Kriegshinterbliebenen).

17. On the wartime demands of the *Kriegsopfer*, see Diehl, "Organization," and

Whalen, *Bitter Wounds*, chapter 8. For details on the changes in the system, see Helmut Rühland, "Entwicklung, heutige Gestaltung und Problematik der Kriegsopferversorgung in der Bundesrepublik Deutschland" (Inaugural dissertation, Universität Köln, 1957), pp. 37–61, and Whalen, *Bitter Wounds*, chapters 9–10.

18. On the hardships suffered by German war widows, see, in addition to Whalen, *Bitter Wounds*, Karin Hausen, "The German Nation's Obligations to the Heroes' Widows of World War I," in *Behind the Lines: Gender and the Two World Wars*, edited by Margaret Randolph Higonnet et al. (New Haven, 1987).

19. Michael Geyer, "Ein Vorbote des Wohlfahrtsstaates: Die Kriegsopferversorgung in Frankreich, Deutschland und Grossbritannien nach dem Ersten Weltkrieg," *Geschichte und Gesellschaft* 9/2 (1983): 252, 255; Whalen, *Bitter Wounds*, pp. 133–36.

20. Political conflict was avoided, but the war victims did not necessarily gain as a result; above all, they failed to achieve one of their major wartime objectives: to be colegislators and not merely the objects of postwar legislation dealing with war victims. On the whole, as Michael Geyer has noted, the nature of the RVG served to diminish rather than to enhance the political position of German war victims. Geyer, "Vorbote," pp. 248–49, 255–58.

21. Ibid., pp. 237–41, 256.

22. For more on these omissions, see text at n. 36.

23. Whalen, *Bitter Wounds*, pp. 136–38, 142–43, 149, 162–65; Geyer, "Vorbote," pp. 248–49, 256–58.

24. Rühland, "Entwicklung," pp. 62–65; Whalen, *Bitter Wounds*, pp. 146–47, 151.

25. Whalen, *Bitter Wounds*, pp. 150–51, 170–71. The concern about "pension psychosis" predated the RVG. See Devine, *Disabled Soldiers*, p. 291.

26. *Bericht des Bundesvorstandes*, pp. 17, 33.

27. For discussions of war victims' organizations, see Diehl, "Germany," pp. 151–52, and Whalen, *Bitter Wounds*, pp. 126–28.

28. In 1922 the various organizations representing the war-disabled were proportionately represented in the National Committee for the Welfare of the War-Disabled as follows: Reichsbund, 13; Zentralverband, 5; and Einheitsverband, Internationaler Bund, and Kyffhäuserbund, 4 each. In 1921 an unsuccessful attempt was made to unite all of the groups; the record of the negotiations provides a revealing insight into the differences between them. See *Protokoll über Einigungsverhandlungen der Kriegsbeschädigten- und Kriegshinterbliebenen-Organisationen am 16. und 17. April in Weimar* (Berlin, [1921]). See also Whalen, *Bitter Wounds*, pp. 128, 151–52.

29. An exception was the Bund deutscher Militäranwärter, founded in 1890, which represented former professional soldiers, primarily noncommissioned officers, who were eligible for jobs in the civil service. It was reorganized and renamed the Reichsbund der Zivildienstberechtigten in 1923. Franz Schwede-Coburg, "Der Reichstreubund ehemaliger Berufssoldaten," in *Das Dritte Reich im Aufbau* (Berlin, 1939), 3:172–73.

30. Before the war, most ex-officers refused to join the veterans' associations, for

example, feeling that they were too plebeian. See Saul, "Der 'Deutsche Kriegerbund,'" and Höhn, *Sozialismus und Heer*.

31. Brief sketches of the DOB and other officers' associations can be found in Dieter Fricke, et al., eds., *Die bürgerlichen Parteien in Deutschland. Handbuch der Geschichte der bürgerlichen Parteien und anderer bürgerlicher Interessenorganisationen vom Vormärz bis zum Jahre 1945*, 2 Bände (Leipzig, 1968).

32. Quoted in ibid., 2:447.

33. On the promotion of enlisted men to officers and the attendant problems, see Robert G. L. Waite, *Vanguard of Nazism: The Free Corps Movement in Postwar Germany, 1918–1923* (New York, 1969), pp. 46–47.

34. For a biased but essentially correct account of the Republic's treatment of former officers, see Hans Ernst Fried, *The Guilt of the German Army* (New York, 1942), pp. 98–161; also cf. Waite, *Vanguard of Nazism*, p. 262.

35. Richard Bessel, "The Great War in German Memory: The Soldiers of the First World War, Demobilization, and Weimar Political Culture," *German History* 6/1 (1988). Bessel notes that although the myth largely reflected the view of officers, others also supported it because it provided a much more heroic image of the returning soldier than had been the case in reality.

36. Both the Kyffhäuserbund and the Verband Nationalgesinnter Soldaten struck medals. That of the latter was modeled on a design for an official medal that was made in 1917. Kurt-Gerhard Klietmann, "The German Honor Medal of World War I," *Medal Collector* 20/4 (April 1969), and "Die deutsche Ehrendenkmünze des Weltkrieges, 1917–1934, Deutsche Ehrenlegion," *Ordenskunde*, Nr. 44 (1975).

37. On the failure to create a national war memorial and the conflicts over the form of war memorials, see Wolfgang Ribbe, "Flaggenstreit und Heiliger Hain. Bemerkungen zur nationalen Symbolik in der Weimarer Republik," in *Aus Theorie und Praxis der Geschichtswissenschaft. Festschrift für Hans Herzfeld zum 80. Geburtstag*, herausgegeben von Dietrich Kurze (Berlin, 1982), pp. 181–87, and Meinhold Lurz, *Kriegerdenkmäler in Deutschland*, Band 4, *Weimarer Republik* (Heidelberg, 1985).

38. On the polarized dichotomy of pacifist and militarist responses to the war, see Wilhelm Karl Pfeiler, *War and the German Mind: The Testimony of Men of Fiction Who Fought at the Front* (New York, 1941).

39. See Eric J. Leed, *No Man's Land: Combat and Identity in World War I* (Cambridge, 1979), especially chapter 6.

40. See, for example, Ward, *The War Generation*. On veterans' anger toward women, who they felt had unfairly benefited from male sacrifice, see Sandra M. Gilbert, "Soldier's Heart: Literary Men, Literary Women, and the Great War," in *Behind the Lines: Gender and the Two World Wars*, edited by Margaret Randolph Higonnet et al. (New Haven, 1987). For the prevalence of misogynist feelings among German veterans, especially those active in the Free Corps, see the idiosyncratic and fascinating study by Klaus Theleweit, *Male Fantasies*, 2 vols. (Minneapolis, 1987, 1989).

41. In addition to Waite, *Vanguard of Nazism*, see Theleweit, *Male Fantasies*, 2:388ff.

42. Bessel, "Great War," p. 30.

43. Cf. Wilhelm Deist, "Der militärische Zusammenbruch des Kaiserreichs. Zur Realität der 'Dolchstosslegende,'" in *Das Unrechtsregime. Internationale Forschung über den Nationalsozialismus. Festschrift für Werner Jochmann zum 65. Geburtstag*, herausgegeben von Ursula Büttner, Band 1 (Hamburg, 1986).

44. Diehl, "Organization," pp. 171–78; Elliott, "Kriegervereine," pp. 118, 125; Karl Rohe, *Das Reichsbanner Schwarz Rot Gold. Ein Beitrag zur Geschichte und Struktur der politischen Kampfverbände zur Zeit der Weimarer Republik* (Düsseldorf, 1966), pp. 126–27. In 1921 the Bund was reorganized and given a more centralized leadership, and in 1922 it changed its name to the Deutscher Reichskriegerbund "Kyffhäuser" (German National Combatants' League, "Kyffhäuser").

45. Of these only about 10 percent were war-disabled veterans, a figure that clearly reflects the Kyffhäuserbund's failure—or lack of interest—in this field of activity in spite of its propaganda to the contrary. On the eve of the First World War, the Kyffhäuserbund claimed over 2,860,000 members. Of these approximately one-half were recalled to active duty during the war. By 1921 the Bund's membership had returned to nearly 2,200,000, and by 1929 it had risen to over 2,500,000. Although the Kyffhäuserbund was therefore able to achieve a postwar membership that was nearly equal to its prewar membership, in view of the enormous number of new veterans created by the war, the Bund's postwar record was at best only a relative success and clearly reflects a failure to appeal to large numbers of the new generation of veterans.

46. The following account of the VNS is based primarily on material in R43 I/766, Militärvereine, 1921–23, BAK.

47. The best general accounts of the Stahlhelm are Volker R. Berghahn, *Der Stahlhelm, Bund der Frontsoldaten, 1918–1935* (Düsseldorf, 1966), and Alois Klotzbücher, "Der politische Weg des Stahlhelm, Bund der Frontsoldaten, in der Weimarer Republik. Ein Beitrag zur Geschichte der 'Nationalen Opposition,' 1918–1933" (Inaugural dissertation, Erlangen-Nürnberg, 1964). See also James M. Diehl, *Paramilitary Politics in Weimar Germany* (Bloomington, 1977).

48. Seldte to Georg Escherich, 8 April 1920, quoted in Diehl, *Paramilitary Politics*, p. 80.

49. Peter Fritzsche, in his recent study of bourgeois political mobilization in the Weimar Republic, overlooks this and portrays the Stahlhelm in too benign a light, underplaying the violent nature of its activity. Peter Fritzsche, *Rehearsals for Fascism: Populism and Political Mobilization in Weimar Germany* (New York, 1990).

50. See Diehl, *Paramilitary Politics*, chapters 1–4, for details.

51. Waite, *Vanguard of Nazism*, p. 42.

52. The term "military desperados" is from Wolfgang Sauer, "National Socialism: Totalitarianism or Fascism?," *American Historical Review* 73 (1963). On the development of the individual groups, see Diehl, *Paramilitary Politics*.

53. Quoted in Otto-Ernst Schüddekopf, *Das Heer und die Republik. Quellen zur Politik der Reichswehrführung, 1918 bis 1933* (Hannover, 1955), p. 130.

54. Berghahn, *Der Stahlhelm*, pp. 33, 100; Klotzbücher, "Der politische Weg," p. 41.

55. Graham Wootton, *The Politics of Influence: British Ex-Servicemen, Cabinet Decisions, and Cultural Change, 1917–1957* (Cambridge, 1963), p. 107; cf. ibid., pp. 120–22.

56. This change was expressed in a report drawn up for the Prussian minister of interior in October 1926. Noting that the so-called nationalist organizations had originally concentrated primarily on military activity and left politics to others, it continued: "Since 1924 a change has been noticeable. . . . The organizations no longer—or no longer exclusively—limit themselves to the field of soldierly activity, but increasingly are becoming engaged in the political struggle and are seeking to obtain political influence and political power." Quoted in Diehl, *Paramilitary Politics*, p. 175.

57. As one political combat league spokesperson put it: "As long as the paramilitary formations simply functioned as recruiting organizations and supporters of the parties' work, they were happily tolerated, [but] since they have made demands for political influence and a share in leadership, they are beginning to get on the nerves of the diehard party politicians." Quoted in ibid., p. 236.

58. The debates between the various combat leagues at times reached a level of acrimony usually reserved for attacks on the left. One of the most heated and prolonged was that between the Young German Order and the Stahlhelm, with the former attacking the latter as being reactionary and allied with plutocratic forces.

59. On the Front Ideology, see Pfeiler, *War and the German Mind*; Kurt Sontheimer, *Antidemokratisches Denken in der Weimarer Republik. Die politischen Ideen des deutschen Nationalismus zwischen 1918 und 1933* (Munich, 1962); and Armin Mohler, *Die Konservative Revolution in Deutschland, 1918–1932. Grundriss ihrer Weltanschauungen* (Stuttgart, 1950). On the growth of war-experience literature in the late 1920s, see Michael Gollbach, *Die Wiederkehr des Weltkrieges in der Literatur. Zu den Frontromanen der späten Zwanziger Jahre* (Kronberg/Ts., 1978), and Wolfram Wette, "Ideologien, Propaganda und Innenpolitik als Voraussetzungen der Kriegspolitik des Dritten Reiches," in *Das Deutsche Reich und der Zweite Weltkrieg*, herausgegeben vom Militärgeschichtlichen Forschungsamt, Band 1 (Stuttgart, 1979). See also George L. Mosse, *Fallen Soldiers: Reshaping the Memory of the World Wars* (New York, 1990); Modris Eksteins, *Rites of Spring: The Great War and the Birth of the Modern Age* (New York, 1989); and Klaus Vondung, ed., *Kriegserlebnis. Der Erste Weltkrieg in der literarischen Gestaltung und symbolischen Deutung der Nationen* (Göttingen, 1980).

60. The enthusiasm that greeted the outbreak of the war and the feeling that it signified the beginning of a new age of domestic unity were graphically depicted many years later by the German historian Friedrich Meinecke:

The exaltation of spirit experienced during the August days of 1914 . . . is one of the most precious, unforgettable memories of the highest sort. All the rifts which had hitherto existed in the German people, both within the bourgeoisie and between the bourgeoisie and the working classes, were suddenly closed in the face of the common danger. . . . And more than that, one perceived in all camps that it was not a matter merely of the unity of a gain-seeking partnership, but that an inner renovation of our whole state and culture was needed. We generally believed, indeed, that this had already commenced and that it would progress further in the common experience of the war.

Friedrich Meinecke, *The German Catastrophe: Reflections and Recollections* (Boston, 1963), p. 25.

61. As Eric Leed puts it, "The cessation of hostilities did not mean the end of the war experience but rather the beginning of a process in which that experience was framed, institutionalized, given ideological content, and relived in political action as well as fiction." Leed, *No Man's Land*, xi. Richard Bessel has observed that the fact that the memory of the war was formed by a conservative minority says much about the basis upon which Weimar politics were stabilized in the late 1920s. Bessel, "Great War," p. 34.

62. The phrase is that of Ernst Jünger, one of the most forceful advocates of a state permanently and totally mobilized for war. For more on Jünger, see Leena Kitzberg Osteraas, "The New Nationalists: Front Generation Spokesmen in the Weimar Republic" (Ph.D. dissertation, Columbia University, 1972); Karl Prümm, *Die Literatur des soldatischen Nationalismus in der 20er Jahre, 1919–1933* (Kronberg/Ts., 1974); Walter Struve, *Elites against Democracy: Leadership Ideas in Bourgeois Political Thought in Germany, 1890–1933* (Princeton, 1973), chapter 12; and Joseph Peter Stern, *Ernst Jünger* (New Haven, 1953).

63. Leed perceptively observes that the feeling of specialness and positive mission was linked to a belief in the collective victimization of soldiers and that as a result it was suffused with anger and a desire for revenge against the home front as well as the external enemy. Leed, *No Man's Land*, pp. 146, 196, 204ff.

64. This belief was widely held among veterans of the radical right. See, for example, Ernst Röhm's autobiography, *Geschichte eines Hochverräters* (Munich, 1928–34). One group, the Frontkrieger in Munich, even demanded that votes be weighed according to the type and length of service performed during the war. Diehl, *Paramilitary Politics*, p. 361, n. 64.

65. Quoted in Diehl, "Germany," p. 176.

66. On the connection between the combat leagues and the prewar youth movement in general, see Ernst Posse, *Die politischen Kampfbünde Deutschlands* (Berlin, 1931). A particularly good example is Artur Mahraun, the head of the Young German Order; see Klaus Hornung, *Der Jungdeutsche Orden* (Düsseldorf, 1958), chapter 1.

67. For a good example of this attitude, see the remarks of Georg Strasser quoted in Jeremy Noakes and G. Pridham, *Nazism, 1919–1945*, vol. 1, *The Rise to Power* (Exeter, 1983), pp. 41–42.

68. Otto-Ernst Schüddekopf, *Linke Leute von Rechts. Nationalbolschewismus in Deutschland von 1918 bis 1933* (Stuttgart, 1960), p. 102; see also ibid., pp. 166–67, 261.

69. The term "social-political milieu" is taken from M. Rainer Lepsius, "Parteiensystem und Sozialstruktur. Zum Problem der Demokratisierung der deutschen Gesellschaft," in *Wirtschaft, Geschichte und Wirtschaftsgeschichte. Festschrift zum 65. Geburtstag von Friedrich Lütge*, herausgegeben von Wilhelm Abel et al. (Stuttgart, 1966). On the hypocritical use of the term "unpolitical," see Fritz Stern, "The Political Consequences

of the Unpolitical German," in *The Failure of Illiberalism: Essays on the Political Culture of Modern Germany* (New York, 1972). On the naive political conceptions of young middle-class officers and the more cynical views of their working-class troops, see Leed, *No Man's Land*.

70. On the problematical character of "front" socialism, see, for example, Leed, *No Man's Land*, pp. 198–200, 210.

71. For an interesting and sympathetic description of the feelings of wartime comradeship from a nonrightist source, see Erich Maria Remarque's *The Road Back* (1930), which also realistically, and regretfully, portrays how prewar socioeconomic differences reasserted themselves once the soldiers returned home from the front.

72. Posse, *Die politischen Kampfbünde*, p. 77. See also Eksteins, *Rites of Spring*.

73. Ernst Nolte's characterization of Charles Maurras, the leader of the Action Française, as being simultaneously "a national warrior and a social pacifist" fits the German political combat leagues as well. Nolte, *Three Faces of Fascism* (New York, 1966), p. 113. See also William S. Allen, "The Appeal of Fascism and the Problem of National Disintegration," in *Reappraisals of Fascism*, edited by Henry Ashby Turner, Jr. (New York, 1975), on the attempt to translate the lessons of the First World War into victory in a second.

74. On the Reichsbanner, see Rohe, *Reichsbanner*, and the relevant chapters in Diehl, *Paramilitary Politics*.

75. The campaign against the Young Plan of 1929, the formation of the Harzburg Front in 1931, the presidential elections of 1932, and, finally, Seldte's inclusion in Hitler's first cabinet all marked the progressive subjugation of the Stahlhelm to Hitler, not, as its leaders had hoped and expected, the reverse. For details, see Berghahn, *Der Stahlhelm*, and Klotzbücher, "Der politische Weg."

76. On the relationship of the SA to the combat leagues, see Diehl, *Paramilitary Politics*, chapters 4 and 8.

77. For pre-1930 appeals to pensioners and disabled veterans, see Thomas Childers, "Inflation and Electoral Politics in Germany 1919–29," in *Inflation through the Ages: Economic, Social, Psychological, and Historical Aspects*, edited by Nathan Schmukler and Edward Marcus (New York, 1983), pp. 377–78, and *The Nazi Voter: The Social Foundations of Fascism in Germany, 1919–33* (Chapel Hill, 1983), pp. 83, 112, 164; for the Nazi cultivation of a pensioner constituency after 1930, see ibid., pp. 208, 225–28.

78. Whalen, *Bitter Wounds*, pp. 168–70. For a description of the cuts, see *Die Rückläufigkeit der Versorgung und Fürsorge für die Kriegsopfer im Zeichen der Notverordnung* (Berlin, 1932), distributed in 1932 to members of the Reichstag and government by the Reichsbund der Kriegsbeschädigten, Kriegsteilnehmer, und Kriegshinterbliebenen.

79. Oberlindober was born in Munich in 1896. His father was an officer in the Bavarian army, and at the outbreak of the war Oberlindober joined the Bavarian army as a Fahnenjunker. In August 1918, while serving as a lieutenant in the Sixteenth Pioneer Company, he was wounded in the knee and was discharged in October 1918. Probably because of his wound, which qualified him for a pension, Oberlindober did

not engage in any Free Corps action. Like many former junior officers, he was employed as a salesman after the war. In 1922 he joined the NSDAP and the SA in Straubing, lower Bavaria, where he remained active in politics until 1928 as an Ortsgruppeleiter, Kreisleiter, and, finally, Gaupropagandaleiter. Apparently an effective public speaker, Oberlindober became a Reichsredner for the party after 1928 and was elected to the Reichstag in the breakthrough election of September 1930, at which time he was also named to head the newly formed section in the national party directorate dealing with disabled veterans.

80. For descriptions and examples of this process of infiltration, see Heinrich A. Winkler, "German Society, Hitler, and the Illusion of Restoration, 1930–33," *Journal of Contemporary History* 11/1 (1976), and Jeremy Noakes, *The Nazi Party in Lower Saxony, 1921–1933* (London, 1971). Similar tactics were also used to win over civil servants. See Jane Caplan, *Government without Administration: State and Civil Service in Weimar and Nazi Germany* (Oxford, 1988), chapter 4, especially p. 110.

81. Hauptgeschäftsstelle der Reichsleitung an alle Gauleitungen, 18 November 1930, Sammlung Schumacher, 255/NSKOV, BAK.

82. Martin to Herrn Reichsorganisationsleiter I, 2 February 1932, ibid. A further argument for intensified activity was that "the N.S.D.A.P. is [gilt als] the party of the front soldiers and must as such direct special attention to the war victims." Ibid.

83. A good summary of the party's arguments is provided in the pamphlet *Nationalsozialismus und Kriegsopfer*, herausgegeben von der NSDAP Reichsorganisationsleiter I, Referat Kriegsopferversorgung (Munich, [1932]); see also *Auch ein armes Vaterland kann dankbar sein. Dem deutschen Soldaten des Weltkrieges und den Seinen zugeeignet*, herausgegeben von der Reichsorganisationsleitung, Abteilung Kriegsopferversorgung (Diessen, 1932), NSD 54/22 and 54/23, BAK.

84. Hauptgeschäftsstelle der Reichsleitung an alle Gauleitungen, 18 November 1930, and Bericht über den Stand der deutschen Kriegsopferversorgung, 26 May 1933, Sammlung Schumacher, 255/NSKOV, BAK; *Nationalsozialismus und Kriegsopfer*, pp. 13–14; Whalen, *Bitter Wounds*, pp. 173–76.

85. *Nationalsozialismus und Kriegsopfer*, pp. 11–15.

86. For examples of the NSDAP's exploitation of the Reichsbund's difficulties, see *Der Dank des Vaterlandes. Rechtsbuch*, herausgegeben von der Reichsleitung der NSDAP Org. Abt. I, Referat Kriegsopferbewegung (Düsseldorf, 1931), p. 105; Martin to Herrn Reichsorganisationsleiter I, 2 February 1932, Sammlung Schumacher, 255/NSKOV, BAK.

Chapter 2

1. See, for example, Walther Kayser, *Die nationalpolitische Bedeutung der Wehrmacht* (Hamburg, 1937), p. 10, where Hitler is portrayed as "the soldierly and political leader who . . . became the executor of the historical legacy of the front soldiers [der zugleich

soldatische und politische Führer, der . . . zum Vollstrecker des geschichtliches Vermächtnisses der Frontsoldaten wurde]."

2. Sebastian Haffner, *The Meaning of Hitler* (Cambridge, 1983), p. 11.

3. The Nazis were not the only ones to appropriate the *Fronterlebnis*. See the discussion on the Front Ideology in chapter 1.

4. For more on the militarization of society in the Third Reich, including the relevant literature, see text following n. 55.

5. See Tim Mason, "The Legacy of 1918 for National Socialism," in *German Democracy and the Triumph of Hitler*, edited by Anthony Nicholls and Erich Matthias (New York, 1971), and William S. Allen, "The Appeal of Fascism and the Problem of National Disintegration," in *Reappraisals of Fascism*, edited by Henry Ashby Turner, Jr. (New York, 1975).

6. Oberlindober and Martin to Hitler, 7 January 1933, Sammlung Schumacher, 255/NSKOV, BAK. The two men were helped greatly in their organizational efforts by the benefits provided to Reichstag deputies, such as salaries and train passes.

7. This account of the *Gleichschaltung* of the *Kriegsopferverbände* is taken primarily from the lengthy report prepared by Oberlindober for Ley dated 26 May 1933, Bericht über den Stand der deutschen Kriegsopferversorgung, Sammlung Schumacher, 255/NSKOV, BAK. See also "Ein Jahr National-Sozialistische Kriegsopferversorgung," *DKOV*, May 1934, and Robert W. Whalen, *Bitter Wounds: German Victims of the Great War, 1914–1939* (Ithaca, N.Y., 1984), pp. 173–76. The final statement is from the *Völkischer Beobachter*, 13 July 1933, quoted in Whalen, *Bitter Wounds*, p. 175.

8. Telegram from Horn of 8 May 1933 and Führerordnung of 21 May 1933, R43 II/824, BAK. Also cf. Christopher James Elliott, "Ex-Servicemen's Organisations and the Weimar Republic" (Ph.D. dissertation, London University, 1971), pp. 301–8.

9. Franz Schwede-Coburg, "Der Reichstreubund ehemaliger Berufssoldaten," in *Das Dritte Reich im Aufbau*, herausgegeben von Paul Meier-Benneckenstein, Band 3 (Berlin, 1939); Elliott, "Ex-Servicemen's Organisations," p. 306.

10. *Völkischer Beobachter*, 26–27 November 1933.

11. Bericht über den Stand der deutschen Kriegsopferversorgung, 26 May 1933, Sammlung Schumacher, 255/NSKOV, BAK.

12. Hans Buchheim, "Die Eingliederung des 'Stahlhelms' in die SA" and "Kyffhäuserbund und SA," in *Gutachten des Institutes für Zeitgeschichte*, Band 1 (Munich, 1958); *Lokal Anzeiger*, 16 February 1934, R43 II/824, BAK.

13. On Oberlindober's and the NSKOV's relation to the "Second Revolution," see text at n. 26.

14. Die Grundlagen eines deutschen Soldatenbundes, 26 November 1934, Sammlung Schumacher, 247/Kyffhäuserbund, BAK. In terms of his ideological presuppositions and imperial ambitions, Oberlindober was remarkably similar to Robert Ley. See Ronald Smelser, *Robert Ley: Hitler's Labor Front Leader* (Oxford, 1988), especially chapters 5–7.

15. These remarks provide another confirmation of the formative impact of the

collapse and Revolution of 1918 on the Nazi leadership's mentality and its preoccupation with the need to prevent a second putative "stab in the back." See Mason, "The Legacy of 1918."

16. To ensure his own position in case his proposal was implemented with someone else as leader, Oberlindober concluded that war victims should continue to have a "special position [Sonderstellung] in such an organization."

17. Evidence of the continued campaign against the leadership of the traditional veterans' groups is provided by a collection of detailed reports on the political views of local Kyffhäuserbund leaders compiled in 1935 (NS20/112, BAK). A good number of these were provided by local NSKOV and SA organizations, which suggests that Oberlindober may have been behind the project.

18. Whether Reinhard actively sought the protection of Himmler or, as is more likely, in his efforts to fend off Oberlindober, simply fell victim to the SS-Reichsführer's own expansionist ambitions is unclear. In any case, Reinhard was made an officer in the SS in 1935 and by 1937 had put the Kyffhäuserbund under the command of Himmler. Reinhard to Himmler, 6 and 15 April 1937, , Records of the Reich Leader of the SS and Chief of German Police, T-175, roll 131, frames 7937–40, NARS.

19. Periodically announcements were made in the *DKOV* stating that membership in the NSKOV was open to all veterans, not just *Kriegsopfer*. See, for example, the November 1935 and April 1936 issues. In his letter of 6 April 1937 to Himmler, Reinhard, for his part, argued that the NSKOV should be fused with the Kyffhäuserbund in a way that clearly implied the subordination of the former to the latter. Records of the Reich Leader of the SS and Chief of German Police, T-175, roll 131, frames 7937–38, NARS.

20. See the material in R43 II/825a, and Niederschrift über die am 26. April 1937 abgehaltene Besprechung über Verbände alter Soldaten, R43 II/1284b, BAK. For more on the ongoing struggle between the two organizations, see text at n. 47.

21. In addition to taking over the property of the Reichsbund, the NSKOV also appropriated its assets, which, according to Oberlindober, consisted of approximately 6 million Reichsmark. Bericht über den Stand der deutschen Kriegsopferversorgung, 26 May 1933, Sammlung Schumacher, 255/NSKOV, BAK.

22. In May 1933, Oberlindober claimed that the membership of the NSKOV was around 1.5 million (ibid.). At this time he apparently expected to bring the Kyffhäuserbund and the DOB, with a combined membership estimated at nearly 500,000, into the new organization, a plan that failed to materialize. Later reports set the membership of the NSKOV at 1.1–1.2 million, of which 1,082,000 were dues-paying members. The breakdown between disabled veterans and next of kin was 700,000 and 450,000, respectively, with 5 percent said to be party members. Reports of 23 and 28 December 1933, Sammlung Schumacher, 255/NSKOV, BAK.

In a memo of 7 January 1933 (ibid.), Oberlindober set the membership of the *Kriegsopferverbände* as follows: Reichsbund, 300,000; Reichsverband, 180,000; Zentralverband, 70,000; and Internationaler Bund, 50,000. How many of these went over to or remained active members of the NSKOV is hard to say. Yet, if the above membership figures for the NSKOV are accurate, a good number must have joined. In his report of 26 May Oberlindober claimed that the Reichsverband had been about 60 percent National Socialist before the merger; he also noted that the transfer of the Reichsbund to the new organization had been completed "without difficulty" and that the leadership of the Reichsbund "in spite of ideological differences had cooperated in the transfer in an honorable and correct manner." It would be interesting to determine what percentage of the leaderships of the coordinated war victims' organizations received positions in the NSKOV, which, according to Dietrich Orlow, had some 25,000 functionaries in 1934. Dietrich Orlow, *History of the Nazi Party, 1933–1945* (Pittsburgh, 1973), p. 92.

23. Hanns Oberlindober, *Ehre und Recht für die deutschen Kriegsopfer* (Berlin, 1933).

24. This unwarranted partisan demand was realized through passage of a law a few months later (Gesetz über die Versorgung der Kämpfer für die nationale Erhebung vom 27. Februar 1934), which extended the benefits of the RVG to members of National Socialist and other nationalist paramilitary organizations.

25. In the regime's early cabinet meetings Göring repeatedly stressed the need for some sort of concessions. See *Akten der Reichskanzlei. Die Regierung Hitler, Teil I, 1933/34*, herausgegeben für die Historische Kommission bei der Bayerischen Akademie der Wissenschaften von Konrad Repgen für das Bundesarchiv von Hans Booms; bearbeitet von Karl-Heinz Minuth (Boppard am Rhein, 1983).

26. The rapid growth of the party affiliates fueled the ambitions of those who resented the old elites and hoped to expand the role of party organizations at the expense of traditional institutions, including those of the state. The NSKOV was no exception to this general trend. Oberlindober's goals were given concrete expression in his memo to Ley of 26 May 1933, in which he foresaw the NSKOV taking over control of the war victims' welfare system from the Labor Ministry. For details, see James M. Diehl, "Victors or Victims?: Disabled Veterans in the Third Reich," *Journal of Modern History* 59/4 (December 1987): n. 38. For glimpses into the behind-the-scenes maneuvering that accompanied the drafting of the law, see Max Wenzel, *Fünfzig Jahre Kriegsopferversorgung—Eine Betrachtung zur historischen Entwicklung. Sonderausdruck aus VdK Mitteilungen*, Heft 12 (1968), p. 17, and the materials in R43 II/1285, BAK.

27. Seldte to Reichskanzlei, 29 May 1934, and Frick to Reichskanzlei, 4 June 1934, R43 II/1285, BAK; *Akten der Reichskanzlei*, 2:1334, n. 2.

28. Seldte to Reichskanzlei, 15 June 1934, R43 II/1285, BAK. This document is reprinted in *Akten der Reichskanzlei*, 2:1333–35. Seldte asked for 125 million Reichsmark and got 30 million.

29. The text of the new law, Gesetz über Änderungen auf dem Gebiete der Reichsversorgung vom 3. Juli 1934, is reprinted in *Neue Wege der deutschen Kriegsopferversorgung*, herausgegeben von der National-Sozialistischen Kriegsopferversorgung (Berlin, 1934), NSD 54/19, BAK, pp. 5–31.

30. In fact, the *Frontzulage* was only awarded to those with a disability of 70 percent or more or those with a disability of 30–70 percent who were over fifty years old. In addition, veterans living in foreign countries or involved in "Marxist activity" were not eligible for the new pension.

31. *Neue Wege*, pp. 2–3. Oberlindober concluded that the attitudes of both the war victims and the general public had to be altered before substantial changes in material benefits would be possible, an argument that was developed in detail in the *DKOV* shortly before the new law was promulgated. See "Ein Rückblick auf die Entstehungs-geschichte des neuen Versorgungsrechts," *DKOV*, May 1934.

32. The Cross of Honor (*Ehrenkreuz*) was awarded in three classes: combatant, noncombatant, and next of kin of those killed. The privileges accorded to bearers of the medals included preferred seating at public functions and preferred treatment at public offices. For details on the issuance of the medal, see *Neue Wege*, pp. 31–32. Also cf. Whalen, *Bitter Wounds*, pp. 176–77.

33. Wenzel, *Fünfzig Jahre Kriegsopferversorgung*, pp. 17–18. While the dropping of psychiatric casualties from the rolls of the RVG accorded with National Socialist prejudices, it also apparently enjoyed the support of the majority of war victims as well, who felt that pensions for the non-physically disabled weakened their case with the public. See ibid., pp. 17–19, and Bundesminister für Arbeit an den Bundestagabgeord-neten Herrn Bruno Leddin, 5 May 1950, B149/1820, BAK.

34. For summaries of the changes, see Wenzel, *Fünfzig Jahre Kriegsopferversorgung*, pp. 17–23, and Franz Seldte, *Sozialpolitik im Dritten Reich, 1933–1938* (Munich, 1939), pp. 215–56. After 1933, the number of disabled veterans receiving pensions began to decline, dropping from nearly 840,000 in 1930 to 806,963 in 1935 and 796,611 in 1936; pension costs decreased by about 40 percent between 1928 and 1935. Whalen, *Bitter Wounds*, p. 178. Also cf. *Statistisches Jahrbuch* (1935), pp. 500–503.

35. Paul Schätzchen to Seldte, 22 July 1935, R43 II/1285, BAK.

36. Mitteilung des Sacharbeiters für Militärversorgung im Reichsfinanzministerium Geheimrat Dr. Fischbach, 29 October 1935, and Vorschlag für Verbesserungen in der Reichsversorgung im Jahre 1936, 30 October 1935, ibid. On the system for the new Wehrmacht, see text following n. 48.

37. Mackensen to Hitler, 5 November 1935, ibid.

38. Aufzeichnung Sieler, n.d., ibid.

39. Aufzeichnung betr. Erweiterung des Kreises der Frontzulageempfänger, 2 December 1935, ibid.

40. Materials detailing the changes are in R43 II/1285, BAK.

41. "Demilitarization" referred not only to the removal of military points of reference in calculating benefits under the RVG but also to the shift in self-image from *Front-soldat* to *Kriegsopfer*, a shift that the NSKOV tried to reverse by emphasizing its role as a *Soldatenbund*. See, for example, *DKOV*, June 1937, pp. 3–5, and note 19 above.

42. *DKOV*, February 1936, pp. 7–12, and May 1936, pp. 5–9.

43. For example, "Das Geschenk des Führers an uns," ibid., June 1939.

44. See David Schoenbaum, *Hitler's Social Revolution: Class and Status in Nazi Germany, 1933–1939* (New York, 1966), and Arthur Schweitzer, *Die Nazifizierung des Mittelstandes* (Stuttgart, 1970). See also Jane Caplan, *Government without Administration: State and Civil Service in Weimar and Nazi Germany* (Oxford, 1988).

45. The phrase "partial fascism" is taken from Arthur Schweitzer, *Big Business in the Third Reich* (Bloomington, 1964).

46. *Völkischer Beobachter*, 22 December 1935; Rudolf Absolon, *Die Wehrmacht im Dritten Reich* (Boppard am Rhein, 1971), 4:30–31.

47. Wilhelm Reinhard, "Der N.S.-Reichskriegerbund," in *Das Dritte Reich im Aufbau*, herausgegeben von Paul Meier-Benneckenstein, Band 3 (Berlin, 1939). On the SA-Wehrmannschaften, see Manfred Messerschmidt, *Die Wehrmacht im NS-Staat. Zeit der Indoktrination* (Hamburg, 1969), pp. 226–32.

48. As the war went on, the position of the party vis-à-vis its erstwhile institutional opponents became stronger. For the radicalizing effects of the war on the relationship between the party and the army, for example, see Jürgen Förster, "Vom Führerheer der Republik zur Nationalsozialistischen Volksarmee. Zum Strukturwandel der Wehrmacht, 1935–1945," in *Deutschland in Europa: Kontinuität und Bruch. Gedenkschrift für Andreas Hillgruber*, herausgegeben von Jost Dülffer et al. (Frankfurt am Main, 1990), pp. 319–20. Messerschmidt characterizes the creation of the SA-Wehrmannschaften as "Eine Art Wiedergutmachung gegen die Wehrmacht für die SA." *Wehrmacht*, p. 231.

49. Until 1938 members of the Reichswehr/Wehrmacht were not covered by the RVG but by the Wehrmachtversorgungsgesetz of 4 August 1921, which regulated both disability and retirement benefits. See Absolon, *Die Wehrmacht*, 2:279–85. On the WFVG and WEFVG, see Helmut Rühland, "Entwicklung, heutige Gestaltung und Problematik der Kriegsopferversorgung in der Bundesrepublik Deutschland" (Inaugural dissertation, Universität Köln, 1957), pp. 73–77; Wenzel, *Fünfzig Jahre Kriegsopferversorgung*, pp. 23–25; and Oskar Georg Fischbach, *Fürsorge- und Versorgungsgesetz und Einsatzfürsorge- und Versorgungsgesetz für die ehemaligen Angehörigen der Wehrmacht und ihre Hinterbliebenen* (Berlin, 1943).

50. The natural antipathy of combatant troops toward rear-echelon forces was deepened and politicized in Germany as a result of defeat, revolution, and the subsequent establishment of the "stab in the back" myth. The sharp distinction between front soldiers and those in the rear that infused Nazi thinking was manifested in the regime's issuance of combatant and noncombatant versions of the *Ehrenkreuz*. The front-rear distinction, which was not recognized in the RVG, was first carried over into the area of war-disability benefits by the Nazis with the introduction of the *Frontzulage*.

51. This had already been decided at a meeting in April 1935. Seldte and members of his staff argued against removing the administration of benefits for the new Wehrmacht from the control of the Labor Ministry on grounds of economy. The war minister, Blomberg, pressed for the transfer and was supported by Hitler, who claimed the financial arguments presented by the Labor Ministry officials were "irrelevant." Aufzeichnung, 11 April 1935, R43 II/1285, BAK.

52. On Wehrmacht benefits, see Absolon, *Die Wehrmacht*, Band 2, chapter 6, and Band 4, chapter 7.

53. On these plans, see Bormann to Lammers, Betrifft: Unterbringung der Kapitulanten der Wehrmacht, 5 January 1941, and Der Reichsminister und Chef der

Reichskanzlei. An alle Obersten Reichsbehörden, 16 January 1941, *Akten der Partei-Kanzlei der NSDAP. Rekonstruktion eines velorgegangen Bestandes*, herausgegeben vom Institut für Zeitgeschichte (Munich, 1983), 101 22426–28 and 101 20176–78. Whether these types of positions were to be offered to other veterans, including those who were disabled, is unclear. On the use of former military personnel in the civil administration in the Kaiserreich, see Reinhard Höhn, *Sozialismus und Heer* (Bad Harzburg, 1969), 3:314–54. On the use of former military personnel as schoolteachers, see Michael Kater, "Hitler in Social Context," *Central European History* 14/3 (September 1981): 255.

54. See Rolf-Dieter Müller, *Hitlers Ostkrieg und die deutsche Siedlungspolitik. Die Zusammenarbeit von Wehrmacht, Wirtschaft und SS* (Frankfurt am Main, 1991). The programs were run by the Wehrmacht, and it appears that the main beneficiaries were high-ranking officers. Some settlements were created for war-disabled veterans, however, and these were heavily publicized. See the newspaper clippings in ZSg 103/4777, BAK.

55. While the party's efforts to take over the state administration in the Reich proper were only partly successful, party and party affiliate personnel played a much larger role in the conquered areas, where German state officials had no established footholds and where Nazi ideological principles and administrative practices prevailed. On the increased party influence in the administration of the eastern territories, see Martin Broszat, *The Hitler State: The Foundation and Development of the Internal Structure of the Third Reich* (London, 1981), pp. 353ff.; Orlow, *History of the Nazi Party*, pp. 381ff.; and Michael Kater, *The Nazi Party: A Social Profile of Members and Leaders, 1919–1945* (Cambridge, 1983), pp. 215–16.

56. On the development and cultivation of the Front Fighter (*Frontkämpfer*) myth, see James H. McRandle, *The Track of the Wolf: Essays on National Socialism and Its Leader Adolf Hitler* (Evanston, Ill., 1965), chapter 3. On the distortion of military virtues and the militarization of civilian society, see Hans Ernst Fried, *The Guilt of the German Army* (New York, 1942), pp. 198ff., and "Fascist Militarization and Education for War," in *The Third Reich* (London, 1955); also cf. Kayser, *Die nationalpolitische Bedeutung der Wehrmacht*, pp. 13–14, 32, 37ff. On propaganda glorifying military life and presenting soldiers as role models, see Jutta Sywottek, *Mobilmachung für den totalen Krieg. Die propagandistische Vorbereitung der deutschen Bevölkerung auf den Zweiten Weltkrieg* (Opladen, 1976), pp. 54–59; David Welch, *Propaganda and the German Cinema, 1933–1945* (Oxford, 1983), chapter 6; and Ernst Kris and Hans Speier, *German Radio Propaganda: Report on Home Broadcasts during the War* (London, 1944), pp. 37–38, 68–69, 148, 150–63, 165, 204–6.

57. On the Heldengedenktag, as well as the National Socialist efforts to eradicate pacifist elements in post–World War I monuments, see Meinhold Lurz, *Kriegerdenkmäler in Deutschland*, Band 5, *Drittes Reich* (Heidelberg, 1986); on the general celebration of the *Heldentod* in the Third Reich, see Jay W. Baird, *To Die for Germany: Heroes in the Nazi Pantheon* (Bloomington, 1990).

58. Hedwig Wachenheim, "Allowances for Dependants of Mobilised Men in Germany," *International Labour Review*, March 1944. To defuse discontent—and expecting

a short war—the National Socialist government established an extensive and generous system of benefits for military dependents, including parents. When the hopes for a short war ended and the regime began to try to mobilize women for the war effort, these benefits worked as an economic disincentive for wives—at least those of middle-class soldiers—to enter the work force.

59. This was clear in the practices of the major Nazi welfare organization, the Nationalsozialistische Volkswohlfahrt (NSV), which focused its efforts on helping the "healthy" elements of society, while abandoning the racially inferior, sick, and elderly to the care of the churches and local authorities. The purpose of the NSV was not to aid the poor but to strengthen those who could still make a productive contribution to the state, as well as to enable a greater allocation of the state's resources to rearmament. See Thomas Erich Joachim De Witt, "The Nazi Party and Social Welfare, 1919–1939" (Ph.D. dissertation, University of Virginia, 1972), pp. 171–73, 289–96, and Mark Alan Siegel, "The National Socialist People's Welfare Organization, 1933–1939: The Political Manipulation of Welfare" (Ph.D. dissertation, University of Cincinnati, 1976), pp. 20–22.

60. On the work ethic foundations of the RVG, see Michael Geyer, "Ein Vorbote des Wohlfahrtsstaates. Die Kriegsopferversorgung in Frankreich, Deutschland und Gross-britannien nach dem Ersten Weltkrieg," *Geschichte und Gesellschaft* 9/2 (1983): 245–48. On the Nazi view of work in general, see Joan Campbell, *Joy in Work, German Work: The National Debate, 1800–1945* (Princeton, 1989), chapters 13–14. On the way in which the work ethic and the equation of work with freedom and self-worth were applied to war-disability payments, see the Bormann memo cited in note 76 below. On the shortcomings of National Socialist legislation in this regard, see Wenzel, *Fünfzig Jahre Kriegsopferversorgung*, pp. 24, 29–31.

61. For a detailed comparison of *Kriegsopferverbände* publications, see Ludwig Plank, "Die Entstehung der Kriegsopferzeitschrift in Deutschland" (Inaugural dissertation, Ludwig-Maximilians-Universität, München, 1950).

62. See, for example, the picture of Hitler's wartime hospital room, which appears to have been converted into a shrine, *DKOV*, December 1934, p. 19.

63. Telegram of the Landesleitung Mitteldeutschland, reprinted in *DKOV*, December 1933, p. 2. For pictures and an account of events in Berlin, see ibid., p. 3, and January 1934, pp. 2–3. The NSV was also mobilized during plebiscites. Siegel, "The National Socialist People's Welfare Organization," p. 48.

64. Hanns Oberlindober, "Der 12. November," *DKOV*, December 1933, p. 1.

65. Ibid., November 1933, July and October 1934, January 1935.

66. See, for example, Oberlindober's lead article in *5 Jahre Arbeit für Führer und Volk. Ein Rechenschaftsbericht über die Tätigkeit des Hauptamts für Kriegsopfer der N.S.D.A.P. und der Nationalsozialistischen Kriegsopferversorgung e.V. für die Jahre 1933–1938* (Berlin, 1938).

67. The linkage of the "field gray" and "brown" armies and the portrayal of the NSKOV as a *Soldatenbund* and a model for society were themes that continued into the Second World War. For two representative examples of NSKOV propaganda in the

mid-1930s, see "Ein Kampf um Ehre und Recht," celebrating Oberlindober's fortieth birthday (*DKOV*, March 1936), and the report of Oberlindober's speech at the 1936 party rally (ibid., October 1936).

68. Ibid., May and August 1935, April and July 1936, February, April, August, and September 1937.

69. See Oberlindober's "Versailles 1939," ibid., July 1939, and, in the same issue, the report of Hitler's speech at the Reichskriegertag in Kassel.

70. The interview was published in ibid., December 1939. While the Labor Ministry was able to block the NSKOV's attempts to take over the administration of welfare benefits under the RVG, it was unable to thwart the Wehrmacht's desire to institute—and administer—the WFVG/WEFVG. See Wenzel, *Fünfzig Jahre Kriegsopferversorgung*, pp. 23–25, and the materials in R43 II/1285, BAK.

71. *DKOV*, November and December 1939, January, August, and September 1940, October/November 1941. The Strength through Joy section of the German Labor Front was also active in these efforts. See the materials in ZSg 103/4739, BAK.

72. For general accounts of Nazi propaganda during the war, see Jay W. Baird, *The Mythical World of Nazi War Propaganda, 1939–1945* (Minneapolis, 1974), and Robert E. Herzstein, *The War That Hitler Won: The Most Infamous Propaganda Campaign in History* (New York, 1978).

73. *DKOV*, November 1939, January, March, and August 1940, January and October/November 1941, December 1941/January 1942. See also "Der Dank des Vaterlandes," by Hans Hertel, in ZSg 103/4777, BAK.

74. See, for example, "Soldatische Haltung der Frau," *DKOV*, February 1940.

75. Wenzel, *Fünfzig Jahre Kriegsopferversorgung*, pp. 28–30. For details on the treatment of the war-disabled during the war, see ibid., pp. 28–34; Rühland, "Entwicklung," pp. 77–85; and Reinhold W. Staib, "Das deutsche Versorgungsrecht während des Krieges, 1939–1945, und seine Entwicklung nach dem 8. Mai 1945" (Inaugural dissertation, Eberhard Karls-Universität, Tübingen, 1951), part 1.

76. The original text of this quotation from Bormann's memo is as follows:

> Im Vordergrund des WFVG steht daher auch der Gedanke der Arbeitsfürsorge. Mit allen Mitteln soll der Verletzte, sofern er seinen alten Beruf nicht mehr ausüben kann, umgeschult und einem neuen Beruf zugeführt werden, damit er wieder voll arbeitsfähig wird. Das Gesetz geht dabei von dem richtigen Gedanken aus, dass es wesentlich nationalsozialistischer ist, einen Beschädigten wieder voll arbeitsfähig zu machen, als ihn lediglich mit Renten abzuspeisen, und es dem Zufall zu überlassen, ob er wieder Arbeit findet.
>
> Bei der Verschiedenartigkeit der Grundsätze der beiden Gesetze ist es nicht zu vermeiden, dass bei dem Vorliegen derselben Beschädigung nach dem neuen Gesetz niedrigere Beträge gezahlt werden als nach dem RVG.
>
> Es muss daher Aufgabe der Parteidienststellen sein, diejenigen Volksgenossen, die sich hinsichtlich ihrer Versorgung gegenüber den Weltkriegsbeschädigten be-

nachteiligt fühlen, auf die Gründe dieser unterschiedlichen Behandlung hinzu-weisen und ihnen den Vorzug der neuen Versorgungsart (Umschulung und Arbeitsfürsorge statt Rentenzahlung) klar zu machen.

StdF 18.1.1941. Bekanntsgabe. Betrifft: Versorgung von Kriegsbeschädigten und Kriegshinterbliebenen, *Akten der Partei-Kanzlei der NSDAP*, 107 00294. See also Ley to Oberlindober, 26 June 1941, ibid., 117 08293–97.

77. On these programs, see the materials in ZSg 103/4777, BAK.

78. Wenzel, *Fünfzig Jahre Kriegsopferversorgung*, pp. 28–33. Also cf. the report com-piled by the labor minister in February 1950, which details the changes made in the RVG between 1920 and 1945. B136/390, BAK.

79. OKW. An die NSDAP, Reichsleitung. Betr.: Änderung auf dem Gebiet der Hinterbliebenenversorgung der Wehrmachtsfürsorge- und -versorgungsgesetze, Feb-ruary 1943, R2/22425, BAK; Begründung zum Entwurf eines Erlasses über Änderung des Wehrmachtsfürsorge- und -versorgungsgesetzes und des Einsatzfürsorge- und -versorgungsgesetzes auf dem Gebiete der Beschädigtenversorgung, R2/22429, BAK.

80. Authorities were warned not to be too strict in processing requests and to be generous in cases in which children were involved or the fiancée was pregnant. Der Reichsminister des Innern. Betr.: Nachträgliche Eheschliessung, 15. Juni 1943, R2/22426, BAK.

81. Such benefits were repeatedly noted, both during and after the war, as the area where cutbacks were most justified. See, for example, the discontent expressed by Oberlindober in his speech cited in note 82 below.

82. "Kein blosses Rentensystem," *Deutsche Allgemeine Zeitung*, 24 June 1944, ZSg 103/4777, BAK. A full text of Oberlindober's remarks is in R2/22427, BAK.

83. The bankruptcy of the war-disability system reflected the bankruptcy of the Third Reich as a whole. In the six wartime budget years, the Reich spent 685 billion Reichs-mark, of which nearly three-quarters (some 510 billion Reichsmark) went for the war and armaments proper. See Gustav Stolper et al., *The German Economy: 1870 to the Present* (New York, 1967), p. 165. The expenditures for disabled veterans and survivors naturally increased dramatically, especially after 1942. In August 1938, 1.6 million Germans were eligible for pensions under the RVG and WFVG. Expenditures for the two systems totaled 937 million Reichsmark, with 99 percent going to beneficiaries of the RVG. In 1944 expenditures for the war-disabled and survivors had increased to 3,491 million Reichsmark, of which 62 percent was being paid to victims of the Second World War. See *Die Versorgung der Kriegsopfer in der Bundesrepublik Deutschland (Das Bundesversorgungsgesetz) Stand 30.9.1952*, herausgegeben vom Presse- und Informations-amt der Bundesregierung (Bonn, [1952]), pp. 15–16. An additional war-related social expenditure was the generous allowances paid to military dependents in order to shore up morale (see note 58 above). Only a very small part of the skyrocketing costs of the war effort was covered by taxes. Instead, the regime employed a system of so-called "noiseless" war financing, which consisted of borrowing (i.e., forcing loans) from

public corporations, social security funds, and various party agencies; the exploitation of conquered foreign assets; and, above all, as in the First World War, deficit financing. As a result, the Reich debt, which had been about 30 billion Reichsmark at the outset of the war, had risen to nearly 400 billion Reichsmark by the war's end. See Stolper, *The German Economy*, pp. 147–49, 164–66, and Karl Hardach, *The Political Economy of Germany in the Twentieth Century* (Berkeley, 1980), p. 85. The inflationary consequences of National Socialist financial practices were largely hidden through rigid wage and price controls, but with the collapse of the Third Reich, the fiscal sleight of hand could no longer be continued or concealed. Long-established social insurance systems such as old-age, sickness, and industrial accident disability, which had access to independent and continuing sources of fiscal support like pension funds (insofar as they had not been totally depleted by government raids) and member contributions, were able to reestablish themselves after the war, though with considerable difficulty. Programs dependent solely on public funds, such as those for war victims and military dependents, whose spiraling costs had been covered primarily by the printing press were, however, like the Third Reich, bankrupt.

84. Ian Kershaw, *Popular Opinion and Political Dissent in the Third Reich: Bavaria, 1933–1945* (New York, 1983), p. 294. According to Albert Speer, when Hitler, sitting in his private train, saw some wounded soldiers outside, he immediately pulled down the blind. John Hiden and John Farquharson, *Explaining Hitler's Germany: Historians and the Third Reich* (Totowa, N.J., 1983), p. 30.

85. Oberlindober agreed to give up 100 employees (41 male and 59 female), but at the same time he tried to gain assurances that the employees would be returned to the NSKOV at the end of the war, since the amount of social work (*Betreuungsarbeit*) would be enormous and there would not be time to train new workers in the field. Oberlindober to Schwarz, 7 April 1943, Sammlung Schumacher, 255/NSKOV, BAK.

86. In particular, Oberlindober had used 585,861 Reichsmark of propaganda funds to purchase paintings that were given to Hitler, Göring, and Schwarz, the party treasurer. See Schwarz to Bormann, 8 March 1943, ibid.

87. U.S. Military Intelligence Report on the NSKOV, OMGUS, RG 260, box 377, folder 31, NARS.

88. I have been unable to determine with certainty what happened to Oberlindober after the war. The documents I obtained from the Berlin Document Center provide no information on his activities after 1944. A letter, discovered by chance in the Bundesarchiv (B149/1802), possibly sheds some light on his fate, however. The letter, from the Hilfswerk der Evangelischen Kirchen to the Verwaltung für Arbeit and dated 1 December 1949, was written on behalf of a Frau Oberlindober, whose husband, Hans, a native of Munich and a disabled World War I veteran (as was the NSKOV leader), had been interned in Dachau after the war and then, as a result of a name mixup, mistakenly extradicted in 1947 to Poland, where he died in a Warsaw prison on 6 April 1949. Since the letter fails to give either the Christian or maiden name of the woman in question, it is impossible to identify her positively as Oberlindober's wife, whose maiden name was

Karoline Knauer, or to be certain that the fate of her husband was that of the NSKOV's leader. There is good reason to believe that this was the case, however. Because of his high-ranking positions in the NSKOV and SA, Oberlindober was liable to arrest, and because he gave testimony that was used at the Nuremberg trials, it is certain that he was captured by Allied forces and probably interned, quite possibly at Dachau.

89. This was especially hard on younger veterans, who either had not worked or had only worked for a few years before the outbreak of the war. Since their contributions to accident and/or social security pension systems were small, their pension benefits were meager or nonexistent. On pension provisions in the immediate postwar years, see chapter 3 and Wenzel, *Fünfzig Jahre Kriegsopferversorgung*, pp. 34–36; Rühland, "Entwicklung," pp. 86–119; and Staib, "Das deutsche Versorgungsrecht," part 2.

Chapter 3

1. Developments in the French zone have recently been clarified by the work of Rainer Hudemann, *Sozialpolitik im deutschen Südwesten zwischen Tradition und Neuordnung, 1945–1953. Sozialversicherung und Kriegsopferversorgung im Rahmen französischer Besatzungspolitik* (Mainz, 1988). The opening of former East German archives that has followed German unification will soon remedy the deficit of materials for the former Soviet zone and enable historians to reconstruct events there.

2. See, for example, Edwin Hartrich, *The Fourth and Richest Reich: How the Germans Conquered the Postwar World* (New York, 1980), chapter 3.

3. According to Edward N. Peterson, "Demilitarization was welcomed by most, resisted by none." *The American Occupation of Germany: Retreat to Victory* (Detroit, 1977), p. 138.

4. Gerhard Wettig, *Entmilitarisierung und Wiederbewaffnung in Deutschland, 1943–1955. Internationale Auseinandersetzungen um die Rolle der Deutschen in Europa* (Munich, 1967), chapter 1. For the text of JCS 1067, see *Documents on Germany under Occupation, 1945–1954*, edited by Beate Ruhm von Oppen (London, 1955), pp. 13–27. On the genesis of JCS 1067 and its implementation, see John Gimbel, *The American Occupation of Germany: Politics and the Military, 1945–1949* (Stanford, 1968), and Earl F. Ziemke, *The U.S. Army in the Occupation of Germany* (Washington, D.C., 1985); also cf. Hudemann, *Sozialpolitik im deutschen Südwesten*, pp. 400–402.

5. *Documents on Germany*, p. 16.

6. Wettig, *Entmilitarisierung*, pp. 23–24; Kurt Tauber, *Beyond Eagle and Swastika: German Nationalism since 1945* (Middletown, Conn., 1967), 1:255; Eugene Davidson, *The Trial of the Germans: An Account of the Twenty-Two Defendants before the International Military Tribunal at Nuremberg* (New York, 1966), p. 22. The link between nazism and militarism and the priority of the latter were also emphasized in U.S. and British newsreels. See K. R. M. Short and Stephan Dolzel, eds., *Hitler's Fall: The Newsreel Witness* (London, 1988), pp. 11, 30, 35–37.

7. Wettig, *Entmilitarisierung*, p. 23.

8. Ibid., p. 106. The phrase is equally euphonious in German: "Es heisst färben oder sterben."

9. U.S. Group Control Council Joint Intelligence Staff, German Officer Corps, 25 June 1945, OMGUS, RG 260, box 123, folder 34, NARS.

10. Although the report conceded that there had not been any signs of resistance, it cited events in Aachen, as well as the resistance to Nazi occupation, as reasons to fear German resistance to Allied occupation. Ibid., pp. 6–7.

11. Disposition of Potentially Dangerous Officers of German Armed Forces, 9 August 1945, OMGUS, RG 260, box 135, NARS.

12. Ibid., TAB A, Specifications for Determining Those Officers of the German Armed Forces Who Should Be Subject to Restrictive Measures. Exactly how this figure was calculated is unclear. Group I, the officers that were considered to be "the most potentially dangerous," were drawn from three categories: officers of "Flag rank," that is, major general and above, General Staff officers, and "Other Officers of Marked Potential Danger." While the criteria for determining the first two categories were fairly precise, those for the third were considerably more vague, including, for example, early indoctrination in German military tradition as a result of birth and position, formal military training, prewar military activity, and wartime military record.

13. Ibid., TAB B, Analysis of Proposed Plans for Disposal of German Officers Who Must Be Subject to Restrictive Measures.

14. The extent to which this control was actually implemented is uncertain.

15. Control Commission for Germany (British Element), Chief of Staff's (British Zone) Conference, Payment of Pensions in Germany, 12 July 1945, and Extracts from First and Second Reports of the Working Party on the Payment of Pensions in Germany, FO944/313, PRO.

16. Fourth Meeting of Working Party on the Payment of Pensions in Germany, 10 September 1945, ibid.

17. Ibid.

18. Ibid.

19. Cited in Third Report of the Working Party on the Payment of Pensions in Germany, with covering letters dated 5 and 9 October 1945, ibid.

20. Ibid.

21. The Working Party clinched its argument by noting that German pension officials had expressed the view that even if Germany had won the war it would have been unable to pay the pensions to which it was committed by legislation.

22. Since all veterans, including former POWs and the war-disabled, were organized in Nazi affiliate organizations, the banning of Nazi organizations and the arrest and internment of many of their functionaries deprived veterans of existing organizations and potential leaders. The implementation of JCS 1067, which ordered "the total dissolution of all military and paramilitary organizations . . . together with all associations which might serve to keep alive the military tradition in Germany," prohibited the formation of new groups. Control Council Law 34 sealed the process by disbanding,

completely dissolving, and declaring illegal the General Staff, officers corps, reserve corps, military schools, as well as "war veteran organizations, and all other military and quasi-military organizations, together with all clubs and associations which serve to keep alive the military tradition in Germany." On the demilitarization decrees of the Allies, see Wettig, *Entmilitarisierung*, pp. 102–6; for the text of Control Council Law 34, see *Documents on Germany*, pp. 151–52.

23. The following quotations from the British report (as well as the American response) are taken from *Information Control Intelligence Summary*, No. 55, 17 August 1946, OMGUS, RG 319, box 699, NARS.

24. Sammlung Ritter von Schramm. Materialien zu einer Geschichte der deutschen Berufssoldaten zwischen 1945 und 1955: Schicksale Deutscher Berufssoldaten von 1945–1955, MSg 118/1, BAF, pp. 25, 34–35.

25. Leeb to McNary, 23 October 1946, OMGUS, RG 260, box 130, and Lequis to Länderrat, Stuttgart, 19 February 1947, and Lequis to OMGUS, Berlin, March 1947, OMGUS, RG 260, box 56, folder 15, NARS.

26. While Hansen was quick to point out that the court had judged the General Staff and Supreme Command not guilty, he was silent about the fact that it had based its verdict on the technical consideration that they were, in fact, not groups or organizations as indicted. Equally overlooked by the admiral was the stinging statement that accompanied the court's finding: "Many of these men have made a mockery of the soldier's oath of obedience to military orders. When it suits their defense they say they had to obey; when confronted with Hitler's brutal crimes, which are shown to have been within their general knowledge, they say they disobeyed. The truth is that they actively participated in all these crimes, or sat silent and acquiescent, witnessing the commission of crimes on a scale larger and more shocking than the world has ever had the misfortune to know." Quoted in Davidson, *The Trial of the Germans*, p. 563.

27. On the controversy over the meaning of the 20 July 1944 assassination attempt on Hitler, see chapter 7.

28. For a representative collection of Hansen's arguments, see his letters to Hermann Pünder, the director of the Wirtschaftsrat, in Z13/338, Band 1, BAK; see also Sammlung Ritter von Schramm. Materialien zu einer Geschichte der deutschen Berufssoldaten zwischen 1945 und 1955: Zwei Handakten des Admirals Hansen, MSg 118/5, BAF. In published form, the arguments of Hansen and his associates can be found in *Der Notweg. Wirtschaftlicher Wegweiser für versorgungsberechtige ehemalige Angehörige der Wehrmacht und deren Hinterbliebene*, first published in April 1949.

29. An extensive and representative collection of these can be found in Z13/338, Band 2, BAK; also see Sammlung Ritter von Schramm: Einzelerlebnisse, MSg 118/4, BAF, and the material from the Nachlass Donat cited in Georg Meyer, "Zur Situation der deutschen militärischen Führungsschicht im Vorfeld des westdeutschen Verteidigungsbeitrages, 1945–50/51," in *Anfänge westdeutscher Sicherheitspolitik, 1945–1956*, herausgegeben vom Militärgeschichtlichen Forschungsamt, Band 1, *Von der Kapitulation bis zum Pleven-Plan* (Munich, 1982), p. 637, n. 135.

30. See, for example, Kobe v. Koppenfels to Pünder, 1 April 1948, Z13/338, Band 2, BAK.

31. Reports of such suicides, especially in the wake of the currency reform, were a standard staple of the petitions and memoranda of the former professional soldiers. An example that was repeatedly cited was the report that forty-three former officers had committed suicide in the Regierungsbezirk Lüneburg within a period of a hundred days. For this and other examples, see Sammlung Ritter von Schramm: Schicksale Deutscher Berufssoldaten von 1945–1955, MSg 118/1, BAF, pp. 60–61. Also see Meyer, "Zur Situation," p. 637, n. 135.

32. Concluding sentences of a two-page memorandum on military pensions prepared by Gerhard Gieren, a retired major from Hameln, dated 15 June 1948, Z13/338, Band 1, BAK. For another example of this type of complaint, see Meyer, "Zur Situation," p. 638.

33. "Durch die Einstellung der Zahlungen nach dem Waffenstillstand . . . sind die Angehörigen dieses Berufsstandes in eine unverschuldete Notlage geraten, die grösser ist als die der Juden während der Herrschaft des Nationalsozialismus, weil diesen die Unterstützung des Weltjudentums sicher war, während für den Stand der Berufs- soldaten sich erst jetzt einzelne Deutsche einzusetzen wagen." Generalmajor a. D. Gerhard Müller to the Landtagsfraktion of the SPD Rheinland-Pfalz, 16 November 1948, Z13/338, Band 2, BAK. For similar views, see the letter of Hugo Oster (3 July 1948) and the memo accompanying the letter of Anita Sievert (26 August 1948) in ibid.

34. Meyer, "Zur Situation," p. 646; see Pensions—Instructions in Force in the French Zone, Z40/68, BAK, which gives the conditions for granting pensions in the French zone.

35. See the statements quoted by Meyer, "Zur Situation," p. 638; see also the letters of the former officers in Z13/338, Band 2, BAK.

36. Regional Government Coordinating Office to Erich Rossmann, Director of the Länderrat. Subject: Maintenance Grants to Career Military Personnel, 15 March 1948, Z1/296, BAK.

37. See, for example, Stellungnahme des Unterausschusses Sozialversicherung zum Entwurf eines Gesetzes über die Zahlung von Unterhaltsbeträgen an berufsmässige Wehrmachtsangehörigen und ihre Hinterbliebenen, TO. 24.6.1948, Anlage 2, Z1/296, BAK, and Bericht über die Sitzung des Parlamentarischen Rates in Stuttgart am 19. Juli zum Entwurf eines Gesetzes über die Zahlung von Unterhaltsbeträgen an berufs- mässige Wehrmachtsangehörigen und deren Hinterbliebene. 20. Juli 1948, Z1/297, BAK. On the origins and passage of compensation legislation, see Hans-Dieter Krei- kamp, "Zur Entstehung des Entschädigungsgesetzes der amerikanischen Besatzungs- zone," in *Wiedergutmachung in der Bundesrepublik Deutschland*, herausgeben von Lu- dolf Herbst und Constantin Goschler (Munich, 1989).

38. See point 4 of the memorandum prepared by the social insurance section of the Labor Ministry in the British zone, Zentralamt für Arbeit in der britischen Zone. Hauptabteilung IV Sozialversicherung IVa/821/48, 8. Juni 1948, Z40/68, BAK.

39. Bericht über die Sitzung des Parlamentarischen Rates in Stuttgart am 19. Juli [1948] zum Entwurf eines Gesetzes über die Zahlung von Unterhaltsbeträgen an berufsmässige Wehrmachtsangehörigen und deren Hinterbliebene, Z1/297, BAK.

40. The guidelines accompanying the military government's permission to provide the *Unterhaltsbeträge* had suggested that the legislation be coordinated among the states, so as to avoid substantial variations that would then necessitate strict residence requirements in order to prevent migration from one state to another by recipients seeking better payments. In the U.S. zone, the Finance Committee of the Länderrat produced a draft law in late May, which then circulated through the Länderrat's legislative apparatus. After much wrangling among the committees and the states, a final law, scheduled to take effect on 1 January 1949, was passed by the Länderrat and submitted to the military government in September 1948. In April 1949 the Germans were informed by the military government that a zonal law was unnecessary and that the *Unterhaltsbeträge* were a matter for state legislation. The responsibility was formally transferred to the states of the Federal Republic in July 1949. In the meantime, a number of states, using the Länderrat law as a model, had begun to pass their own legislation. On developments in the U.S. zone, see the materials in Z1/296–97, BAK. The process in the British zone was somewhat different, but the outcome was the same; see the materials in Z40/68, BAK.

41. Krafft Freiherr Schenck zu Schweinsberg, "Die Soldatenverbände in der Bundesrepublik," in *Studien zur politischen und gesellschaftlichen Situation der Bundeswehr*, herausgegeben von Georg Picht (Witten, 1965), p. 98; Sammlung Ritter von Schramm: Schicksale von deutscher Berufssoldaten, MSg 118/1, BAF, pp. 88–89; Meyer, "Zur Situation," pp. 643–44.

42. Meyer, "Zur Situation," pp. 642–45; Anhang zur Verzeichnis der Akten Admiral a.D. Hansen, 1945–56: Beiträge zu einer Geschichte des BvW, VdS/BvW und Vds, Findleiter, Nachlass Hansen, N222, BAF.

43. See Hansen to Pünder and accompanying documents, 25 September 1948, Z13/338, Band 1, BAK.

44. *Documents on Germany*, pp. 445–46.

45. Schenck zu Schweinsberg, "Die Soldatenverbände," pp. 99–100; Meyer, "Zur Situation," p. 645. According to Hansen the BvW was not really founded until July. Sitzungsprotokoll der Vertreterversammlung des BvW v. 19/21.5.51, Nachlass Hansen, N222/228, BAF, p. 6. Allied High Commission Law 16 still prohibited "organizations which require any of their members to be war veterans," but this restriction was circumvented by the inclusion in the BvW's membership of survivors of former professional soldiers who had died. For more on the development of the BvW, see chapters 7, 8, and Conclusion.

46. Anhang zur Verzeichnis der Akten Admiral a.D. Hansen, 1945–56: Beiträge zu einer Geschichte des BvW, VdS/BvW und Vds, Findleiter, Nachlass Hansen, N222, BAF.

47. Arthur L. Smith, *Heimkehr aus dem Zweiten Weltkrieg. Die Entlassung der deutschen Kriegsgefangenen* (Stuttgart, 1985), p. 11; Ziemke, *The U.S. Army in the Occupation of Germany*, pp. 291ff. Also cf. Peterson, *The American Occupation of Germany*, pp. 114–16, and *Freiheit ohne Furcht. Zehn Jahre Heimkehrerverband*, herausgegeben vom Verband der Heimkehrer, Kriegsgefangenen, und Vermisstenangehörigen Deutschlands (Bad Godesberg, [1960]), p. 41.

48. In 1989 Canadian author James Bacque caused a minor sensation with the publication of a book in which he maintained that the Americans and the French, as the result of a policy deliberately implemented by General Dwight D. Eisenhower, allowed nearly a million German POWs to starve to death. James Bacque, *Other Losses: An Investigation into the Mass Deaths of German Prisoners of War at the Hands of the French and Americans after World War II* (Toronto, 1989). A conference at the Eisenhower Center located at the University of New Orleans investigated Bacque's charges and found them to be totally unsubstantiated. Although there were cases of maltreatment of the prisoners and their rations were meager, there was no deliberate policy to starve German POWs to death. Bacque overlooks the enormity of the logistical problems facing the Allies, especially the critical food shortage in Europe in the postwar years, and his handling of statistical materials is seriously flawed. For a rebuttal of his arguments based on the findings of the conference, see Stephan E. Ambrose, "Ike and the Disappearing Atrocities," *New York Times Book Review*, 24 February 1991.

49. Smith, *Heimkehr*, pp. 11, 24–25.

50. Hartrich, *Fourth and Richest Reich*, p. 30. On the different treatment of German POWs by the Allied powers, see Smith, *Heimkehr*, chapter 4.

51. Smith, *Heimkehr*, pp. 94–95.

52. Ibid., pp. 62–63, 83, 91.

53. Ibid., p. 73.

54. Ibid., chapter 2.

55. Ibid., pp. 116–17; "Some Problems of Repatriation and Resettlement of German Prisoners of War," FO945/223, PRO.

56. *Information Control Weekly Review*, No. 10 (14 December 1946) and No. 28 (21 June 1947), OMGUS, RG 260, box 281, and *Information Control Intelligence Summary*, No. 53 (3 August 1946), OMGUS, RG 319, box 699, NARS.

57. Smith, *Heimkehr*, p. 182.

58. *Political Intelligence Summary*, No. 9 (1 September 1945), FO371/46934, BAOR, *Fortnightly Intelligence Summary*, No. 11 (22 September 1945), FO371/46935, and Intelligence Control Staff, Berlin, *Fortnightly Political Intelligence Report*, 3 January 1946, FO371/55879, PRO; *Information Control Weekly Review*, No. 10 (14 December 1946) and No. 28 (21 June 1947), OMGUS, RG 260, box 281, and *Information Control Intelligence Summary*, No. 6 (17 August 1945) and No. 53 (3 August 1946), OMGUS, RG 319, box 699, NARS.

59. Smith, *Heimkehr*, pp. 111–12, 122, 125–26; Julian Bach, *America's Germany: An Account of the Occupation* (New York, 1946), p. 62.

60. "The Repatriated Prisoners of War," FO939/384, and "Some Problems of Repatriation and Resettlement of German Prisoners of War," FO945/223, PRO.

61. "Some Problems of Repatriation and Resettlement of German Prisoners of War," FO945/223, and Intelligence Control Staff, Berlin, *Intelligence Summary*, No. 62 (21 September 1946), FO371/55882, PRO; *Information Control Weekly Review*, No. 10 (14 December 1946), OMGUS, RG 260, box 281, and *Information Control Intelligence*

Summary, No. 5 (10 August 1945) and No. 8 (31 August 1945), OMGUS, RG 319, box 699, NARS.

62. Situation Report on Conditions in Germany, 17 August 1945, FO371/46934, PRO.

63. Smith, *Heimkehr*, pp. 110–11.

64. *Information Control Intelligence Summary*, No. 31 (16 February 1946), OMGUS, RG 319, box 699, NARS. The belief that there was an impending rearmament that would utilize German volunteers was reinforced by the existence of the so-called work battalions, composed of demobilized German soldiers, in the American and British zones. On these battalions, see Heinz-Ludiger Borgert, "Zur Entstehung, Entwicklung und Struktur der Dienstgruppen in der britischen und amerikanischen Besatzungszone Westdeutschlands, 1945–1950," in *Dienstgruppen und westdeutscher Verteidigungsbeitrag. Vorüberlegungen zur Bewaffnung der Bundesrepublik Deutschland*, herausgegeben vom Militärgeschichtlichen Forschungsamt (Boppard am Rhein, 1982).

65. Twenty-first Army Group, *Weekly Political Intelligence Summary*, No. 5 (4 August 1945), FO371/46933, PRO.

66. Smith, *Heimkehr*, pp. 49–50. The names on the gravestones in the French cemetery at Dien Bien Phu provide silent testimony to the success of French recruitment efforts in Germany. For this information, I am indebted to my colleague, William B. Cohen.

67. "Europe 1946," FO371/55879, PRO; Bach, *America's Germany*, pp. 16–17, 252–53, 291; Hartrich, *Fourth and Richest Reich*, pp. 29–30; Douglas Botting, *From the Ruins of the Reich: Germany, 1945–1949* (New York, 1985), p. 130.

68. Earl R. Beck, *Under the Bombs: The German Home Front, 1942–1945* (Lexington, 1986); Wilbur H. Morrison, *Fortress without a Roof: The Allied Bombing of the Third Reich* (New York, 1982).

69. For examples of positive reactions to the return of soldiers, see P.I.D. German and Austrian Intelligence, *Germany, Weekly Background Notes*, No. 1 (8 January 1945), FO371/46933, and *Political Intelligence Summary*, No. 8 (24 August 1945), FO371/46934, PRO. For examples of negative responses, see GS Headquarters British Troops, Berlin, *Intelligence Summary*, No. 44 (16 May 1946), FO371/55879, PRO; *Information Control Weekly Review*, No. 10 (8 February 1947) and No. 28 (21 June 1947), OMGUS, RG 260, box 281; *Information Control Intelligence Summary*, No. 6 (17 August 1945), OMGUS, RG 319, box 699, NARS; Smith, *Heimkehr*, pp. 33–34, 131–32; and Wolf Donner, *Die sozial- und staatspolitische Tätigkeit der Kriegsopferverbände. Ein Beitrag zur Verbandsdiskussion* (Berlin, 1960), p. 19.

70. Smith, *Heimkehr*, p. 192. This theme, as well as others connected with the return of veterans to postwar Germany, is poignantly captured in the early short stories of Heinrich Böll.

71. On the problems of reunited veteran families, see Sibylle Meyer and Eva Schulze, *Von Liebe sprach damals keiner. Familienalltag in der Nachkriegszeit* (Munich, 1985),

chapter 6, and Klaus-Jörg Ruhl, *Frauen in der Nachkriegszeit, 1945–1963* (Munich, 1988), chapter 1.

72. "Some Problems of Repatriation and Resettlement of German Prisoners of War," FO945/223, PRO; David Rodnick, *Postwar Germans: An Anthropologist's Account* (New Haven, 1948), chapter 9; Smith, *Heimkehr*, pp. 110–11.

73. Intelligence Control Staff, Berlin, *Intelligence Summary*, No. 53 (17 July 1946), FO371/55880, PRO.

74. Ibid.

75. On the Allied strictures against veterans' organizations, see note 22 above.

76. On these early organizational efforts, see Smith, *Heimkehr*, pp. 137–41.

77. Ibid., p. 195.

78. Ibid., pp. 35–36, 42–44, 65–68, 170ff.

79. For a glimpse of the difficult situation of the war-disabled in finding adequate health care, see Betr.: Krankenanstalten und- Einrichten für den Versehrte, 20 March 1948, Z40/194, BAK. The problem is graphically captured in the 1949 British film *The Third Man*, whose villian, Harry Lime, is involved in the black market sale of penicillin.

80. Rainer Hudemann has argued convincingly that although the black market, or parallel economy, was not as important as it has become in the collective memory, it did play a key role and those who were excluded from the parallel market were at a disadvantage, a fact that obviously affected the war victims, especially the war-disabled. *Sozialpolitik im deutschen Südwesten*, chapter 1, especially pp. 108–23. Also cf. Dietrich Hilger, "Die mobilisierte Gesellschaft," in *Die zweite Republik. 25 Jahre Bundesrepublik Deuthschland—Eine Bilanz*, herausgegeben von Richard Löwenthal und Hans-Peter Schwarz (Stuttgart, 1974).

81. Gedanken zur Betreuung der Kriegsopfer and Bemerkungen zur Denkschrift der bisherigen Hauptabteilung für die Kriegsopferversorgung im ehemaligen Reichsarbeitsministerium über die künftige Betreuung der Kriegsopfer, R2/22417, BAK; Die Versorgung der Kriegsbeschädigten und ihrer Hinterbliebenen in Deutschland, OMGUS, RG 260, box 56, folder 13, NARS; *Die Versorgung der Kriegsopfer in der Bundesrepublik Deutschland (Das Bundesversorgungsgesetz) Stand 30.9.1952*, herausgegeben vom Presse- und Informationsamt der Bundesregierung (Bonn, [1952]).

82. See Gedanken zur Betreuung der Kriegsopfer, R2/22417, BAK, pp. 2–4; and Die Versorgung der Kriegsbeschädigten und ihrer Hinterbliebenen in Deutschland, OMGUS, RG 260, box 56, folder 13, p. 20, and *Information Control Intelligence Summary*, No. 6 (17 August 1947), OMGUS, RG 319, box 699, NARS, on unemployment. For a statistical profile of the physically disabled in the early years of the Federal Republic, see "Die Körperbehinderten im Bundesgebiet. Ergebnisse der Volkszählung vom 13. September 1950," *Wirtschaft und Statistik* (December 1952).

83. Bemerkungen zur Denkschrift der bisherigen Hauptabteilung für die Kriegsopferversorgung im ehemaligen Reichsarbeitsministerium über die künftige Betreuung der Kriegsopfer, R2/22417, BAK, p. 1.

84. For the texts of JCS 1067 and Control Council Law 34, see *Documents on Germany*, pp. 13–27, 151–52.

85. War Pensions in Connection with Demilitarization, ACo19(MD), 8 January 1947, OMGUS RG 260, box 56, folder 10, NARS.

86. According to one estimate, between 25 and 30 percent of the population in the three Western zones needed monetary assistance. Fritz Blücher, "Financial Situation and Currency Reform in Germany," *Annals* 260 (November 1948): 64.

87. For details of French occupation policies, see Hudemann, *Sozialpolitik im deutschen Südwesten*.

88. See ibid., pp. 402–10.

89. Ibid., pp. 410–12.

90. On the treatment of war victims in the Soviet zone and the German Democratic Republic, see Helmut Rühland, "Entwicklung, heutige Gestaltung und Problematik der Kriegsopferversorgung in der Bundesrepublik Deutschland" (Inaugural disserta-tion, Universität Köln, 1957), pp. 98–103, 191–99, and "Tatsachen hinter dem eisernen Vorhang," *Ostinformationsdienst der Bundespressestelle des DGB*, no. 9 (19 December 1963).

91. For overviews of the treatment of war victims in the Western zones, see Rühland, "Entwicklung," pp. 88–98, 103–19; *Die Versorgung. Stand 30.9.1952*, pp. 18–19; and Leonhard Trometer, "Die Kriegsopferversorgung nach 1945," in *Sozialpolitik nach 1945. Geschichte und Analysen*, herausgegeben von Reinhart Bartholomäi et al. (Bonn, 1977), pp. 192–93.

92. In a survey conducted in the U.S. zone in April 1946 to sample German opinion regarding support for the claims of various categories of those who had suffered losses as a result of the war, the war-disabled were placed at the head of the list of those deserving support (84 percent favoring aid), followed by those who had been bombed out (75 percent), expellees (70 percent), refugees (65 percent), dependents of war victims (61 percent), Jews (47 percent), victims of political persecution (47 percent), and displaced persons (39 percent). *Information Control Intelligence Summary*, No. 45 (8 June 1946), OMGUS, RG 319, box 699, NARS. Another poll, taken later in the year, produced similar results, with 63 percent placing war casualties at the top of the list of those deserving aid. Ann J. Merritt and Richard L. Merritt, *Public Opinion in Occupied Germany: The OMGUS Surveys, 1945–1949* (Urbana, 1970), p. 121.

93. German authorities were aware of the need to cut levels of benefits, but they opposed the wholesale restructuring of the old system, especially the subordination of war victims to other programs. See Gedanken zur Betreuung der Kriegsopfer and Bemerkungen zur Denkschrift der bisherigen Hauptabteilung für die Kriegsopferver-sorgung im ehemaligen Reichsarbeitsministerium über die künftige Betreuung der Kriegsopfer, R2/22417, BAK, and Hudemann, *Sozialpolitik im deutschen Südwesten*, pp. 442–50.

94. War Pensions in Connection with Demilitarization, ACo19(MD), 8 January 1947, OMGUS, RG 260, box 56, folder 10, NARS.

95. Rühland, "Entwicklung," pp. 88–96; Hudemann, *Sozialpolitik im deutschen Süd-westen*, pp. 444–50.

96. For details, see Hudemann, *Sozialpolitik im deutschen Südwesten*, chapter 8.

97. French generosity in the payment of social pensions was facilitated by the refusal to accept expellees in the French zone, which removed an enormous social welfare burden. In the U.S. zone, for example, 28 percent of welfare payments went to expellees. OMGUS, Monthly Report, *Public Welfare*, No. 9 (20 April 1946), p. 2.

98. In order to prevent such fears from becoming reality, the military governments decreed that the additional costs incurred by the social insurance programs as a result of their taking over war-disability payments were to be covered by general tax revenues, not pension funds. Moreover, to keep the additional costs as low as possible, eligibility requirements for war-disability pensions were more stringent in many areas than those employed by the general program; for example, for regular members of the industrial accident insurance program, disability payments began with a disability of 25 percent, whereas disabled veterans only began to receive pensions with a disability of more than 40 percent. For a contemporary account of the difficulties confronting the various social insurance systems in postwar Germany, see Rudolf Wissel, "Social Insurance in Germany," *Annals* 260 (November 1948), especially pp. 128–30. A comprehensive account of the rebuilding of the German social insurance system after the war is provided in Hans Günter Hockerts, *Sozialpolitische Entscheidungen im Nachkriegsdeutschland. Allierte und deutsche Sozialversicherungspolitik 1945 bis 1957*, (Stuttgart, 1980); see also Hudemann, *Sozialpolitik im deutschen Südwesten*.

99. The following is based on Rühland, "Entwicklung," pp. 103–10.

100. For details and examples, see ibid., pp. 111–19.

101. Control Council Law 2, *Documents on Germany*, p. 79.

102. Ibid, p. 151.

103. Donner, *Die sozial- und staatspolitische Tätigkeit*, p. 20; Hudemann, *Sozialpolitik im deutschen Südwesten*, pp. 415–16. Union personnel were especially active in organizing efforts. Ibid., pp. 419–20.

104. See note 126 below.

105. See chapter 1.

106. *Chronik in Daten. Der Reichsbund, 1917–1933 und 1946–1971* (Bonn, 1971); Das Organisationsbild des Reichsbundes: Ein kurzgefasster geschichtlicher Überblick, Z40/326, BAK.

107. Die Einigungsverhandlungen zwischen dem VdK und dem Reichsbund, Nachlass Erich Rossmann, Lfd. Nr. 49, BAK, p. 4.

108. While the French were willing to grant more generous benefits than the other Allies, their fears of a resurgence of German militarism was just as great, if not greater, and this produced an even stronger aversion to manifestations of the organization of German veterans. Hudemann, *Sozialpolitik im deutschen Südwesten*, p. 463.

109. For more on these efforts, see text at n. 114.

110. Die Einigungsverhandlungen zwischen dem VdK und dem Reichsbund, Nachlass Erich Rossmann, Lfd. Nr. 49, BAK, pp. 6–7.

111. Ibid., pp. 8–9.

112. Ibid., pp. 9–12.

113. French authorities allowed their zone's war victims' organizations to send

representatives but not to join the league; in January 1949, however, they were permitted to become members. Hudemann, *Sozialpolitik im deutschen Südwesten*, p. 427.

114. Liberalization of Benefits to Widows of War-Killed, 4 April 1947, OMGUS, RG 260, box 51, folder 2, NARS; Rühland, "Entwicklung," pp. 91, 94–95. Cf. Hudemann, *Sozialpolitik im deutschen Südwesten*, pp. 449–50.

115. For information on the committee's activities, see Z40/120 and Z40/147, BAK.

116. On the formation of the VfA, see Walter Vogel, *Westdeutschland, 1945–1950. Der Aufbau von Verfassungs- und Verwaltungseinrichtungen über den Ländern der drei westlichen Besatzungszonen*, Teil 3, *Einzelne Verwaltungszweige* (Boppard am Rhein, 1983), pp. 398ff. According to its director, Anton Storch, the VfA, although technically not allowed to work for the war victims, had begun to prepare the ground for the later Bundesversorgungsgesetz (BVG). Anton Storch, *Abgeordnete des deutschen Bundestages. Aufzeichnungen und Erinnerungen* (Boppard am Rhein, 1983), 2:329.

117. Rühland, "Entwicklung," p. 92; *Akten zur Vorgeschichte der Bundesrepublik Deutschland, 1945–1949*, herausgegeben von der Bundesarchiv und Institut für Zeitgeschichte (Munich, 1981), 5:604, 652. Also cf. Hockerts, *Sozialpolitische Entscheidungen*, pp. 101–2. For the debate in the Wirtschaftsrat, see *Wörtliche Berichte und Drucksachen des Wirtschaftsrats des Vereinigten Wirtschaftsgebietes, 1947–1949*, herausgegeben vom Institut für Zeitgeschichte und dem Deutschen Bundestag (Munich, 1977), 3:1666–67, 1825, 1935–41, 1988–89.

118. Rühland, "Entwicklung," pp. 92–95; *Die Versorgung. Stand 30.9.1952*, pp. 18–19.

119. On developments in Baden, see Hudemann, *Sozialpolitik im deutschen Südwesten*, pp. 460–74. Attempts to introduce additional cuts following those connected with the denazification of the RVG remained halfhearted and foundered on public opposition and the unwillingness of French military government officials to press for their implementation.

120. On developments in Rhineland-Palatinate, see ibid., pp. 475–500. In Rhineland-Palatinate, as in the other states of the French zone, German officials played an important role in the shaping of war victim legislation. While the Germans accepted the need for some changes and cuts in the old system, they adamantly resisted the idea of completely subordinating the war victim benefits system to the industrial accident program and French officials did not insist that this be done.

121. On the friction among the Allies, as well as the conflict between the French and the Germans over the rates, not the structure, of the law, see ibid., pp. 490ff.

122. On developments in Württemberg-Hohenzollern, see ibid., pp. 501–40.

123. That the formulation and implementation of occupation policy involved considerable give and take in areas other than social legislation is confirmed in James F. Tent, *Mission on the Rhine: Reeducation and Denazification in American-Occupied Germany* (Chicago, 1982), and Peterson, *The American Occupation of Germany*. The amount of German influence in determining zonal policies varied from zone to zone. It was greatest in the U.S. zone, where an independent German position was reinforced by the Länderrat, whose competence was greater than that of the analagous institutions in the other zones, such as the Zonenbeirat of the British zone. As Rainer Hudemann has

recently shown, German input into social legislation in the French zone, as opposed to political matters, was greater than has generally been supposed.

124. The ongoing dialogue between German and U.S. military government officials can be traced in the protocols of the Länderrat Subcommittee on Social Insurance, OMGUS, RG 260, boxes 102 and 107, and the OMGUS Manpower Division policy papers, boxes 51, 52, and 56, NARS. For the French zone, developments in the Rhineland-Palatinate offer a good example of German input into the legislative process. See Hudemann, *Sozialpolitik im deutschen Südwesten*, pp. 475–500.

125. See, for example, Länderrat Unterausschuss Sozialversicherung: Sitzung am 10.4.1946, pp. 3–4, and Sitzung am 9. und 10.10.1946, p. 15, OMGUS, RG 260, box 107, folder 8; Estimates of Expenditures Arising for Pensions for War Wounded, Widows, and Orphans of Deceased Soldiers, 16 May 1946, pp. 4–5, box 56, folder 12; and War Pensions and Social Insurance, 9 August 1946, p. 2, and Amendment of Military Government Regulations, 9 August 1946, TAB C, box 56, folder 16, NARS.

126. The extremes to which U.S. military government officials were willing to go in order to root out all vestiges of past, ostensibly militaristic, practices are shown by their response to the Länderrat's final draft of the new law, in which they demanded that the term *Versorgung* be replaced since it "has been used in the past to mean the war pensions and special assistance to war veterans which are now prohibited by Military Government Regulations," and by their opposition to a war victims' organization using the terms *Schwerkriegsbeschädigten* and *Kriegshinterbliebenen*. OMGUS Action on Länderrat Proposals, 27 November 1946, OMGUS, RG 260, box 56, folder 16, and Use of Terminology Distinguishing between War Disabled or War Survivors on the One Hand and Civilian Disabled or Survivors on the Other, 28 May 1947, box 56, folder 11, NARS. When German officials discussed plans to set aside 12 percent of jobs for the seriously disabled in late 1946, U.S. military government officials expressed concern that this could lead to a "Hineinströmung von Militaristen" into German public administration and factories. See Länderrat: Sozialpolitischer Ausschuss, 17 September 1946, ibid., box 102, folder 7.

127. For the mood of the war victims, see *Die Fackel*, July 1949.

Chapter 4

1. Hans-Peter Schwarz, *Die Ära Adenauer. Gründerjahre der Republik, 1949–1957* (Stuttgart, 1981), pp. 34–35.

2. On the negotiations preceding the formation of Adenauer's first cabinet, see *Auftakt zur Ära Adenauer. Koalitionsverhandlungen und Regierungsbildung, 1949*, bearbeitet von Udo Wengst (Düsseldorf, 1985), and Udo Wengst, *Staatsaufbau und Regierungspraxis, 1948–1953. Zur Geschichte der Verfassungsorgane der Bundesrepublik Deutschland* (Düsseldorf, 1984).

3. The protracted negotiations that accompanied the Wirtschaftrat's passage of veterans' legislation had already begun to cause unrest. When the military government

refused to approve the Wirtschaftrat's laws, arguing that the soon-to-be-formed Federal Republic had to pass legislation in these areas, the pressure to act was transferred to the federal government. For another example of this process, see the discussion of the 131 Law in chapter 6.

4. On the formation of the Ministry of Labor, see Wengst, *Staatsaufbau*; Walter Vogel, *Westdeutschland, 1945–1950. Der Aufbau von Verfassungs- und Verwaltungseinrichtungen über den Ländern der drei westlichen Besatzungszonen*, Teil 3, *Einzelne Verwaltungszweige* (Boppard am Rhein, 1983); and Hans Günter Hockerts, *Sozialpolitische Entscheidungen im Nachkriegsdeutschland. Allierte und deutsche Sozialversicherungspolitik 1945 bis 1957* (Stuttgart, 1980). According to Storch, the VfA "fulfilled nearly all of the functions of the old Reich Labor Ministry and, against the original intent of the occupying powers, legislation for the war-disabled was covertly [stillschweigend] prepared." Anton Storch, *Abgeordnete des deutschen Bundestages. Aufzeichnungen und Erinnerungen* (Boppard am Rhein, 1983), 2:329.

5." On the relationship of Storch and Adenauer and the debate surrounding Storch's appointment, see Hockerts, *Sozialpolitische Entscheidungen*; Storch, *Abgeordnete*; and Wengst, *Staatsaufbau*.

6. For details, see Hockerts, *Sozialpolitische Entscheidungen*.

7. For Storch's views, see 9. Sitzung des Organisationsauschusses der Ministerpräsidenten 2.7.49, *Akten zur Vorgeschichte der Bundesrepublik Deutschland, 1945–1949*, herausgegeben von der Bundesarchiv und Institut für Zeitgeschichte (Munich, 1981), 5:733–38.

8. See Storch's account of his talk with Sauerborn in Storch, *Abgeordnete*, 2:332–33; Wengst, *Staatsaufbau*, pp. 131–32; *Auftakt*, pp. 451–55; and Hockerts, *Sozialpolitische Entscheidungen*, which discusses Sauerborn's background and significance.

9. For the early history of the postwar war victims' organizations, see chapter 3.

10. According to the figures provided by Wolf Donner in *Die sozial- und staatspolitische Tätigkeit der Kriegsopferverbände. Ein Beitrag zur Verbandsdiskussion* (Berlin, 1960), p. 7, the percentaqe of civilian disabled was 10 percent. Rupert Breitling, *Die Verbände in der Bundesrepublik. Ihre Arten und ihre Wirkungsweise* (Meisenheim am Glan, 1955), p. 239, n. 321, sets the figure at 5 percent.

11. Whether this was done out of the conviction that the nonmilitary social pensioners now truly belonged or out of the fear that their exclusion would only drive them into the arms of rival organizations is unclear. Simple inertia was probably the decisive factor.

12. On the origins of the BDKK, see Breitling, *Verbände*, p. 72, and Donner, *Die sozial- und staatspolitische Tätigkeit*, pp. 22, 196.

13. Breitling, *Verbände*, p. 72; Donner, *Die sozial- und staatspolitische Tätigkeit*, pp. 7, 197. The BDKK's lack of appeal is a good illustration of the change in the atmosphere of veterans' politics following the Second World War. For more on this, see the Conclusion.

14. On the Bund der Kriegsblinden, see Donner, *Die sozial- und staatspolitische Tätigkeit*, pp. 7, 22, 196, and Rainer Hudemann, *Sozialpolitik im deutschen Südwesten*

zwischen Tradition und Neuordnung, 1945–1953. Sozialversicherung und Kriegsopferversorgung im Rahmen französischer Besatzungspolitik (Mainz, 1988), pp. 432–34.

15. On the history and development of the Bund, see Donner, *Die sozial- und staatspolitische Tätigkeit*, pp. 22, 197, and Hudemann, *Sozialpolitik im deutschen Südwesten*, pp. 434–39.

16. See, for example, I/87B, Anlage 4, PAB.

17. Die Praxis der Einigungsbestrebungen, Nachlass Rossmann, Lfd. Nr. 50, BAK.

18. The formation of the VdK also preempted attempts of the Reichsbund to pick off isolated *Landesverbände* of the Bund. Die Eingigungsverhandlungen zwischen dem VdK und dem Reichsbund, Nachlass Rossmann, Lfd. Nr. 49, BAK, p. 15.

19. Ibid., p. 16.

20. Sitzung des Reichsbundes der Kriegsbeschädigten, Hinterbliebenen, und Sozialrentner, Hamburg am 20. April 1950, Nachlass Rossmann, Lfd. Nr. 49, BAK.

21. For details on the negotiations, see chapter 7.

22. For an overview of the situation of the former POWs in the immediate postwar years, see Arthur L. Smith, *Heimkehr aus dem Zweiten Weltkrieg. Die Entlassung der deutschen Kriegsgefangenen* (Stuttgart, 1985).

23. Ibid., pp. 139–40.

24. Manfred Teschner, "Entwicklung eines Interessenverbandes. Ein empirischer Beitrag zum Problem der Verselbständigung von Massenorganisationen" (Inaugural dissertation, Johann-Wolfgang-Goethe-Universität, Frankfurt am Main, 1961), p. 5.

25. Ibid., pp. 5–6, 12–13.

26. On the founding of the VdH, see the facsimile of the second issue of *Der Heimkehrer* in *Freiheit ohne Furcht. Zehn Jahre Heimkehrerverband*, herausgegeben vom Verband der Heimkehrer, Kriegsgefangenen, und Vermisstenangehörigen Deutschlands (Bad Godesberg, [1960]), pp. 21–22, and Teschner, "Entwicklung," pp. 4–17.

27. See chapter 3, note 92.

28. *Chronik in Daten. Der Reichsbund, 1917–1933 und 1946–1971* (Bonn, 1971), p. 46.

29. See Donner, *Die sozial- und staatspolitische Tätigkeit*, pp. 28–29, for information on the number of Bundestag deputies who belonged to war victims' organizations in the second and third Bundestags and their distribution among the parties.

30. *DBDr*, Nr. 30, 16 September 1949.

31. *VDB*, 20 September 1949, pp. 23, 26.

32. Ibid., p. 26. This had also been the policy in the Weimar Republic and the Third Reich. See chapters 1 and 2.

33. See Hans-Hermann Hartwich, *Sozialstaatspostulat und gesellschaftlicher status quo* (Cologne, 1970).

34. *DBDr*, Nr. 36, 27 September 1949.

35. Ibid., Nr. 107, 18 October 1949.

36. Ibid., Nr. 108, 18 October 1949.

37. *VDB*, 4 November 1949, pp. 356–58; *DBDr*, Nr. 130, 27 October 1949.

38. Renner was referring to recent raises in the Maintenance Grants to former

officers in North Rhine–Westphalia and the military pensions connected with the legislation associated with article 131 of the Basic Law. See chapter 6.

39. Discussions on the law began in the Labor Ministry on 5 December, and a draft proposal was submitted to the cabinet on 19 December. *Die Versorgung der Kriegsopfer in der Bundesrepublik Deutschland. Stand 31.1.1952*, herausgegeben von der Bundesregierung, Schriftenreihe des BfA (Bonn, [1952]), p. 32.

40. *Die Kabinettsprotokolle der Bundesregiegung*, herausgegeben für das Bundesarchiv von Hans Booms, Band 1 (1949) (Boppard am Rhein, 1982), p. 265.

41. *DBDr*, Nr. 308, 9 December 1949.

42. Ibid., Nr. 340, 15 December 1949.

43. *Kabinettsprotokolle*, Band 1 (1949), p. 274.

44. *VDB*, 16 December 1949, pp. 758ff.

45. For the war victims' response, see *Die Fackel*, January 1950.

46. *VDB*, 20 January 1950, p. 905. The concern that cuts would prompt counterproposals by the Bundestag was expressed by Storch at the cabinet meeting of 17 January 1950. *Kabinettsprotokolle*, Band 2 (1950), p. 136.

47. *VDB*, 20 January 1950, pp. 900–910.

48. Bundesminister für Arbeit, 27. Januar 1950. Vermerk zu den finanziellen Auswirkungen des Entwurfs eines Gesetzes zur Verbesserung von Leistungen an Kriegsopfer, I/20A, Lfd. 11, PAB.

49. *Kabinettsprotokolle*, Band 2 (1950), pp. 175–76.

50. Ausführungen der Bundesminister Schäffer und Storch zum Entwurf eines Gesetzes zur Verbesserungen von Leistungen an Kriegsopfer in der gemeinsamen Sitzung des Haushaltsausschusses und des Ausschusses für Kriegsopfer und Kriegsgefangenen am 31. Januar 1950, I/20A, Lfd. 14, PAB.

51. *DBDr*, Nr. 484, 31 January 1950.

52. Ibid., Nr. 491, 2 February 1950.

53. *VDB*, 2 February 1950, p. 1064.

54. Ibid., pp. 1073–74.

55. Ibid., p. 1075.

56. Ibid., pp. 1076–79.

57. For details on legislation concerning POW benefits during the occupation, see *DBDr*, Nr. 631, 28 February 1950, p. 9.

58. Smith, *Heimkehr*, pp. 142–45.

59. For background on the drafting of the HKG, see *Kabinettsprotokolle*, Band 1 (1949), pp. 45, 200, 224, 278.

60. Smith, *Heimkehr*, p. 143. For more on POW compensation legislation, see chapter 7.

61. Denkschrift der Heimkehrer Organisationen der amerikanischen Zone für den 21er Ausschuss, I/35A, Lfd. 10, PAB.

62. The fear of losing out to better-organized interests was a constant theme of *Heimkehrer* demands. Former POWs were not included among the groups mentioned in polls ranking those in need of aid. See chapter 3, note 92.

63. Denkschrift der Heimkehrer Organisationen der amerikanischen Zone and Hilfsmassnahmen für Heimkehrer, I/35A, Lfd. 10, PAB.

64. On the Prisoner of War Compensation Law, see chapter 7.

65. *VDB*, 17 March 1950, pp. 1643–53.

66. Whereas legislation for the war-disabled and survivors involved over DM 3 billion, the HKG cost DM 74 million; moreover, the main costs associated with the HKG were largely one-time expenses, unlike those connected with the war victims.

67. *DBDr*, Nr. 831, 19 April 1950; *VDB*, 26 April 1950, pp. 2144–51.

68. *VDB*, 26 April 1950, p. 2149.

69. Ibid., pp. 2163–71.

70. There were considerable discrepancies between the composition of state legislatures and the Bundestag in the early years of Republic, and the state governments played a more important role in national politics than was the case later. See Schwarz, *Ära Adenauer*, pp. 48ff., and Dietrich Thränhardt, *Geschichte der Bundesrepublik Deutschland* (Frankfurt am Main, 1986), pp. 113ff.

71. In the cabinet meeting of 24 March 1950, the finance minister stated that he was willing to approve a raise in the *Entlassungsgeld*, but only if the sum for goods was reduced. *Kabinettsprotokolle*, Band 2 (1950), p. 290.

72. See *Der Heimkehrer*, passim.

73. Teschner, "Entwicklung," pp. 20–21. For the results of this campaign, see chapter 7.

74. *Die Fackel*, March 1950, p. 1. On origins of the phrase, see text preceding n. 53.

75. *Die Fackel*, March, April, and May 1950; see also the materials in I/87, PAB, and B149/1820, BAK.

76. Die Eingigungsverhandlungen zwischen dem VdK und dem Reichsbund, Nachlass Rossmann, Lfd. Nr. 49, BAK, pp. 16ff. For more on these unification efforts, see chapter 7.

Chapter 5

1. Rainer Hudemann, *Sozialpolitik im deutschen Südwesten zwischen Tradition und Neuordnung, 1945–1953. Sozialversicherung und Kriegsopferversorgung im Rahmen französischer Besatzungspolitik* (Mainz, 1988), pp. 514–15. For a statistical overview of the numbers affected by the BVG and the attendant costs from 1950 to 1960, see Waldemar Schönleiter, *Die Kriegsopferversorgung* (Stuttgart, 1961), Anlagen 2 and 3.

2. See James M. Diehl, "Social Legislation and the Legitimation of the Federal Republic," paper presented at the conference, "A Framework for Democracy: Forty Years of Experience with the Grundgesetz of the Federal Republic of Germany," Philadelphia, April 1989 (Cambridge, forthcoming).

3. The paradoxical role of social legislation, especially of the BVG, in the "reform versus restoration" controversy is discussed in ibid.

4. On the problem of corporatism and neocorporatism after the two world wars,

see, in general, Charles Maier, *Recasting Bourgeois Europe: Stabilization in France, Germany, and Italy in the Decade after World War I* (Princeton, 1975); Suzanne D. Berger, ed., *Organizing Interests in Western Europe: Pluralism, Corporatism, and the Transformation of Politics* (Cambridge, 1981); and Philippe C. Schmitter and Gerhard Lehmbruch, eds., *Trends toward Corporatist Intermediation* (Beverly Hills, Calif., 1979). For a recent account of corporatism in the Federal Republic, see M. Donald Hancock, *West Germany: The Politics of Democratic Corporatism* (Chatham, N.J., 1989).

5. See, for example, the exchange between the state secretary of interior in the Chancellor's Office, 10 March 1950, and Schönleiter of the Labor Ministry, n.d., B149/1824, BAK.

6. The invitation was issued on 25 February. A copy is in B149/1823, BAK. See also *Die Versorgung der Kriegsopfer in der Bundesrepublik Deutschland. Stand 31.1.1952*, herausgegeben von der Bundesregierung, Schriftenreihe des BfA (Bonn, [1952]), p. 33.

7. Niederschrift über die Besprechung mit den Vertretern der Kriegsbeschädigtenorganisationen über die Neuordnung der Kriegsopferversorgung am 3., 7. und 8. März 1950, B149/1823, BAK.

8. The desire to limit aid to parents was in reaction to the profligate policies of Nazis in this area.

9. The disagreement on this point was fudged over in the reports of the first two meetings, apparently in an effort to create the impression of unanimity. In a letter of 25 April 1950 (B149/1823, BAK), the Reichsbund insisted that its opposition be noted. The debate over this question was to remain a point of contention between the Reichsbund and the VdK, on the one hand, and the Reichsbund and the Labor Ministry, on the other.

10. Niederschrift über die Besprechungen mit den Vertretern der obersten Arbeitsbehörden der Länder über die Neuordnung der Kriegsopferversorgung am 23. und 24. März 1950, ibid.

11. While the federal government assumed responsibility for all *Kriegsfolgelasten* and bore the administative costs for the related programs, the states were required to make a contribution (*Interessenquote*) of 15 percent.

12. For a statistical breakdown, see *Die Versorgung der Kriegsopfer in der Bundesrepublik Deutschland (Das Bundesversorgungsgesetz) Stand 30.9.1952*, herausgegeben vom Presse- und Informationsamt der Bundesregierung (Bonn, [1952]), p. 21. Also cf. "Die Körperbehinderten im Bundesgebiet. Ergebnisse der Volkszählung vom 13. September 1950," *Wirtschaft und Statistik* (December 1952), pp. 482–86.

13. On the actions of the Bundesrat and the cabinet concerning the coverage of the lightly disabled in the ÜBG, see chapter 4. That the Labor Ministry would, if necessary, consider a short-term suspension of benefits to the lightly disabled was clear in the remarks of its representative at the meeting with members of the war victims' organizations in March. Niederschrift über die Besprechung mit den Vertretern der Kriegsbeschädigtenorganisationen über die Neuordnung der Kriegsopferversorgung am 3., 7. und 8. März 1950, B149/1823, BAK, pp. 5–6.

14. Ibid., p. 5; Zusammenfassung des Ergebnisses der Besprechungen am 3., 7. und 8. März 1950, ibid., p. 2.

15. The Bavarian representative remained convinced that the lightly disabled would accept a temporary suspension of benefits if they believed that the continuation of benefit payments to them would endanger coverage of the severely disabled, but the general consensus was that pensions should be provided to the lightly disabled.

16. Copies of the Vorläufiger Referentenentwurf and Storch's letter of invitation to the meeting are in B136/389, BAK.

17. It was requested that this information be relayed by the representative of the Chancellor's Office to the chancellor. Vermerk, 23 May 1950, B136/389, BAK.

18. Ibid.; Vermerk Eckert, 24 May 1950, B149/1823, BAK.

19. The threats of action by the war victims' organizations were given further impetus by the efforts to unite the VdK and Reichsbund that were taking place at this time. See chapter 7.

20. See the correspondence cited in note 5 above.

21. *Die Versorgung. Stand 31.1.1952*, p. 33. For an outline of the Beirat's final form, see I/87B, Lfd. 108, PAB, p. 5.

22. The protocols of the meetings, arranged by date, are in B149/2601, BAK.

23. In fact, new claims were recognized, and the official number of war victims receiving benefits did not peak until 1952. See *Die Versorgung. Stand 30.9.1952*, pp. 20, 44, and Schönleiter, *Kriegsopferversorgung*, p. 29.

24. The Advisory Council's final figure thus squared with the Labor Ministry's figure presented at the interministerial conference discussed above, which was supported by everyone but the finance minister.

25. "Ächtung des Krieges durch Ächtung seiner Opfer?," *Die Fackel*, June 1950. For examples of the letters to the Chancellor's Office, see B136/389, BAK.

26. *Neue Zeitung*, 30 June 1950, B149/1820, and Brönner to Storch, 23 June 1950, B149/1824, BAK.

27. *Die Versorgung. Stand 31.1.1952*, p. 33. Apparently it was originally planned to coordinate the introduction of the BVG with that of the LAG and the 131 Law, but this plan was abandoned. See *Die Kabinettsprotokolle der Bundesregierung*, herausgegeben für das Bundesarchiv von Hans Booms, Band 2 (1950) (Boppard am Rhein, 1984), pp. 523–24.

28. With some modifications this version became the proposal submitted by the government to the Bundestag as *DBDr*, Nr. 1333, 12 September 1950. Materials related to the draft and the changes made before its submission to the Bundestag are located in B136/389, BAK.

29. Schäffer's objections are outlined in detail in his memo to the state secretary of interior in the Chancellor's Office, Bezug: Kabinettsvorlage des Herrn Bundesministers für Arbeit vom 21. und 24. Juli 1950, 25 July 1950, B136/389, BAK.

30. Zu Punkt 4 der T.O. der 86. Kabinettssitzung am 25.7 1950, 24. Juli 1950, ibid.

31. *Kabinettsprotokolle*, Band 2 (1950), pp. 575–78.

32. According to Dr. Petz of the Bundeskanzleramt, "The pension payments have been brought so close to prevailing wage levels through increases that further raises by the Bundesrat and Bundestag cannot be accepted because of salary policy and financial

considerations." Zu Punkt 4 der T.O. der 86. Kabinettssitzung am 25.7. 1950, 24. Juli 1950, B136/389, BAK.

33. *Kabinettsprotokolle*, Band 2 (1950), p. 588; Zu Punkt 8 der T.O. für die 87. Kabinettssitzung am 28.7.50, 27. Juli 1950, B136/389, BAK.

34. The 15 percent contribution was required by the general law regulating the financial relations between the federal and state governments, not by the ÜBG per se.

35. The dispute amused the Finance Committee's members but understandably infuriated the Labor Ministry's representatives, who felt that they had to defend the proposal "not only against the states' representatives but against the Finance Ministry." Vermerk über die Sitzung des Finanzauschusses des Bundesrats am 8.8.1950, B149/4422, BAK.

36. These included across-the-board cuts of base pensions, exclusion of payments to the lightly disabled and some widows, reduction of the outside income threshold to DM 400, and the striking of article 89, which provided for the increase of the states' contribution from 15 to 25 percent. Ibid. and Änderungsvorschläge des Finanzauschusses des Deutschen Bundesrats, 8. August 1950, ibid.

37. Vermerk über die Sitzung des Finanzauschusses des Bundesrats am 10. August 1950, and Kurzbericht über die 22. Sitzung des Finanzauschusses des Deutschen Bundesrats am 10. August 1950, ibid.

38. Vermerk über die Sitzung des Sozialpolitischen Ausschusses des Bundesrats am 10. und 11. August 1950, ibid.

39. Vermerk über die Plenarsitzung des Bundesrats am 18. August 1950, ibid.

40. Der Staatssekretär des Innern im Bundeskanzleramt an den Herrn Bundesminister für Arbeit, 26. August 1950, and Stellungsnahme der Bundesregierung zu den Abänderungsvorschlägen des Bundesrats vom 18. August 1950, ibid.; Zu Punkt 1 der Tagesordnung der 95. Kabinettssitzung am 8.9.50 [actually 12 September 1950], B136/391, BAK.

41. *Kabinettsprotokolle*, Band 2 (1950), p. 682.

42. Schäffer to the state secretary of interior in the Chancellor's Office, 5 September 1950, B136/391, BAK. The reason for his agreement was tied to the date that the law would go into effect. Schäffer claimed that the Bundesrat was assuming that the law would go into effect on 1 January 1951, which would reduce costs and make the raising of the states' contributions unnecessary. With the provision that the 1 January date would be retained, he agreed to withdraw his opposition to the reduction of the states' contributions. At the cabinet meeting of 12 September the Finance Ministry's representative agreed to the Bundesrat's striking of article 89a, which provided for the raise.

43. *VDB*, 13 September 1950, pp. 3165–67.

44. Ibid., pp. 3167–70.

45. Leddin was also a prominent leader of the VdK.

46. *VDB*, 13 September 1950, pp. 3170–72.

47. Ibid., pp. 3173, 3179, 3176.

48. Ibid., pp. 3174–76. The figure actually given in the stenographic report (p. 3175) is DM 1,800, but this appears to be a typographical error.

49. The war victims' organizations also opposed article 8.

50. Ibid., pp. 3177–79.

51. *VDB*, 13 September 1950, pp. 3180–81. The only dissenter was the right-wing extremist, Franz Richter (Fritz Rössler).

52. For examples, see I/87B, Anlagen 2–30, and I/87A, Anlagen 1–12, PAB.

53. 26. Ausschuss Protokoll Nr. 29, I/87A, Lfd. 9, PAB.

54. Stellungnahme des Hauptgeschäftsführers des VdK Max Wuttke vor dem 26er Auschuss für Kriegsopfer und Kriegsgefangenenfragen 20.9.1950, I/87A, Anlage 10, PAB; for the Reichsbund position, see ibid., Anlage 7.

55. 26. Ausschuss Protokoll Nr. 29, I/87A, Lfd. 9, PAB, pp. 4–10. Throughout his presentation Schäffer spoke of supporting the law as it stood and implied that money could be found to fund it if no changes were made. At the same time he stuck to the figure of DM 2.684 billion and refused to let himself be pinned down to a figure that would have permitted the funding of the BVG as presented by the labor minister, that is, DM 3.034 billion. The finance minister hoped to make up the difference either through the temporary suspension of some benefits or, as this became more unlikely, through postponement of the law's enactment. See, for example, the section on Finanzielle Auswirkungen at the end of the bill presented to the Bundestag, *DBDr*, Nr. 1333, 12 September 1950, p. 72.

56. 26. Ausschuss Protokoll Nr. 29, I/87A, Lfd. 9, PAB, p. 10.

57. Ibid., p. 13. "Please give the *Kriegsopfer* the impression that we all together, Bundestag and government, really have done all that we can [Bitte, lassen Sie den Kriegsopfer doch den Eindruck, dass wir alle zusammen, Bundestag und Regierung, wirklich bis an die Grenze des Möglichen gegangen sind]." See also n. 92.

58. Ibid., pp. 14–15.

59. *Die Verhandlungen des (26.) Ausschusses für Kriegsopfer- und Kriegsgefangenen-fragen des Deutschen Bundestages über das Bundesversorgungsgesetz*, I/87A, Lfd. 10, PAB. Interestingly, while the committee used the document to put the ministerial representatives on record, the published minutes did not reveal the names of the committee members or their political affiliations but simply referred to them as deputies (*Abgeordneter*). Fortunately, the original typewritten protocols are also available (I/87A, Lfd. 12–30, PAB), from which the name and political party of each speaker can be ascertained.

60. The article numbers used in the following discussions refer to those in the draft proposal. Because of additions and deletions, the numbers of the equivalent articles in the final version of the BVG are often different.

61. *Verhandlungen des (26.) Ausschusses*, I/87A, Lfd. 10, PAB, p. 35. The Reichsbund was demanding DM 30 and DM 50.

62. Ibid., p. 56.

63. Ibid., p. 110.

64. Ibid., pp. 110–11.

65. Ibid. The Reichsbund was demanding DM 35 and DM 50.

66. Ibid., p. 112. Mende supported the raises; Arndgen abstained.

67. This is not clear in the printed protocol. As noted above (n. 59), it does not designate the name or political affiliation of the speaker. The gender of the speaker is concealed as well by the uniform usage of the male form of the word for deputy (*Abgeordneter*). The original typewritten protocols identify the speakers by name, and the names can be checked against the list of Bundestag members to ascertain speakers' party affiliation and gender.

68. *Verhandlungen des (26.) Ausschusses*, I/87A, Lfd. 10, PAB, p. 57C.

69. Ibid., pp. 85–86B.

70. Ibid., p. 86B.

71. See chapter 2.

72. *Verhandlungen des (26.) Ausschusses*, I/87A, Lfd. 10, PAB, p. 113C.

73. Ibid., p. 107A.

74. Ibid., p. 107B.

75. Ibid., p. 107D.

76. Ibid., p. 113.

77. Here she was referring to the provisions of the National Socialist legislation for military dependents that were designed to assure social stability and as a consequence were not uniform. For more on this, see chapter 2.

78. *Verhandlungen des (26.) Ausschusses*, I/87A, Lfd. 10, PAB, p. 113.

79. Ibid., p. 112.

80. Ibid., p. 118B.

81. Ibid., pp. 144–45. The provision was dropped after the Labor Ministry representative promised that enforcement of existing laws would prevent injustices, a good example of the effectiveness of the committee's strategy of having the protocols of meetings recorded and published in order to hold officials to their word and to cover for the committee's failure to get more provisions introduced directly into the law.

82. According to Arnold, the number involved was 80,000. Ibid., p. 107D.

83. See text preceding n. 40.

84. *Verhandlungen des (26.) Auschusses*, I/87A, Lfd. 10, PAB, p. 144.

85. See Schäffer's remarks in his letter to the state secretary of interior in the Chancellor's Office, in which he agreed to accept the Bundesrat's rejection of the raise of the states' contributions to 25 percent, 5 September 1950, B136/391, BAK.

86. *Verhandlungen des (26.) Ausschusses*, I/87A, Lfd. 10, PAB, pp. 96D-97.

87. Referat I/7, 4 October 1950, B136/391, BAK.

88. When and among whom this agreement was made is not clear.

89. *Verhandlungen des (26.) Ausschusses*, I/87A, Lfd. 10, PAB, p. 118C.

90. Ibid., pp. 145–46.

91. Ibid., p. 147.

92. Paul Lücke, for example, claimed that "the unanimous passage of the law by parliament will make a more long-lasting impression on the war victims than the fulfillment of this perhaps justified demand for retroactive dating. The achievement of unanimity will prove to be a greater service to democracy, as well as, above all, to the war disabled." Ibid., p. 147B. See also the remarks of Heinrich Hoefler, ibid., p. 148.

93. The vote was 9 to 9. The seven SPD members of the committee were probably joined by the members of the Bavarian and Center parties.

94. See the reports of Selbach to Petz, 28 September–13 October 1950, B136/391, BAK.

95. *DBDr*, Nr. 1466, 13 October 1950.

96. A copy of the telegram is in B136/391, BAK.

97. Vermerk. Betr: Bundesversorgungsgesetz, 17. Oktober 1950, ibid.

98. *Kabinettsprotokolle*, Band 2 (1950), pp. 752–53.

99. *VDB*, 19 October 1950, pp. 3442–55.

100. Schäffer to the state secretary of interior in the Chancellor's Office, Betrifft: Deckungsvorschag für die durch das Bundesversorgungsgesetz entstehenden Mehraufwendungen im Rechnungsjahr 1950, 19 October 1950, B136/391, BAK; *Kabinettsprotokolle*, Band 2 (1950), pp. 756–58.

101. Referat I/7 (Petz), 3 November 1950, B136/391, BAK.

102. Ibid. In dealing with future "proposals that cost money," the report concluded, it would be wise to avoid such situations by including in advance a "certain amount of financial elbow room."

103. *Kabinettsprotokolle*, Band 2 (1950), p. 814.

104. Ibid., p. 823, n. 37.

105. Ibid., pp. 823–24.

106. Ibid., p. 831.

107. Ibid., p. 839.

108. Ibid, p. 839, n. 31.

109. Ibid., p. 875; *DBDr*, Nr. 1680, 6 December 1950; *VDB*, 14 December 1950, pp. 4020–30.

110. According to Minister-Rat Grau of the Bundeskanzleramt, Schäffer had discussed the situation with the coalition parties and felt the cabinet could give its approval. Therefore, "in view of the extraordinary political and social significance attached to a quick promulgation of the law, approval is to be granted." Betr.: Gesetz über die Versorgung der Opfer des Kriegs. Hier Zustimmung der Bundesregierung gemäss Artikel 113 des Grundgesetzes, 15. Dezember 1950, B136/391, BAK.

111. *Kabinettsprotokolle*, Band 2 (1950), p. 898; *Bundesgesetzblatt*, 1950, Nr. 53 (21 December 1950).

Chapter 6

1. Arnold Brecht, "Personnel Management," in *Governing Postwar Germany*, edited by Edward H. Lichtfield et al. (Ithaca, N.Y., 1953), 1:263–64; Theodor Eschenburg, "Der bürokratische Rückhalt," in *Die zweite Republik. 25 Jahre Bundesrepublik Deutschland—Eine Bilanz*, herausgegeben von Richard Löwenthal und Hans-Peter Schwarz (Stuttgart, 1974), p. 67.

2. Wolfgang Benz, "Versuche zur Reform des öffentlichen Dienstes in Deutschland, 1945–1952," *Vierteljahrshefte für Zeitgeschichte* 29/2 (April 1981): 218–19.

3. Brecht, "Personnel Management," pp. 266ff.; Eschenburg, "Der bürokratische Rückhalt," pp. 66–70.

4. Particular points of concern were the limited access to careers in the German bureaucracy, including the so-called lawyers' monopoly (*Juristenmonopol*), the lack of effective centralized control, which insulated the German bureaucracy from the public, the sharp differences in the status of personnel within the bureaucracy, and the lack of restrictions on political activity by German civil servants. Brecht, "Personnel Management," pp. 272ff.; Benz, "Versuche zur Reform," p. 217.

5. For an excellent, comprehensive account of the Allied attempts to reform the German bureaucracy and the evolution of the Beamtengesetz of 1953, see Udo Wengst, *Beamtentum zwischen Reform und Tradition. Beamtengesetzgebung in der Gründungsphase der Bundesrepublik Deutschland, 1948–1953* (Düsseldorf, 1988).

6. Lutz Niethammer, "Zum Verhältnis von Reform und Rekonstruktion in der US-Zone am Beispiel der Neuordnung des öffentlichen Dienstes," *Vierteljahrshefte für Zeitgeschichte* 21/2 (April 1973): 178.

7. Benz, "Versuche zur Reform," p. 235; Wengst, *Beamtentum*, pp. 57–58, 61–65.

8. Eschenburg, "Der bürokratische Rückhalt," pp. 81–85; Wengst, *Beamtentum*, p. 33. While the SPD on the whole supported this action, its support was not total and the party was well aware of the problematical consequences of supporting such a drastic and unpopular move by military authorities. Since the Social Democrats expected to win a majority in the upcoming elections to the Bundestag, they did not push too hard for reform, believing they could implement their reform plans after the Federal Republic was created.

9. Since the SPD rejected the concept of "collective guilt," it logically opposed the blanket prohibition of military pensions by the occupying powers. In the debate over the 131 Law, the Social Democrats were the most forceful advocates of the expansion of benefits for former noncommissioned officers, many of whom came from working-class backgrounds. Increasing numbers of regular officers were also drawn from the ranks of the working class as a result of the war's voracious manpower demands. On the social democratization of the officer corps under the Third Reich, see Bernhard R. Kroener, "Auf dem Weg zu einer 'nationalsozialistischen Volksarmee.' Die soziale Öffnung des Heeresoffizierkorps im Zweiten Weltkrieg," in *Von Stalingrad zur Währungsreform. Zur Sozialgeschichte des Umbruchs in Deutschland*, herausgegeben von Martin Broszat et al. (Munich, 1988), and Jürgen Förster, "Vom Führerheer der Republik zur nationalsozialistischen Volksarmee. Zum Strukturwandel der Wehrmacht, 1935–1945," in *Deutschland in Europa: Kontinuität und Bruch. Gedenkschrift für Andreas Hillgruber*, herausgegeben von Jost Dülffer et al. (Frankfurt am Main, 1990). The main source of SPD opposition to the law was the extension of affirmative hiring quotas (and the accompanying penalties for noncompliance) to the municipal and communal levels of government, where Social Democratic officials often held sway and

sought to provide employment for members of their own party, who had traditionally been excluded from civil service positions.

10. Gesetz zur Regelung der Rechtsverhältnisse der unter Artikel 131 des Grundgesetzes fallenden Personen. For details on the background, formulation, and passage of the law, see Wengst, *Beamtentum,* chapter 4.

11. See chapter 3.

12. For an overview of the activities of Hansen and his supporters in the months preceeding the Republic's founding, see Anhang zur Verzeichnis der Akten Admiral a.D. Hansen 1945–56: Beiträge zu einer Geschichte des BvW, VdS/BvW und VdS, Findleiter, Nachlass Hansen, N222, BAF. See also Sitzungsprotokoll der Vertreterversammlung des B.v.W. v. 9/21.5.51, Nachlass Hansen, N222/228, BAF, from which the quotation is taken.

13. Aktenvermerk (9.10.49) über den Inhalt des beim Herrn Bundesfinanzminister am 7.10.49 durch General d. Inf. a.D. Koch gehaltenen Vortrages, B136/529, BAK.

14. For example, the former officers claimed that if civilian bureaucrats were to continue being governed by the 1937 Civil Service Law, then soldiers should be covered by the 1938 WFVG.

15. Aktenvermerk (9.10.49), Zusatz, B136/529, BAK.

16. Koch to Schäffer, 30 November 1949, ibid.

17. Besprechungsnotizen vom 4.11.49, Nachlass Donat, N571/60, BAF.

18. This estimate was not too far off, though it appears that Linde did not really expect things to drag out so long, since in his covering letter to the report he said his response had been a tactical ploy.

19. On the military promotion policies in the Third Reich, see Kroener, "Auf dem Weg," pp. 673–78.

20. At the end of the meeting, Meyer asked Linde if he would be interested in drafting the new law; Linde said he would be willing, if he were given the necessary staff and economic guarantees, most preferably a civil service position. It is unclear if or to what extent Linde worked directly for the government. The Verzeichnis notes that he had been involved in the drafting of the WFVG and gives the impression that he was currently working in a ministry, though he remained a lobbyist for the BvW. It is possible that he worked as an unofficial or semiofficial adviser.

21. Wengst, *Beamtentum,* pp. 154–59; Der Bundesminister der Finanzen, I BR 1112–44/50, 10. Februar 1950, B136/505, BAK.

22. Schrag to Veiel, 13 March 1950, Nachlass Donat, N571/62, BAF.

23. Linde to General Veiel, 30 March 1950, Nachlass Donat, N571/60, BAF.

24. I/156A, Anlage 2 zu Protokoll Nr. 17 (17. Sitzung. 25. Auschuss. 17. März 1950), PAB.

25. Ibid., Anlage 3 zu Protokoll Nr. 17.

26. At the time the 131 Law was being drafted, efforts were under way to restore the cuts in civil service salaries that had been made under Brüning's Emergency Economic Decrees and that were still in effect. The early drafts of the 131 Law, in particular those made by the finance minister, foresaw taking one-half of the scheduled 6 percent salary

increase as a mandatory contribution to help fund the benefits to be provided by the 131 Law. For details of the scheme and the violent opposition to it among civil servants, see Wengst, *Beamtentum*, chapter 4.

27. I/156A, Anlage 2 zu Protokoll Nr. 17, PAB.

28. See Wengst, *Beamtentum*, chapter 4, for the sources and nature of this pressure. The main source of pressure from inside the CDU came from Linus Kather, the leader of the largest expellees' organization. On Kather's role, see, in addition to Wengst, *Beamtentum*, *Die Kabinettsprotokolle der Bundesregierung*, herausgegeben für das Bundesarchiv von Hans Booms, Band 2 (1950) (Boppard am Rhein, 1984), pp. 276–77.

29. Ibid., p. 277. Until this point, each ministry had worked out its own draft, and that of the Finance Ministry, because of its more stringent terms, had become the target of considerable negative criticism.

30. Adenauer to the Ministers of Interior, Finance, and Expellees, 28 March 1950, B136/505, BAK.

31. Der Bundesminister des Innern, II3–451/50, 28.2.50, ibid.; Wengst, *Beamtentum*, p. 162.

32. Herrn Oberregierungsrat Gumbel, 21.6.50, B136/532, BAK.

33. Ibid.

34. For the Finance Ministry's response, see Der Bundesminister der Finanzen. Persönlicher Referent, 5.7.50, B136/508, BAK.

35. Aktenvermerk, 31.7.50, Nachlass Donat, N571/60, BAF.

36. See note 28 above. While the former officers hoped to exploit Kather's organization to achieve their own goals, they wanted to retain their independence and not be taken "in tow [aber nicht im Schlepptau nehmen lassen]" by it.

37. For details of the protests, see Wengst, *Beamtentum*, pp. 188ff.

38. Aufzeichnung. Die Versorgung der Berufssoldaten nach dem Gesetzentwurf zu Artikel 131, 23.8.50 and Entw. eines Gesetzes zur Regelung der Rechtsverhältnis der unter Art. 131 GG fallenden Personen. Hier: Abschnitt Berufssoldaten, B136/509, BAK.

39. The law set the day of German capitulation as the final day for entitlement, which meant that officers who had entered service after 8 May 1935 were not eligible for retirement pensions since they had not served ten years. This effectively eliminated the prospect of a pension for the mass of new officers created after the enlargement of the Wehrmacht following Germany's rejection of the disarmament provisions of the Treaty of Versailles in March 1935. This provision also worked to the disadvantage of officers who had served earlier and then been recalled to service, as well as those who had been imprisoned after the war and who would have been entitled to pensions if at least some of this time were included in the calculation of pension entitlement. In order to increase the numbers eligible for pensions, the BvW argued that the earlier date should be disregarded and that the latter deadline should be extended to cover the period of postwar imprisonment or, at the very least, to August 1946, when Control Council Law 34 went into effect.

40. Notiz für Herrn Bundeskanzler [from Wirmer], 25.8.50 and Gumbel to Wirmer, 25 August 1950, B136/509, BAK.

41. Press notice (Pressenotiz) of the 25 August 1950 meeting, ibid.

42. This resolution came about at the NATO Council meeting in New York in mid-September 1950. See chapter 7.

43. Dem Herrn Bundeskanzler vorzulegen—Gumbel, 31.8.50, B136/509, BAK. See also the report cited above (n. 32) on Gumbel's meeting with the BvW delegation.

44. Der Bundesminister des Innern. Kabinettssache!, 29.9.50, B136/510, BAK.

45. According to Heinemann, there were around 35,000 noncommissioned officers with ten to twelve years of service.

46. While many categories of civil servants who were recalled after 1933 were allowed to use World War I service in calculating pension entitlements and rates, soldiers could not. This particularly affected former officers who were recalled as training officers (*E-Offiziere*).

47. *Kabinettsprotokolle*, Band 2 (1950), p. 733.

48. Vermerk für die Kabinettssitzung am 6. Oktober 1950, B136/510, BAK.

49. BvW Geschäftsstelle. Abschliessende Zusammenstellung der Ereignisse der Besprechungen, 19.9.50, Nachlass Donat, N571/60, BAF.

50. The 131 Law was introduced for its first reading on 13 September 1950. For the parliamentary debate on the law, see text following n. 60.

51. In discussing the changes that had been obtained, Linde sought to accentuate the successes and to minimize the failures. In the case of the agreement to include POW time in the calculation of pensions, he went beyond what government officials had promised, asserting that it could also be used to acquire entitlement. Linde's account of the negotiations also brought up some other interesting points. The question of benefits for Waffen-SS veterans who had earlier belonged to the Wehrmacht was a "hot potato" and had to be handled delicately. One had to feel out the parties before going any further; in any case, the BvW had to present itself as the defender not of the SS, but of those who had been ordered into the Waffen-SS.

52. See, for example, Zusammenfassung. Aktenbestand: Arbeitsangebote und Vermittlung von Arbeitsstellen, Nachlass Donat, N571/45, BAF; see also Sammlung Ritter von Schramm. Materialien zu einer Geschichte der deutschen Berufssoldaten zwischen 1945 und 1955: Schicksale Deutscher Berufssoldaten von 1945–1955, MSg 118/1, BAF.

53. Anhang zur Verzeichnis der Akten Admiral a.D. Hansen 1945–56: Beiträge zu einer Geschichte des BvW, VdS/BvW und VdS, Findleiter, 21.6.46, 29.10.47, 20.8.49, MSg 118/1, BAF, p. 89; BvW, Der Geschäftsführer, 28.7.50, Besprechung bei Dr. Schumacher, SPD, am 26.7.50, N571/60, BAF.

54. Gordon D. Drummond, *The German Social Democrats in Oppositon: The Case against Rearmament* (Norman, 1982), p. 57. Also, like the former officers, the SPD leader rejected the charge of collective guilt.

55. See, for example, the letters of Otto E. Flies to the SPD Parteivorstand of 17 November and 2 December 1947, Nachlass Donat, N571/45, BAF.

56. Hansen, for example, seemed to be on good terms with Schumacher but was constantly fulminating against the reluctance of the SPD in Schleswig-Holstein to grant or raise Maintenance Grants.

57. Zusammenfassung. Aktenbestand: Arbeitsangebote und Vermittlung von Arbeitsstellen, Nachlass Donat, N571/45, BAF. The issue was also discussed at the 9 September meeting with Schäffer. Ibid.

58. Blankenhorn to Schlafejew, 15 September 1950, BW9/3103, BAF. Gerhard Graf von Schwerin had been appointed by Adenauer as the chancellor's military adviser and headed what would later become the Defense Ministry. See chapter 7.

59. Bundeskanzleramt. Zentrale für Heimatdienst. Vortragsnotiz für Herrn Min.-Dir. Dr. Globke, 28.10.50, B136/510, BAK.

60. The outcome of these meetings and the effectiveness of the recommended measures remain unclear. The leadership of the BvW apparently remained unconvinced that enough was being done and called for its local groups to compile a "Boykott-Chronik," similar to the earlier "Not-Chronik," in order to convince authorities of the magnitude of the problem and to force further action. According to BvW officials, the continued pressure eventually had the desired effect, since after mid-1952 "the Arbeitsboycott clearly subsided." Zusammenfassung. Aktenbestand: Arbeitsangebote und Vermittlung von Arbeitsstellen, Nachlass Donat, N571/45, BAF.

61. *VDB*, 13 September 1950, pp. 3142–61. The protests of the expelled civil servants were especially vehement. For details, see Wengst, *Beamtentum*, chapter 4. Schäffer was so angry he considered filing lawsuits against the instigators of the protests.

62. For a statistical breakdown of those covered, see *Statistische Berichte: Verdrängte Beamte und ehemalige Wehrmachtangehörige. Statistische Erhebung über den unter Artikel 131 des Grundgesetzes fallenden Personenkreis. Endgültige Gesamtergebnisse für das Bundesgebiet*, Statistisches Amt des Vereinigten Wirtschaftsgebietes mit der Führung der Statistik für Bundeszwecke beauftragt, 10.6.1950, I/156A, Anlage 1, PAB.

63. *VDB*, 13 September 1950, p. 3145. The ten-year rule was a return to the old German Civil Service Law, which, Heinemann argued, had been manipulated and distorted by the Nazis.

64. See Wengst, *Beamtentum*, chapter 2.

65. The more hostile environment that was encountered by the former officers was reflected in the fact that Heinemann's references to Hitler's role elicited catcalls about the role of the generals—and these do not appear to have come only from the far left. Also see General Veiel's letters to the BvW headquarters and Linde of 11 November and 13 December 1950 expressing his concern over the fact that the former officers were not as well organized or active as the other interest groups and were therefore falling behind in the struggle for benefits. Nachlass Donat, N571/60, BAF.

66. Stenographisches Protokoll über die 64. Sitzung des Ausschusses für Beamtenrecht am Montag, dem 20.11.50, I/156A, PAB.

67. Ibid., pp. 20–27. At this point it apparently was decided not to include former Waffen-SS members in the 131 Law but to let the claims of those transferred from the Wehrmacht to the Waffen-SS be handled by the administrative regulations for the implementation of the law. The final version of the law did provide for those who had been transferred, though other Waffen-SS members continued to be excluded.

68. Ibid., pp. 30–33.

69. Stenographisches Protokoll der 103. Sitzung des Ausschusses für Beamtenrecht am Freitag, den 9.3.51, I/156A, PAB; see also the minutes of the 92d and 101st meetings of 7 February and 1 March 1951, ibid.

70. *DBDr*, Nr. 2075, 16 March 1951, p. 28.

71. *VDB*, 5 April 1951, pp. 4983–5017, and 6 April 1951, pp. 5020–47. For Linde's views on the course of events, see Stellungnahme zu einigen wichtigen noch nicht oder unbefriedigend gelösten Versorgungsproblemen im Gesetzentwurf gem. Artikel 131 Grundgesetz, 20.3.51, BW9/3085, BAF.

72. *VDB*, 5 April 1950, pp. 4983–84.

73. Ibid., 6 April 1950, p. 5021. Kleindinst also made the point that many men who were not professional soldiers had served in the Wehrmacht for ten years and yet had no pension claims.

74. Ibid., p. 5027.

75. Ibid., pp. 5031–32. Schmid went on to discuss the reemergence of organizations such as the Stahlhelm, which was being reported in the press. Their slogans, he noted, "are exactly the same as those after 1919." If the new organizations appeared to be developing along lines similar to their predecessors, he warned, to loud applause from his and the coalition parties, then they must be destroyed. Ibid.

76. Ibid. According to the stenographic report, Schmid's remarks were accompanied by "continuing enthusiastic applause by the SPD and deputies of the government coalition parties [Anhaltender lebhafter Beifall bei der SPD und Abgeordneter der Regierungsparteien]."

77. Ibid., p. 5110.

Chapter 7

1. On the LAG, see Reinhold Schillinger, *Der Entscheidungsprozess beim Lastenausgleich, 1945–1952* (St. Katharinen, 1985); see also Peter Paul Nahm, *Der Lastenausgleich* (Stuttgart, 1961) and "Lastenausgleich und Integration der Vertriebenen und Geflüchteten," in *Die zweite Republik. 25 Jahre Bundesrepublik Deutschland—Eine Bilanz*, herausgegeben von Richard Löwenthal und Hans-Peter Schwarz (Stuttgart, 1974).

2. The first amendment to the BVG was passed in March 1952. For a chronological table of social legislation, see Reinhart Bartholomäi et al., eds., *Sozialpolitik nach 1945. Geschichte und Analysen* (Bonn, 1977), pp. 287–91.

3. Rupert Breitling, *Die Verbände in der Bundesrepublik. Ihre Arten und ihre Wirkungsweise* (Meisenheim am Glan, 1955), p. 69.

4. Ibid., p. 70.

5. See the Conclusion.

6. As Breitling puts it: "With a satisfactory compensation, the organization's goal would often be fulfilled. In order to prevent its dissolution, the organization [Geschädigtenverband] then would interpret the negative experience that had been the cause of its founding [das Schadensereignis] as a positive 'sacrifice for the state [Staatsopfer]'

and from this develop a Citizens' Ideology [Staatsbürgerideologie] and new tasks."
Verbände, p. 70.

7. See chapter 4.

8. See the letter of the Hessen *Landesverband* of the VdK to the VdK Württemberg-Baden (and Rossmann) of 22 July 1950, Nachlass Rossmann, Lfd. 50, BAK; on the founding of the BDKK, see chapter 4.

9. See chapter 4.

10. Die Einigungsverhandlungen zwischen dem VdK und dem Reichsbund, pp. 13, 17, and Erste Sitzung der Einigungskommission des V.d.K. und des Reichbundes in Stuttgart am 15. Juli 1950, Nachlass Rossmann, Lfd. 49, BAK.

11. Erste Sitzung der Einigungskommission des V.d.K. und des Reichbundes in Stuttgart am 15. Juli 1950, Nachlass Rossmann, Lfd. 49, BAK, p. 28.

12. Die Einigungsverhandlungen zwischen dem VdK und dem Reichsbund, Nachlass Rossmann, Lfd. 49, BAK, pp. 17–20.

13. Ibid., pp. 20–24.

14. See chapter 5.

15. Die Einigungsverhandlungen zwischen dem VdK und dem Reichsbund, Nachlass Rossmann, Lfd. 49, BAK, p. 24. Rossmann himself favored the two-tier plan. Ibid., p. 25.

16. Ibid.

17. Ibid., p. 36.

18. Ibid, p. 46.

19. Ibid., pp. 55–74. See also Wolf Donner, *Die sozial- und staatspolitische Tätigkeit der Kriegsopferverbände. Ein Beitrag zur Verbandsdiskussion* (Berlin, 1960), pp. 99–102.

20. Die Einigungsverhandlungen zwischen dem VdK und dem Reichsbund, Nachlass Rossmann, Lfd. 49, BAK, p. 74. Breitling also notes that the larger role of salaried employees in the Reichsbund may have made its cadre less interested in fusion. Breitling, *Verbände*, p. 239, n. 324.

21. Die Einigungsverhandlungen zwischen dem VdK und dem Reichsbund, Nachlass Rossmann, Lfd. 49, BAK, pp. 76–77. See also Rossmann's letters to Weltersbach, 10 October 1950, and Nitsche, 26 October 1950, Nachlass Rossmann, Lfd. 50, BAK.

22. Donner, *Die sozial- und staatspolitische Tätigkeit*, pp. 30–32; see also Karl Weishäupl, "Die Bedeutung des VdK für die Nachkriegsgeschichte der deutschen Sozialpolitik," and Rudolf Kleine, "Die Geschichte des Reichsbundes in ihrer Bedeutung für die Nachkriegsentwicklung der Sozialpolitik," in *Sozialpolitik nach 1945. Geschichte und Analysen*, herausgegeben von Reinhart Bartholomäi et al. (Bonn, 1977), pp. 489–96, 495–511.

23. Donner, *Die sozial- und staatspolitische Tätigkeit*, pp. 33–62.

24. Ibid., pp. 82–89, 132–91.

25. Ibid., pp. 24, 89–93. The familial role was especially pronounced in the immediate postwar years.

26. *Die Fackel*, April 1949.

27. Ibid., May 1949.

28. Ibid., July 1949.

29. Ibid., October 1949.

30. Ibid., July 1949.

31. Ibid.

32. The advertisements were printed in the women's section. There was considerable debate over whether it was desirable for two disabled persons to marry or not. On the one hand, it was felt that it would ensure empathy. On the other hand, there was concern that such an arrangement would only double the burden. One male writer felt the best wife would be a sister of a war-disabled veteran, since she would be experienced with the problems of a disabled veteran and at the same time would be able to bear the full burdens of a housewife. Ibid., October 1949.

33. For details of these reforms, see Bartholomäi et al., *Sozialpolitik*; Waldemar Schönleiter, *Die Kriegsopferversorgung* (Stuttgart, 1961), Anlage 5; and Hermann-Josef Becker, *Die Beschäftigung Schwerbeschädigter* (Stuttgart, 1961).

34. See, for example, the remarks of Helmut Bazille at the VdK's 1951 Verbandstag in Trier, "Kriegsopferversorgung vor Wehrbeitrag," *Die Fackel*, November 1951. Also cf. Donner, *Die sozial- und staatspolitische Tätigkeit*, pp. 102–9.

35. See, for example, the facsimile of the lead article in *Der Heimkehrer*, April 1950, "Ein neuer Heimkehrerverband?," reprinted in *Freiheit ohne Furcht. Zehn Jahre Heimkehrerverband* (Bad Godesberg, [1960]), pp. 21–22.

36. For details of the law and its improvements, see Kurt Draeger, *Heimkehrer-Recht. Heimkehrergesetz, Kriegsgefangenenentschädigungsgesetz, Häftlingshilfegesetz und sonstiges Heimkehrerrecht* (Berlin, 1956).

37. This campaign is traced in the excellent study by Manfred Teschner, "Entwicklung eines Interessenverbandes. Ein empirischer Beitrag zum Problem der Verselbständigung von Massenorganisationen" (Inaugural dissertation, Johann-Wolfgang-Goethe-Universität, Frankfurt am Main, 1961).

38. Ibid., pp. 32–38. Between 1950 and 1954 approximately 56,000 German POWs were released from captivity. During the same time, some 350,000 former POWs joined the VdH. The mass of the new members obviously came from the ranks of former POWs who had returned before 1950, that is, those who presumably had been reintegrated into society. Ibid., pp. 36–37.

39. Ibid., pp. 14–15, 28–31.

40. Ibid., pp. 22–25.

41. *VDB*, 27 November 1952, p. 11080. The VdH had submitted a proposal to the government in April. The first discussion in the Bundestag took place on 9 October 1952.

42. *DBDr*, Nr. 4316, 6 May 1953.

43. *DBDr*, Nr. 4318, 15 May 1953. The SPD proposal was quickly followed by one from the German Party and one from the FDP (in combination with the German Party). *DBDr*, Nr. 4426, 3 June 1953, and Nr. 4446, 10 June 1953.

44. *DBDr*, Nr. 4629, 30 June 1953; *VDB*, 12 January and 2 July 1953.

45. On the use of article 113 by the cabinet to block undesired legislation, see chapter 5.

46. Teschner, "Entwicklung," p. 26.

47. Ibid., p. 27. For details of the law, see Draeger, *Heimkehrer-Recht*.

48. Quoted in Teschner, "Entwicklung," p. 28.

49. Ibid., pp. 38–42.

50. Ibid., pp. 62–63.

51. Ibid., pp. 44–45.

52. Ibid., pp. 47–48. Cf. the statement of Breitling, quoted in note 6 above.

53. See the Conclusion for more on this.

54. Teschner, "Entwicklung," p. 46.

55. Ibid., p. 65.

56. Ibid., pp. 49–53.

57. Ibid., pp. 54, 63, 66, 98–99, 110. Membership dropped from a high of 500,000 in 1954/55 to 200,000 by 1958.

58. Ibid., p. 73.

59. Ibid., pp. 73–75. For a list of these meetings and their participants, see *Politische Bildung im Verband der Heimkehrer Deutschlands: 200 Diskussionswochen, 1954–1977. Auf dem Weg nach Europa. Die politische Bildungsarbeit des Verbandes der Heimkehrer, Kriegsgefangenen und Vermisstenangehörigen Deutschlands e.V.* (Bonn/Bad Godesberg, 1977).

60. Teschner, "Entwicklung," pp. 78–88.

61. Ibid., p. 82.

62. This was clear at the BvW's first general meeting, held in May 1951. For details, see chapter 8.

63. Like the BVG, and unlike the Heimkehrer legislation, the 131 Law provided for pensions instead of lump sum settlements. Moreover, like the BVG, the 131 Law only provided minimal assistance to large groups (e.g., widows and noncommissioned officers), whose needs provided grounds for continued lobbying. Finally, in both laws future improvements were linked to improved fiscal conditions, which meant that the expansion of the economy spurred further pressure for improvements.

64. On the one hand, many of those whose interests had been met by the law now no longer saw any reason to continue their membership; on the other, many whose interests had not been met, for example, noncommissioned officers and officers with less than ten years of service, became discouraged and dropped out of the BvW. See, for example, the material dealing with membership fluctuations in the Baden-Württemberg *Landesverband* contained in Nachlass Donat, N571/45, BAF.

65. Hans-Adolf Jacobsen, "Zur Rolle der öffentlichen Meinung bei der Debatte um die Wiederbewaffnung, 1950–1955," in *Aspekte der deutschen Wiederbewaffnung bis 1955,* Militärgeschichte seit 1945, Band 1, herausgegeben vom Militärgeschichtlichen Forschungsamt (Boppard am Rhein, 1975), pp. 86–89; Thomas Alan Schwartz, "Die Begnadigung deutscher Kriegsverbrecher. John J. McCloy und die Häftlinge von Landsberg," *Vierteljahrshefte für Zeitgeschichte* 38/3 (July 1990); Frank M. Buscher, "The U.S. High Commission and German Nationalism, 1949–52," *Central European History* 23/1 (March 1990): 67–75.

66. The phrase *military subculture* comes from Roland G. Foerster, "Innenpolitische

Aspekte der Sicherheit Westdeutschlands," in *Anfänge westdeutscher Sicherheitspolitik, 1945–56*, herausgegeben vom Militärgeschichtlichen Forschungsamt, Band 1, *Von der Kapitulation bis zum Pleven-Plan* (Munich, 1982), p. 471.

67. The most comprehensive and up-to-date account of German rearmament at present is provided in *Anfänge westdeutscher Sicherheitspolitik, 1945–56*, herausgegeben vom Militärgeschichtlichen Forschungsamt, Band 1, *Von der Kapitulation bis zum Pleven-Plan* (Munich, 1982), and Band 2, *Die EVG-Phase* (Munich, 1990); further volumes are planned. A major, definitive study of the topic, *Germans to the Front: West German Rearmament in the Adenauer Era*, by David C. Large, is forthcoming.

68. Klaus von Schubert, *Wiederbewaffnung und Westintegration. Die innere Auseinandersetzung um die militärische und aussenpolitische Orientierung der Bundesrepublik, 1950–1952* (Stuttgart, 1970); Christian Greiner, "Die allierten Militärstrategischen Planungen zur Verteidigung Westeuropas, 1947–1950," in *Anfänge westdeutscher Sicherheitspolitik*, 1:287–91; Norbert Wiggershaus, "Die Entscheidung für einen Westdeutschen Verteidigungsbeitrag 1950," in ibid.

69. In addition to the works cited in notes 65–68, see the older but still valuable work by Arnulf Baring, *Im Anfang war Adenauer. Die Entstehung der Kanzlerdemokratie* (Munich, 1982), originally published in 1969 under the title *Aussenpolitik in Adenauers Kanzlerdemokratie. Bonns Beitrag zur Europäischen Verteidigungsgemeinschaft.*

70. Foerster, "Innenpolitische Aspekte"; Georg Meyer, "Zur Situation der deutschen militärischen Führungsschicht im Vorfeld des westdeutschen Verteidigungsbeitrages, 1945–1950/51," and Hans-Jürgen Rautenberg, "Zur Standortsbestimmung für künftige deutsche Streitkräfte, 1945–1956," in *Anfänge westdeutscher Sicherheitspolitik*, Band 1. See also Donald Abenheim, *Reforging the Iron Cross: The Search for Tradition in the West German Armed Forces* (Princeton, 1988).

71. On the Himmerod meeting, see Foerster, "Innenpolitische Aspekte," pp. 506–7; Rautenberg, "Zur Standortsbestimmung," pp. 783–85; Hans-Jürgen Rautenberg and Norbert Wiggershaus, "Die 'Himmeroder Denkschrift' vom Oktober 1950. Politische und militärische Überlegungen für einen Beitrag der Bundesrepublik zur westeuropäischen Verteidigung," *Militärgeschichtliche Mitteilungen*, 1977/1; and Abenheim, *Reforging the Iron Cross*, pp. 52–63.

72. Foerster, "Innenpolitische Aspekte," p. 506.

73. See chapter 6.

74. For examples of these attitudes, see the interviews with former military personnel in Hans Speier, *From the Ashes of Defeat: A Journal from Germany, 1945–1955* (Amherst, 1981).

75. "Hiwis" were the Russian auxiliary forces used by the Wehrmacht on the eastern front.

76. Hansen's covering letter accompanying the resolution to Adenauer stated that the resolution "should serve as proof that for us, despite the previous deprivation of rights and defamation of the former professional members of the German armed forces, the need of our country takes precedence over our own need." Copies of the resolution and Hansen's letter are in BW9/3103, BAF.

77. See David C. Large, "'A Gift to the German Future?': The Anti-Nazi Resistance Movement and West German Rearmament," *German Studies Review* 7/3 (October 1984).

78. On the reasons for the building of this myth and its eventual dismantling, see ibid., pp. 505–6. The most thorough and devastating critiques of the Wehrmacht's behavior have been provided in Christian Streit, *Keine Kameraden. Die Wehrmacht und die sowjetischen Kriegsgefangenen, 1941–1945* (Stuttgart, 1978), and Omer Bartov, *The Eastern Front, 1941–1945: German Troops and the Barbarisation of Warfare* (New York, 1986), and *Hitler's Army: Soldiers, Nazis, and War in the Third Reich* (New York, 1991).

79. Large, "'A Gift to the German Future?,'" p. 507, n. 31.

80. Cf. Abenheim, *Reforging the Iron Cross*, pp. 140–47.

81. Large, "'A Gift to the German Future?,'" p. 512.

82. Division over the issue was not limited to veterans who were still on the outside. There was also division in the Dienststelle Blank. Ibid., p. 519, and Abenheim, *Reforging the Iron Cross*, pp. 142–44.

83. On the Stahlhelm, see Kurt Tauber, *Beyond Eagle and Swastika: German Nationalism since 1945* (Middletown, Conn., 1967), 1:316–32; Manfred Jenke, *Verschwörung von Rechts? Ein Bericht über den Rechtsradikalismus in Deutschland nach 1945* (Berlin, 1961), pp. 302–11; and Krafft Freiherr Schenck zu Schweinsberg, "Die Soldatenverbände in der Bundesrepublik," in *Studien zur politischen und gesellschaftlichen Situation der Bundeswehr*, herausgegeben von Georg Picht (Witten, 1965).

84. On the former Waffen-SS veterans and the formation of their interest group, the HIAG, see Tauber, *Beyond Eagle and Swastika*, 1:346–62; Jenke, *Verschwörung von Rechts?*, pp. 311–20; and David C. Large, "Reckoning without the Past: The HIAG of the Waffen-SS and the Politics of Rehabilitation in the Bonn Republic, 1950–1961," *Journal of Modern History* 59/1 (March 1987).

85. "Vorsitzende pariert Spott gegen BLITZMÄDEL," ZA-PV, HQ 99, Soldatenbünde, AdsD/FES.

86. Accounts of Eisenschink's activities often note that he had a license from the Americans, but the extent of U.S. support is unclear.

87. Sitzungsprotokoll der Vertreterversammlung des BvW v. 19/21.5.51, Nachlass Hansen, N222/228, BAF, p. 6.

88. Der Informationsdienst, 24 March 1951, BW9/3085, BAF.

89. Hansen to Schwerin, 13 October 1950, and Schwerin to Hansen, 25 October 1950, BW9/3103, BAF. Schwerin saw himself "as the middleman between the federal government and all of the interest groups of former professional soldiers." Schwerin to Schulte, 10 October 1950, ibid.

90. On the founding of the BDS and the DSZ, see Tauber, *Beyond Eagle and Swastika*, 1:271–75, and Jenke, *Verschwörung von Rechts?*, pp. 347–48.

91. Krakau to Hansen, 16 March 1951, and Hansen to Krakau, 21 March 1951, BW9/3085, BAF.

92. Hansen to Blank, 10 April 1951, ibid.

93. Schenck zu Schweinsberg, "Die Soldatenverbände," p. 100; Aufzeichnung, Nr. 54/51, 5 July 1951, BW9/3085, and An die Landesverbandsvorsitzenden des VDS (DDSB), 14 November 1951, BW9/3086, BAF.

94. Yet, at the same time, many young officers remained uninterested in the BvW since its primary concern was to obtain and improve pensions for which they were not eligible. A prime target for an expanded BvW, therefore, would be those young officers who had had a career in the enlarged Wehrmacht after 1935 but did not qualify for pensions.

95. Hansen's tone irritated many in the government and the Dienststelle Blank, including those who supported his goals. The former officers' selfish demands during the early stages of the drafting of the 131 Law also created ill will, as did the not-so-subtle efforts of some elements of the veterans' movement to blackmail the government on the rearmament issue. See, for example, the draft of a letter by Blank to a local CDU leader who was upset about the government's failure to respond to the demands of former soldiers. Blank to Ostermann, 26 January 1951, BW9/3086, BAF.

96. See, for example, the article by Joachim Joesten, "Is Hitlerism Wearing a New Veteran's Uniform?," that appeared in the *Washington Star* of 23 September 1951 and was read into the *Congressional Record* (volume 97, number 178) the following day. A copy is in BW9/3086, BAF.

97. See, for example, Vortragsnotiz, 5.12.50, Anlage 2A, Vorschläge zur Sprachregelung, BW9/3103, and Holtz to Hansen, 25 April 1951, BW9/3085, BAF.

98. Authors discussing Adenauer's modus operandi, particularly his activities connected with rearmament, repeatedly note his penchant for secrecy. One reflection of this is that there is little direct material in the Bundeskanzleramt files detailing its ties to veterans' organizations. The papers of Otto Lenz, who was the main link, remain closed. His diary, which has recently been published, reveals some details, but most of the material concerning his dealings with the veterans' organizations has either been edited out, removed earlier, or, quite likely, never entered. The main problem is that which faces all historians of contemporary events, namely, that it is easy for participants involved in sensitive issues to avoid leaving a paper trail by conducting business in person or by phone.

99. On Schwerin's fall, see Foerster, "Innenpolitische Aspekte," pp. 564–70; Abenheim, *Reforging the Iron Cross*, pp. 78–79; and Baring, *Im Anfang war Adenauer*, pp. 51–57.

100. When Hansen tried to get the Dienststelle to work on the BDS in April 1951, his request was refused. Holtz to Hansen, 10 April 1951, BW9/3085, BAF.

101. Some opponents wanted a united organization in order to oppose more effectively the government's policies and to block rearmament; see, for example, Tauber's account of Gert Spindler's activities in *Beyond Eagle and Swastika*, 1:278–83. For an example of Hansen's efforts to ward off accusations that the BvW was too close to the government, see An alle Mitglieder des erweiterten Vorstandes des BvW, 18 March 1951, BW9/3085, BAF.

Chapter 8

1. Sitzungsprotokoll der Vertreterversammlung des BvW v. 19./20.5.51, Nachlass Hansen, N222/228, BAF.

2. Ibid., pp. 13–22.

3. Ibid., pp. 22–23.

4. This position was supported by the Bund's legal committee the next day. Eventually, lawsuits were filed in the hopes of improving the terms of the law and increasing the benefits it provided. See, for example, Linde's report of 9 January 1952 on the Vertreterversammlung in Hannover on 5–6 January, Nachlass Donat, N571/209, BAF.

5. Sitzungsprotokoll der Vertreterversammlung des BvW v. 19./20.5.51, pp. 10–11. According to Hansen, the Wehrmacht's defamation had been ended by Eisenhower's statement during his visit to Germany in early 1951 and by the chancellor's statement to the Bundestag on 5 April.

6. D. Schmoeckel, "Eingliederung in das Volksganze," ibid., pp. 26–36.

7. According to Schmoeckel, the majority of the people looked at the state "with the eyes of a creditor, who has a claim to benefits, but no reciprocal responsibilities." Most did not realize that "also a milk cow must be fed, cared for, and protected." This, however, according to Schmoeckel, did not apply to the "old Prussian state official and soldier, who have always known that the opposite was true." Ibid., pp. 30–32.

8. Ibid., p. 37.

9. Ibid., p. 81.

10. Ibid., pp. 98–112.

11. Ibid., p. 102. See also Suchrow's earlier remarks during the first day's meeting. Ibid., pp. 55–58.

12. Ibid., pp. 103–8.

13. An die Landesverbände und den Vorstand, 26. Juni 1951, BW9/3085, BAF. For details on the debate over the name and the structure of the new organization, see the separately bound file entitled "Wie der Soldatenbund aussehen soll," in Nachlass Hansen, N222/240, BAF.

14. According to a report prepared in the Dienststelle Blank (by Oster) in July 1951, the Dienststelle was observing the *Soldatenbünde* to identify movements within them that "could lead to radicalism." The report made it clear, however, that the Dienststelle had no intention of becoming involved in any forms of "active" influence: "If under 'active protection of the constitution' a sympathetic [verständnisvolle] influencing of groups for the purpose of contributing to their deradicalization is envisioned, then this falls under the jurisdiction of Cologne [i.e., the Federal Office for the Protection of the Constitution]." Aufzeichnung Nr. 54/51, 5. Juli 1951, BW9/3085, BAF.

15. Dethleffsen and the Wirtschaftspolitische Gesellschaft von 1947 were closely associated with the *Frankfurter Allgemeine Zeitung*. See Georg Meyer, "Soldaten ohne Armee," in *Von Stalingrad zur Währungsreform. Zur Sozialgeschichte des Umbruchs in Deutschland*, herausgegeben von Martin Broszat et al. (Munich, 1988), p. 740.

16. This account is based on the letter of General Helge Auleb to Hansen of 26 June 1951 and the minutes of a later meeting of BvW leaders in Kiel, Aus den Besprechungen mit Sapauschke in Kiel am 1.7.51, both in Nachlass Hansen, N222/240, BAF.

17. Sapauschke was invited by Dethleffsen, but as a private individual; neither the BvW, as such, nor Hansen, were invited. Some prominent military figures who were invited but did not attend were Heinz Guderian, Franz Halder, and Friedrich Hossbach.

18. Aus den Besprechungen mit Sapauschke in Kiel am 1.7.51, Nachlass Hansen, N222/240, BAF.

19. Ibid. Lenz, according to Röhlke, had instructed him to make clear to the Bund's leaders that the BvW should create as quickly as possible the foundations for a general veterans' organization, a "Hansen-Bund ehemaliger Soldaten." If desired, the Bundesregierung would provide financial help. Hansen rejected this proposal, claiming he wanted to retain independence, though the possibility of the government's providing office space was not excluded. Bonn's apparent eagerness to support Hansen's efforts obviously provided the admiral with a certain grim satisfaction. "Finally," he exclaimed, "the Bundeskanzler has realized that he made a mistake [etwas verspielt hat]." Lenz's published diary, *Im Zentrum der Macht. Das Tagebuch von Staatssekretär Lenz, 1951–1953*, bearbeitet von Klaus Gotto et al. (Düsseldorf, 1989), makes no reference of this particular meeting with Röhlke, but many of the meetings with representatives of veterans' organizations, which clearly did take place, are either unrecorded or omitted from the published version of the diary.

20. On a number of occasions Hansen made it clear that his first choice to be his successor was Field Marshall Albert von Kesselring, who, however, was still serving a prison sentence for war crimes committed in Italy. Friessner's dogged campaign to exonerate and free the military war criminals, which paralleled the admiral's fight against the "defamation" of the military, may have helped gain Hansen's support.

21. Hansen to Friessner, 2 July 1951, Nachlass Hansen, N222/240, BAF. Hansen also sent a copy to Manteuffel.

22. Manteuffel to Friessner, 17 July 1951, Nachlass Friessner, N528/38, BAF.

23. On Spindler and his activities, see Kurt Tauber, *Beyond Eagle and Swastika: German Nationalism since 1945* (Middletown, Conn., 1967), 1:275–89.

24. Ibid., 1:279. Cf. Meyer, "Soldaten ohne Armee," p. 740.

25. Tauber, *Beyond Eagle and Swastika*, 1:280; Betr. Besprechung Altenberg am 21./22.7.1951, Nachlass Friessner, N528/35, BAF.

26. According to Tauber, Spindler wanted to block rearmament. A third meeting was held in Altenberg in late August for the purpose of maneuvering Guderian into the leadership of the impending organization and politicizing it along the lines Spindler and his colleagues desired, but this came to naught. Tauber, *Beyond Eagle and Swastika*, 1:288–89. See also the clipping from Spindler's paper, *Der Fortschritt*, 23 November 1951, in BW9/3086, BAF.

27. Reise des Adm. nach Bonn u. Düsseldorf 6./7. Juli, Nachlass Hansen, N222/240, BAF.

28. Events of these two meetings have been reconstructed from a variety of minutes and notes located in ibid. The major sources are Anregungen für Ausstattung des BvW, Düsseldorf 23.7.51; v. Manteuffel's Tagung im Weinhaus B., 25.7.51; Zusammenkunft in Düsseldorf am 24. Juli 1951 auf Einladung von Gen. v. Manteuffel im Weinhaus Bettermann; Tagung des erweiterten Vorstandes Juli 1951; Beitrag für Ansprache Adm. Hansen am 28.7.51 in Bonn; Besprechungspunkte für die Sitzung des erweiterten Vorstandes am 28/29.7.1951 in Bonn; Sitzung des erweiterten Vorstandes des BvW in Bonn am 28.7.51; and Worum geht es letztlich? 29.7.51 (memo prepared by Captain Rollmann).

29. Captain Rollmann, Hansen's aide, also appears to have been present but apparently was not considered to be a representative of the BvW per se.

30. These remarks by Dethleffsen are quoted from Beitrag für Ansprache Adm. Hansen. In the corresponding passage cited in Sitzung des erweiterten Vorstandes, Dethleffsen appears to be more concerned with the "baggage" of Weimar than that of the Third Reich: "Wir Soldaten sind nicht vorbelastet durch Gepäck von vor 33 bzw. noch nicht politische tätig gewesen."

31. Zusammenkunft in Düsseldorf am 24. Juli 1951 auf Einladung von Gen. v. Manteuffel im Weinhaus Bettermann, Nachlass Hansen, N222/240, BAF.

32. Beitrag für Ansprache Adm. Hansen am 28.7.51 in Bonn, ibid.

33. The following account is taken from Protokoll der erweiterten Vorstandssitzung des BvW in Bonn am 28. und 29.7.1951, ibid.

34. Ibid., p. 2.

35. Ibid., p. 7.

36. Ibid., p. 9.

37. Copies of the letter and accompanying materials Hansen sent to Lenz as well as of his letter to the *Landesverbände* are in BW9/3085, BAF.

38. Hansen to Speidel, 6 August 1951, ibid. Hansen concluded that he was convinced that the BvW/DDSB must remain in existence and that the BDS and *Waffengemeinschaften* must join it. The composition of the executive committee could be settled later. The admiral saw Friessner as the executive secretary and Kesselring as his own successor.

39. Hansen to Friessner, 30 July 1951, Nachlass Hansen, N222/240, BAF.

40. Friessner to Hansen, 1 August 1951, ibid.

41. A copy of Hansen's response, apparently sent by him to Speidel, is in BW9/3085, BAF.

42. Hansen to Friessner, 5 August 1951, Nachlass Hansen, N222/240, BAF.

43. See, for example, Manteuffel to Friessner, 17 July 1951, Nachlass Friessner, N528/48, BAF.

44. Dethleffsen to Friessner, 5 July 1951, Nachlass Friessner, N528/43, and Manteuffel to Friessner, 29 July and 17 August 1951, Nachlass Friessner, N528/48, BAF.

45. Manteuffel to Friessner, 29 July and 17 August 1951, Nachlass Friessner, N528/48, BAF.

46. The *Deutsche Soldaten Zeitung* attracted interest from a number of quarters. Its

aggressive nationalism, anticommunism, and hysterical attacks against purported acts of "defamation" of the former Wehrmacht made it an effective tool of recruitment for the BDS, especially among younger veterans who were unconcerned about the problems of pensionable officers, which occupied the pages of the BvW's paper, *Der Notweg*. Leaders of the BvW were envious of the *DSZ*, and officials in the government and the Dienststelle Blank wanted to gain influence over it in order to win support for their rearmament policies. Government subsidies were provided for the *DSZ* during the 1950s but were withdrawn once the rearmament crisis passed and the *DSZ* began to take on a more radical cast. On the debate over the need for a soldiers' newspaper and the *DSZ* in the Dienststelle Blank, see BW9/3085 and BW9/3086, BAF. On the *DSZ*, see Tauber, *Beyond Eagle and Swastika*, especially 1:300–301, and Manfred Jenke, *Verschwörung von Rechts? Ein Bericht über den Rechtsradikalismus in Deutschland nach 1945* (Berlin, 1961), pp. 347–48, 382–83.

47. Trettner über Aussprache in Frankfurt 9.8 mit Friessner, Dethleffsen, v. Kalben; An die Landesverbände und den Vorstand des DDSB, 19 August 1951; and Hansen an Hausser et al., 22 August 1951, Nachlass Hansen, N222/240, BAF.

48. Hansen to Friessner, 22 August 1951, ibid., and 1 September 1951, Nachlass Hansen, N222/241, BAF.

49. Friessner to Hansen, 31 August 1951, Nachlass Hansen, N222/241, BAF.

50. Dethleffsen to Friessner, 1 September 1951, Nachlass Friessner, N528/43, and Friessner to Manteuffel, 24 and 30 August 1951, Nachlass Friessner, N528/48, BAF; Friessner to Hansen, 31 August 1951, Nachlass Hansen, N222/241, BAF.

51. Friessner to Manteuffel, 24 and 30 August 1951, Nachlass Friessner, N528/48, BAF.

52. See, for example, Koller to Hansen, 1 July 1951, and Hansen to Koller, 12 July 1951, Nachlass Hansen, N222/240, BAF.

53. Stellungnahme des Landesverbandes Württ./Baden zu den neuen Absichten des 1. Vorsitzenden des BvW vom 26.6.51, Nachlass Hansen, N222/241, BAF. See also the letter of Veiel to Hansen, 30 August 1951, ibid.

54. See chapter 3, text following n. 40. The pressure for rearmament also seemed to be greater in the north. According to a BvW observer from Stuttgart who was traveling in the north, the mood there was more radical ("scheint hier eine ziemlich nazistische Einstellung vorzuherrschen") because of the proximity of the Russians, whereas in the south, which was a greater distance from the Russians, the mood was more relaxed and veterans were more skeptical about becoming involved in political activity. See Meyer, "Soldaten ohne Armee," p. 737.

55. Versammlung der Vorsitzenden der süddeutschen Landesverbände am 6.9.1951 in Bonn, Nachlass Donat, N571/209, BAF.

56. Minutes of the meeting (and of the following day's), entitled DDSB-VDS, are in Nachlass Hansen, N222/241, BAF. More information, including the reactions and views of the southern groups, is provided in the minutes made by General Donat, Vollsitzung sämtlicher BvW Landesvorsitzenden am 7.9, Nachlass Donat, N571/209, BAF.

57. According to Donat, while the majority of the *Landesverbände* were for the

changes, in terms of membership the six opposing *Landesverbände* had a majority of nearly 2 to 1 (47,800 to 25,000).

58. There are several accounts of the meeting. Copies of the official minutes produced by the VdS, entitled Protokoll der Tagung am 9. [*sic*] September 1951 in Bonn, which were distributed by the VdS Geschäftsstelle and dated 17 September 1951, are scattered throughout the various *Nachlässe*. The copy I have used was obtained at the Archiv der Deutschen Gesellschaft für Auswärtige Politik in Bonn. There is also a short version in DDSB-VDS, pp. 3–4, Nachlass Hansen, N222/241, BAF, and a longer, twenty-page version, entitled Hauptsitzung am 8.9, in the Donat Nachlass, N571/209, BAF. In the discussion that follows, I rely mostly on the VdS minutes, Protokoll der Tagung.

59. Fifty-one names are listed in the official protocol. Their affiliation breaks down as follows: DDSB, 24; *Traditionsverbände*, 12, including Manteuffel, Ramcke, and Kurt Student; Stahlhelm, 4; BDS, 3; Waffen-SS, 1; unaffiliated, 7. Donat's account says there were nearly a hundred participants.

60. Protokoll der Tagung, pp. 2–6.

61. Ibid., p. 6.

62. The first two questions were asked by Otto Mosbach, Hansen's deputy, and Mosbach probably asked the third, although this is unclear—even in the BvW minutes.

63. Protokoll der Tagung, pp. 6–7.

64. Hauptsitzung am 8.9, Donat Nachlass, N571/209, BAF, pp. 18–19.

65. Protokoll der Tagung, p. 7. This apparently was done in agreement with Friessner, since Hansen asked the questions in the latter's name. It is likely that Hansen spoke with Friessner, as well as members of his own organization, during the break.

66. See chapter 7.

67. Protokoll der Tagung, pp. 7–9.

68. Ibid., pp. 9–10. According to Dethleffsen the average age of members of the Fourth Army in 1944 was twenty-six, which meant they were now thirty-three.

69. Ibid., p. 10.

70. Ibid., pp. 11–12.

71. Ibid., p. 12.

72. Hauptsitzung am 8.9, Nachlass Donat, N571/209, BAF, p. 22. The VdS account of Guderian's remarks makes no mention of this threat. Protokoll der Tagung, pp. 12–13.

73. Protokoll der Tagung, pp. 13–14.

74. Ibid., p. 14. According to Georg Meyer, Dethleffsen's role in the creation of the VdS "can hardly be underestimated." "Soldaten ohne Armee," p. 742.

75. Protokoll der Tagung, p. 16. Ruoff was appointed to the committee.

76. Ibid., p. 18. What exactly had been decided was still unclear. There was confusion as to what was to be done and how it was to be accomplished. The name Der Deutsche Soldatenbund had been submitted to the Verein registration office but apparently had not yet been certified. It was agreed to withdraw the petition or to resubmit it. Meanwhile, the DDSB leaders were to resign and to serve provisionally as leaders of the new group until it was reorganized.

77. Guderian's role at the meeting is emphasized much more in Donat's account than in the official one. In general, the southern BvW leaders felt that Friessner and his supporters had dictated the course of the meeting and imposed their ideas on the delegates, including Hansen. See the following account of the BvW leaders' meeting on 9 September 1951 and Hansen's meeting in Stuttgart with leaders of the southern *Landesverbände* on 15 October.

78. Protokoll der Tagung, pp. 19–20.

79. Ibid., p. 20.

80. Ibid., pp. 21–22. After twelve names, all officers, had been proposed and accepted, Mosbach noted (drily?) that he would consider it desirable if not only generals but noncommissioned officers and representatives of other interested groups, for example, Wehrmachtbeamte, were chosen. This was followed by a scramble of the various groups to name their token noncommissioned officers to the committee. Donat's version of the selection of the executive committee is less flattering than the official one and probably closer to the truth. Hauptsitzung am 8.9, Nachlass Donat, N571/209, BAF, pp. 31–32.

81. Protokoll der Tagung, pp. 21–23.

82. Ibid., p. 23.

83. As Hansen put it later, "That Friessner launched a hostile mutiny [feindliche Meute] in no way changes the correctness of the decision to found the VdS." Hansen to Raven, 5 October 1951, Nachlass Hansen, N222/241, BAF.

84. This account of the meeting is based on minutes made by Donat, DDSB-(BvW) Sitzung am 9.9, Nachlass Donat, N571/209, BAF.

85. Manteuffel to Friessner, 11 September 1951, Nachlass Friessner, N528/48, BAF.

86. Friessner to Manteuffel, 15 September 1951, ibid.

87. Spindler to Friessner, 11 September 1951, Nachlass Friessner, N528/38, BAF.

88. In the early stages of the occupation, the Allies had prohibited the wearing of any decorations or orders by the Germans. In 1949 the High Commission loosened this blanket prohibition but still banned the wearing of orders and decorations from the two world wars. In 1953 a special commission, headed by the former Weimar defense minister, Otto Gessler, and including representatives of veterans' organizations, decided that the wearing of military orders and decorations, with the swastika removed, should be permitted. This proposal was adopted by the Bundestag in 1957.

89. Tauber, *Beyond Eagle and Swastika*, 1:282; Friessner's marginal comments in Spindler to Friessner, 11 September 1951, Nachlass Friessner, N528/38, BAF; Dethleffsen to Spindler, Nachlass Friessner, N528/43, BAF. Cf. Meyer, "Soldaten ohne Armee," p. 742.

90. For Friessner's account of the meetings, see Sitzungsprotokoll des Präsidiums des VdS am 14. Oktober 1951 in Königswinter, Nachlass Friessner, N528/38, BAF, and Sitzung des komm. Präsidiums einschl. LV in Königswinter Gold. Stern am 14.10.51, Nachlass Hansen, N222/241, BAF. While he could boast that he had forcefully presented the VdS's conditions for support of the government's policy, Friessner apparently had irritated the chancellor; at the conclusion of his interview, when he asked "what effectively the other side would provide in return," he received no answer. See

also "Über die Uneinigkeit zwischen den Soldatenbünde," an undated, unsigned manuscript probably written by Ernst Riggert in early 1952. ZA-PV, HQ 99, Soldaten-bünde, AdsD/FES, pp. 7, 10.

91. Tauber, *Beyond Eagle and Swastika*, 1:293–94.

92. Ibid., p. 295. Tauber mistakenly identifies Gümbel as the Bavarian leader of the VdS, when in fact, as he himself notes earlier, Gümbel was a founder and leader of the BDS.

93. Ibid.; Krafft Freiherr Schenck zu Schweinsberg, "Die Soldatenverbände in der Bundesrepublik," in *Studien zur politischen und gesellschaftlichen Situation der Bundes-wehr*, herausgegeben von Georg Picht (Witten, 1965), p. 103. For examples, see the newspaper clipping collections dealing with German veterans' organizations at the AdsD/FES (ZA-PV, HQ 99) and the Wiener Library (G8C2), now located at the Leo Baeck Institute, New York.

94. Schenck zu Schweinsberg, "Die Soldatenverbände," pp. 103–4.

95. Tauber, *Beyond Eagle and Swastika*, 1:289, 295–96.

96. For examples, see Nachlass Friessner, N528/39–40, BAF, especially Keim's letter in the latter file.

97. A letter from Heinz Trettner, who had been present at the press conference, to Hansen in early October accurately reflected the mood. Trettner noted that following their "brilliant start, the interview had caused a serious setback." There was no ques-tion, however, "that the entire affair had been unfair." Friessner's prepared statements had gone well and had been met with applause. Then, Trettner claimed, in spite of requests to "draw a line through the past," to focus on "the common goal of creating a unified front against the East," and not to take Friessner's "plain and outspoken soldier's words" amiss, the press went on the attack: "One noticed immediately from the journalists' questions that they were motivated by ill will and unwilling to free themselves from the spirit of '45." The questions were fired at such a rate that there was no time for thought, and Friessner's "unskilled formulations," which made sense in relation to his speech, were then quoted out of context. Trettner did not think Friessner should resign, however, since it would be impossible to begin work effectively in the face of such a setback. Gümbel's remarks, which were "even more deplorable" than those of Friessner, had exacerbated the situation. Trettner concluded, "It is clear that the rush with which we proceeded was both unnecessary and inexpedient." Trettner to Hansen, 3 October 1951, Nachlass Hansen, N222/241, BAF.

98. Sitzungsprotokoll des Präsidiums des VdS am 14. Oktober 1951 in Königswinter, Nachlass Friessner, N528/38, BAF, and Sitzung des komm. Präsidiums einschl. LV in Königswinter Gold. Stern am 14.10.51, Nachlass Hansen, N222/241, BAF.

99. Hansen to Raven, 5 October 1951, Nachlass Hansen, N222/241, BAF.

100. Sitzungsprotokoll des Präsidiums des VDS am 14. Oktober 1951 in Königswin-ter, Nachlass Friessner, N528/38, BAF, pp. 13–14.

101. Ibid., pp. 17–18.

102. See the minutes of the meeting, Stuttgart 15.10.51, Nachlass Hansen, N222/241, BAF.

103. Hansen apparently was still in Stuttgart but did not attend the evening meeting.

104. Friessner responded to the founding of the *Arbeitsgemeinschaft* by ordering the formation of new BvW branches in the rebellious areas. Tauber, *Beyond Eagle and Swastika*, 1:296.

105. Hansen to Raven, 5 October 1951, Nachlass Hansen, N222/241, BAF. Initially Linde did not seem especially upset either. See Linde to Hansen, 30 September 1951, ibid.

106. Tauber, *Beyond Eagle and Swastika*, 1:295–96; Lenz, *Im Zentrum der Macht*, pp. 138–39; *Die Kabinettsprotokolle der Bundesregierung*, herausgegeben für das Bundesarchiv von Hans Booms, Band 4 (1951) (Boppard am Rhein, 1988), pp. 670–71.

107. *VDB*, 16 October 1951, p. 6884.

108. *DBDr*, Nr. 2784, 8 November 1951.

109. Claes compiled his letters in a memorandum that was circulated to interested parties. A copy is in BW9/3086, BAF.

110. An die Landesverbandsvorsitzenden des V.D.S. (D.D.S.B.), 14 November 1951, ibid.

111. Schenck zu Schweinsberg, "Die Soldatenverbände," p. 104; Ernst Riggert, Betrifft: Deutsche Soldatenbünde, ZA-PV, HQ 99, Soldatenbünde, AdsD/FES; Aufzeichnung Nr. 72/51, Betr: Soldatenbünde, 1.9.51, BW9/3085, BAF; Lenz, *Im Zentrum der Macht*, p. 135.

112. Geyr had discussed his plans with Lenz and Globke, who apparently had encouraged him. Aktennotiz Betr: Soldatenbünde, 2 September 1951, BW9/3085, BAF.

113. Noack had been involved in the creation of Geyr's Deutscher Frontkämpferbund, founded in Hamburg the previous June, and the two men were in constant contact thereafter. See Nachlass Geyr, IfZ.

114. This account is based on two reports of the meeting located in BW9/3086, BAF: Bericht über die Goslaer Tagung der soldatischen Verbände, prepared by Schwerin, and an untitled report apparently prepared by Manteuffel or one of his representatives.

115. The remarks of the representatives of the *Traditionsverbände* make it clear that their organizations had either backed away from or already left the VdS.

116. Farke met regularly with Lenz to discuss developments in the *Soldatenbünde*. For examples, see Lenz's diary, *Im Zentrum der Macht*.

117. Bericht über die Bildung eines Arbeitsausschusses für die Zusammenarbeit soldatischer und gleichartiger Verbände in Goslar am 10. und 11.11.1951, BW9/3086, BAF.

118. *Der Fortschritt*, 23.11.51, ibid.

119. Betr: Situation des Verbandes Deutschen Soldaten (VDS), Ende November 1951, ibid.

120. Hansen to Friessner, 17 November 1951, Nachlass Friessner, N528/45, BAF. The relevant sentence was underlined and heavily marked in the margin by Friessner.

121. Aktennotiz der Besprechung in Hannover am 21.11.51, Nachlass Friessner, N528/38, BAF.

122. Manteuffel to Friessner, 21 November 1951, Nachlass Friessner, N528/48, BAF. Spindler's group also abandoned Friessner. Aktenvermerk 3. Dez. 1951, BW9/3086, BAF. Friessner's anger and bitterness at his treatment by his erstwhile allies is reflected in his response to Manteuffel, 1 December 1951, Nachlass Friessner, N528/48, BAF.

123. See, in addition to the report by Claes (n. 109), Admiral Mewis's evaluation of the situation following meetings with Hansen and State Secretaries Lehr and Lenz on 4 and 5 December 1951. Mewis to Friessner, 17 December 1951, Nachlass Friessner, N528/40, BAF. Following Friessner's resignation, Dethleffsen, in a discussion with Lenz, noted that there had been a rumor going around in the veterans' organizations that Lenz had said there would be no further action on military pensions until Friessner resigned and that this had caused his resignation. The state secretary replied that he had heard "something similar" from Hansen and that he had told the admiral "that [the rumor] was pure nonsense [heller Unsinn]." Lenz, *Im Zentrum der Macht*, p. 194. Lenz's disavowal notwithstanding, it seems likely that the government was not loath to promote such a rumor and certainly did little to discourage it. Cf. Tauber, *Beyond Eagle and Swastika*, 1:296.

124. At a meeting with Lenz on 5 December Hansen had said that Friessner's resignation was "fairly certain [ziemlich feststehe]." The admiral proposed that Alexander von Falkenhausen be Friessner's successor, an idea opposed by Lenz because of the "incidents" that had arisen following Falkenhausen's return from captivity in Belgium. Lenz urged Hansen to take over the position vacated by Friessner, which he eventually did. Lenz, *Im Zentrum der Macht*, pp. 186–87.

125. The original German is as follows:

Nach den Erfahrungen der letzten Monate habe ich den Eindruck gewonnen, dass sich bei der ganz heterogenen Einstellung des ehem. Deutschen Offizierkorps in Besonderen und der ehem. Soldaten überhaupt eine Sammlungs- und Einigungsbewegung mit einheitlicher Gesinnungsbildung in den grossen Fragen des Soldatentums, wie wir uns das vorgestellt haben, einfach heutzutage nicht mehr zustande bringen lässt. Es wird wohl höchstens ein Nebeneinander von verschiedenen "Interessenverbänden" möglich sein, wie "Berufssoldaten," "Heimkehrer," "VdK," "Kriegsopfer," "Kyffhäuser," "Traditionsverbände," u.s.w. Ich kann noch nicht erkennen, ob dazu überhaupt noch ein "Dach" nötig ist. Welchen Zweck und welche Befugnisse sollte es haben?

Friessner to Hansen, 12 January 1952, Nachlass Friessner, N528/45, BAF.

126. For an account of the Hannover meeting, see *Der Notweg*, January 1952, and VDS/BVW, Betr.: Vertreterversammlung des BvW am 5. und 6. Januar 1952 in Hannover, Nachlass Donat, N571/209, BAF.

127. *Der Notweg*, January 1952, pp. 1–2.

128. VdS/BvW. Jahresbericht 1952, Nachlass Hansen, N222/230, BAF.

129. Ernst Riggert, "Gescheiterte Soldatenbünde," *Der Telegraf*, 8 May 1952, ZA-PV, HQ 99, Soldatenbünde, AdSD/FES.

130. Ernst Riggert, "Betrifft: Deutsche Soldatenbünde," 12 August 1951, ibid.; Meyer, "Soldaten ohne Armee," p. 734.

131. See n. 80.

132. *Der Notweg*, January 1952.

133. Otto Mosbach, "Getrennt marschiern?" and *Unteroffiziere im Verband deutscher Soldaten*, Nachlass Donat, N571/62, BAF.

134. Ernst Riggert, "Gescheiterte Soldatenbünde," *Der Telegraf*, 8 May 1952, ZA-PV, HQ 99, Soldatenbünde, AdSD/FES; Schenck zu Schweinsberg, "Die Soldatenverbände," pp. 104–5.

135. By the beginning of the new year, the initial optimism of the leaders of the Goslar project had already begun to wane and was replaced by deep pessimism over the prospects of the upcoming meeting in Wiesbaden. See, for example, the covering letter and Noack's report to Geyr on the VdH's executive committee meeting of 20 January, as well as his letter of 7 March 1952, Nachlass Geyr, IfZ.

136. On 6 December Geyr visited Lenz and discussed the plans developed at Goslar. When he told Lenz that the Goslar group refused to work with the VdS, Lenz replied: "I told Schweppenburg that for our part we would have no interest in seeing the veterans divided into two camps composed of a strongly rightist veterans' organization and a moderate one [Ich erklärte Schweppenburg, dass wir auf der anderen Seite keine Interesse daran hätten, dass ein scharf rechts gerichteter Soldatenverband und ein gemässigter Soldatenverband das soldatische Lager in zwei Teile aufspalte]." Lenz, *Im Zentrum der Macht*, p. 187.

137. For a biased, but generally accurate, account of these developments, see VdS/BvW. An die Vorsitzenden der Landesverbände. Das Verhältnis des VdW/BvW zum Kyffhäuserbund, 18. September 1951. VERTRAULICH!, Nachlass Hansen, N222/152, BAF.

138. Although the federal government could not intervene directly in restoring the Kyffhäuserbund's assets (which consisted mostly of property) since it was a matter of state jurisdiction, it could give general guidelines, and it and the coalition parties made it clear that they supported the Bund's claims. See, for example, *VDB*, 17 January 1952, pp. 7914–19. When an SPD speaker reminded the deputies of the Kyffhäuserbund's earlier complicity in the fall of the Weimar Republic and its role in the Third Reich, coalition party speakers evaded the issue by taking narrowly legalistic positions. Like many other organizations (and individuals), the Kyffhäuserbund sought to whitewash its unsavory past by claiming it had been a victim of national socialism and implying that it had been opposed to the regime. It asserted that the dissolution of the Bund had been illegal and that it had been caused by the Bund's refusal to bow to the demands of the Nazis. The argument was, of course, false, but such specious arguments were given widespread currency in postwar Germany. For an example of the Kyffhäuser line, see *Deutscher Soldatenbund-Kyffhäuser, e.V. Geschichte, Leitsätze, Anschriften* ([1957]), p. 3. A copy is in the Bundestag Bibliothek.

139. For an up-to-date account of the HIAG and the relevant literature, see David C. Large, "Reckoning without the Past: The HIAG of the Waffen-SS and the Politics of

Rehabilitation in the Bonn Republic, 1950–1961," *Journal of Modern History* 59/1 (March 1987): 79–113.

140. Ibid., 90, 95–102. Schumacher's position was a result of his rejection of collective guilt and his determination not to allow the SPD to again be labeled as "unnational." Although he condemned the criminal acts of individuals within the organization, he refused to denounce the entire Waffen-SS. See, in addition to ibid., "Über die Uneinigkeit zwischen den Soldatenbünde," ZA-PV, HQ 99, Soldatenbünde, AdsD/FES, pp. 10–12.

141. Local HIAG groups had begun to emerge much earlier than 1951. Although a newspaper, *Der Freiwillige,* was being published and Generals Gille and Hauser were widely perceived as the national spokespersons for the former Waffen-SS troops, at the time of the founding of the VdS a national organization still did not formally exist (see Gille's remarks at the September meeting cited in text preceding n. 73). Bylaws for the HIAG were not officially drawn up and accepted until May 1952.

142. See VdS/BvW. Jahresbericht 1952 and the protocols for the 1953 *Vertreterversammlung* in Nachlass Hansen, N222/230, BAF, and the materials on the 1954 *Vertreterversammlung* in Nachlass Hansen, N222/231, BAF.

143. For details, see the copious materials in Nachlass Hansen, especially Soldatische Verbände, Kyffhäuser I, and Kyffhäuser II, N222/209–11, and Arbeitsgemeinschaft-Protokolle, N222/227, BAF. An agreement was finally reached in 1973, but it did not produce a true fusion of the two organizations.

144. Schenck zu Schweinsberg, "Die Soldatenverbände," pp. 105–6; Ernst Riggert, "Zur Lage in den deutschen Soldatenbünden," *Gewerkschaftliche Monatshefte,* January 1953, pp. 39–44.

Conclusion

1. The Reichstag committee that was created to investigate the causes of Germany's defeat can be seen as a post–World War I German analogue to the Nuremberg trials.

2. Marlis Steinert, *Hitlers Krieg und die Deutschen* (Düsseldorf, 1970), chapters 3 and 4. The contrast to 1918 was expressed by an elderly countess in 1950, who remarked that "Germany's collapse [in 1918] was for us a much more severe experience than that of 1945, even if objectively it was not so thorough," since it was "more unexpected." Quoted in Johannes Rogalla von Bieberstein, "Adel und Revolution 1918/1919," in *Mentalitäten und Lebensverhältnisse* (Göttingen, 1982), p. 247.

3. On the impact of Allied bombing, see Earl R. Beck, *Under the Bombs: The German Home Front, 1942–1945* (Lexington, 1986). The relief felt by the German population following the cessation of the bombing was noted in Allied intelligence reports; see, for example, *Information Control Intelligence Summary,* Numbers 18 and 19 (10 and 17 November 1945), OMGUS, RG 165, box 1296, NARS.

4. On the mood in Germany at the outbreak of the war, see Albert Speer, *Inside the*

Third Reich (New York, 1971), pp. 229–30, and Omer Bartov, *Hitler's Army: Soldiers, Nazis, and War in the Third Reich* (New York, 1991), pp. 179–80.

5. German tin soldiers of the Second World War not only depicted the usual poses of military action but also portrayed soldiers who were wounded, amputees, and dead. George L. Mosse, *Fallen Soldiers: Reshaping the Memory of the World Wars* (New York, 1990), p. 144.

6. A. J. P. Taylor, *The Origins of the Second World War* (New York, 1963), p. 18.

7. Edwin Hartrich, *The Fourth and Richest Reich: How the Germans Conquered the Postwar World* (New York, 1980), p. 29; Friedrich Freiherr Hiller von Gaertringen, "'Dolchstoss'-Diskussion und 'Dolchstoss-legende' im Wandel von vier Jahrzehnten," in *Geschichte und Gegenwartsbewusstsein. Historische Betrachtungen und Untersuchungen. Festschrift für Hans Rothfels*, herausgegeben von Waldemar Besson et al. (Göttingen, 1963), pp. 145–46; Hans Schröder, *Das Ende der Dolchstosslegende. Geschichtliche Erkenntnis und politische Verantwortung* (Hamburg, 1946), pp. 18–19. Cf. Barbara Marshall, "German Reactions to Military Defeat, 1945–1947: The British View," in *Germany in the Age of Total War*, edited by Volker R. Berghahn and Martin Kitchen (London, 1981), pp. 224–25.

8. Ian Kershaw, *Popular Opinion and Political Dissent in the Third Reich: Bavaria, 1933–1945* (New York, 1983), p. 310.

9. Military government officials feared the growth of a new, reverse stab-in-the-back legend: "Contrary to the post–World War I period, German nationalists . . . will probably compete for a new stab-in-the-back legend in reverse: to have stabbed Hitler in the back [20 July 1944] may be exploited by these forces in an effort to whitewash Germany morally and nationally in the eyes of the world." *Information Control Review*, Number 10 (8 February 1947), OMGUS, RG 260, box 281, folder 107, NARS. This, in fact, did occur. See David C. Large, "Uses of the Past: The Anti-Nazi Resistance Legacy in the Federal Republic of Germany," in *Contending with Hitler: Varieties of German Resistance in the Third Reich* (Cambridge, 1992), pp. 163–82.

10. Wolf Donner, *Die sozial- und staatspolitische Tätigkeit der Kriegsopferverbände. Ein Beitrag zur Verbandsdiskussion* (Berlin, 1960), p. 19.

11. See Marshall, "German Reactions," pp. 225–26.

12. The intelligence reports from both the U.S. and British zones, as well as the accounts of journalists, all comment on the Germans' lack of a sense of responsibility or shame for what had happened. For examples, see ibid.

13. See, for example, John D. Montgomery, *Forced to Be Free: The Artificial Revolutions in Germany and Japan* (Chicago, 1957). To be fair, Montgomery's conclusions were more ambiguous than his title suggests, but, as he later observed at a conference on the U.S. occupation experience in Germany and Japan, a general perception that the occupations had been successful emerged after the fact, even though it was "a conclusion that seems to defy much of the opinion expressed in this conference." Robert Wolfe, ed., *Americans as Proconsuls: United States Military Government in Germany and Japan, 1944–1952* (Carbondale, 1984), p. 437.

14. On the problem of reform versus restoration and the relevant literature, see

Diethelm Prowe, "Socialism as a Crisis Response: Socialization and the Escape from Poverty and Power in Post–World War II Germany," *German Studies Review* 15/1 (February 1992): 65–85; see also Hans-Jürgen Rautenberg, "Zur Standortsbestimmung für künftige deutsche Streitkräfte, 1945–1956," in *Anfänge westdeutscher Sicherheitspolitik, 1945–56*, herausgegeben vom Militärgeschichtlichen Forschungsamt, Band 1, *Von der Kapitulation bis zum Pleven-Plan* (Munich, 1982), pp. 765ff.

15. Under the circumstances of the 1920s (physically intact country and widespread belief that Germany had not been defeated or that the present government was responsible for defeat) it was difficult, if not impossible, for the government to demand sacrifice; everyone was convinced that he or she had suffered but no one else had. After 1945, with the country in ruins and virtually every segment of society in some way harmed by the war, it was easier for the government to convince citizens of the need to make sacrifices for the common good. The best expression of the changed atmosphere was the Lastenausgleichsgesetz, which levied special taxes on those who had suffered less material loss as a result of the war in order to provide support for those who had lost virtually everything.

16. Barbara Marshall, "German Attitudes to British Military Government, 1945–47," *Journal of Contemporary History* 15 (1980): 677; Alfred Grosser, *Germany in Our Time: A Political History of the Post-War Years* (New York, 1971), p. 53.

17. German self-confidence was also restored by the blunders of the Allied military governments. Marshall, "German Attitudes," p. 668. The overturn in the early years of the Federal Republic of unpopular legislation imposed by the Allies during the occupation period also helped greatly to legitimize and consolidate the new regime. For more on this, see text at n. 55.

18. In many cases the new leaders of 1945 were the same as those of 1918, but now enriched with experience, able to draw upon the lessons of the past, and bolstered by the support of the occupation powers.

19. To take but one example: direct efforts at denazification were largely a failure. Indeed, Allied attempts at denazification, especially those of the United States, were probably the major catalyst for neo-Nazi activity in the immediate postwar years and helped to generate among the populace at large sympathy for former Nazis that had previously been lacking. For further examples, see James F. Tent, *Mission on the Rhine: Reeducation and Denazification in American-Occupied Germany* (Chicago, 1982), and Edward N. Peterson, *The American Occupation of Germany: Retreat to Victory* (Detroit, 1978).

20. Dietrich Thränhardt, *Geschichte der Bundesrepublik Deutschland* (Frankfurt am Main, 1986), pp. 17–20, 35–36, 126–29. Although there was widespread support for the nationalization of heavy industry among all classes of Germans, attempts at socialization were blocked by the U.S. military government. Critics of U.S. policy often overestimate the nature and strength of German support for socialization. Many Germans simply saw no other alternative to socialization in view of the discreditization of capitalism through the cooperation of German big business with the Nazi regime. Even among its strongest proponents—the SPD and the unions—socialization was

seen more as a means to an end—the revival of economic life—than as an end in itself. See Lutz Niethammer, "Zum Verhältnis von Reform und Rekonstruktion am Beispiel der Reform des öffentlichen Dienstes," in *Die Bundesrepublik Deutschland. Entstehung, Entwicklung, Struktur*, herausgegeben von Wolf-Dieter Narr und Dietrich Thränhardt (Königstein/Ts., 1984), p. 55, n. 3; Diethelm Prowe, "Economic Democracy in Post–World War II Germany: Corporatist Crisis Response, 1945–1948," *Journal of Modern History* 57 (September 1985), and "Socialism as a Crisis Response."

21. Jane Caplan, *Government without Administration: State and Civil Service in Weimar and Nazi Germany* (Oxford, 1988), chapter 5; Udo Wengst, *Beamtentum zwischen Reform und Tradition. Beamtengesetzgebung in der Gründungsphase der Bundesrepublik Deutschland, 1948–1953* (Düsseldorf, 1988), chapter 1 and pp. 313–14, and *Staatsaufbau und Regierungspraxis, 1948–1953. Zur Geschichte der Verfassungsorgane der Bundesrepublik Deutschland* (Düsseldorf, 1984), pp. 180–81; Niethammer, "Zum Verhältnis," in *Die Bundesrepublik Deutschland*, p. 54; Rautenberg, "Zur Standortsbestimmung," pp. 771ff. For a fuller exposition on the positive effects of "restorative" social legislation, see James M. Diehl, "Social Legislation and the Legitimation of the Federal Republic," paper presented at the conference, "A Framework for Democracy: Forty Years of Experience with the Grundgesetz of the Federal Republic of Germany," Philadelphia, April 1989 (Cambridge, forthcoming).

22. See Eric J. Leed, *No Man's Land: Combat and Identity in World War I* (Cambridge, 1979), especially chapter 6.

23. For example, veterans were to keep to themselves what they had seen and done in the East, which justified Soviet actions and repelled the Western powers.

24. On the contrast between the reception of soldiers in the two world wars and the relation between veterans and civilians, see Julian Bach, *America's Germany: An Account of the Occupation* (New York, 1946), pp. 252–53, 291; Douglas Botting, *From the Ruins of the Reich: Germany, 1945–1949* (New York, 1985), p. 130; Arthur L. Smith, *Heimkehr aus dem Zweiten Weltkrieg. Die Entlassung der deutschen Kriegsgefangenen* (Stuttgart, 1985), pp. 33–34, 131–32; *Information Control Review*, Numbers 10 (8 February 1947) and 28 (21 June 1947), OMGUS, RG 260, box 281, folders 107 and 108, and *Information Control Intelligence Summary*, Numbers 1 (5 July 1945), 5 (10 August 1945), 6 (17 August 1945), and 53 (3 August 1946), OMGUS, RG 165, box 1296, and RG 319, box 699, NARS. See also Mosse, *Fallen Soldiers*, chapter 10.

25. Krafft Freiherr Schenck zu Schweinsberg, "Die Soldatenverbände in der Bundesrepublik," in *Studien zur politischen und gesellschaftlichen Situation der Bundeswehr*, herausgegeben von Georg Picht (Witten, 1965), pp. 171ff., and Hans-Erich Volkmann, "Die innenpolitische Dimension Adenauerscher Sicherheitspolitik in der EVG-Phase," in *Anfänge westdeutscher Sicherheitspolitik, 1945–1956*, herausgegeben vom Militärgeschichtlichen Forschungsamt, Band 2, *Die EVG-Phase* (Munich, 1990), p. 596. This failure of veterans to become a significant political force after the war was true not only for Germany but for Europe as a whole. See Charles S. Maier, *In Search of Stability: Explorations in Historical Political Economy* (Cambridge, 1987), pp. 157–58.

26. See chapter 1, as well as Leed, *No Man's Land*, and Mosse, *Fallen Soldiers*. That the

actual circumstances surrounding the return of German veterans after the First World War was rather less glorious than portrayed in the myth has been shown in Richard Bessel, "The Great War in German Memory: The Soldiers of the First World War, Demobilization, and Weimar Political Culture," *German History* 6/1 (1988).

27. See note 57 below.

28. W. L. White, *Report on the Germans* (New York, 1947), p. 143; John Dornberg, *Schizophrenic Germany* (New York, 1961), p. 206; Herbert Frey, "The German Guilt Question after the Second World War: An Overview," (Ph.D. dissertation, University of Washington, 1979), p. 21.

29. Bartov, *Hitler's Army*, p. 183; Annemarie Tröger, "German Women's Memories of World War II," in *Behind the Lines: Gender and the Two World Wars*, edited by Margaret Randolph Higonnet et al. (New Haven, 1987), pp. 298–99.

30. See chapter 3, text at n. 33.

31. Adolf Rieth, cited in Mosse, *Fallen Soldiers*, p. 215. In the Federal Republic, evangelical ministers were instructed to include all victims of the war in the dedication ceremonies of memorials for fallen soldiers. Volkmann, "Die innenpolitische Dimension," p. 591. On the changing iconography of German war memorials from 1918 to the present, see Meinhold Lurz, *Kriegerdenkmäler in Deutschland*, Band 4, *Weimarer Republik*, Band 5, *Drittes Reich*, Band 6, *Bundesrepublik* (Heidelberg, 1985–87).

32. This was true not only for the VdS, as described in chapter 8, but for the HIAG as well. See David C. Large, "Reckoning without the Past: The HIAG of the Waffen-SS and the Politics of Rehabilitation in the Bonn Republic, 1950–1961," *Journal of Modern History* 59/1 (March 1987), pp. 79–113.

33. Müller-Brandenburg had begun his career before the First World War as a publicist for the Deutscher Wehrverein.

34. Müller-Brandenburg to Schützinger, 4 June 1951, BW9/3086 BAF.

35. Müller-Brandenburg, "Nein, so geht das nicht!," ibid.

36. An die Herren Vorsitzenden der Landersverbände des BVW, 22 December 1951, ibid.

37. Noack to Spindler, 23 November 1951, ibid.

38. See Kurt Tauber, *Beyond Eagle and Swastika: German Nationalism since 1945* (Middletown, Conn., 1967), 1:16–32.

39. On the *Landser-Hefte*, see Walter Nutz, "Der Krieg als Abenteuer und Idylle. Landser-Hefte und triviale Kriegsromane," in *Gegenwartsliteratur und Drittes Reich. Deutsche Autoren in der Auseinandersetzung mit der Vergangenheit*, herausgegeben von Hans Wagener (Stuttgart, 1977), pp. 265–83, and Mosse, *Fallen Soldiers*, p. 218.

40. Schenck zu Schweinsberg, "Die Soldatenverbände"; Ernst Riggert, "Zur Lage in den deutschen Soldatenbünden," *Gewerkschaftliche Monatshefte*, January 1953.

41. "Wo Stehen die Ehemaligen Soldaten heute?," BW9/3086, BAF.

42. See Large, "Reckoning without the Past," and Riggert, "Zur Lage."

43. Above all, the war had democratized the officer corps. Not only had the social differences between officers and troops been reduced, but the congruence of Germany's military forces and German society at large had been increased. See Bernhard R.

Kroener, "Auf dem Weg zu einer 'nationalsozialistischen Volksarmee.' Die soziale Öffnung des Heeresoffizierskorps im Zweiten Weltkrieg," in *Von Stalingrad zur Wäh-rungsreform. Zur Sozialgeschichte des Umbruchs in Deutschland*, herausgegeben von Martin Broszat et al. (Munich, 1988), pp. 352–53, 362, 678, and Jürgen Förster, "Vom Führerheer der Republik zur nationalsozialistischen Volksarmee: Zum Strukturwandel der Wehrmacht, 1935–1945," in *Deutschland in Europa: Kontinuität und Bruch. Gedenk-schrift für Andreas Hillgruber*, herausgegeben von Jost Dülffer et al. (Frankfurt am Main, 1990), pp. 315–16, 319–20.

44. As Georg Meyer notes, this had always been true and had been compounded by the war. "Soldaten ohne Armee," in *Von Stalingrad zur Währungsreform. Zur Sozialge-schichte des Umbruchs in Deutschland*, herausgegeben von Martin Broszat et al. (Munich, 1988), pp. 721–22.

45. The strongest factor in the government's favor was the hiatus in the existence of the military. Much more than was the case for other German institutions, there was a genuine break in continuity in military developments. This meant that, unlike in 1918, the government could control events and could play off competing interests within the military establishment in order to achieve its ends.

46. A comprehensive and up-to-date account of the West German rearmament is provided by the forthcoming study by David C. Large, *Germans to the Front: West German Rearmament in the Adenauer Era*.

47. In a similar manner, the fragmentation and individualization of the German working class under the Third Reich may also have worked to promote the integration of workers into postwar society. See Detlev J. K. Peukert, *Inside Nazi Germany: Conformity, Opposition, and Racism in Everyday Life* (New Haven, 1987), pp. 117, 182.

48. There were 3.9 million recipients in 1950 and 5.5 million in 1955. Hans Günter Hockerts, "Integration der Gesellschaft," in *Entscheidung für den Westen*, herausge-geben von Manfred Funke (Bonn, 1988), p. 42.

49. Hockerts, "Integration," p. 39.

50. Hans-Peter Schwarz, *Die Ära Adenauer. Gründerjahre der Republik, 1949–1957* (Stuttgart, 1981), p. 120.

51. *VDB*, 20 September 1949, p. 23.

52. Richard Löwenthal, "Prolog. Dauer und Verwandlung," in *Die zweite Republik. 25 Jahre Bundesrepublik Deutschland—Eine Bilanz*, herausgegeben von Richard Löwen-thal und Hans-Peter Schwarz (Stuttgart, 1974), p. 12. See also Christoph Klessmann, *Die doppelte Staatsgründung. Deutsche Geschichte, 1945–1955* (Bonn, 1986), p. 236, which refers to social legislation as "sozialpolitische Integrationsklammern."

53. Detlev Zöllner, "Sozialpolitik," in *Die Bundesrepublik Deutschland. Geschichte in drei Bänden*, herausgegeben von Wolfgang Benz, Band 2, *Gesellschaft* (Frankfurt am Main, 1983), p. 300. For a list of the laws passed, see Reinhart Bartholomäi et al., eds. *Sozialpolitik nach 1945. Geschichte und Analysen* (Bonn, 1977), pp. 287–91.

54. Hockerts, "Integration," pp. 48–50; Peter Paul Nahm, *Der Lastenausgleich* (Stutt-gart, 1961) and "Lastenausgleich und Integration der Vertriebenen und Geflüchteten," in *Die zweite Republik. 25 Jahre Bundesrepublik Deutschland—Eine Bilanz*, herausge-

geben von Richard Löwenthal und Hans-Peter Schwarz (Stuttgart, 1974). The main beneficiaries of the law were the *Vertriebenen*, who constituted nearly 20 percent of the Federal Republic's population, but others, such as those whose houses had been bombed out and those who had suffered severe losses as a result of the currency reform of 1948, were also given assistance.

55. On the efforts to reform the German social security system, see Hans Günter Hockerts, *Sozialpolitische Entscheidungen in Nachkriegsdeutschland. Alliierte und deutsche Sozialversicherungspolitik 1945 bis 1957* (Stuttgart, 1980).

56. According to Wengst, *Beamtentum*, p. 304, there was "an almost optimal representation of the interests of the German bureaucracy in the first years of the Federal Republic." For examples, see ibid., pp. 87–101. The war victims were also well represented. Many of the Twenty-sixth Committee's members were associated with either the Verband der Kriegsbeschädigten or the Reichsbund. For a breakdown of the representation of the two *Kriegsopferverbände* in the parties of the second Bundestag, see Donner, *Die sozial- und staatspolitische Tätigkeit*, p. 29. For an example of the situation in the VdH, see *Freiheit ohne Furcht. Zehn Jahre Heimkehrerverband*, herausgegeben vom Verband der Heimkehrer, Kriegsgefangenen, und Vermisstenangehörigen (Bad Godesberg, [1960]), pp. 46–47.

57. As David Schoenbaum has shown in *Hitler's Social Revolution: Class and Status in Nazi Germany, 1933–1939* (New York, 1966), chapter 8, the link between social and political position had begun to be erased during the Third Reich, and the process was intensified in the general uprooting and dislocation that followed in the aftermath of the fall of the regime. Germans from all classes were hurt and suffering was not class specific. Old social categories were replaced with new ones: "Social categories determined by class, profession, education, and religion receded in favor of categories of fate [Schicksalskategorien] such as *Heimkehrer, Flüchtling, Kriegsgefangener, Kriegswitwe*, Displaced Person, *KZ-Häftling*." Friedrich H. Tenbruck, "Alltagsnormen und Lebensgefühle in der Bundesrepublik," in *Die zweite Republik. 25 Jahre Bundesrepublik Deutschland—Eine Bilanz*, herausgegeben von Richard Löwenthal und Hans-Peter Schwarz (Stuttgart, 1974), p. 291. As an SPD deputy put it during the debate over the 131 Law, "The task of our legislative work must be an equalization of fate [Ausgleich des Schicksals], which has blindly struck down one person, while sparing the other." *VDB*, 10 April 1951, p. 5092.

58. In social legislation, especially during the first legislative period, pragmatism generally overcame ideological considerations and there was considerable cooperation between the SPD and the CDU. This is clear both in the protocols of the Bundestag committee meetings and in the Bundestag debates. See Hockerts, "Integration," pp. 44–45, who quotes Werner Conze's description of the situation as being a "Krypto-Grosskoalition." The SPD also frequently joined with other small parties of the center and right-center in order to put pressure on the coalition parties to increase benefits or to embarrass them if they did not. In at least one instance, the FDP, exasperated by the maneuvering of the CSU, praised the SPD for being more reliable and responsible than its coalition partner. *VDB*, 26 April 1950, p. 2147.

59. Thränhardt, *Geschichte*, pp. 23–26.

60. For anticommunism's role as a "Legitimationsideologie" in general, see Klessmann, *Die doppelte Staatsgründung*, pp. 251–57.

61. Such exchanges were most prevalent during the first readings of bills, when the discussion was more general, political, and ideological. For a good example, see the first reading of the BVG, *VDB*, 13 September 1950, pp. 3165ff.

62. On the use of *"Wahlgeschenke"* before Bundestag elections, see Thränhardt, *Geschichte*, pp. 124–25. Aside from the KgfEG, discussed in chapter 7, the second and sixth *Novellen* of the BVG (August 1953 and July 1957), the second *Novelle* of the 131 Law (July 1957), as well as the opening of the 131 Law to former Waffen-SS officers in June 1961 would qualify as such "election gifts." Since unpopular restrictions on the level of benefits were repeatedly imposed by the weak and uncertain state of the economy, the drafters of the laws, in order to demonstrate their goodwill, promised improvements with the coming of an improved economy. See, for example, the discussion of war widows' pensions in *Die Verhandlungen des (26.) Ausschusses für Kriegsopfer- und Kriegsgefangenenfragen des Deutschen Bundestages über das Bundesversorgungsgesetz*, I/87A, Lfd. 10, PAB. As a result, the laws were like sails and the *Wirtschaftswunder* rapidly filled them. Amendments to the laws followed quickly, and the process culminated in the *Dynamisierung* of social pensions. For a chronological listing of social legislation, including the *Novellen*, see Bartholomäi et al., *Sozialpolitik*, pp. 287–91.

National Archives and Records Service, Washington, D.C. (NARS)
  Office of Military Government, United States (OMGUS)
    RG 165
    RG 260
    RG 319
  Records of the Reich Leader of the SS and Chief of German Police (T-175)
Parlamentsarchiv, Bonn (PAB)
  I/20 Gesetz zur Verbesserung von Leistungen an Kriegsopfer vom 27. März 1950
  I/35 Gesetz über Hilfsmassnahmen für Heimkehrer (Heimkehrergesetz) vom 19. Juni 1950
  I/87 Gesetz über die Versorgung der Opfer des Krieges (Bundesversorgungsgesetz) vom 20. Dezember 1950
  I/156 Gesetz zur Regelung der Rechtsverhältnisse der unter Artikel 131 des Grundgesetzes fallenden Personen vom 11. Mai 1951
  I/544 Gesetz über die Entschädigung ehemaliger deutscher Kriegsgefangenen (Kriegsgefangenenentschädigungsgesetz) vom 30. Januar 1954
Public Record Office, Kew, England (PRO)
  FO371 General Corrrespondence of the Foreign Office: Germany, 1945–49
  FO939 Control Office for Germany and Austria: Prisoners of War
  FO944 Control Office for Germany and Austria: Finance
  FO945 Control Office for Germany and Austria: General Department
Wiener Library, Leo Baeck Institute, New York
  G8C2 Revival of Nazism: Soldiers' Leagues

Published Documents

Akten der Partei-Kanzlei der NSDAP. Rekonstruktion eines velorgegangen Bestandes. Herausgegeben vom Institut für Zeitgeschichte unter Mitwirkung von Volker Dahm, Hildegard von Kotze, Gerhard Weiher, und Reinhilde Staude. Munich: R. Oldenbourg, 1983.

Akten der Reichskanzlei. Die Regierung Hitler. Teil I, *1933/34.* 2 Bände. Herausgegeben für die Historische Kommission bei der Bayerischen Akademie der Wissenschaften von Konrad Repgen für das Bundesarchiv von Hans Booms; bearbeitet von Karl-Heinz Minuth. Boppard am Rhein: Harald Boldt, 1983.

Akten zur Vorgeschichte der Bundesrepublik Deutschland, 1945–1949. 5 Bände. Herausgegeben von der Bundesarchiv und Institut für Zeitgeschichte. Munich: R. Oldenburg, 1976–81.

Auftakt zur Ära Adenauer. Koalitionsverhandlungen und Regierungsbildung, 1949. Bearbeitet von Udo Wengst. Quellen zur Geschichte des Parlamentarismus und der politischen Parteien. Vierte Reihe: Deutschland seit 1955, Band 3. Herausgegeben von Karl Dietrich Bracher et al. Düsseldorf: Droste, 1985.

BIBLIOGRAPHY

Archives

Archiv der Deutschen Gesellschaft für Auswärtige Politik, Bonn
Archiv der sozialen Demokratie/Friedrich-Ebert-Stiftung, Bonn/Bad Godesberg
  (AdsD/FES)
  ZA-PV HQ 99 Soldatenbünde
Bundesarchiv, Koblenz (BAK)
  B106 Bundesministerium des Innern
  B136 Bundeskanzleramt
  B141 Bundesministerium der Justiz
  B149 Bundesministerium für Arbeit und Sozialordnung
  R2 Reichsfinanzministerium
  R43 Reichskanzlei
  Z1 Länderrat des amerikanischen Besatzungsgebietes
  Z13 Direktorialkanzlei des Verwaltungsrates des Vereinigten Wirtschaftsgebietes
  Z40 Zentralamt für Arbeit in der Britischen Zone
  NSD Drucksachen der NSDAP
  NS20 Kleine Erwerbungen NSDAP
  NS26 Hauptarchiv der NSDAP
  Sammlung Schumacher zur Geschichte des Nationalsozialismus
  ZSg 103 Pressausschnitt-Sammlung Lauterbach
  NL11 Nachlass Erich Rossmann
Bundesarchiv-Militärarchiv, Freiburg im Breisgau (BAF)
  BW9 Deutsche Dienstellen zur Vorbereitung der Europäischen Verteidigungsge-
    meinschaft
  N222 Nachlass Gottfried Hansen
  N528 Nachlass Johannes Friessner
  N571 Nachlass Hans von Donat
  MSg 118 Sammlung Ritter von Schramm
Institut für Zeitgeschichte, Munich (IfZ)
  Nachlass Leo Freiherr Geyr von Schweppenburg

Deutscher Bundestag
  Verhandlungen des Deutschen Bundestags. I. Wahlperiode 1949. Stenographische
    Berichte (VDB)
  Anlagen zu den Stenographische Berichten. Drucksache (DBDr)
Documents on Germany under Occupation, 1945–1954. Edited by Beate Ruhm von Oppen. London: Oxford University Press, 1955.
Die Kabinettsprotokolle der Bundesregierung. Herausgegeben für das Bundesarchiv von Hans Booms.
  Band 1 (1949), bearbeitet von Ulrich Enders und Konrad Reiser. Boppard am Rhein: Harald Boldt, 1982.
  Band 2 (1950), bearbeitet von Ulrich Enders und Konrad Reiser. Boppard am Rhein: Harald Boldt, 1984.
  Band 4 (1951), bearbeitet von Ursula Hüllbüsch. Boppard am Rhein: Harald Boldt, 1988.
  Band 5 (1952), bearbeitet von Kai von Jena. Boppard am Rhein: Harald Boldt, 1989.
  Band 6 (1953), bearbeitet von Ulrich Enders und Konrad Reiser. Boppard am Rhein: Harald Boldt, 1989.
Wörtliche Berichte und Drucksachen des Wirtschaftsrats des Vereinigten
  Wirtschaftsgebietes, 1947–1949. 6 Bände. Herausgegeben vom Institut für Zeitgeschichte und dem Deutschen Bundestag, Wissenschaftliche Dienste; bearbeitet von Christoph Weisz und Hans Woller. Munich: R. Oldenbourg, 1977.

Government and Organization Publications

Auch ein armes Vaterland kann dankbar sein. Dem deutschen Soldaten des Weltkrieges und den Seinen zugeeignet. Herausgegeben von der Reichsorganisationsleitung, Abteilung Kriegsopferversorgung. Diessen, 1932.
Bericht des Bundesvorstandes mit Protokoll der Verhandlungen des 2. Reichsbundestages, Würzburg, 11.–15. Mai. Herausgegeben vom Reichsbund der Kriegsbeschädigten, Kriegsteilnehmer, und Kriegshinterbliebenen. Berlin, [1920].
Bundesgesetzblatt.
Chronik in Daten. Der Reichsbund, 1917–1933 und 1946–1971. Reichsbund der Kriegs- und Zivilbeschädigten, Sozialrentner, und Hinterbliebenen. Bonn, 1971.
Der Dank des Vaterlandes. Rechtsbuch. Herausgegeben von der Reichsleitung der NSDAP, Org. Abt. I, Referat Kriegsopferbewegung. Düsseldorf, 1931.
Deutsche Kriegsopferversorgung.
Deutscher Soldatenbund-Kyffhäuser, e.V. Geschichte, Leitsätze, Anschriften. [1957].
Die Fackel.
Freiheit ohne Furcht. Zehn Jahre Heimkehrerverband. Verband der Heimkehrer, Kriegsgefangenen, und Vermisstenangehörigen Deutschlands. Bad Godesberg, [1960].

Der Heimkehrer.

5 Jahre Arbeit für Führer und Volk. Ein Rechenschaftsbericht über die Tätigkeit des Hauptamts für Kriegsopfer der N.S.D.A.P. und der Nationalsozialistischen Kriegsopferversorgung e.V. für die Jahre 1933–1938. Berlin, 1938.

Nationalsozialismus und Kriegsopfer. Herausgegeben von der NSDAP Reichsorganisationsleiter I, Referat Kriegsopferversorgung. Munich, [1932].

Neue Wege der deutschen Kriegsopferversorgung. Herausgegeben von der National-Sozialistischen Kriegsopferversorgung. Berlin, 1934.

Der Notweg.

Politische Bildung im Verband der Heimkehrer Deutschlands: 200 Diskussionswochen, 1954–1977. Auf dem Weg nach Europa. Die politische Bildungsarbeit des Verbandes der Heimkehrer, Kriegsgefangenen und Vermisstenangehörigen Deutschlands e.V. Schriftenreihe des VdH, Nr. 60/1977. Bonn/Bad Godesberg, 1977.

Protokoll über Einigungsverhandlungen der Kriegsbeschädigten- und Kriegshinterbliebenen-Organisationen am 16. und 17. April in Weimar. Herausgegeben vom Reichsbund der Kriegsbeschädigten, Kriegsteilnehmer, und Kriegshinterbliebenen. Berlin, [1921].

Der Reichsbund.

Die Rückläufigkeit der Versorgung und Fürsorge für die Kriegsopfer im Zeichen der Notverordnung. Herausgegeben vom Reichsbund der Kriegsbeschädigten, Kriegsteilnehmer, und Kriegshinterbliebenen. Berlin, 1932.

Statistisches Jahrbuch.

Die Versorgung der Kriegsopfer in der Bundesrepublik Deutschland (Das Bundesversorgungsgesetz) Stand 31.1.1952. Herausgegeben von der Bundesregierung. Schriftenreihe des BfA. Bonn, [1952].

Die Versorgung der Kriegsopfer in der Bundesrepublik Deutschland (Das Bundesversorgungsgesetz) Stand 30.9.1952. Herausgegeben vom Presse- und Informationsamt der Bundesregierung. Bonn, [1952].

Secondary Works

Abenheim, Donald. *Reforging the Iron Cross: The Search for Tradition in the West German Armed Forces.* Princeton: Princeton University Press, 1988.

Absolon, Rudolf. *Die Wehrmacht im Dritten Reich.* Schriften des Bundesarchivs, 16. 4 Bände. Boppard am Rhein: Harald Boldt, 1969–79.

Allen, William S. "The Appeal of Fascism and the Problem of National Disintegration." In *Reappraisals of Fascism*, edited by Henry Ashby Turner, Jr. New York: New Viewpoints, 1975.

Ambrose, Stephan E. "Ike and the Disappearing Atrocities." *New York Times Book Review*, 24 February 1991.

Anfänge westdeutscher Sicherheitspolitik, 1945–56. Herausgegeben vom Militärgeschichtlichen Forschungsamt. Band 1, *Von der Kapitulation bis zum Pleven-Plan.* Munich:

R. Oldenbourg Verlag, 1982. Band 2, *Die EVG-Phase*. Munich: R. Oldenbourg Verlag, 1990.

Aspekte der deutschen Wiederbewaffnung bis 1955. Militärgeschichte seit 1945, Band 1. Herausgegeben vom Militärgeschichtlichen Forschungsamt. Boppard am Rhein: Harald Boldt Verlag, 1975.

Bach, Julian. *America's Germany: An Account of the Occupation*. New York: Random House, 1946.

Bacque, James. *Other Losses: An Investigation into the Mass Deaths of German Prisoners of War at the Hands of the French and Americans after World War II*. Toronto: Stoddart, 1989.

Baird, Jay W. *The Mythical World of Nazi War Propaganda, 1939–1945*. Minneapolis: University of Minnesota Press, 1974.

———. *To Die for Germany: Heroes in the Nazi Pantheon*. Bloomington: Indiana University Press, 1990.

Baring, Arnulf. *Im Anfang war Adenauer. Die Entstehung der Kanzlerdemokratie*. Munich: Deutscher Taschenbuch Verlag, 1982.

Bartholomäi, Reinhart, et al., eds. *Sozialpolitik nach 1945. Geschichte und Analysen*. Bonn: Verlag Neue Gesellschaft, 1977.

Bartov, Omer. *The Eastern Front, 1941–1945: German Troops and the Barbarisation of Warfare*. New York: St. Martin's Press, 1986.

———. *Hitler's Army: Soldiers, Nazis, and War in the Third Reich*. New York: Oxford University Press, 1991.

Beck, Earl R. *Under the Bombs: The German Home Front, 1942–1945*. Lexington: University of Kentucky Press, 1986.

Becker, Hermann-Josef. *Die Beschäftigung Schwerbeschädigter*. Sozialpolitik in Deutschland, Band 4. Stuttgart: Kohlhammer Verlag, 1961.

Becker, Winfried, ed. *Die Kapitulation von 1945 und der Neubeginn in Deutschland*. Cologne: Böhlau Verlag, 1987.

Benz, Wolfgang. "Versuche zur Reform des öffentlichen Dienstes in Deutschland, 1945–1952." *Vierteljahrshefte für Zeitgeschichte* 29/2 (April 1981).

Berger, Suzanne D., ed. *Organizing Interests in Western Europe: Pluralism, Corporatism, and the Transformation of Politics*. Cambridge: Cambridge University Press, 1981.

Berghahn, Volker R. *Der Stahlhelm, Bund der Frontsoldaten, 1918–1935*. Düsseldorf: Droste, 1966.

Bessel, Richard. "The Great War in German Memory: The Soldiers of the First World War, Demobilization, and Weimar Political Culture." *German History* 6/1 (1988).

Blücher, Fritz. "Financial Situation and Currency Reform in Germany." *Annals* 260 (November 1948).

Borgert, Heinz-Ludiger. "Zur Entstehung, Entwicklung und Struktur der Dienstgruppen in der britischen und amerikanischen Besatzungszone Westdeutschlands, 1945–1950." In *Dienstgruppen und westdeutscher Verteidigungsbeitrag*.

Vorüberlegungen zur Bewaffnung der Bundesrepublik Deutschland. Militärgeschichte seit 1945, Band 6. Herausgegeben vom Militärgeschichtlichen Forschungsamt. Boppard am Rhein: Harald Boldt, 1982.

Botting, Douglas. *From the Ruins of the Reich: Germany, 1945–1949.* New York: Crown, 1985.

Brecht, Arnold. "Personnel Management." In *Governing Postwar Germany,* edited by Edward H. Lichtfield et al. Vol. 1. Ithaca, N.Y.: Cornell University Press, 1953.

Breitling, Rupert. *Die Verbände in der Bundesrepublik. Ihre Arten und ihre Wirkungsweise.* Meisenheim am Glan: Verlag Anton Hain, 1955.

Broszat, Martin. *The Hitler State: The Foundation and Development of the Internal Structure of the Third Reich.* London: Longman, 1981.

Buchheim, Hans. "Die Eingliederung des 'Stahlhelms' in die SA." In *Gutachten des Institutes für Zeitgeschichte.* Band 1. Munich: Selbstverlag des Instituts für Zeitgeschichte, 1958.

———. "Kyffhäuserbund und SA." In *Gutachten des Institutes für Zeitgeschichte.* Band 1. Munich: Selbstverlag des Instituts für Zeitgeschichte, 1958.

Buscher, Frank M. "The U.S. High Commission and German Nationalism, 1949–52." *Central European History* 23/1 (March 1990).

Campbell, Joan. *Joy in Work, German Work: The National Debate, 1800–1945.* Princeton: Princeton University Press, 1989.

Caplan, Jane. *Government without Administration: State and Civil Service in Weimar and Nazi Germany.* Oxford: Oxford University Press, 1988.

Chickering, Roger. *Imperial Germany and a World without War: The Peace Movement and German Society, 1892–1914.* Princeton: Princeton University Press, 1975.

Childers, Thomas. "Inflation and Electoral Politics in Germany, 1919–29." In *Inflation through the Ages: Economic, Social, Psychological, and Historical Aspects,* edited by Nathan Schmukler and Edward Marcus. New York: Brooklyn College Press, 1983.

———. *The Nazi Voter: The Social Foundations of Fascism in Germany, 1919–33.* Chapel Hill: University of North Carolina Press, 1983.

Coetzee, Marilyn Shevin. *The German Army League: Popular Nationalism in Wilhelmine Germany.* Oxford: Oxford University Press, 1990.

Davidson, Eugene. *The Trial of the Germans: An Account of the Twenty-Two Defendants before the International Military Tribunal at Nuremburg.* New York: Collier, 1966.

Deist, Wilhelm. "Der militärische Zusammenbruch des Kaiserreichs. Zur Realität der 'Dolchstosslegende.'" In *Das Unrechtsregime. Internationale Forschung über den Nationalsozialismus. Festschrift für Werner Jochmann zum 65. Geburtstag,* herausgegeben von Ursula Büttner. Band 1. Hamburg: Christians, 1986.

Devine, Edward T. *Disabled Soldiers and Sailors Pensions and Training.* Carnegie Endowment for International Peace, Preliminary Economic Studies of the War, no. 12. New York: Oxford University Press, 1919.

De Witt, Thomas Erich Joachim. "The Nazi Party and Social Welfare, 1919–1939." Ph.D. dissertation, University of Virginia, 1972.

Diehl, James M. "Germany: Veterans' Politics under Three Flags." In *The War Generation: Veterans of the First World War*, edited by Stephen R. Ward. Port Washington, N.Y.: Kennikat Press, 1975.

———. "The Organization of German Veterans, 1917–1919." *Archiv für Sozialgeschichte* 11 (1971).

———. *Paramilitary Politics in Weimar Germany*. Bloomington: Indiana University Press, 1977.

———. "Social Legislation and the Legitimation of the Federal Republic." Paper presented at the conference, "A Framework for Democracy: Forty Years of Experience with the Grundgesetz of the Federal Republic of Germany," Philadelphia, April 1989. Cambridge: Cambridge University Press, forthcoming.

———. "Victors or Victims?: Disabled Veterans in the Third Reich." *Journal of Modern History* 59/4 (December 1987).

Donner, Wolf. *Die sozial- und staatspolitische Tätigkeit der Kriegsopferverbände. Ein Beitrag zur Verbandsdiskussion*. Berlin: Duncken und Humblot, 1960.

Dornberg, John. *Schizophrenic Germany*. New York: Macmillan, 1961.

Draeger, Kurt. *Heimkehrer-Recht. Heimkehrergesetz, Kriegsgefangenenentschädigungsgesetz, Häftlingshilfegesetz und sonstiges Heimkehrerrecht*. Berlin: Franz Vahlen, 1956.

Drummond, Gordon D. *The German Social Democrats in Opposition: The Case against Rearmament*. Norman: University of Oklahoma Press, 1982.

Eksteins, Modris. *Rites of Spring: The Great War and the Birth of the Modern Age*. New York: Doubleday, 1989.

Elliott, Christopher James. "Ex-Servicemen's Organisations and the Weimar Republic." Ph.D. dissertation, London University, 1971.

———. "The Kriegervereine and the Weimar Republic." *Journal of Contemporary History* 10/1 (January 1975).

Eschenburg, Theodor. "Der bürokratische Rückhalt." In *Die zweite Republik. 25 Jahre Bundesrepublik Deutschland—Eine Bilanz*, herausgegeben von Richard Löwenthal und Hans-Peter Schwarz. Stuttgart: Seewald, 1974.

Fischbach, Oskar Georg. *Fürsorge- und Versorgungsgesetz und Einsatzfürsorge- und Versorgungsgesetz für die ehemaligen Angehörigen der Wehrmacht und ihre Hinterbliebenen*. Berlin: Walter de Gruyter, 1943.

Foerster, Roland G. "Innenpolitische Aspekte der Sicherheit Westdeutschlands." In *Anfänge westdeutscher Sicherheitspolitik, 1945–56*, herausgegeben vom Militärgeschichtlichen Forschungsamt. Band 1, *Von der Kapitulation bis zum Pleven-Plan*. Munich: R. Oldenbourg Verlag, 1982.

Förster, Jürgen. "Vom Führerheer der Republik zur nationalsozialistischen Volksarmee. Zum Strukturwandel der Wehrmacht, 1935–1945." In *Deutschland in Europa: Kontinuität und Bruch. Gedenkschrift für Andreas Hillgruber*, herausgegeben von Jost Dülffer et al. Frankfurt am Main: Propyläen, 1990.

Frey, Herbert. "The German Guilt Question after the Second World War: An Overview." Ph.D. dissertation, University of Washington, 1979.

Fricke, Dieter, et al., eds. *Die bürgerlichen Parteien in Deutschland. Handbuch der Geschichte der bürgerlichen Parteien und anderer bürgerlicher Interessenorganisationen vom Vormärz bis zum Jahre 1945*. 2 Bände. Leipzig: VEB Bibliographisches Institut, 1968.

Fried, Hans Ernst. "Fascist Militarization and Education for War." In *The Third Reich*. International Council for Philosophy and Humanistic Studies. London: Wiedenfeld and Nicholson, 1955.

———. *The Guilt of the German Army*. New York: Macmillan, 1942.

Fritzsche, Peter. *Rehearsals for Fascism: Populism and Political Mobilization in Weimar Germany*. New York: Oxford University Press, 1990.

Geyer, Michael. "German Strategy in the Age of Machine Warfare." In *Makers of Modern Strategy from Machiavelli to the Nuclear Age*, edited by Peter Paret. Princeton: Princeton University Press, 1986.

———. "Ein Vorbote des Wohlfahrtsstaates. Die Kriegsopferversorgung in Frankreich, Deutschland und Grossbritannien nach dem Ersten Weltkrieg." *Geschichte und Gesellschaft* 9/2 (1983).

Gilbert, Sandra M. "Soldier's Heart: Literary Men, Literary Women, and the Great War." In *Behind the Lines: Gender and the Two World Wars*, edited by Margaret Randolph Higonnet et al. New Haven: Yale University Press, 1987.

Gimbel, John. *The American Occupation of Germany: Politics and the Military, 1945–1949*. Stanford: Stanford University Press, 1968.

Gollbach, Michael. *Die Wiederkehr des Weltkrieges in der Literatur. Zu den Frontromanen der späten Zwanziger Jahre*. Kronberg/Ts.: Scriptor Verlag, 1978.

Greiner, Christian. "Die alliierten militärstrategischen Planungen zur Verteidigung Westeuropas, 1947–1950." In *Anfänge westdeutscher Sicherheitspolitik, 1945–56*, herausgegeben vom Militärgeschichtlichen Forschungsamt. Band 1, *Von der Kapitulation bis zum Pleven-Plan*. Munich: R. Oldenbourg Verlag, 1982.

Grosser, Alfred. *Germany in Our Time: A Political History of the Post-war Years*. New York: Praeger, 1971.

Haffner, Sebastian. *The Meaning of Hitler*. Cambridge: Harvard University Press, 1983.

Hancock, M. Donald. *West Germany: The Politics of Democratic Corporatism*. Chatham, N.J.: Chatham House, 1989.

Hardach, Karl. *The Political Economy of Germany in the Twentieth Century*. Berkeley: University of California Press, 1980.

Hartrich, Edwin. *The Fourth and Richest Reich: How the Germans Conquered the Post-war World*. New York: Macmillan, 1980.

Hartwich, Hans-Hermann. *Sozialstaatspostulat und gesellschaftlicher status quo*. Cologne: Westdeutscher Verlag, 1970.

Hausen, Karin. "The German Nation's Obligations to the Heroes' Widows of

World War I." In *Behind the Lines: Gender and the Two World Wars*, edited by Margaret Randolph Higonnet et al. New Haven: Yale University Press, 1987.

Heinz, Grete, and Agnes F. Peterson, eds. *NSDAP Hauptarchiv: Guides to the Hoover Institution Microfilm Collection*. Hoover Institution Bibliographical Service, vol. 17. Stanford: Hoover Institution, 1964.

Herzstein, Robert E. *The War That Hitler Won: The Most Infamous Propaganda Campaign in History*. New York: G. P. Putnam, 1978.

Hiden, John, and John Farquharson. *Explaining Hitler's Germany: Historians and the Third Reich*. Totowa, N.J.: Barnes and Noble, 1983.

Hilger, Dietrich. "Die mobilisierte Gesellschaft." In *Die zweite Republik. 25 Jahre Bundesrepublik Deutschland—Eine Bilanz*, herausgegeben von Richard Löwenthal und Hans-Peter Schwarz. Stuttgart: Seewald, 1974.

Hiller von Gaertringen, Friedrich Freiherr. "'Dolchstoss'-Diskussion und 'Dolchstosslegende' im Wandel von vier Jahrzehnten." In *Geschichte und Gegenwartsbewusstsein. Historische Betrachtungen und Untersuchungen. Festschrift für Hans Rothfels*, herausgegeben von Waldemar Besson et al. Göttingen: Vandenhoeck and Ruprecht, 1963.

Hockerts, Hans Günter. "Integration der Gesellschaft." In *Entscheidung für den Westen*, herausgegeben von Manfred Funke. Bonn: Bouvier, 1988.

———. *Sozialpolitische Entscheidungen im Nachkriegsdeutschland. Alliierte und deutsche Sozialversicherungspolitik 1945 bis 1957*. Stuttgart: Klett-Cotta, 1980.

Höhn, Reinhard. *Sozialismus und Heer*. Band 3. Bad Harzburg: Verlag für Wissenschaft, Wirtschaft, und Technik, 1969.

Hornung, Klaus. *Der Jungdeutsche Orden*. Düsseldorf: Droste, 1958.

Hudemann, Rainer. *Sozialpolitik im deutschen Südwesten zwischen Tradition und Neuordnung, 1945–1953. Sozialversicherung und Kriegsopferversorgung im Rahmen französischer Besatzungspolitik*. Mainz: v. Hase und Koehler Verlag, 1988.

Jacobsen, Hans-Adolf. "Zur Rolle der öffentlichen Meinung bei der Debatte um die Wiederbewaffnung, 1950–1955." In *Aspekte der deutschen Wiederbewaffnung bis 1955*. Militärgeschichte seit 1945, Band 1. Herausgegeben vom Militärgeschichtlichen Forschungsamt. Boppard am Rhein: Harald Boldt Verlag, 1975.

Jenke, Manfred. *Verschwörung von Rechts? Ein Bericht über den Rechtsradikalismus in Deutschland nach 1945*. Berlin: Colloquium Verlag, 1961.

Kater, Michael. "Hitler in Social Context." *Central European History* 14/3 (September 1981).

———. *The Nazi Party: A Social Profile of Members and Leaders, 1919–1945*. Cambridge: Harvard University Press, 1983.

Kayser, Walther. *Die nationalpolitische Bedeutung der Wehrmacht*. Hamburg: Hanseatische Verlagsanstalt, 1937.

Kehr, Eckart. "Zur Genesis des Königlich Preussischen Reserveoffiziers." In Eckart Kehr, *Der Primat der Innenpolitik. Gesammelte Aufsätze zur preussisch-deutschen Sozialgeschichte im 19. und 20. Jahrhundert*, herausgegeben und eingeleitet von Hans-Ulrich Wehler. Berlin: De Gruyter, 1965.

Kershaw, Ian. *Popular Opinion and Political Dissent in the Third Reich: Bavaria, 1933–1945*. New York: Oxford University Press, 1983.

Kitchen, Martin. *The German Officer Corps, 1890–1914*. London: Oxford University Press, 1968.

Kleine, Rudolf. "Die Geschichte des Reichsbundes in ihrer Bedeutung für die Nachkriegsentwicklung der Sozialpolitik." In *Sozialpolitik nach 1945. Geschichte und Analysen*, herausgegeben von Reinhart Bartholomäi et al. Bonn: Verlag Neue Gesellschaft, 1977.

Klessmann, Christoph. *Die doppelte Staatsgründung. Deutsche Geschichte, 1945–1955*. Bonn: Bundeszentrale für politische Bildung, 1986.

Klietmann, Kurt-Gerhard. "Die deutsche Ehrendenkmünze des Weltkrieges, 1917–1934, Deutsche Ehrenlegion." *Ordenskunde* Nr. 44 (1975).

———. "The German Honor Medal of World War I." *Medal Collector* 20/4 (April 1969).

Klotzbücher, Alois. "Der politische Weg des Stahlhelm, Bund der Frontsoldaten, in der Weimarer Republik. Ein Beitrag zur Geschichte der 'Nationalen Opposition,' 1918–1933." Inaugural dissertation, Friedrich-Alexander-Universität, Erlangen-Nürnberg, 1964.

"Die Körperbehinderten in Bundesgebiet. Ergebnisse der Volkszählung vom 13. September 1950." *Wirtschaft und Statistik* (December 1952).

Kreikamp, Hans-Dieter. "Zur Entstehung des Entschädigungsgesetzes der amerikanischen Besatzungszone." In *Wiedergutmachung in der Bundesrepublik Deutschland*, herausgegeben von Ludolf Herbst und Constantin Goschler. Munich: R. Oldenbourg, 1989.

Kris, Ernst, and Hans Speier. *German Radio Propaganda: Report on Home Broadcasts during the War*. London: Oxford University Press, 1944.

Kroener, Bernhard R. "Auf dem Weg zu einer 'nationalsozialistischen Volksarmee.' Die soziale Öffnung des Heeresoffizierskorps im Zweiten Weltkrieg." In *Von Stalingrad zur Währungsreform. Zur Sozialgeschichte des Umbruchs in Deutschland*, herausgegeben von Martin Broszat et al. Munich: R. Oldenbourg Verlag, 1988.

Large, David C. *Germans to the Front: West German Rearmament in the Adenauer Era*. Forthcoming.

———. "'A Gift to the German Future?': The Anti-Nazi Resistance Movement and West German Rearmament." *German Studies Review* 7/3 (October 1984).

———. "Reckoning without the Past: The HIAG of the Waffen-SS and the Politics of Rehabilitation in the Bonn Republic, 1950–1961." *Journal of Modern History* 59/1 (March 1987).

———. "Uses of the Past: The Anti-Nazi Resistance Legacy in the Federal Republic of Germany." In *Contending with Hitler: Varieties of German Resistance in the Third Reich*. Cambridge: Cambridge University Press, 1992.

Leed, Eric J. *No Man's Land: Combat and Identity in World War I*. Cambridge: Cambridge University Press, 1979.

Lenz, Otto. *Im Zentrum der Macht. Das Tagebuch von Staatssekretär Lenz, 1951–1953*, bearbeitet von Klaus Gotto et al. Forschung und Quellen zur Zeitgeschichte. Im Auftrag der Konrad-Adenauer-Stiftung, herausgegeben von Klaus Gotto et al., Band 11. Düsseldorf: Droste, 1989.

Lepsius, M. Rainer. "Parteiensystem und Sozialstruktur. Zum Problem der Demokratisierung der deutschen Gesellschaft." In *Wirtschaft, Geschichte und Wirtschaftsgeschichte. Festschrift zum 65. Geburtstag von Friedrich Lütge*, herausgegeben von Wilhelm Abel et al. Stuttgart: G. Fischer, 1966.

Linton, Derek S. *Who Has the Youth Has the Future: The Campaign to Save Young Workers in Imperial Germany*. Cambridge: Cambridge University Press, 1991.

Löwenthal, Richard. "Prolog. Dauer und Verwandlung." In *Die zweite Republik. 25 Jahre Bundesrepublik Deutschland—Eine Bilanz*, herausgegeben von Richard Löwenthal und Hans-Peter Schwarz. Stuttgart: Seewald, 1974.

Lurz, Meinhold. *Kriegerdenkmäler in Deutschland*. Band 4, *Weimarer Republik*. Band 5, *Drittes Reich*. Band 6, *Bundesrepublik*. Heidelberg: Esprint, Druckerei, und Verlag, 1985–87.

McRandle, James H. *The Track of the Wolf: Essays on National Socialism and Its Leader Adolf Hitler*. Evanston, Ill.: Northwestern University Press, 1965.

Maier, Charles S. *Recasting Bourgeois Europe: Stabilization in France, Germany, and Italy in the Decade after World War I*. Princeton: Princeton University Press, 1975.

———. *In Search of Stability: Explorations in Historical Political Economy*. Cambridge: Cambridge University Press, 1987.

Marshall, Barbara. "German Attitudes to British Military Government, 1945–47." *Journal of Contemporary History* 15 (1980).

———. "German Reactions to Military Defeat, 1945–1947: The British View." In *Germany in the Age of Total War*, edited by Volker R. Berghahn and Martin Kitchen. London: Croom Helm, 1981.

Mason, Tim. "The Legacy of 1918 for National Socialism." In *German Democracy and the Triumph of Hitler*, edited by Anthony Nicholls and Erich Matthias. New York: St. Martins, 1971.

Mayer, Arno J. *Political Origins of the New Diplomacy, 1917–1918*. New York: Random House, 1970.

Meinecke, Friedrich. *The German Catastrophe: Reflections and Recollections*. Boston: Beacon Press, 1963.

Merritt, Ann J., and Richard L. Merritt. *Public Opinion in Occupied Germany: The OMGUS Surveys, 1945–1949*. Urbana: University of Illinois Press, 1970.

Messerschmidt, Manfred. *Die Wehrmacht im NS-Staat. Zeit der Indoktrination*. Hamburg: R. v. Decker's Verlag, G. Schenk, 1969.

Meyer, Georg. "Soldaten ohne Armee." In *Von Stalingrad zur Währungsreform. Zur Sozialgeschichte des Umbruchs in Deutschland*, herausgegeben von Martin Broszat et al. Munich: R. Oldenbourg Verlag, 1988.

———. "Zur Situation der deutschen militärischen Führungsschicht im Vorfeld des westdeutschen Verteidigungsbeitrages, 1945–50/51." In *Anfänge westdeutscher Sicherheitspolitik, 1945–56*, herausgegeben vom Militärgeschichtlichen Forschungsamt. Band 1, *Von der Kapitulation bis zum Pleven-Plan*. Munich: R. Oldenbourg Verlag, 1982.

Meyer, Sibylle, and Eva Schulze. *Von Liebe sprach damals keiner. Familienalltag in der Nachkriegszeit*. Munich: C. H. Beck, 1985.

Mohler, Armin. *Die Konservative Revolution in Deutschland, 1918–1932. Grundriss ihrer Weltanschauungen*. Stuttgart: Friedrich Vorwerk, 1950.

Montgomery, John D. *Forced to Be Free: The Artificial Revolutions in Germany and Japan*. Chicago: University of Chicago Press, 1957.

Morrison, Wilbur H. *Fortress without a Roof: The Allied Bombing of the Third Reich*. New York: St. Martin's Press, 1982.

Mosse, George L. *Fallen Soldiers: Reshaping the Memory of the World Wars*. New York: Oxford University Press, 1990.

Müller, Rolf-Dieter. *Hitlers Ostkrieg und die deutsche Siedlungspolitik. Die Zusammenarbeit von Wehrmacht, Wirtschaft und SS*. Frankfurt am Main: Fischer Taschenbuch Verlag, 1991.

Nahm, Peter Paul. *Der Lastenausgleich*. Sozialpolitik in Deutschland, Band 50. Stuttgart: Kohlhammer Verlag, 1961.

———. "Lastenausgleich und Integration der Vertriebenen und Geflüchteten." In *Die zweite Republik. 25 Jahre Bundesrepublik Deutschland—Eine Bilanz*, herausgegeben von Richard Löwenthal und Hans-Peter Schwarz. Stuttgart: Seewald, 1974.

Niethammer, Lutz. "Zum Verhältnis von Reform und Rekonstruktion in der US-Zone am Beispiel der Neuordnung des öffentlichen Dienstes." *Vierteljahrshefte für Zeitgeschichte* 21/2 (April 1973).

———. "Zum Verhältnis von Reform und Rekonstruktion am Beispiel der Reform des öffentlichen Dienstes." In *Die Bundesrepublik Deutschland. Entstehung, Entwicklung, Struktur*, herausgegeben von Wolf-Dieter Narr und Dietrich Thränhardt. Königstein/Ts., 1984.

Noakes, Jeremy. *The Nazi Party in Lower Saxony, 1921–1933*. London: Oxford University Press, 1971.

Noakes, Jeremy, and G. Pridham. *Nazism, 1919–1945*. Vol. 1, *The Rise to Power*. Exeter: University of Exeter, 1983.

Nolte, Ernst. *Three Faces of Fascism*. New York: Holt, Rinehart, and Winston, 1966.

Nutz, Walter. "Der Krieg als Abenteuer und Idylle. Landser-Hefte und triviale Kriegsromane." In *Gegenwartsliteratur und Drittes Reich. Deutsche Autoren in der Auseinandersetzung mit der Vergangenheit*, herausgegeben von Hans Wagener. Stuttgart: Philipp Reclam jun., 1977.

Oberlindober, Hanns. *Ehre und Recht für die deutschen Kriegsopfer*. Berlin: Verlag Deutscher Kriegsopferversorgung, 1933.

Orlow, Dietrich. *History of the Nazi Party, 1933–1945*. Pittsburgh: University of Pittsburgh Press, 1973.

Osteraas, Leena Kitzberg. "The New Nationalists: Front Generation Spokesmen in the Weimar Republic." Ph.D. dissertation, Columbia University, 1972.

Peterson, Edward N. *The American Occupation of Germany: Retreat to Victory*. Detroit: Wayne State University Press, 1978.

Peukert, Detlev J. K. *Inside Nazi Germany: Conformity, Opposition, and Racism in Everyday Life*. New Haven: Yale University Press, 1987.

Pfeiler, Wilhelm Karl. *War and the German Mind: The Testimony of Men of Fiction Who Fought at the Front*. New York: Columbia University Press, 1941.

Plank, Ludwig. "Die Entstehung der Kriegsopferzeitschrift in Deutschland." Inaugural dissertation, Ludwig-Maximilians-Universität, Munich, 1950.

Posse, Ernst. *Die politischen Kämpfbünde Deutschlands*. Berlin: Junker und Dünnhaupt, 1931.

Prowe, Diethelm. "Economic Democracy in Post–World War II Germany: Corporatist Crisis Response, 1945–1948." *Journal of Modern History* 57 (September 1985).

———. "Socialism as a Crisis Response: Socialization and the Escape from Poverty and Power in Post–World War II Germany." *German Studies Review* 15/1 (February 1992).

Prümm, Karl. *Die Literatur des soldatischen Nationalismus in der 20er Jahre, 1919–1933*. Kronberg/Ts., 1974.

Rabinowitch, Alexander. "The Petrograd Garrison and the Bolshevik Seizure of Power." In *Revolution and Politics in Russia: Essays in Memory of B. I. Nicolaevsky*, edited by Alexander Rabinowitch and Janet Rabinowitch. Bloomington: Indiana University Press, 1972.

Rautenberg, Hans-Jürgen. "Zur Standortsbestimmung für künftige deutsche Streitkräfte, 1945–1956." In *Anfänge westdeutscher Sicherheitspolitik, 1945–56*, herausgegeben vom Militärgeschichtlichen Forschungsamt. Band 1, *Von der Kapitulation bis zum Pleven-Plan*. Munich: R. Oldenbourg Verlag, 1982.

Rautenberg, Hans-Jürgen, and Norbert Wiggershaus. "Die 'Himmeroder Denkschrift' vom Oktober 1950. Politische und militärische Überlegungen für einen Beitrag der Bundesrepublik zur westeuropäischen Verteidigung." *Militärgeschichtliche Mitteilungen*, 1977/1.

Reinhard, Wilhelm. "Der N.S.-Reichskriegerbund." In *Das Dritte Reich im Aufbau*, herausgegeben von Paul Meier-Benneckenstein. Band 3. Berlin: Junker und Dünnhaupt, 1939.

Ribbe, Wolfgang. "Flaggenstreit und Heiliger Hain. Bemerkungen zur nationalen Symbolik in der Weimarer Republik." In *Aus Theorie und Praxis der Geschichtswissenschaft. Festschrift für Hans Herzfeld zum 80. Geburtstag*, herausgegeben von Dietrich Kurze. Berlin: Walter de Gruyter, 1982.

Riggert, Ernst. "Zur Lage in den deutschen Soldatenbünden." *Gewerkschaftliche Monatshefte*, January 1953.

Rodnick, David. *Postwar Germans: An Anthropologist's Account*. New Haven: Yale University Press, 1948.

Rogalla von Bieberstein, Johannes. "Adel und Revolution 1918/1919." In *Mentalitäten und Lebensverhältnisse. Beispiele aus der Sozialgeschichte der Neuzeit. Rudolf Vierhaus zum 60. Geburtstag*. Göttingen: Vandenhoeck and Ruprecht, 1982.

Rohe, Karl. *Das Reichsbanner Schwarz Rot Gold. Ein Beitrag zur Geschichte und Struktur der politischen Kampverbände zur Zeit der Weimarer Republik.* Düsseldorf: Droste, 1966.

Röhm, Ernst. *Geschichte eines Hochverräters.* Munich: Franz Eher, 1928–34.

Ruhl, Klaus-Jörg. *Frauen in der Nachkriegszeit, 1945–1963.* Munich: Deutscher Taschenbuch Verlag, 1988.

Rühland, Helmut. "Entwicklung, heutige Gestaltung und Problematik der Kriegsopferversorgung in der Bundesrepublik Deutschland." Inaugural dissertation, Universität Köln, 1957.

Sauer, Wolfgang. "National Socialism: Totalitarianism or Fascism?" *American Historical Review* 73 (1963).

Saul, Klaus. "Der 'Deutsche Kriegerbund.' Zur innenpolitischen Funktion eines 'nationalen' Verbandes im kaiserlichen Deutschland." *Militärgeschichtliche Mitteilungen,* 1969/1.

———. "Der Kampf um die Jugend zwischen Volksschule und Kaserne. Ein Beitrag zur 'Jungendpflege' im Wilhelminischen Reich, 1890–1914." *Militärgeschichtliche Mitteilungen,* 1971/1.

Schenck zu Schweinsberg, Krafft Freiherr. "Die Soldatenverbände in der Bundesrepublik." In *Studien zur politischen und gesellschaftlichen Situation der Bundeswehr,* herausgegeben von Georg Picht. Witten: Eckart Verlag, 1965.

Schillinger, Reinhold. *Der Entscheidungsprozess beim Lastenausgleich, 1945–1952.* St. Katharinen: Scripta Mercaturae Verlag, 1985.

Schmitter, Philippe C., and Gerhard Lehmbruch, eds. *Trends toward Corporatist Intermediation.* Beverly Hills, Calif.: Sage, 1979.

Schoenbaum, David. *Hitler's Social Revolution: Class and Status in Nazi Germany, 1933–1939.* New York: Norton, 1966.

Schönleiter, Waldemar. *Die Kriegsopferversorgung.* Sozialpolitik in Deutschland, Band 42. Stuttgart: Kohlhammer Verlag, 1961.

Schröder, Hans. *Das End der Dolchstosslegende. Geschichtliche Erkenntnis und politische Verantwortung.* Hamburg: Hammerich und Lesser, 1946.

Schubert, Klaus von. *Wiederbewaffnung und Westintegration. Die innere Auseinandersetzung um die militärische und aussenpolitische Orientierung der Bundesrepublik, 1950–1952.* Stuttgart: Deutsche Verlags-Anstalt, 1970.

Schüddekopf, Otto-Ernst. *Das Heer und die Republik. Quellen zur Politik der Reichswehrführung, 1918 bis 1933.* Hannover: Norddeutsche Verlagsanstalt O. Goedel, 1955.

———. *Linke Leute von Rechts. Nationalbolschewismus in Deutschland von 1918 bis 1933.* Stuttgart: Kohlhammer Verlag, 1960.

Schwartz, Thomas Alan. "Die Begnadigung deutscher Kriegsverbrecher. John J. McCloy und die Häftlinge von Landsberg." *Vierteljahrshefte für Zeitgeschichte* 38/3 (July 1990).

Schwarz, Hans-Peter. *Die Ära Adenauer. Gründerjahre der Republik, 1949–1957.* Geschichte der Bundesrepublik Deutschland, Band 2, herausgegeben von Karl Dietrich Bracher et al. Stuttgart: Deutsche Verlags-Anstalt, 1981.

Schwede-Coburg, Franz. "Der Reichstreubund ehemaliger Berufssoldaten." In *Das Dritte Reich im Aufbau*, herausgegeben von Paul Meier-Benneckenstein. Band 3. Berlin: Junker und Dünnhaupt, 1939.

Schweitzer, Arthur. *Big Business in the Third Reich*. Bloomington: Indiana University Press, 1964.

―――. *Die Nazifizierung des Mittelstandes*. Stuttgart: Ferdinand Enke Verlag, 1970.

Seldte, Franz. *Sozialpolitik im Dritten Reich, 1933–1938*. Munich: C. H. Beck'sche Verlagsbuchhandlung, 1939.

Short, K. R. M., and Stephan Dolzel, eds. *Hitler's Fall: The Newsreel Witness*. London: Croom Helm, 1988.

Siegel, Mark Alan. "The National Socialist People's Welfare Organization, 1933–1939: The Political Manipulation of Welfare." Ph.D. dissertation, University of Cincinnati, 1976.

Smelser, Ronald. *Robert Ley: Hitler's Labor Front Leader*. Oxford: Berg, 1988.

Smith, Arthur L. *Heimkehr aus dem Zweiten Weltkrieg. Die Entlassung der deutschen Kriegsgefangenen*. Stuttgart: Deutsche Verlags-Anstalt, 1985.

Sontheimer, Kurt. *Antidemokratisches Denken in der Weimarer Republik. Die politischen Ideen des deutschen Nationalismus zwischen 1918 und 1933*. Munich: Nymphenburger, 1962.

Speer, Albert. *Inside the Third Reich*. New York: Avon, 1971.

Speier, Hans. *From the Ashes of Defeat: A Journal from Germany, 1945–1955*. Amherst: University of Massachusetts Press, 1981.

Staib, Reinhold W. "Das deutsche Versorgungsrecht während des Krieges, 1939–1945, und seine Entwicklung nach dem 8. Mai 1945." Inaugural dissertation, Eberhard Karls-Universität, Tübingen, 1951.

Stegemann, Dirk. "Zwischen Repression und Manipulation. Konservative Machteliten und Arbeiter- und Angestelltenbewegung, 1910–1918." *Archiv für Sozialgeschichte* 12 (1972).

Steinert, Marlis. *Hitlers Krieg und die Deutschen*. Düsseldorf: Econ, 1970.

Stern, Fritz. "The Political Consequences of the Unpolitical German." In *The Failure of Illiberalism: Essays on the Political Culture of Modern Germany*. New York: Knopf, 1972.

Stern, Joseph Peter. *Ernst Jünger*. New Haven: Yale University Press, 1953.

Stolper, Gustav, et al. *The German Economy: 1870 to the Present*. New York: Harcourt, Brace and World, 1967.

Storch, Anton. *Abgeordnete des deutschen Bundestages. Aufzeichnungen und Erinnerungen*. Band 2. Boppard am Rhein: Harald Boldt Verlag, 1983.

Streit, Christian. *Keine Kameraden. Die Wehrmacht und die sowjetischen Kriegsgefangenen, 1941–1945*. Stuttgart: Deutsche Verlags-Anstalt, 1978.

Struve, Walter. *Elites against Democracy: Leadership Ideas in Bourgeois Political Thought in Germany, 1890–1933*. Princeton: Princeton University Press, 1973.

Sywottek, Jutta. *Mobilmachung für den totalen Krieg. Die propagandistische Vorbereitung der deutschen Bevölkerung auf den Zweiten Weltkrieg*. Opladen: Westdeutscher Verlag, 1976.

"Tatsachen hinter dem eisernen Vorhang." *Ostinformationsdienst der Bundespressestelle des DGB*, no. 9 (19 December 1963).

Tauber, Kurt. *Beyond Eagle and Swastika: German Nationalism since 1945.* 2 vols. Middletown, Conn.: Wesleyan University Press, 1967.

Taylor, A. J. P. *The Origins of the Second World War.* New York: Fawcett, 1963.

Tenbruck, Friedrich H. "Alltagsnormen und Lebensgefühle in der Bundesrepublik." In *Die zweite Republik. 25 Jahre Bundesrepublik Deutschland—Eine Bilanz*, herausgegeben von Richard Löwenthal und Hans-Peter Schwarz. Stuttgart: Seewald, 1974.

Tent, James F. *Mission on the Rhine: Reeducation and Denazification in American-Occupied Germany.* Chicago: University of Chicago Press, 1982.

Teschner, Manfred. "Entwicklung eines Interessenverbandes. Ein empirischer Beitrag zum Problem der Verselbständigung von Massenorganisationen." Inaugural dissertation, Johann-Wolfgang-Goethe-Universität, Frankfurt am Main, 1961.

Theleweit, Klaus. *Male Fantasies.* 2 vols. Minneapolis: University of Minnesota Press, 1987, 1989.

Thränhardt, Dietrich. *Geschichte der Bundesrepublik Deutschland.* Frankfurt am Main: Suhrkamp, 1986.

Tröger, Annemarie. "German Women's Memories of World War II." In *Behind the Lines: Gender and the Two World Wars*, edited by Margaret Randolph Higonnet et al. New Haven: Yale University Press, 1987.

Trometer, Leonhard. "Die Kriegsopferversorgung nach 1945." In *Sozialpolitik nach 1945. Geschichte und Analysen*, herausgegeben von Reinhart Bartholomäi et al. Bonn: Verlag Neue Gesellsch"aft, 1977.

Vogel, Walter. *Westdeutschland, 1945–1950. Der Aufbau von Verfassungs- und Verwaltungseinrichtungen über den Ländern der drei westlichen Besatzungszonen.* Teil 3, *Einzelne Verwaltungszweige.* Boppard am Rhein: Harald Boldt, 1983.

Volkmann, Hans-Erich. "Die innenpolitische Dimension Adenauerscher Sicherheitspolitik in der EVG-Phase." In *Anfänge westdeutscher Sicherheitspolitik, 1945–1956*, herausgegeben vom Militärgeschichtlichen Forschungsamt. Band 2, *Die EVG-Phase.* Munich: R. Oldenbourg, 1990.

Vondung, Klaus, ed. *Kriegserlebnis. Der Erste Weltkrieg in der literarischen Gestaltung und symbolischen Deutung der Nationen.* Göttingen: Vandenhoeck und Ruprecht, 1980.

Wachenheim, Hedwig. "Allowances for Dependants of Mobilized Men in Germany." *International Labour Review*, March 1944.

Waite, Robert G. L. *Vanguard of Nazism: The Free Corps Movement in Postwar Germany, 1918–1923.* New York: Norton, 1969.

Ward, Stephen R., ed. *The War Generation: Veterans of the First World War.* Port Washington, N.Y.: Kennikat Press, 1975.

Weishäupl, Karl. "Die Bedeutung des VdK für die Nachkriegsgeschichte der deutschen Sozialpolitik." In *Sozialpolitik nach 1945. Geschichte und Analysen*, herausgegeben von Reinhart Bartholomäi et al. Bonn: Verlag Neue Gesellschaft, 1977.

Welch, David. *Propaganda and the German Cinema, 1933–1945.* Oxford: Oxford University Press, 1983.

Wengst, Udo. *Beamtentum zwischen Reform und Tradition. Beamtengesetzgebung in der Gründungsphase der Bundesrepublik Deutschland, 1948–1953.* Düsseldorf: Droste, 1988.

———. *Staatsaufbau und Regierungspraxis, 1948–1953. Zur Geschichte der Verfassungsorgane der Bundesrepublik Deutschland.* Düsseldorf: Droste, 1984.

Wenzel, Max. *Fünfzig Jahre Kriegsopferversorgung—Eine Betrachtung zur historischen Entwicklung. Sonderausdruck aus VdK Mitteilungen,* Heft 12 (1968).

Westphal, Alfred. "Die Kriegervereine." In *Deutschland als Weltmacht. Vierzig Jahre Deutsches Reich,* herausgegeben vom Kaiser-Wilhelm-Dank. Berlin: Kameradschaft, 1911.

Wette, Wolfram. "Ideologien, Propaganda und Innenpolitik als Voraussetzungen der Kriegspolitik des Dritten Reiches." In *Das Deutsche Reich und der Zweite Weltkrieg.* Band 1, *Ursachen und Voraussetzungen der deutschen Kriegspolitik,* herausgegeben vom Militärgeschichtlichen Forschungsamt. Stuttgart: Deutsche Verlags-Anstalt, 1979.

Wettig, Gerhard. *Entmilitarisierung und Wiederbewaffnung in Deutschland, 1943–1955. Internationale Auseinandersetzungen um die Rolle der Deutschen in Europa.* Munich: R. Oldenbourg Verlag, 1967.

Whalen, Robert W. *Bitter Wounds: German Victims of the Great War, 1914–1939.* Ithaca, N.Y.: Cornell University Press, 1984.

White, W. L. *Report on the Germans.* New York: Harcourt, Brace, 1947.

Wiggershaus, Norbert. "Die Entscheidung für einen Westdeutschen Verteidigungsbeitrag 1950." In *Anfänge westdeutscher Sicherheitspolitik, 1945–56,* herausgegeben vom Militärgeschichtlichen Forschungsamt. Band 1, *Von der Kapitulation bis zum Pleven-Plan.* Munich: R. Oldenbourg Verlag, 1982.

Winkler, Heinrich A. "German Society, Hitler, and the Illusion of Restoration, 1930–33." *Journal of Contemporary History* 11/1 (1976).

Wissel, Rudolf. "Social Insurance in Germany." *Annals* 260 (November 1948).

Wolfe, Robert, ed. *Americans as Proconsuls: United States Military Government in Germany and Japan, 1944–1952.* Carbondale: Southern Illinois University Press, 1984.

Wootton, Graham. *The Politics of Influence: British Ex-Servicemen, Cabinet Decisions, and Cultural Change, 1917–1957.* Cambridge: Harvard University Press, 1963.

Ziemke, Earl F. *The U.S. Army in the Occupation of Germany.* Washington, D.C.: Center of Military History, United States Army, 1985.

Zöllner, Detlev. "Sozialpolitik." In *Die Bundesrepublik Deutschland. Geschichte in drei Bänden,* herausgegeben von Wolfgang Benz. Band 2, *Gesellschaft.* Frankfurt am Main: Fischer Taschenbuch Verlag, 1983.

INDEX

liger Wehrmachtsangehöriger und deren Hinterbliebenen (BvW), 215, 216, 217, 240; creation of, 65; and 131 Law, 146–47, 150, 151, 153, 177, 186–87, 195–96; expansion of goals, 164, 169, 171, 177–78, 186–98, 201–2; defends Wehrmacht, 177, 180; and rearmament, 177–78, 179, 180–82; and Adenauer, 180; and meaning of 20 July 1944, 181–82; rivalry with other veterans' organizations, 181–84; attempts to unify veterans' organizations, 182, 183, 190–91, 192–98; and merger with BDS, 183, 194–95, 196; relations with government, 183–84; first general meeting of, 186–90; north-south divisions within, 189–90, 195–97, 201–2, 203, 207, 300 (n. 54); and DDSB, 190, 197, 199, 201–2, 203, 207, 209; and Hattenheim meeting, 190–91; and Waffen-SS, 196, 202, 225, 288 (n. 51); and LAG, 197; rivalry with BDS, 198–201, 209; and VdS, 209, 213, 215, 220–22. *See also* Hansen, Admiral Gottfried

BVG. *See* Bundesversorgungsgesetz

BvW. *See* Bund versorgungsberechtigter ehemaliger Wehrmachtsangehöriger und deren Hinterbliebenen

Center Party (Zentrumspartei), 105

Christian Democratic Union (Christlich-Demokratische Union [CDU]), 83, 87, 149; and ÜBG, 94; and HKG, 105; and BVG, 128, 129, 135–36, 192

Christian Social Union (Christlichsoziale Union [CSU]), 83, 87, 105, 106

Civil Service Law (Beamtenrecht), 142, 160, 239

Claes, Heinrich, 214–16, 217

Combat leagues (Kampfbünde), 23–24, 25, 26–27

Communist Party (Kommunistische Partei Deutschlands [KPD]), 87, 94, 98, 104, 137

Control Council. *See* Allied Control Council

Control Council Law Number 34, 62, 63, 74, 143; effect on war pensions, 60, 73; officers' critique of, 61–62; replaced by Allied High Commission Law 16, 65; ban on military organizations, 78, 264–65 (n. 22)

Defense Ministry, 178, 184. *See also* Dienststelle Blank; Zentrale für Heimatdienst

Demilitarization: and military pensions, 52, 53, 58, 59, 72, 78; as Allied goal, 54, 55; and German officers, 56; and treatment of war victims, 73, 74; in Western occupation zones, 201–2. *See also* Control Council Law Number 34; Joint Chiefs of Staff Document 1067

Dethleffsen, General Erich, 190, 192, 194, 206, 207, 208, 211

Deutsche Kriegsopferversorgung (DKOV), 28, 46–48, 50

Deutscher Gewerkschaftsbund (DGB), 150, 155

Deutscher Offiziersbund (DOB), 16, 33, 34, 35, 188

Deutsche Soldatenbund (DDSB): creation, 190; and efforts to unify veterans' organizations, 195, 196, 197; relations with BDS, 198–201, 207, 209, 216; debate over use of name, 206–8; and VdS, 209, 212, 216–17. *See also* Bund versorgungsberechtigter ehemaliger Wehrmachtsangehöriger und deren Hinterbliebenen

Deutsche Soldaten Zeitung (DSZ), 194,

Nationale Kampfgemeinschaft deutscher Kriegsopferverbände, 33. *See also* National-Sozialistische Kriegsopferversorgung

National Socialist German Workers' Party (Nationalsozialistische Deutsche Arbeiterpartei [NSDAP]): and veterans in Weimar Republic, 27, 28; and RVG, 29; and veterans' organizations, 29, 42; and disabled veterans, 51. *See also* National-Sozialistische Kriegsopferversorgung

National Socialist War Victims' Association. *See* National-Sozialistische Kriegsopferversorgung

National Social Security Law (Reichsversicherungsordnung [RVO]), 77, 112, 113, 116

National-Sozialistische Kriegsopferversorgung (NSKOV): creation and goals of, 28; as interest group, 28, 42, 48; and veterans, 28–29, 47–48; and war victims, 29–30, 46, 47; and *Gleichschaltung* of rivals, 32–33; and Kyffhäuserbund, 33, 34, 35, 36; and POWs, 36–37; and RVG, 37, 38, 39, 40–41; and veterans' benefits, 37, 38, 48, 49; finances of, 37, 52; membership of, 37, 254 (n. 22); and universal conscription, 42; propagandistic functions of, 46–47, 48, 49; and home front, 48–49; effects of World War II on, 48–49, 52; and Wehrmacht, 49; dissolution of, 78. See also *Deutsche Kriegsopferversorgung*; Oberlindober, Hanns

National-Sozialistischer Deutscher Reichskriegerbund, Kyffhäuser. *See* Kyffhäuserbund

National-Sozialistischer Reichsverband deutscher Kriegsopfer, 32–33. *See also* National-Sozialistische Kriegsopferversorgung

Nationalsozialistische Volkswohlfahrt, 259 (n. 59)

Nationalverband Deutscher Offiziere (NDO), 16–17, 20–21, 34, 188

National War Victims' Benefits Law. *See* Reichsversorgungsgesetz

Neumann, Paul, 81, 90–91

Noack, Werner, 217–18, 219, 235

Noncommissioned officers: Hitler's support of, 44; and WFVG/WEFVG, 44; and 131 Law, 152–53, 158

Notweg, Der, 65, 222. *See also* Bund versorgungsberechtigter ehemaliger Wehrmachtsangehöriger und deren Hinterbliebenen

NSKOV. *See* National-Sozialistische Kriegsopferversorgung

Oberlindober, Hanns, 28, 43; and *Gleichschaltung* of Weimar *Kriegsopferverbände*, 32, 33; populism of, 33, 34; and DOB, 33, 34, 35; and Kyffhäuserbund, 33, 34, 35; and efforts to unify veterans' organizations, 33, 34, 35–36, 41–42; and Röhm, 33, 34–35; and SA, 33, 34–35; and Hitler, 35, 36; on possible uses of veterans, 35–36; and veterans' benefits, 37–38; and RVG reforms, 37–41; on *Frontzulage*, 39; and war victims, 40; and Reinhard, 41–42; rivalry with Wehrmacht, 42, 49; and unification of disability programs, 51; misuse of NSKOV funds, 52, 262 (n. 88); background of, 251–52 (n. 79); fate of, 262–63 (n. 88). *See also* National-Sozialistische Kriegsopferversorgung

Occupation Statute, 142

Office of Military Government, United States (OMGUS). *See* U.S. Military Government

Officers: post–World War I concerns of,